THE COLLECTED WORKS OF APHRA BEHN

(Volume 1 of 6)

Edited by MONTAGUE SUMMERS

A Digireads.com Book
Digireads.com Publishing

The Collected Works of Aphra Behn (Volume 1 of 6)
Edited by Montague Summers
ISBN: 1-4209-3774-X

Please visit *www.digireads.com*

VOLUME I

CONTENTS

PREFACE.

It is perhaps not altogether easy to appreciate the multiplicity of difficulties with which the first editor of Mrs. Behn has to cope. Not only is her life strangely mysterious and obscure, but the rubbish of half-a-dozen romancing biographers must needs be cleared away before we can even begin to see daylight. Matter which had been for two centuries accepted on seemingly the soundest authority is proven false; her family name itself was, until my recent discovery, wrongly given; the very question of her portrait has its own vexed (and until now unrecognized) dilemmas. In fine there seems no point connected with our first professional authoress which did not call for the nicest investigation and the most incontrovertible proof before it could be accepted without suspicion or reserve. The various collections of her plays and novels which appeared in the first half of the eighteenth century give us nothing; nay, they rather cumber our path with the trash of discredited *Memoirs*. Pearson's reprint (1871) is entirely valueless: there is no attempt, however meagre, at editing, no effort to elucidate a single allusion; moreover, several of the Novels—and the Poems in their entirety—are lacking. I am happy to give (Vol. V) one of the Novels, and that not the least important, *The History of the Nun*, for the first time in any collected edition. Poems, in addition to those which appeared in Mrs. Behn's lifetime, and were never reprinted after, have been gathered with great care from many sources (of which some were almost forgotten).

It is hoped that this new issue of Mrs. Behn may prove adequate. Any difficulties in the editing have been more than amply compensated for by the interest shown by many friends. Foremost, my best thanks are due to Mr. Bullen, whose life-long experience of the minutiæ of editing our best dramatic literature, has been ungrudgingly at my service throughout, to the no small advantage of myself and my work. Mr. Edmund Gosse, C.B., has shown the liveliest interest in the book from its inception, and I owe him most grateful recognition for his kindly encouragement and aid. Nay, more, he did not spare to lend me treasured items from his library so rich in first, and boasting unique, editions of Mrs. Behn. Mr. G. Thorn Drury, K.C., never wearied of answering my enquiries, and in discussion solved many a knotty point. To him I am obliged for the transcript of Mrs. Behn's letter to Waller's daughter-in-law, and also the Satire on Dryden. He even gave of his valuable time to read through the Memoir and from the superabundance of his knowledge made suggestions of the first importance. The unsurpassed library of Mr. T. J. Wise, the well-known bibliographer, was freely at my disposal. In other cases where I have received any assistance in clearing a difficulty I have made my acknowledgement in the note itself.

MEMOIR OF MRS. BEHN.

The personal history of Aphra Behn, the first Englishwoman to earn her livelihood by authorship, is unusually interesting but very difficult to unravel and relate. In dealing with her biography writers at different periods have rushed headlong to extremes, and we now find that the pendulum has swung to its fullest stretch. On the one hand, we have prefixed to a collection of the *Histories and Novels*, published in 1696, 'The Life of Mrs. Behn written by one of the Fair Sex', a frequently reprinted (and even expanded) compilation crowded with romantic incidents that savour all too strongly of the Italian novella, with sentimental epistolography and details which can but be accepted cautiously and in part. On the other there have recently appeared two revolutionary essays by Dr. Ernest Bernbaum of Harvard, 'Mrs. Behn's *Oroonoko*', first printed in *Kittredge Anniversary Papers*, 1913; and—what is even more particularly pertinent—'Mrs. Behn's Biography a Fiction,' *Publications of the Modern Language Association of America*, 3: both afterwards issued as separate pamphlets, 1913. In these, the keen critical sense of the writer has apparently been so jarred by the patent incongruities, the baseless fiction, nay, the very fantasies (such as the fairy pavilion seen floating upon the Channel), which, imaginative and invented flotsam that they are, accumulated and were heaped about the memory of Aphra Behn, that he is apt to regard almost every record outside those of her residence at Antwerp [1] with a suspicion which is in many cases surely unwarranted and undue. Having energetically cleared away the more peccant rubbish, Dr. Bernbaum became, it appears to us, a little too drastic, and had he then discriminated rather than swept clean, we were better able wholly to follow the conclusions at which he arrives. He even says that after '1671' [2] when 'she began to write for the stage ... such meagre contemporary notices as we find of her are critical rather than biographical'. This is a very partial truth; from extant letters, [3] to which Dr. Bernbaum does not refer, we can gather much of Mrs. Behn's literary life and circumstances. She was a figure of some note, and even if we had no other evidence it seems impossible that her contemporaries should have glibly accepted the fiction of a voyage to Surinam and a Dutch husband named Behn who had never existed.

Ayfara, or Aphara [4] (Aphra), Amis or Amies, the daughter of John and Amy Amis or Amies, was baptized together with her brother Peter in the Parish Church of SS. Gregory and Martin, Wye, 10 July, 1640, presumably by Ambrose Richmore, curate of Wye at that date. [5] Up to this time Aphra's maiden name has been stated to be Johnson, and she is asserted to have been the daughter of a barber, John Johnson. That the name was not Johnson (an ancient error) is certain from the baptismal register, wherein, moreover, the 'Quality, Trade, or Profession' is left blank; that her father was a barber rests upon no other foundation than a MS. note of Lady Winchilsea. [6] Mr. Gosse, in a most valuable article (*Athenæum*, 6 September, 1884), was the first to correct the statement repeatedly made that Mrs. Behn came from 'the City of Canterbury in Kent'. He tells how he acquired a folio volume containing the MS. poems of Anne, Countess of Winchilsea, [7] 'copied about 1695 under her eye and with innumerable notes and corrections in her autograph'. In a certain poem entitled *The Circuit of Apollo* [8] the following lines occur:—

> And standing where sadly he now might descry
> From the banks of the Stowre the desolate Wye,
> He lamented for Behn, o'er that place of her birth,
> And said amongst Women there was not on the earth,
> Her superior in fancy, in language, or witt,
> Yet own'd that a little too loosely she writt.

To these is appended this note: 'Mrs. Behn was Daughter to a Barber, who liv'd formerly in Wye, a little Market Town (now much decay'd) in Kent. Though the account of her life before her Works pretends otherwise; some Persons now alive Do testify upon their Knowledge that to be her Original.' It is a pity that whilst the one error concerning Aphra's birthplace is thus remedied, the mistake as to the nature of her father's calling should have been initiated.

Aphra Amis, then, was born early in July, 1640, at Wye, Kent. When she was of a tender age the Amis family left England for Surinam; her father, who seems to have been a relative of Francis, Lord Willoughby of Parham, sometime administrator of several British colonies in the West Indies, having been promised a post of some importance in these dependencies. John Amis died on the voyage out, but his widow and children necessarily continued their journey, and upon their arrival were accommodated at St. John's Hill, one of the best houses in the district. Her life and adventures in Surinam Aphra has herself realistically told in that wonderfully vivid narrative, *Oroonoko*. [9] The writer's bent had already shown itself. She kept a journal as many girls will, she steeped herself in the interminable romances fashionable at that time, in the voluminous *Pharamond, Cléopatre, Cassandre, Ibrahim*, and, above all, *Le Grand Cyrus*, so loved and retailed to the annoyance of her worthy husband by Mrs. Pepys; with a piece of which Dorothy Osborne was 'hugely pleased'.

It was perhaps from the reading of La Calprenède and Mlle de Scudéri Aphra gained that intimate knowledge of French which served her well and amply in after years during her literary life; at any rate she seems early to have realized her dramatic genius and to have begun a play drawn from one of the most interesting episodes in *Cléopatre*, the love story of the Scythian King Alcamène, scenes which, when they had 'measured three thousand leagues of spacious ocean', were, nearly a quarter of a century later, to be taken out of her desk and worked up into a baroque and fanciful yet strangely pleasing tragi-comedy, *The Young King*.

In Surinam she witnessed the fortunes and fate of the Royal Slave, Oroonoko, of whom she writes (with all due allowance for pardonable exaggeration and purely literary touches), so naturally and feelingly, that 'one of the Fair Sex' with some acerbity makes it her rather unnecessary business to clear Aphra from any suspicion of a liaison. It was Surinam which supplied the cognate material for the vivid comedy, the broad humor and early colonial life, photographic in its realism, of *The Widow Ranter; or, The History of Bacon in Virginia*. Mistakes there may be, errors and forgetfulness, but there are a thousand touches which only long residence and keen observation could have so deftly characterized.

We now approach a brief yet important period in Mrs. Behn's life, which unless we are content to follow (with an acknowledged diffidence and due reservations) the old Memoir and scattered tradition, we find ourselves with no sure means whatsoever of detailing. It seems probable, however, that about the close of 1663, owing no doubt to the Restoration and the subsequent changes in affairs, the Amis family returned to England, settling in London, where Aphra, meeting a merchant of Dutch extraction named Behn, so fascinated him by her wit and comeliness that he offered her his hand and fortune. During her married life she is said to have been in affluence, and even to have appeared at the gay licentious Court, attracting the notice of and amusing the King himself by her anecdotes and cleverness of repartee; but when her husband died, not impossibly of the plague in the year of mortality, 1665, she found herself helpless, without friends or funds. In her distress it was to the Court she applied for assistance; and owing to her cosmopolitan experience and still more to the fact that her name was Dutch, and that she had been by her husband brought into close contact with the Dutch, she was selected as a meet political agent to visit Holland and there be employed in various secret and semi-official capacities. The circumstance that her position and work could never be openly recognized nor acknowledged by the English government was shortly to involve her in manifold difficulties, pecuniary and otherwise, which eventually led to her perforce abandoning so unstable and unsatisfactory a commission.

In the old *History of the Life and Memoirs of Mrs. Behn* (1696; and with additions 1698, &c.), ushered into the world by Charles Gildon, a romance full as amorous and sensational as any novel of the day, has been woven about her sojourn at Antwerp. A 'Spark whom we must call by the name of *Vander Albert* of *Utrecht*' is given to Aphra as a fervent lover, and from him she obtains political secrets to be used to the English advantage. He has a rival, an antique yclept Van Bruin, 'a *Hogen Mogen ... Nestorean*' admirer, and the intrigue becomes fast and furious. On one occasion Albert, imagining he is possessing his mistress, is cheated with a certain Catalina; and again when he has bribed an ancient duenna to admit him to Aphra's bed, he is surprised there by a frolicsome gallant. [10] There are even included five letters from Mrs. Behn and a couple of ridiculous effusions purporting to be Van Bruin's. It would seem that all this pure fiction, the sweepings of Aphra's desk, was intended by her to have been worked up into a novel; both letters and narrative are too good to be the unaided composition of Gildon himself, but possibly Mrs. Behn in her after life may have elaborated and told him these erotic episodes to conceal the squalor and misery of the real facts of her early Dutch mission. It is proved indeed in aim and circumstance to have been far other.

Her chief business was to establish an intimacy with William Scott, son of Thomas Scott, the regicide who had been executed 17 October, 1660. This William, who had been made a fellow of All Souls by the Parliamentary Visitors of Oxford, and graduated B.C.L. 4 August, 1648, was quite ready to become a spy in the English service and to report on the doings of the English exiles who were not only holding treasonable correspondence with traitors at home and plotting against the King, but even joining with the Dutch foe to injure their native land. Scott was extremely anxious for his own pardon and, in addition, eager to earn any money he could.

Aphra then, taking with her some forty pounds in cash, all she had, set sail with Sir Anthony Desmarces [11] either at the latter end of July or early in August, 1666, and on 16 August she writes from Antwerp to say she has had an interview with William Scott (dubbed in her correspondence Celadon), even having gone so far as to take coach and ride a day's journey to see him secretly. Though at first diffident, he is very ready to undertake the service, only it will be necessary for her to enter Holland itself and reside on the spot, not in Flanders, as Colonel Bampfield, who was looked upon as head of the exiled English at the Hague, watched Scott with most jealous care and a growing suspicion. Aphra, whose letters give a vivid picture of the spy's life with its risks and impecuniosity, addresses herself to two correspondents, Tom Killigrew and James Halsall, cupbearer to the King.

On 27 August she was still at Antwerp, and William Scott wrote to her there but did not venture to say much lest the epistle might miscarry. He asks for a cypher, a useful and indeed necessary precaution in so difficult circumstances. It was about this time that Mrs. Behn began to employ the name of Astrea, which, having its inception in a political code, was later to be generally used by her and recognized throughout the literary world. Writing to Halsall, she says that she has been unable to effect anything, but she urgently demands that money be sent, and confesses she has been obliged even to pawn her ring to pay messengers. On 31 August she writes to Killigrew declaring she can get no answer from Halsall, and explaining that she has twice had to disburse Scott's expenses, amounting in all to £20, out of her own pocket, whilst her personal debts total another £25 or £30, and living itself is ten guilders a day. If she is to continue her work satisfactorily, £80 at least will be needed to pay up all her creditors; moreover, as a preliminary and a token of good faith, Scott's official pardon must be forwarded without compromise or delay. Scott himself was, it seems, playing no easy game at this juncture, for a certain Carney, resident at Antwerp, 'an unsufferable, scandalous, lying, prating fellow', piqued at not being able to ferret out the intrigue, had gone so far as to molest poor Celadon and threaten him with death, noising up and down meanwhile the fact of his clandestine rendezvous with Aphra. No money, however, was forthcoming from England, and on 4 September Mrs. Behn writing again to Killigrew tells him plainly that she is reduced to great straits, and unless funds are immediately provided all her work will be nugatory and vain. The next letter, dated 14 September, gives Halsall various naval information. On 17 September she is obliged to importune Killigrew once more on the occasion of sending him a letter from Scott dealing with political matters. Halsall, she asserts, will not return any answer, and although she is only in private lodgings she is continually being thwarted and vilipended by Carney, 'whose tongue needs clipping'. Four days later she transmits a five page letter from Scott to Halsall. On 25 September she sends under cover yet another letter from Scott with the news of De Ruyter's illness. Silence was her only answer. Capable and indeed ardent agent as she was, there can be no excuse for her shameful, nay, criminal, neglect at the hands of the government she was serving so faithfully and well. Her information [12] seems to have been received with inattention and disregard; whether it was that culpable carelessness which wrecked so many a fair scheme in the second Charles' days, or whether secret enemies at home steadfastly impeded her efforts remains an open question. In any case on 3 November she sends a truly piteous letter to Lord Arlington, Secretary of State, and informs him she is suffering the extremest want and penury. All her goods are pawned, Scott is in prison for debt, and she herself seems on the point of going to the common gaol. The day after Christmas Aphra wrote to Lord Arlington for the last time. She asks for a round £100 as delays have naturally doubled her expenses and she has had to obtain credit. Now she is only anxious to return home, and she declares that if she did not so well know the justness of her cause and complaint, she would be stark wild with her hard treatment. Scott, she adds, will soon be free. [13] Even this final appeal obtained no response, and at length—well nigh desperate—Mrs. Behn negotiated in England, from a certain Edward Butler, a private loan of some £150 which enabled her to settle her affairs and start for home in January, 1667.

But the chapter of her troubles was by no means ended. Debt weighed like a millstone round her neck. As the weary months went by and Aphra was begging in vain for her salary, long overdue, to be paid, Butler, a harsh, dour man with heart of stone, became impatient and resorted to drastic measures, eventually flinging her into a debtor's prison. There are extant three petitions, undated indeed, but which must be referred to the early autumn of 1668, from Mrs. Behn to Charles II. Sadly complaining of two years' bitter sufferings, she prays for an order to Mr. May [14] or Mr. Chiffinch [15] to satisfy Butler, who declares he will stop at nothing if he is not paid within a week. In a second document she sets out the reasons for her urgent claim of £150. Both Mr. Halsall and Mr. Killigrew know how justly it is her due, and she is hourly threatened with an execution. To this is annexed a letter from the poor distracted woman to Killigrew, which runs as follows:—

Sr.

if you could guess at the affliction of my soule you would I am sure Pity me 'tis tomorrow that I must submitt my self to a Prison the time being expird & though I indeauerd all day yesterday to get a ffew days more I can not because they say they see I am dallied wth all & so they say I shall be for euer: so I can not reuoke my doome I haue cryd myself dead & could find in my hart to break through all & get to ye king & neuer rise till he weare pleasd to pay this; but I am sick & weake & vnfitt for yt; or a Prison; I shall go tomorrow: But I will send my mother to ye king wth a Pitition for I see euery body are words: & I will not perish in a Prison from whence he swears I shall not stirr till ye uttmost farthing be payd: & oh god, who considers my misery & charge too, this is my reward for all my great promises, & my indeauers. Sr if I have not the money tonight you must send me som thing to keepe me in Prison for I will not starue.

A. Behn.

Endorsed:
For Mr. Killigrew this.

There was no immediate response however, even to this pathetic and heart-broken appeal, and in yet a third petition she pleads that she may not be left to suffer, but that the £150 be sent forthwith to Edward Butler, who on Lord Arlington's declaring that neither order nor money had been transmitted, threw her straightway into gaol.

It does not seem, however, that her imprisonment was long. Whether Killigrew, of whom later she spoke in warm and admiring terms, touched at last, bestirred himself on her behalf and rescued her from want and woe, whether Mrs. Amy Amis won a way to the King, whether help came by some other path, is all uncertain. In any case the debt was duly paid, and Aphra Behn not improbably received in addition some compensation for the hardships she had undergone.

'The rest of her Life was entirely dedicated to Pleasure and Poetry; the Success in which gain'd her the Acquaintance and Friendship of the most Sensible Men of the Age, and the Love of not a few of different Characters; for tho' a Sot have no Portion of Wit of his own, he yet, like old Age, covets what he cannot enjoy.'

More than dubious and idly romancing as the early *Memoirs* are, nevertheless this one sentence seems to sum up the situation thenceforth pretty aptly, if in altogether too general terms. Once extricated from these main difficulties Mrs. Behn no doubt took steps to insure that she should not, if it lay in her power, be so situated again. I would suggest, indeed, that about this period, 1669, she accepted the protection of some admirer. Who he may have been at first, how many more there were than one, how long the various amours endured, it is idle to speculate. She was for her period as thoroughly unconventional as many another woman of letters has been since in relation to later times and manners, as unhampered and free as her witty successor, Mrs. de la Riviere Manley, who lived for so long as Alderman Barber's kept mistress and died in his house. Mrs. Behn has given us poetic pseudonyms for many of her lovers, Lycidas, Lysander, Philaster, Amintas, Alexis, and the rest, but these extended over many years, and attempts at identification, however interesting, are fruitless. [16]

There has been no more popular mistake, nor yet one more productive, not merely of nonsense and bad criticism but even of actual malice and evil, than the easy error of confounding an author with the characters he creates. Mrs. Behn has not been spared. Some have superficially argued from the careless levity of her heroes: the Rover,

Cayman, Wittmore, Wilding, Frederick; and again from the delightful insouciance of Lady Fancy, Queen Lucy, and the genteel coquette Mirtilla, or the torrid passions of Angelica Bianca, Miranda and la Nuche; that Aphra herself was little better, in fact a great deal worse, than a common prostitute, and that her works are undiluted pornography.

In her own day, probably for reasons purely political, a noisy clique assailed her on the score of impropriety; a little later came Pope with his jaded couplet

> The stage how loosely does Astrea tread
> Who fairly puts all characters to bed;

and the attack was reinforced by an anecdote of Sir Walter Scott and some female relative who, after having insisted upon the great novelist lending her Mrs. Behn, found the *Novels* and *Plays* too loose for her perusal, albeit in the heyday of the lady's youth they had been popular enough. As one might expect, Miss Julia Kavanagh, in the mid-Victorian era [17] (*English Women of Letters* 1863), is sad and sorry at having to mention Mrs. Behn—'Even if her life remained pure, [18] it is amply evident her mind was "tainted to the very core. Grossness was congenial to her.... Mrs. Behn's indelicacy was useless and worse than useless, the superfluous addition of a corrupt mind and vitiated taste".' One can afford to smile at and ignore these modest outbursts, but it is strange to find so sound and sane a critic as Dr. Doran writing of Aphra Behn as follows: 'No one equalled this woman in downright nastiness save Ravenscroft and Wycherley.... With Dryden she vied in indecency and was not overcome.... She was a mere harlot, who danced through uncleanness and dared them [the male dramatists] to follow.' Again, we have that she was 'a wanton hussy'; her 'trolloping muse' shamefacedly 'wallowed in the mire'; but finally the historian is bound to confess 'she was never dull'.

The morality of her plays is *au fond* that of many a comedy of to-day: that the situations and phrasing in which she presents her amorous intrigues and merry cuckoldoms do not conform with modern exposition of these themes we also show yet would not name, is but our surface gloss of verbal reticence; we hint, point, and suggest, where she spoke out broad words, frank and free; the *motif* is one and the same. If we judge Mrs. Behn's dramatic output in the only fair way by comparing it legitimately with the theatre of her age, we simply shall not find that superfluity of naughtiness the critics lead us to expect and deplore. There are not infrequent scenes of Dryden, of Wycherley, of Vanbrugh, Southerne, Otway, Ravenscroft, Shadwell, D'Urfey, Crowne, full as daring as anything Aphra wrote; indeed, in some instances, far more wanton. Particularizing, it has been objected that although in most Restoration comedies the hero, however vicious (even such a mad scrapegrace as Dryden's Woodall), is decently noosed up in wedlock when the curtain is about to fall, Mrs. Behn's Willmore (*Rover II*), Gayman (*The Lucky Chance*), Wittmore (*Sir Patient Fancy*) end up without a thought of, save it be jest at, the wedding ring. But even this freedom can be amply paralleled. In the Duke of Buckingham's clever alteration of *The Chances* (1682), we have Don John pairing off with the second Constantia without a hint of matrimony; we have the intrigue of Bellmour and Laetitia in Congreve's *The Old Bachelor* (1693), the amours of Horner in *The Country Wife* (1675), of Florio and Artall in Crowne's *City Politics* (1683), and many another beside. As for the cavilling crew who carped at her during her life Mrs. Behn has answered them and she was thoroughly competent so to do. Indeed, as she somewhat tartly remarked to Otway on the occasion of certain prudish dames pleasing to take offence at *The Soldier's Fortune*, she wondered at the impudence of any of her sex that would pretend to understand the thing called bawdy. A clique were shocked at her; it was not her salaciousness they objected to but her success.

In December, 1670, Mrs. Behn's first play, [19] *The Forc'd Marriage; or, the Jealous Bridegroom*, was produced at the Duke's Theatre, Lincoln's Inn Field's, with a strong cast. It is a good tragi-comedy of the bastard Fletcherian Davenant type, but she had not hit upon her happiest vein of comedy, which, however, she approached in a much better piece, *The Amorous Prince*, played in the autumn of 1671 by the same company. Both these had excellent runs for their day, and she obtained a firm footing in the theatrical world. In 1673 [20] *The Dutch Lover* [21] was ready, a comedy which has earned praise for its skilful technique. She here began to draw on her own experiences for material, and Haunce van Ezel owes not a little to her intimate knowledge of the Hollanders.

These three plays brought her money, friends, and reputation. She was already beginning to be a considerable figure in literary circles, and the first writers of the day were glad of the acquaintance of a woman who was both a wit and a writer. There is still retailed a vague, persistent, and entirely baseless tradition that Aphra Behn was assisted in writing her plays by Edward Ravenscroft, [22] the well known dramatist. Mrs. Behn often alludes in her prefaces to the prejudice a carping clique entertained against her and the strenuous efforts that were made to damn her comedies merely because they were 'writ by a woman'. Accordingly, when her plays succeeded, this same party, unable to deny such approved and patent merit, found their excuse in spreading a report that she was not inconsiderably aided in her scenes by another hand. Edward Ravenscroft's name stands to the epilogue of *Sir Timothy Tawdrey*, and he was undoubtedly well acquainted with Mrs. Behn. Tom Brown (I suggest) hints at a known intrigue, [23] but, even if my surmise be correct, there is nothing in this to warrant the oft repeated statement that many of her scenes are actually due to his pen. On the other hand, amongst Aphra's intimates was a certain John Hoyle, a lawyer, well known about the town as a wit. John Hoyle was the son of Thomas Hoyle, Alderman and Lord Mayor of, and M.P. for York, who hanged himself [24] at the same hour as Charles I was beheaded. In the Gray's Inn Admission Register we have: '1659/60 Feb. 27. John Hoyle son and heir of Thomas H. late of the city of York, Esq. deceased.' Some eighteen years after he was admitted to the Inner Temple: '1678/9 Jan. 26. Order that John Hoyle formerly of Gray's Inn be admitted to this society *ad eundem statum*. (*Inner Temple Records*, iii, 131.) There are allusions not a few to him in Mrs. Behn's poems; he is the Mr. J. H. of *Our Cabal*; and in 'A Letter to Mr. Creech at Oxford*, Written in the last great Frost,' which finds a place in the *Miscellany* of 1685, the following lines occur:—

> To Honest H——le I shou'd have shown ye,
> A Wit that wou'd be proud t' have known ye;
> A Wit uncommon, and Facetious,
> A great admirer of *Lucretius*.

There can be no doubt he was on terms of the closest familiarity [25] with Mrs. Behn, and he (if any), not Ravenscroft, assisted her (though we are not to suppose to a real extent) in her plays. There is a very plain allusion to this in Radcliffe's *The Ramble: News from Hell* (1682):—

Amongst this Heptarchy of Wit
The censuring Age have thought it fit,
To damn a Woman, 'cause 'tis said
The Plays she vends she never made.
But that a *Greys Inn* Lawyer does 'em
Who unto her was Friend in Bosom,
So not presenting Scarf and Hood
New Plays and Songs are full as good. [26]

Unfortunately Hoyle was reputed to be addicted to the grossest immorality, and rumours of a sinister description were current concerning him. [27] There is, in fact, printed a letter [28] of Mrs. Behn's wherein she writes most anxiously to her friend stating that the gravest scandals have reached her ears, and begging him to clear himself from these allegations. Hoyle was murdered in a brawl 26 May, 1692, and is buried in the vault belonging to the Inner Temple, which is presumably in the ground attached to the Temple Church. The entry in the Register runs as follows: 'John Hoyle, esq., of the Inner Temple was buried in the vault May ye 29, 1692.' Narcissus Luttrell in his *Diary*, Saturday, 28 May, 1692, has the following entry: 'Mr. Hoil of the Temple on Thursday night was at a tavern with other gentlemen, and quarrelling with Mr. Pitts' eldest son about drinking a health, as they came out Mr. Hoil was stabb'd in the belly and fell down dead, and thereon Pitts fled; and the next morning was taken in a disguise and is committed to Newgate.' [29] 30 June, 1692, the same record says: 'This day Mr. Pitts was tried at the Old Bailey for the murder of Mr. Hoil of the Temple, and the jury found it manslaughter but the next heir has brought an appeal.'

In September, 1676, *The Town Fop* was acted with applause, and the following year Mrs. Behn was very busy producing two comedies (of which one is a masterpiece) and one tragedy. *The Debauchee*, which was brought out this year at the Duke's House, a somewhat superficial though clever alteration of Brome's *Mad Couple Well Match'd*, is no doubt from her pen. It was published anonymously, 4to, 1677, and all the best critics with one accord ascribe it to Mrs. Behn. In the autumn of 1677 there was produced by the Duke's Company a version of Middleton's *No Wit, No Help Like a Woman's*, entitled, *The Counterfeit Bridegroom; or, The Defeated Widow* (4to, 1677); it is smart and spirited. Genest was of opinion it is Aphra's work. He is probably right, for we know that she repeatedly made use of Middleton, and internal evidence fully bears out our stage historian. [30] Both *Abdelazer* [31] and *The Town Fop* evidence in a marked degree her intimate knowledge of the earlier dramatists, whilst *The Rover (I)* is founded on Killigrew. None the less, here she has handled her materials with rare skill, and successfully put new wine into old bottles. The critics, however, began to attack her on this point, and when *The Rover (I)* appeared in print (4to 1677), she found it necessary to add a postscript, defending her play from the charge of merely being '*Thomaso* alter'd'. With reference to *Abdelazer* there is extant a very interesting letter [32] from Mrs. Behn to her friend, Mrs. Emily Price. She writes as follows:—

My Dear,
In your last, you inform'd me, that the World treated me as a *Plagiery*, and, I must confess, not with Injustice: But that Mr. *Otway* shou'd say, my Sex wou'd not prevent my being pull'd to Pieces by the Critics, is something odd, since whatever Mr. *Otway* now declares, he may very well remember when last I saw him, I receiv'd more than ordinary

Encomiums on my *Abdelazer*, But everyone knows Mr. *Otway's* good Nature, which will not permit him to shock any one of our Sex to their Faces. But let that pass: For being impeach'd of murdering my *Moor*, I am thankful, since, when I shall let the World know, whenever I take the Pains next to appear in Print, of the mighty Theft I have been guilty of; But however for your own Satisfaction, I have sent you the Garden from whence I gather'd, and I hope you will not think me vain, if I say, I have weeded and improv'd it. I hope to prevail on the Printer to reprint *The Lust's Dominion*, &c., that my theft may be the more public. But I detain you. I believe I sha'n't have the Happiness of seeing my dear *Amillia* 'till the middle of *September*: But be assur'd I shall always remain as I am,

Yours, A. Behn.

The Rover (I) is undoubtedly the best known of Aphra Behn's comedies. It long remained a popular favorite in the theatre, its verve, bustle and wit, utterly defiant of the modest Josephs and qualmy prudes who censured these lively scenes. Steele has mention of this in an archly humorous paper, No. 51, *Spectator*, Saturday, 28 April, 1711. He pictures a young lady who has taken offence at some negligent expression in that chastest of ice-cold proprieties, *The Funeral*, and he forthwith more or less seriously proceeds to defend his play by quoting the example of both predecessors and contemporaries. Amongst the writers who are 'best skilled in this luscious Way', he informs us that 'we are obliged to the Lady who writ *Ibrahim* [33] for introducing a preparatory Scene to the very Action, when the Emperor throws his Handkerchief as a Signal for his Mistress to follow him into the most retired Part of the Seraglio.... This ingenious Gentlewoman in this piece of Baudry refined upon an Author of the same Sex, who in *The Rover* makes a Country Squire strip to his Holland Drawers. For *Blunt* is disappointed, and the Emperor is understood to go on to the utmost.... It is not here to be omitted, that in one of the above-mentioned Female Compositions the *Rover* is very frequently sent on the same Errand; as I take it above once every Act. This is not wholly unnatural; for, they say, the Men-Authors draw themselves in their Chief Characters, and the Women-Writers may be allowed the same Liberty.'

Early in 1678, in either the first or second week of January, *Sir Patient Fancy* was received with great applause. A hint from Brome, more than a hint from Molière, much wit, vivacity, and cleverness make up this admirable comedy. Throughout the whole of her career it is amply evident that Mrs. Behn, an omnivorous reader, kept in constant touch with and profited by the French literature and theatre of her day. The debt of the English stage to France at this period is a fact often not sufficiently acknowledged, but one which it would really be difficult to over-emphasize. No adequate critical knowledge of much of our English song, fiction and drama of the Restoration can be attained without a close study of their French models and originals.

During the latter part of this year Mrs. Behn found time to revise and write up the romantic scenes she had composed two decades before as a girl in Surinam, and the result was a tragi-comedy, *The Young King*, which won considerable favor. Produced in March or early April, [34] 1679, it was not published till 1683, but a second edition was called for in 1698. [35]

In March, *The Feign'd Courtezans*, one of Mrs. Behn's happiest efforts, appeared on the boards of the Duke's House. Not one tittle is borrowed, and its success gives striking proof of the capacity of her unaided powers. When printed, the comedy was dedicated in adulatory terms to Nell Gwynne. With the great Betterton, handsome Will Smith, Nokes, Underhill, Leigh, an inimitable trio, the famous Mrs. Barry, pretty and piquante Betty

Currer, the beautiful and serenely gracious Mrs. Mary Lee, in the cast, it had a perfect galaxy of genius to give it life and triumph.

In 1681 a second part continued the adventures of *The Rover*, and surprisingly good the sequel is.

From 1678 to 1683 were years of the keenest political excitement and unrest. Fomented to frenzy by the murderous villainies of Gates and his accomplices, aggravated by the traitrous ambition and rascalities of Shaftesbury, by the deceit and weakness of Monmouth, and the open disloyalty of the Whiggish crew, party politics and controversy waxed hotter and fiercer until riots were common and a revolution seemed imminent. Fortunately an appeal in a royal declaration to the justice of the nation at large allayed the storm, and an overwhelming outburst of genuine enthusiasm ensued. Albeit the bill against him was thrown out with an 'ignoramus' by a packed jury 24 November, 1681, a year later, 28 November, 1682, Shaftesbury found it expedient to escape to Holland. Monmouth, who had been making a regal progress through the country, was arrested. Shortly after he was bailed out by his political friends, but he presently fled in terror lest he should pay the penalty of his follies and crimes, inasmuch as a true bill for high treason had been found against him. It was natural that at such a crisis the stage and satire (both prose and rhyme), should become impregnated with party feeling; and the Tory poets, with glorious John Dryden at their head, unmercifully pilloried their adversaries. In 1682 Mrs. Behn produced three comedies, two of which are mainly political. *The Roundheads*, a masterly pasquinade, shows the Puritans, near ancestors of the Whigs, in their most odious and veritable colours. *The City Heiress* lampoons Shaftesbury and his cit following in exquisite caricature. The wit and humor, the pointed raillery never coarsening into mere invective and zany burlesque, place this in the very front rank of her comedies. [36] *The False Count*, the third play of this year, is non-political, and she has herein borrowed a suggestion from Molière. It is full of brilliant dialogue and point, whilst the situations are truly ludicrous and entertaining. As might well be surmised, *The Roundheads* and *The City Heiress* were not slow to wake the rancour of the Whigs, who looked about for an opportunity of vengeance which they shortly found. On 10 August, 1682, there was produced at the Duke's Theatre an anonymous tragedy *Romulus and Hersilia; or, The Sabine War*. It is a vigorous play of no small merit and attracted considerable attention at the time. [37] Mrs. Behn contributed both Prologue and Epilogue, the former being spoken by that sweet-voiced blonde, winsome Charlotte Butler, the latter by Lady Slingsby, who acted Tarpeia. There was matter in the Epilogue which reflected upon the disgraced Duke of Monmouth, for whom, in spite of his known treachery and treasons, Charles still retained the fondest affection. Warm representations were made in high quarters, and the following warrant was speedily issued:—

Whereas the Lady Slingsby Comoedian and Mrs. Aphaw Behen have by acting and writeing at his Royall Highnesse Theatre committed severall Misdemeanors and made abusive reflections upon persons of Quality, and have written and spoken scandalous speeches without any License or Approbation of those that ought to peruse and authorize the same, These are therefore to require you to take into yor Custody the said Lady Slingsby and Mrs. Aphaw Behen and bring them before mee to answere the said Offence, And for soe doeing this shalbe yor sufficient Warr^t. Given und^r my hand and seale this 12'th day of August, 1682.

To Henry Legatt Messenger
of His Mat'ties Chamber, etc.

The lines particularly complained of ran as follows:

> of all Treasons, mine was most accurst;
> Rebelling 'gainst a KING and FATHER first.
> A Sin, which Heav'n nor Man can e're forgive;
> Nor could I *Act* it with the face to live.
> . . . .
> There's nothing can my Reputation save
> With all the *True*, the *Loyal* and the *Brave*;
> Not my Remorse or death can Expiate
> With them a Treason 'gainst the KING and State.

Coming from the mouth of the perjured Tarpeia they were of course winged with point unmistakable. It is not probable, however, that either authoress or actress was visited with anything more than censure and a fright. In any case their detention [38] (if brought about) must have been very shortliv'd, for the partizans of Monmouth, although noisy and unquiet, were not really strong, and they met with the most effective opposition at every turn.

In this same year the Whigs in spite of their utmost efforts signally failed to suppress, and could only retard the production of Dryden and Lee's excellent tragedy *The Duke of Guise*, first performed 4 December. The play created a furore, and its political purport as a picture of the baffled intrigues of Shaftesbury in favor of Lucy Walter's overweening son is obvious, nor is it rendered less so by Dryden's clever and caustic *Vindication of the Duke of Guise* (1683). It is interesting to note that Lady Slingsby, who played the Queen Mother, Catherine de' Medici, in this play, has some very sardonic speeches put in her mouth; indeed, as Henri III aptly remarks, 'she has a cruel wit'.

In 1684 were published the famous *Love Letters between a Nobleman and his Sister*. The letters, supposed to have passed between Forde, Lord Grey, [39] and his sister-in-law Lady Henrietta Berkeley, fifth daughter of the Earl, are certainly the work of Mrs. Behn. Romantic and sentimental, with now and again a pretty touch that is almost lyrical in its sweet cadence, they enjoyed the same extraordinary popularity which very similar productions have attained at a recent date. A third edition was called for in 1707.

Mrs. Behn was also busy seeing her poems through the press. The title page is dated 1684, and they were issued with a dedication to the Earl of Salisbury. [40] In the same volume is included her graceful translation of the Abbé Tallemant's *Le Voyage de l'Isle d'Amour*, entitled, *A Voyage to The Isle of Love*.

The following undated letter (preserved at Bayfordbury) addressed to Jacob Tonson, and first published in the *Gentleman's Magazine*, May, 1836, pleads hard for an extra payment of five pounds for her book. She writes:—

Deare Mr. Tonson
I am mightly obleg'd to you for ye service you have don me to Mr. Dryden; in whose esteeme I wou'd chose to be rather then any bodys in the world; and I am sure I never, in thought, word, or deed merritted other from him, but if you had heard w^t was told me,

you wou'd have excus'd all I said on that account. Thank him most infinitly for ye hon. he offers, and I shall never think I can do anything that can merritt so vast a glory; and I must owe it all to you if I have it. As for Mr. Creech, I would not have you afflict him wth a thing can not now be help'd, so never let him know my resentment. I am troubled for ye line that's left out of Dr. Garth, [41] and wish yor man wou'd write it in ye margent, at his leasure, to all you sell.

As for ye verses of mine, I shou'd really have thought 'em worth thirty pound; and I hope you will find it worth 25l; not that I shou'd dispute at any other time for 5 pound wher I am so obleeged; but you cannot think w^t a preety thing ye Island will be, and w^t a deal of labor I shall have yet with it: and if that pleases, I will do the 2nd Voyage, wch will compose a little book as big as a novel by itself. But pray speake to yor Bro^r to advance the price to one 5lb more, 'twill at this time be more then given me, and I vow I wou'd not aske it if I did not really believe it worth more. Alas I wou'd not loose my time in such low gettings, but only since I am about it I am resolv'd to go throw wth it tho I shou'd give it. I pray go about it as soone as you please, for I shall finish as fast as you can go on. Methinks ye Voyage shou'd com last, as being ye largest volume. You know Mr. Couly's Dauid is last, because a large poem, and Mrs. Philips her Plays for ye same reason. I wish I had more time, I wou'd ad something to ye verses y^t I have a mind too, but, good deare Mr. Tonson, let it be 5lb more, for I may safly swere I have lost ye getting of 50lb by it, tho that's nothing to you, or my satisfaction and humor: but I have been wthout getting so long y^t I am just on ye poynt of breaking, espesiall since a body has no creditt at ye Playhouse for money as we usd to have, fifty or 60 deepe, or more; I want extreamly or I wo'd not urge this.

Yo^{rs} A. B.

Pray send me ye loose papers to put to these I have, and let me know wch you will go about first, ye songs and verses or that. Send me an answer to-day.

It is probable that about this date, 1683-4, she penned her little novel *The Adventure of the Black Lady*, and also that excellent extravaganza *The King of Bantam*. [42] Both these and *The Unfortunate Happy Lady* are written as if they had certainly been completed before the death of Charles II, in which case they must have lain by, MSS, in Mrs. Behn's desk.

The King, at the height of his power, after a short illness, died 6 February, 1685, an event that together with the accession of James naturally evoked a plethora of State Poems, to which flood Mrs. Behn contributed. Her Pindarics rank high amongst the semi-official, complimentary, threnodic or pastoral pseudo-Dithyrambs, of which the age was so bounteous; but it needed the supreme genius of a Dryden sustainedly to instil lyric fire and true poetry into these hybrid forms. [43] The nadir is sounded by the plumbeous productions of Shadwell, Nahum Tate, and 'Persons of Quality'. Aphra's *Pindarick on the Death of Charles II* ran through two editions in 1685, and her *Poem to the Queen Dowager Catherine* was published the same year. James II was crowned on St. George's Day, and she greeted her new monarch and old patron with a *Poem on the Happy Coronation of His Sacred Majesty*. A little later she published a *Miscellany* of poems by various hands: amongst whom were Etheredge, Edmund Arwaker, Henry Crisp, and Otway, including not a few from her own pen, 'Together with Reflections on Morality, or Seneca Unmaskd. Translated from the Maximes of the Duke de la Rochefoucauld', a number of clever apophthegms tersely turned.

The following note, [44] however, affords ample evidence that at this juncture, maugre her diligence and unremitting toils, she was far from being in easy circumstances:—

'Where as I am indebted to Mr. Bags the sum of six pownd for the payment of which Mr. Tonson has obleged himself. Now I do here by impowre Mr. Zachary Baggs, in case the said debt is not fully discharged before Michaelmas next, to stop what money he shall hereafter have in his hands of mine, upon the playing my first play till this aforesaid debt of six pownd be discharged. Witness my hand this 1st August, —85.

A. Behn.'

Early in 1686 a frolicksome comedy of great merit, *The Lucky Chance*, was produced by her at the Theatre Royal, the home of the United Companies. A Whiggish clique, unable to harm her in any other way, banded together to damn the play and so endeavoured to raise a pudic hubbub, that happily proved quite ineffective. *The Lucky Chance*, which contends with *The Rover (I)*, and *The Feign'd Courtezans* for the honor of being Mrs. Behn's highest flight of comic genius, has scenes admittedly wantoning beyond the bounds of niggard propriety, but all are alive with a careless wit and a brilliant humor that prove quite irresistible. Next appeared those graceful translations from de Bonnecorse's *La Montre ... seconde partie contenant La Boëte et Le Miroir*, which she termed *The Lover's Watch* and *The Lady's Looking-Glass*.

In 1687 the Duke of Albemarle's voyage to Jamaica [45] to take up the government in the West Indies gave occasion for a Pindaric, but we only have one dramatic piece from Mrs. Behn, *The Emperor of the Moon*, a capital three act farce, Italian in sentiment and origin. For some little time past her health had begun to trouble her. [46] Her three years of privation and cares had told upon her physically, and since then, 'forced to write for bread and not ashamed to own it,' she had spared neither mind nor bodily strength. Graver symptoms appeared, but yet she found time to translate from Fontenelle his version of Van Dale's *De Oraculis Ethnicorum* as *The History of Oracles and the Cheats of the Pagan Priests*, a book of great interest. There was also published in 1687 an edition in stately folio of *Æsop's Fables with his Life in English, French and Latin*, 'illustrated with One hundred and twelve Sculptures' and 'Thirty One New Figures representing his Life', by Francis Barlow, the celebrated draughtsman of birds and animals. Each plate to the Life has a quatrain appended, and each fable with its moral is versified beneath the accompanying picture. In his brief address to the Reader Barlow writes: 'The Ingenious Mrs. A. Behn has been so obliging as to perform the English Poetry, which in short comprehends the Sense of the Fable and Moral; Whereof to say much were needless, since it may sufficiently recommend itself to all Persons of Understanding.' To this year we further assign the composition of no fewer than four novels, *The Unfortunate Bride*, *The Dumb Virgin*, *The Wandering Beauty*, *The Unhappy Mistake*. She was working at high pressure, and 1688 still saw a tremendous literary output. Waller had died 21 October, 1687, at the great age of eighty-one, and her Elegiac Ode to his Memory begins:—

How to thy Sacred Memory, shall I bring
(Worthy thy Fame) a grateful Offering?
I, who by Toils of Sickness, am become
Almost as near as thou art to a Tomb?
While every soft and every tender strain
Is ruffl'd, and ill-natur'd grown with Pain.

This she sent to his daughter-in-law with the following letter:—[47]

Madam,

At such losses as you have sustain'd in that of yor Glorious ffather in Law M^r. Waller, the whole world must wait on your sighs & mournings, tho' we must allow yours to be the more sensible by how much more (above your Sex) you are Mistriss of that Generous Tallent that made him so great & so admird (besids what we will allow as a Relation) tis therfore at your ffeet Madam we ought to lay all those Tributary Garlands, we humbler pretenders to the Muses believe it our Duty to offer at his Tombe—in excuse for mine Madam I can only say I am very ill & have been dying this twelve month, that they want those Graces & that spiritt wch possible I might have drest em in had my health & dulling vapors permitted me, howeuer Madam they are left to your finer judgment to determin whether they are worthy the Honor of the Press among those that cellibrat M^r. Wallers great fame, or of being doomed to the fire & whateuer you decree will extreamly sattisfy

I humbly beg pardon
for my yll writing
Madam for tis with
a Lame hand scarce
able to hold a pen.

Madam
yor most Devoted &
most Obeadient
Seruant
A. BEHN.

Her weakness, lassitude, and despondency are more than apparent; yet bravely buckling to her work, and encouraged by her success with Fontenelle, she Englished with rare skill his *Theory of the System of Several New Inhabited Worlds*, prefixing thereto a first-rate 'Essay on Translated Prose.' She shows herself an admirable critic, broad-minded, with a keen eye for niceties of style. *The Fair Jilt* (licensed 17 April, 1688), [48] *Oroonoko*, and *Agnes de Castro*, followed in swift succession. She also published *Lycidus, a Voyage from the Island of Love*, returning to the Abbé Tallemant's dainty preciosities. On 10 June, James Francis Edward, Prince of Wales, was born at St. James's Palace, and Mrs. Behn having already written a *Congratulatory Poem* [49] to Queen Mary of Modena on her expectation of the Prince, was ready with a Poem on his Happy Birth.

One of the most social and convivial of women, a thorough Tory, well known to Dryden, Creech, Otway and all the leading men of her day, warm helper and ally of every struggling writer, Astrea began to be completely overpowered by the continual strain, the unremittent tax upon both health and time. Overworked and overwrought, in the early months of 1689 she put into English verse the sixth book (*of Trees*) from Cowley's *Sex Libri Plantarum* (1668). Nahum Tate undertook Books IV and V and prefaced the translation when printed. As Mrs. Behn knew no Latin no doubt some friend, perhaps

Tate himself, must have paraphrased the original for her. She further published *The Lucky Mistake* and *The History of the Nun; or, The Fair Vow Breaker*, [50] licensed 22 October, 1688. On the afternoon of 12 February, Mary, wife of William of Orange, had with great diffidence landed at Whitehall Stairs, and Mrs. Behn congratulated the lady in her Poem *To Her Sacred Majesty Queen Mary on her Arrival in England*. One regrets to find her writing on such an occasion, and that she realized the impropriety of her conduct is clear from the reference to the banished monarch. But she was weary, depressed, and ill, and had indeed for months past been racked with incessant pain. An agonizing complication of disorders now gave scant hope of recovery. It is in the highest degree interesting to note that during her last sickness Dr. Burnet, a figure of no little importance at that moment, kindly enquired after the dying woman. The Pindaric in which she thanks him, and which was printed March, 1689, proved the last poem she herself saw through the press. At length exhausted nature failed altogether, and she expired 16 April, 1689, the end hastened by a sad lack of skill in her physician. She is buried in the east cloisters of Westminster Abbey. A black marble slab marks the spot. On it are graven 'Mrs. Aphra Behn Dyed April, 16, A.D. 1689,' and two lines, 'made by a very ingenious Gentleman tho' no Poet':—[51]

> Here lies a Proof that Wit can never be
> Defence enough against Mortality. [52]

'She was of a generous and open Temper, something passionate, very serviceable to her Friends in all that was in her Power; and could sooner forgive an Injury, than do one. She had Wit, Honor, Good-Humor, and Judgment. She was Mistress of all the pleasing Arts of Conversation, but us'd 'em not to any but those who love Plain-dealing.' So she comes before us. A graceful, comely woman, [53] merry and buxom, with brown hair and bright eyes, candid, sincere, a brilliant conversationalist in days when conversation was no mere slipshod gabble of slang but cut and thrust of poignant epigram and repartee; warm-hearted, perhaps too warm-hearted, and ready to lend a helping hand even to the most undeserving, a quality which gathered all Grub Street round her door. At a period when any and every writer, mean or great, of whatsoever merit or party, was continually assailed with vehement satire and acrid lampoons, lacking both truth and decency, Aphra Behn does not come off scot-free, nobody did; and upon occasion her name is amply vilified by her foes. There are some eight ungenerous lines with a side reference to the 'Conquests she had won' in Buckingham's *A Trial of the Poets for the Bays*, and a page or two of insipid spiritless rhymes, *The Female Laureat*, find a place in *State Poems*. The same collection contains *A Satyr on the Modern Translators*. 'Odi Imitatores servum pecus,' &c. By Mr. P——r, [54] 1684. It begins rather smartly:—

> Since the united Cunning of the Stage,
> Has balk'd the hireling Drudges of the Age;
> Since *Betterton* of late so thrifty 's grown,
> Revives Old Plays, or wisely acts his own;

the modern poets

> Have left Stage-practice, chang'd their old Vocations,
> Atoning for bad Plays with worse Translations.

In some instances this was true enough, but when the writer attacks Dryden he becomes ridiculous and imprecates

> May he still split on some unlucky Coast,
> And have his Works or Dictionary lost:
> That he may know what *Roman Authors* mean,
> No more than does our blind Translatress *Behn*, [55]
> The Female Wit, who next convicted stands,
> Not for abusing *Ovid's* verse but *Sand's*:
> She might have learn'd from the ill-borrow'd Grace,
> (Which little helps the Ruin of her Face)
> That Wit, like Beauty, triumphs o'er the Heart
> When more of Nature's seen, and less of Art:
> Nor strive in *Ovid's* Letters to have shown
> As much of Skill, as Lewdness in her own.
> Then let her from the next inconstant Lover,
> Take a new Copy for a second Rover.
> Describe the Cunning of a jilting Whore,
> From the ill Arts herself has us'd before;
> Thus let her write, but *Paraphrase* no more.

These verses are verjuiced, unwarranted, unfair. Tom Brown too in his *Letters from the Dead to the Living* has a long epistle 'From worthy Mrs. Behn the Poetess, to the famous Virgin Actress,' (Mrs. Bracegirdle), in which the Diana of the stage is crudely rallied. 'The Virgin's Answer to Mrs. Behn' contains allusions to Aphra's intrigue with some well-known dramatic writer, perhaps Ravenscroft, and speaks of many an other amour beside. But then for a groat Brown would have proved Barbara Villiers a virgin, and taxed Torquemada with unorthodoxy. Brown has yet another gird at Mrs. Behn in his *The Late Converts Exposed, or the Reason of Mr. Bays's Changing his Religion &c.* Considered in a Dialogue (1690, a quarto tract; and reprinted in a Collection of Brown's *Dialogues*, 8vo, 1704). Says Eugenius: 'You may remember Mr. Bays, how the famed *Astrea*, once in her Life-time unluckily lighted upon such a Sacred Subject, and in a strange fit of Piety, must needs attempt a Paraphrase on the Lord's Prayer. But alas poor Gentlewoman! She had scarce travell'd half way, when *Cupid* served her as the Cut-Purse did the Old Justice in *Bartholmew* Fair, tickled her with a Straw in her Ear, and then she could not budge one foot further, till she had humbly requested her Maker to grant her a private Act of Toleration for a little Harmless Love, otherwise called Fornication.' There is a marginal note to this passage: 'Mrs. *Behn's* Miscell. Printed by *Jos. Hindmarsh*.' In *a Letter from the Dead Thomas Brown to the Living Heraclitus* (1704), a sixpenny tract, this wag is supposed to meet Mrs. Behn in the underworld, and anon establishes himself on the most familiar terms with his 'dear *Afra*'; they take, indeed, 'an extraordinary liking to one another's Company' for 'good Conversation is not so overplentiful in these Parts.' A bitterer attack yet, *An Epistle to Julian* (c. 1686-7), paints her as ill, feeble, dying:—

Doth that lewd Harlot, that Poetick Quean,
Fam'd through *White Fryars*, you know who I mean,
Mend for reproof, others set up in spight,
To flux, take glisters, vomits, purge and write.
Long with a Sciatica she's beside lame,
Her limbs distortur'd, Nerves shrunk up with pain,
And therefore I'll all sharp reflections shun,
Poverty, Poetry, Pox, are plagues enough for one.

In truth, Aphra Behn's life was not one of mere pleasure, but a hard struggle against overwhelming adversity, a continual round of work. We cannot but admire the courage of this lonely woman, who, poor and friendless, was the first in England to turn to the pen for a livelihood, and not only won herself bread but no mean position in the world of her day and English literature of all time. For years her name to a new book, a comedy, a poem, an essay from the French, was a word to conjure with for the booksellers. There are anecdotes in plenty. Some true, some not so reliable. She is said to have introduced milk-punch into England. [56] We are told that she could write a page of a novel or a scene of a play in a room full of people and yet hold her own in talk the while. [57] Her popularity was enormous, and edition after edition of her plays and novels was called for.

In 1690, there was brought out on the stage a posthumous comedy, *The Widow Ranter*. [58] But without her supervision, it was badly cast, the script was mauled, and it failed. In 1696 Charles Gildon, who posed as her favorite protégé (and edited her writings), gave *The Younger Brother*. He had, however, himself tampered with the text. The actors did it scant justice and it could not win a permanent place in the theatrical repertory. In May, 1738, *The Gentleman's Magazine* published *The Apotheosis of Milton*, a paper, full of interest, which ran through several numbers. It is a Vision, in which the writer, having fallen asleep in Westminster Abbey, is conducted by a Genius into a spacious hall, 'sacred to the Spirits of the Bards, whose Remains are buried, or whose Monuments are erected within this Pile. Tonight an Assembly of the greatest Importance is held upon the Admission of the Great Milton into this Society.' The Poets accordingly appear either in the habits which they were wont to wear on earth, or in some suitable attire. We have Chaucer, Drayton, Beaumont, Ben Jonson, and others who are well particularized, but when we get to the laureates and critics of a later period there are some really valuable touches. In 1738 there must have been many alive who could well remember Dryden, Shadwell, Otway, Prior, Philips, Sheffield Duke of Buckinghamshire, Dennis, Atterbury, Lee, Congreve, Rowe, Addison, Betterton, Gay. In the course of his remarks the guide exclaims to the visitor: 'Observe that Lady dressed in the loose *Robe de Chambre* with her Neck and Breasts bare; how much Fire in her Eye! what a passionate Expression in her Motions; And how much Assurance in her Features! Observe what an Indignant Look she bestows on the President [Chaucer] , who is telling her, *that none of her Sex has any Right to a Seat there*. How she throws her Eyes about, to see if she can find out any one of the Assembly who inclines to take her Part. No! not one stirs; they who are enclined in her favor are overawed, and the rest shake their Heads; and now she flings out of the Assembly. That extraordinary Woman is *Afra Behn*.' The passage is not impertinent, even though but as showing how early condemnatory tradition had begun to incrustate around Astrea. Fielding, however, makes his Man of the World tell a friend that the best way for a man to improve his intellect and commend himself to the ladies is by a course of Mrs. Behn's novels. With the oncoming of the ponderous and starched decorum of the third George's reign her vogue waned apace, but she was still read and quoted. On 12 December, 1786, Horace Walpole writes to the Countess of Upper Ossory, 'I am going to Mrs. Cowley's new play, [59] which I suppose is as *instructive* as the *Marriage of Figaro*, for I am told it approaches to those of Mrs. Behn in Spartan delicacy; but I shall see Miss Farren, who, in my poor opinion is the first of all actresses.' Sir Walter Scott admired and praised her warmly. But the pinchbeck sobriety of later times was unable to tolerate her freedom. She was condemned in no small still voice as immoral, loose, scandalous; and writer after writer, leaving her unread, reiterated the charge till it passed into a byword of criticism, and her works were practically taboo in literature, a type and summary of all that was worst and foulest in Restoration days. The absurdities and falsity or this extreme are of course patent now, and it was inevitable the recoil should come.

It is a commonplace to say that her novels are a landmark in the history of fiction. Even Macaulay allowed that the best of Defoe was 'in no respect... beyond the reach of Afra Behn'. Above all *Oroonoko* can be traced directly and indirectly, perhaps unconsciously, in many a descendant. Without assigning her any direct influence on Wilberforce, much of the feeling of this novel is the same as inspired Harriet Beecher Stowe. She has been claimed to be the literary ancestress of Bernardin de Saint-Pierre and Chateaubriand; nor is it any exaggeration to find Byron and Rousseau in her train. Her lyrics, it has been well said, are often of 'quite bewildering beauty', but her comedies represent her best work and she is worthy to be ranked with the greatest dramatists of her day, with Vanbrugh and Etheredge; not so strong as Wycherley, less polished than Congreve. Such faults as she has are obviously owing to the haste with which circumstances compelled her to write her scenes. That she should ever recover her pristine reputation is of course, owing to the passing of time with its change of manners, fashions, thought and style, impossible. But there is happily every indication that—long neglected and traduced—she will speedily vindicate for herself, as she is already beginning to do, her rightful claim to a high and honorable place in our glorious literature.

THE TEXT.

The text of the dramatic work is primarily based upon the edition of 1724, four volumes, by far the best and most reliable edition of the collected theatre. Each play, however, has been carefully collated with the original quartos, some of which are of excessive rarity, and if, in the case of any divergence, the later reading is preferred, reason why is given in the Textual Notes upon that specific passage. To the Dramatis Personae are in each case added those characters which hitherto were negligently omitted: I have, further, consistently numbered the scenes and supplied (where necessary) the locales. In the order of the plays the 1724 edition has been followed as preserving the traditional and accepted arrangement. The only change herein made is the transferring of *The Emperor of the Moon* from Vol. IV to Vol. Ill, and the placing of *The Amorous Prince* before *The Widow Ranter*, so that the two posthumous plays may thus be found in their due order together at the end of Vol. IV.

With regard to metrical division, I have (unless a special note on any one particular line draws attention to the contrary) in this difficult matter followed the first quartos, as at this point 1724 proves not so satisfactory, and prints much as prose which the earlier separate editions give as verse. A notable instance may be found in *The Amorous Prince*. To the above rule I adhere so strictly as even not to divide into lines several scenes in *The Widow Ranter* and *The Younger Brother* which are palpably blank verse, but yet which are not so set in the quartos of 1690 and 1696. I felt that the metrical difficulties and kindred questions involved were so capable of almost infinite variations, that to attempt a new and decisive text in this matter would not merely be hazardous but also unproductive of any real benefit or ultimately permanent result.

The valuable Dedications and Prefaces, never before given in the collected editions, are here reprinted for the first time from the originals. With regard to the novels the first separate edition has in every case been collated. When impossible, however, so to do (as in the exception of *Oroonoko*), the earliest accessible text has been taken, and if any difficulty arose, all editions of any value whatsoever were likewise consulted. For *La Montre* (*The Lover's Watch*), the original edition of 1686 was used. Any difference in text which has been adopted from later editions is duly noted in the textual apparatus to that piece. The Poems have in every case been printed from the first—which are generally the only—editions. Where they appeared as broadsides, these, when traceable, have been collated.

THE PORTRAITS OF MRS. BEHN.

Of Mrs. Behn there exist three portraits, one by Mary Beale, a second by John Riley, and the third by Sir Peter Lely.

The Beale portrait has been engraved: 'Aphra Behn. From a Picture by Mary Beale in the collection of His Grace the Duke of Buckingham. Drawn by T. Uwins. Engraved by J. Fittler, A.R.A. London. 1 March, 1822. Published by W. Walker, 8 Grays Inn Square.' The original oil painting was purchased at the Stow Sale in 1848 (No. 57 in the sale catalogue), by J. S. Caldwell, a literary antiquarian, Linley Wood, Staffordshire. A letter which I wrote to *The Times Literary Supplement* (26 November, 1914) on the subject of these portraits brought me a most courteous permission from Major-General F. C. Heath Caldwell, the present owner of Linley Wood, to view the picture.

With regard to the well-known and most frequently reproduced portrait by Riley, this, engraved by R. Wise, figures as frontispiece to *The Unfortunate Bride* (title page, 1700, and second title page, 1698). It is also given before the *Novels* (1696, 1698, and other editions). Engraved by B. Cole, the same portrait fronts the *Plays*, 4 vols., 1724, and the *Novels*, 2 vols., 1735. It again appears 'H. R. Cook, Sculp.', published 1 August, 1813, by I. W. H. Payne, when it was included as an illustration to the *Lady's Monthly Museum*.

The portrait by Sir Peter Lely, which is reproduced as frontispiece to this edition of Mrs. Behn, was exhibited at the South Kensington Portrait Exhibition of 1866 by Philip Howard, Esq., of Corby Castle, the head of the Corby branch of the Howard family.

The portrait of Mrs. Behn which appears as frontispiece to the *Plays*, 2 vols., 1716, is none other than Christina of Sweden from Sebastian Bourdon's drawing now in the Louvre.

A so-called portrait of Mrs. Behn, 'pub. Rob't Wilkinson', no date, is of no value, being, at best, a bad pastiche from some very poor engraving.

ENDNOTES TO PREFACE and MEMOIR OF MRS. BEHN.

[1] *Kalendar of State Papers, Domestic*, 1666-7.—ed. Mrs. M. A. E. Green (1864).
[2] This is inaccurate. Mrs. Behn's first play, *The Forc'd Marriage*, was produced in December, 1670.
[3] e.g. to Waller's daughter-in-law; to Tonson. cf. also the Warrant of 12 August, 1682; the Pindaric to Burnet, &c.
[4] Aphra now appears on Mrs. Behn's gravestone, and is the accepted form. This is, however, in all probability the third inscription. *The Antiquities of Westminster* (1711), quoting the inscription, gives Aphara. Sometime in the eighteenth century a certain Thomas Waine restored the inscription and added to the two lines two more:—

Great Poetess, O thy stupendous lays
The world admires and the Muses praise.

The name was then Aphara. The *Biog. Brit.*, whilst insisting on Aphara as correct and citing the stone as evidence, none the less prints Apharra. Her works usually have Mrs. A. Behn. One Quarto misprints 'Mrs. Anne Behn'. There are, of course, many variants of the name. Afara, and Afra are common. Oldys in his MS. notes on Langbaine writes Aphra or Aphora, whilst the *Muses Mercury*, September, 1707, has a special note upon a poem by Mrs. Behn to say 'this Poetess' true Name was Apharra.' Even Aphaw (Behen, in the 1682 warrant,) and Fyhare (in a petition) occur.
[5] He died in 1642.
[6] The Vicar of Wye, the Rev. Edgar Lambert, in answer to my inquiries courteously writes: 'In company with Mr. C. S. Orwin, whose book, *The History of Wye Church and College*, has just been published, I have closely examined the register and find no mention of "Johnson", nor of the fact that Aphara Amis' father was a "barber".'
[7] Anne Finch, Countess of Winchilsea (1660-1720), sometime Maid of Honor to Queen Mary of Modena. She had true lyric genius. For a generous appreciation see Gosse, *Gossip in a Library* (1891).
[8] Then unprinted but now included in the very voluminous edition of Lady Winchilsea's *Poems*, ed. M. Reynolds, Chicago, 1903.
[9] In 'Mrs. Behn's *Oroonoko*' Dr. Bernbaum elaborately endeavours to show that this story is pure fiction. His arguments, in many cases advanced with no little subtlety and precision, do not appear (to me at least) to be convincing. We have much to weigh in the contrary balance: Mrs. Behn's manifest first-hand knowledge of, and extraordinary interest in, colonial life; her reiterated asseverations that every experience detailed in this famous novel is substantially true; the assent of all her contemporaries. It must further be remembered that Aphra was writing in 1688, of a girlhood coloured by and seen through the enchanted mists of a quarter of a century. That there are slight discrepancies is patent; the exaggerations, however, are not merely pardonable but perfectly natural. One of Dr. Bernbaum's most crushing arguments, when sifted, seems to resolve itself into the fact that whilst writing *Oroonoko* Mrs. Behn evidently had George Warren's little book, *An Impartial Description of Surinam* (London, 1667), at hand. Could anything be more reasonable

than to suppose she would be intimately acquainted with a volume descriptive of her girlhood's home? Again, Dr. Bernbaum bases another line of argument on the assumption that Mrs. Behn's father was a barber. Hence the appointment of such a man to an official position in Surinam was impossible, and, 'if Mrs. Behn's father was not sent to Surinam, the only reason she gives for being there disappears'. We know from recent investigation that John Amis did not follow a barber's trade, but was probably of good old stock. Accordingly, the conclusions drawn by Dr. Bernbaum from this point cannot now be for a moment maintained.

[10] Both these incidents are the common property of Italian novelle and our own stage. Although not entirely impossible, they would appear highly suspicious in any connection.

[11] He was at Margate 25 July, and at Bruges 7 August.

[12] There do not appear to be any grounds for the oft-repeated assertions that Mrs. Behn communicated the intelligence when the Dutch were planning an attack (afterwards carried out) on the Thames and Medway squadrons, and that her warning was scoffed at.

[13] Had he been imprisoned for political reasons it is impossible that there should have been so speedy a prospect of release.

[14] Baptist May, Esq. (1629-98), Keeper of the Privy Purse.

[15] William Chiffinch, confidential attendant and pimp to Charles II.

[16] Amintas repeatedly stands for John Hoyle. In *Our Cabal*, however (*vide* Vol. VI, p. 160), Hoyle is dubbed Lycidas.

[17] *The Retrospective Review*, however (Vol. I, November, 1852), has an article, 'Mrs. Behn's Dramatic Writings,' which warmly praises her comedies. The writer very justly observes that 'they exhibit a brilliance of conversation in the dialogue, and a skill in arranging the plot and producing striking situations, in which she has few equals.' He frequently insists upon her 'great skill in conducting the intrigue of her pieces', and with no little acumen declares that 'her comedies may be cited as the most perfect models of the drama of the latter half of the seventeenth century.'

[18] Which it certainly was not secundum mid-Victorian morals.

[19] Mr. Gosse in the Dictionary of National Biography basing upon the preface to *The Young King*, says that after knocking in vain for some time at the doors of the theatres with this tragi-comedy that could find neither manager nor publisher, she put it away and wrote *The Forc'd Marriage*, which proved more successful. Dr. Baker follows this, but I confess I cannot see due grounds for any such hypothesis.

[20] The Duke's Company opened at their new theatre, Dorset Garden, 9 November, 1671.

[21] 4to, 1673. Mrs. Behn's accurate knowledge of the theatre and technicalties theatrical as shown in the preface to this early play is certainly remarkable. It is perhaps worth noting that her allusion to the popularity of 1 *Henry IV* was not included in *Shakspere Allusion-Book* (ed. Furnivall and Munro, 1909), where it should have found a place.

[22] In view of the extremely harsh treatment Ravenscroft has met with at the hands of the critics it may be worth while emphasizing Genest's opinion that his 'merit as a dramatic writer has been vastly underrated'. Ravenscroft has a facility in writing, an ease of dialogue, a knack of evoking laughter and picturing the ludicrous, above all a vitality which many a greater name entirely lacks. As a writer of farce, and farce very nearly akin to comedy, he is capital.

[23] *Letters from the Dead to the Living*: The Virgin's [Mrs. Bracegirdle] Answer to Mrs. Behn. 'You upbraid me with a great discovery you chanc'd to make by peeping into the breast of an old friend of mine; if you give yourself but the trouble of examining an old poet's conscience, who went lately off the stage, and now takes up his lodgings in your territories, and I don't question but you'll there find Mrs. *Behn* writ as often in black characters, and stand as thick in some places, as the names of the generation of *Adam* in the first of *Genesis*.' How far credence may be given to anything of Brown's is of course a moot point, but the above passage and much that follows would be witless and dull unless there were some real suggestion of scandal. Moreover, it cannot here be applied to Hoyle, whereas it very well fits Ravenscroft. This letter which speaks of 'the lash of Mr. C———r' must have been written no great time after the publication of Jeremy Collier's *A Short View of the Immorality of the English Stage* (March, 1698), probably in 1701-2. Ravenscroft's last play, *The Italian Husband*, was produced at Lincoln's Inn Fields in 1697, and he is supposed to have died a year or two later, which date exactly suits the detail given by Brown. Ravenscroft's first play, *Mamamouchi*, had been produced in 1672, and the 'an old poet' would be understood.

[24] This occurrence is the subject of some lines in *The Rump* (1662): 'On the happy Memory of Alderman Hoyle that hang'd himself.'

[25] *The Muses Mercury*, December, 1707, refers to verses made on Mrs. Behn 'and her very good friend, Mr. Hoyle'.

[26] My attention was drawn to these lines by Mr. Thorn Drury, who was, indeed, the first to suggest that Hoyle is the person aimed at. I have to thank him, moreover, for much valuable information on this important point.

[27] cf. Luttrell's *Diary*, February, 1686-7, which records that an indictment for misconduct was actually presented against him at the Old Bailey, but the Grand Jury threw out the bill and he was discharged. The person implicated in the charge against Hoyle seems to have been a poulterer, cf. *A Faithful Catalogue of our Most Eminent Ninnies*, said to have been written by the Earl of Dorset in 1683, or (according to another edition of Rochester's works in which it occurs) 1686. In any case the verses cannot be earlier than 1687.

> Which made the wiser Choice is now our Strife,
> *Hoyle* his he-mistress, or the Prince his wife:
> Those traders sure will be beiov'd as well,
> As all the dainty tender Birds they sell.

The 'Prince' is George Fitzroy, son of Charles II by the Duchess of Cleveland, who was created Duke of Northumberland and married Catherine, daughter of Robert Wheatley, a poulterer, of Bracknell, Berks; and relict of Robert Lucy of Charlecote, Warwickshire.

[28] *Familiar Letters of Love, Gallantry, etc.* There are several editions. I have used that of 1718, 2 vols.

[29] In his MS. Commonplace Book (now in the possession of G. Thorn Drury, Esq., K.C.), Whitelocke Bulstrode writes:—

'27 May 92.

'Mr Hoyle of y'e Temple, coming this morning about two of ye Clock frõ ye Young Divel Tavern, was killed wth a sword; He died Instantly: It proceeded frõ a quarrell about Drincking a Health; Killed by Mr Pitt of Graies Inne y^t Dranck wth them. Mr Hoyle was an Atheist, a Sodomite professed, a corrupter of youth, & a Blasphemer of Christ.'

The Young (or Little) Devil Tavern was in Fleet Street, on the south side, near Temple Bar, adjoining Dick's Coffee House. It was called Young (or Little) to distinguish it from the more famous house, The Devil (or Old Devil) Tavern, which stood between Temple Bar and the Inner Temple Gate.

[30] Betterton's adaption of Marston's *The Dutch Courtezan*, which the actor calls *The Revenge; or, A Match in Newgate*, has sometimes been erroneously ascribed to Mrs. Behn by careless writers. She has also been given *The Woman Turn'd Bully*, a capital comedy with some clever characterization, which was produced at Dorset Garden in June, 1675, and printed without author's name the same year. Both Prologue and Epilogue, two pretty songs, *Oh, the little Delights that a Lover takes*; and *Ah, how charming is the shade*, together with a rollicking catch 'O *London*, wicked *London-Town!*' which is 'to be sung *a l'yvronge*, in a drunken humor', might all well be Mrs. Behn's, and the whole conduct of the play is very like her early manner. Beyond this, however, there is no evidence to suggest it is from her pen.

[31] The overture, act-tunes, incidental music, were composed by Henry Purcell.

[32] *Familiar Letters of Love, Gallantry, etc.*, Vol. I (1718), pp. 31-2.

[33] *Ibrahim, the Thirteenth Emperor of the Turks*, produced in 1696 (410, 1696), a commendable tragedy by Mrs. Mary Pix, *née* Griffiths (1666-1720?). The plot is based on Sir Paul Ricaut's continuation of the Turkish history.

[34] The date is fixed by the Epilogue 'at his R.H. second exile into Flanders'. The Duke of York sailed for Antwerp 4 March, 1679. He returned in August owing to the King's illness.

[35] This fact sufficiently explodes the quite untenable suggestion that *The Young King* in earlier days could find neither producer nor publisher. That the quarto did not appear until four years after the play had been seen on the stage is no argument of non-success. Ravenscroft's *Mamamouchi* was produced early in 1672, and 'continu'd Acting 9 Days with a full house'. It specially delighted the King and Court. It was not printed, however, until 1675.

[36] Gould in *The Play House, a Satyr*, stung by Mrs. Behn's success, derides that

> clean piece of Wit
> *The City Heiress* by chaste *Sappho* Writ,
> Where the Lewd Widow comes with Brazen Face,
> Just seeking from a Stallion's rank Embrace,
> T' acquaint the Audience with her Filthy Case.
> Where can you find a Scene for juster Praise,
> In *Shakespear, Johnson*, or in *Fletcher's* Plays?

[37] Publication was delayed. *Brooks' Impartial Mercury*, Friday, 17 Nov., 1682, advertises: 'To be published on Monday next, the last new play called *Romulus*.' The 4to is dated 1683. A broad sheet, 1682, gives both Prologue 'spoken by Mrs. Butler, written by Mrs. Behn,' and Epilogue 'spoken by the Lady Slingsby.' The 4to gives

'Prologue, spoken by Mrs. Butler,' 'Epilogue, Writ by Mrs. A. Behn. Spoken by Tarpeia.'

[38] Curtis' *Protestant Mercury*, August 12-6, 1682, notices that both Lady Slingsby and Mrs. Behn have been ordered into custody in respect of this Epilogue.

[39] Forde, Lord Grey of Werke, Earl of Tankerville, who succeeded to the title in 1675, was married to Lady Mary Berkeley. He eloped, however, with Lady Henrietta Berkley, and great scandal ensued. When he and his minions were brought to trial, 23 November, 1682, his mistress and a number of staunch Whigs boldly accompanied him into court. He was found guilty, but as his friends banded together to resist, something very like a riot ensued. He died 25 June, 1701. Lady Henrietta Berkeley, who never married, survived her lover nine years.

[40]   Astrea with her soft gay sighing Swains
         And rural virgins on the flowery Plains,
         The lavish Peer's profuseness may reprove
         Who gave her Guineas for the *Isle of Love.*
         —*Contemporary Satire,*—(Harleian MSS.)

[41] This of course cannot be correct, but it is so transcribed. In the transcript of this letter made by Malone, and now in the possession of G. Thorn Drury, Esq., K.C., over the word 'Garth's' is written 'Q', and at the foot of the page a note by Mitford says: 'This name seems to have been doubtful in the MSS.' I have thought it best not to attempt any emendation.

[42] Neither of these was printed until eight years after her death. They first appear, each with its separate title page, 1697, bound up in the Third Edition, 'with Large Additions,' of *All the Histories and Novels, Written by the Late Ingenious Mrs. Behn, Entire in One Volume,* 1698. After Nos. vii, viii, ix, *Memoirs of the Court of the King of* Bantam, *The Nun; or, the Perjured Beauty, The Adventure of the Black Lady* follows a note: 'These last three never before published.' Some superficial bibliographers (e.g. Miss Charlotte E. Morgan in her unreliable monograph, *The English Novel till 1749*) have postulated imaginary editions of 1683-4 for *The Little Black Lady* and *The King of Bantam. The Nun; or, the Perjured Beauty* is universally confounded with *The History of the Nun* (*vide* Vol. V, p. 259, Introduction to that novel) and dated 1689.

With reference to *The King of Bantam* we have in the 1698 collected edition of the Novels the following '*Advertisement to the* Reader. The Stile of the Court of the King of *Bantam,* being so very different from Mrs. *Behn's* usual way of Writing, it may perhaps call its being genuine in Question; to obviate which Objection, I must inform the Reader, that it was a Trial of Skill upon a Wager, to show that she was able to write in the Style of the Celebrated *Scarron,* in Imitation of whom 'tis writ, tho' the Story be true. I need not say anything of the other Two, they evidently confessing their admirable Author.'

[43] Swift, although he amply fulfilled Dryden's famous prophecy, 'Cousin Swift, you will never be a Pindaric poet', was doubtless thinking of these Pindarics when in *The Battle of the Books* he wrote: 'Then *Pindar* slew ——, and ——, and *Oldham,* and ——, and *Afra* the *Amazon* light of foot.'

[44] First published in *The Gentleman's Magazine,* May, 1836.

[45] Christopher Monck, second Duke of Albermarle, was appointed Governor-General of Jamaica, 26 November, 1687. He died there early in the following autumn.

[46] '*Sappho* famous for her Gout and Guilt,' writes Gould in *The Poetess, a Satyr.*

[47] Now published for the first time by the courtesy of G. Thorn Drury, Esq., K.C., who generously obliged me with a transcript of the original.

[48] In the original edition of *The Fair Jilt* (1688), we have advertised: 'There is now in the Press, *Oroonoko; or, The History of the Royal Slave*. Written by Madam *Behn*.'

[49] In the second edition (1688), of this *Congratulatory Poem* to Queen Mary of Modena we have the following advertisement:—'On Wednesday next will be Published the most Ingenious and long Expected History of *Oroonoko; or, the Royal Slave. By Mrs. Behn*.'

[50] The title page has 1689, but it was possibly published late in 1688.

[51] Traditionally said to be John Hoyle.

[52] Sam Briscoe, the publisher, in his Dedicatory Epistle to *Familiar Letters of Love, Gallantry, etc.* (2 vols., 1718), says: 'Had the rough Days of K. *Charles* II *newly recover'd from the Confusion of a Civil War*, or the tempestuous Time of *James* the Second, had the same *Sence of Wit* as our *Gentlemen* now appear to have, the first Impressions of *Milton's Paradise Lost* had never been sold for *Waste Paper*; the Inimitable *Hudibras* had never suffered the Miseries of a Neglected Cavalier; *Tom Brown* the merriest and most diverting'st man, had never expir'd so neglected; Mr. *Dryden*'s Religion would never have lost him his *Pension*; or Mrs. *Behn* ever had but *two Lines* upon her *Grave-stone*.'

[53] 'She was a most beautiful woman, and a more excellent poet'. Col. Colepeper. *Adversaria*, Vol. ii (Harleian MSS.)

[54] This piece finds a place in the unauthorised edition of Prior's Poems, 1707, a volume the poet himself repudiated. In the Cambridge edition of Prior's *Works* (1905-7), reason is given, however, to show that the lines are certainly Prior's, and that he withdrew this and other satires (says Curll, the bookseller), owing to 'his great Modesty'. The Horatian tag (Epistles i, xiv, 19) is of course 'O Imitatores servum pecus'.

[55] In his *Preface Concerning Ovid's Epistles* affixed to the translation of the *Heroides* (*Ovid's Epistles*), 'by Several Hands' (1680), Dryden writes: 'The Reader will here find most of the Translations, with some little Latitude or variation from the Author's Sence: That of *Oenone* to *Paris*, is in Mr. Cowley's way of Imitation only. I was desir'd to say that the Author who is of the *Fair Sex*, understood not *Latine*. But if she does not, I am afraid she has given us occasion to be asham'd who do.'

[56] 'Old Mr. John Bowman, the player, told me that Mrs. Behn was the First Person he ever knew or heard of who made the Liquor call'd Milk Punch.'—Oldys; MS. note in Langbaine. In a tattered MS. recipe book, the compilation of a good housewife named Mary Rockett, and dated 1711, the following directions are given how to brew this tipple. 'To make Milk Punch. Infuse the rinds of 8 Lemons in a Gallon of Brandy 48 hours then add 5 Quarts of Water and 2 pounds of Loaf Sugar then Squize the Juices of all the Lemons to these Ingredients add 2 Quarts of new milk Scald hot stirring the whole till it crudles grate in 2 Nutmegs let the whole infuse 1 Hour then refine through a flannel Bag.'

[57] 'She always Writ with the greatest ease in the world, and that in the midst of Company, and Discourse of other matters. I saw her my self write *Oroonoko*, and keep her own in Discoursing with several then present in the Room.'—Gildon: *An Account of the Life of the Incomparable Mrs. Behn*, prefixed to *The Younger Brother* (4to 1696). Southerne says, with reference to *Oroonoko*, 'That she always told his Story, more feelingly than she writ it.'

[58] It is ushered in by one 'G. J. her friend'. This was almost certainly George Jenkins.

[59] *The School for Greybeards*, produced at Drury Lane, 25 November, 1786. It owes much of its business to *The Lucky Chance*. See the Theatrical History of that comedy (Vol. iii, p. 180). Miss Farren acted Donna Seraphina, second wife of Don Alexis, one of the Greybeards. She also spoke the epilogue.

THE ROVER; OR,
THE BANISH'D CAVALIERS.
PART I.

ARGUMENT.

During the exile of Charles II a band of cavaliers, prominent amongst whom are Willmore (the Rover), Belvile, Frederick, and Ned Blunt, find themselves at Naples in carnival time. Belvile, who at a siege at Pampluna has rescued a certain Florinda and her brother Don Pedro, now loves the lady, and the tender feeling is reciprocated. Florinda's father, however, designs her for the elderly Vincentio, whilst her brother would have her marry his friend Antonio, son to the Viceroy. Florinda, her sister Hellena (who is intended for the veil), their cousin Valeria, and duenna Callis surreptitiously visit the carnival, all in maskrade, and there encounter the cavaliers. Florinda arranges to meet Belvile that night at her garden-gate. Meanwhile a picture of Angelica Bianca, a famous courtesan, is publicly exposed, guarded by bravos. Antonio and Pedro dispute who shall give the 1000 crowns she demands, and come to blows. After a short fray Willmore, who has boldly pulled down the picture, is admitted to the house, and declares his love, together with his complete inability to pay the price she requires. Angelica, none the less, overcome with passion, yields to him. Shortly after, meeting Hellena in the street, he commences an ardent courtship, which is detected by the jealous Angelica, who has followed him vizarded. Florinda that night at the garden-gate encounters Willmore, who, having been toping in the town, is far from sober, and her cries at his advances attract her brother and servants, whom she eludes by escaping back to the house. After a brawl, Willmore has to endure the reproaches of Belvile, who has appeared on the scene. During their discussion Antonio makes as about to enter Angelica's house before which they are, and Willmore, jostling him to one side, wounds him. He falls, and the officers who run up at the clash of swords, arrest Belvile, who has returned at the noise, as the assailant, conveying him by Antonio's orders to the Viceroy's palace. Antonio, in the course of conversation, resigns Florinda to his rival, and Belvile, disguised as Antonio, obtains Florinda from Don Pedro. At this moment Willmore accosts him, and the Spaniard perceiving his mistake, soon takes his sister off home. Angelica next comes in hot pursuit of Willmore, but they are interrupted by Hellena, dressed as a boy, who tells a tale of the Rover's amour with another dame and so rouses the jealous courtesan to fury, and the twain promptly part quarrelling. Florinda, meanwhile, who has escaped from her brother, running into an open house to evade detection, finds herself in Ned Blunt's apartments. Blunt, who is sitting half-clad, and in no pleasant mood owing to his having been tricked of clothes and money and turned into the street by a common Cyprian, greets her roughly enough, but is mollified by the present of a diamond ring. His friends and Don Pedro, come to laugh at his sorry case, now force their way into the chamber, and Florinda, whom her brother finally resigns to Belvile, is discovered. She is straightway united to her lover by a convenient priest. Willmore is then surprised by the apparition of Angelica, who, loading him with bitter reproaches for his infidelity, is about to pistol him, when she is disarmed by Antonio, and accordingly parts in a fury of jealous rage, to give place to Hellena who adroitly secures her Rover in the noose of matrimony.

SOURCE.

The entire plan and many details of both parts of *The Rover* are taken openly and unreservedly from Tom Killigrew's *Thomaso, or The Wanderer*, an unacted comedy likewise in two parts, published for the first time in his collected works by Henry Herringman (folio, 1663-4). It is to be noticed, however, that whilst Killigrew's work is really one long play of ten closely consecutive acts, the scene of which is continually laid in Madrid, without any break in time or action, Mrs. Behn, on the other hand, admirably contrives that each separate part of *The Rover* is complete and possesses perfect unity in itself, the locale being respectively, and far more suitably, in two several places, Naples and Madrid, rather than confined to the latter city alone. Mrs. Behn, moreover, introduces new characters and a new intrigue in her second part, thus not merely sustaining but even renewing the interest which in *Thomaso* jades and flags most wearily owing to the author's prolixity and diffuseness.

Killigrew, a royalist to the core, participated in the protracted exile of Charles II, and devoting this interim to literature, wrote *Thomaso* whilst at Madrid, probably about the year 1654-5. Although undeniably interesting in a high degree, and not ill written, it shares in no small measure the salient faults of his other productions, boundless and needless verbosity, slowness of action, unconscionable length.

For all its wit and cleverness, such blemishes would, without trenchant cutting, have been more than sufficient to prohibit it from any actual performance, and, indeed, *Thomaso* may be better described as a dramatic romance than a comedy intended for the boards. Clumsy and gargantuan speeches, which few actors could have even memorized, and none would have ventured to utter on the stage, abound in every scene. This lack of technical acumen (unless, as may well be the case, Killigrew wrote much of these plays without any thought of presentation) is more than surprising in an author so intimately connected with the theatre and, after the Restoration, himself manager of the King's Company.

Nor is *Thomaso* without its patent plagiarisms. Doubtless no small part is simply autobiographical adventuring, but, beside many a reminiscence of the later Jacobeans, Killigrew has conveyed entire passages and lyrics wholesale without attempt at disguise. Thus the song, 'Come hither, you that love,' Act ii, Scene 3, is from Fletcher's *Captain*, Act iv, the scene in Lelia's chamber. Again, the procedure and orations of Lopus the mountebank are but the flimsiest alterations of *Volpone*, Act ii, Scene I, nor could Killigrew change Jonson for anything but the worse. He has even gone so far as to name his quack's spouse Celia, a distinct echo of Corvino's wife.

In dealing with these two plays Mrs. Behn has done a great deal more than merely fit the pieces for the stage. Almost wholly rewriting them, she has infused into the torpid dialogue no small portion of wit and vivacity, whilst the characters, prone to devolve into little better than prosy and wooden marionettes, with only too apparent wires, are given life, vigour movement, individuality and being. In fact she has made the whole completely and essentially her own. In some cases the same names are retained. We find Phillipo, Sancho, Angelica Bianca, Lucetta, Callis, in Killigrew. But as Willmore is a different thing altogether to Thomaso, so Ned Blunt is an infinitely more entertaining figure than his prototype Edwardo. Amongst other details Killigrew, oddly and stupidly enough, gives his English gentlemen foreign names:—Thomaso, Ferdinando, Rogero, Harrigo. [1] This jar is duly corrected in *The Rover*.

Mrs. Behn has further dealt with the Lucetta intrigue in a far more masterly way than Killigrew's clumsily developed episode. In *Thomaso* it occupies a considerable space, and becomes both tedious and brutally unpleasant. The apt conclusion of the amour in *The Rover* with Blunt's parlous mishap is originally derived from Boccaccio, Second Day, Novel 5, where a certain Andreuccio finds himself in the same unsavory predicament as the Essex squireen. However, even this was by no means new to the English stage. In *Blurt Master Constable*, Lazarillo de Tormes, at the house of the courtesan Imperia, meets with precisely the same accident, Act iii, Scene 3, Act iv, Scenes 2 and 3, and it is probable that Mrs. Behn did not go directly to the *Decameron* but drew upon Middleton, of whom she made very ample use on another occasion, borrowing for *The City Heiress* no small portion of *A Mad World, My Masters*, and racily reproducing in extenso therefrom Sir Bounteous Progress, Dick Folly-Wit, the mock grandee, and that most excellent of all burglaries good enough for Fielding at his best.

In dealing with *Thomaso* Astrea did not hesitate, with manifest advantage, to transfer incidents from Part II to Part I, and vice versa. Correcting, pruning, augmenting, enlivening, rewriting, she may indeed (pace the memory of the merry jester of Charles II) be well said to have clothed dry bones with flesh, and to have given her creation a witty and supple tongue.

THEATRICAL HISTORY.

The first part of *The Rover* was produced at the Duke's House, Dorset Gardens, in the summer of 1677, and licensed for printing on 2 July of the same year. It met, as it fully deserved, with complete success, and remained one of the stock plays of the company. Smith, the original Willmore, and the low comedian Underhill as Blunt were especially renowned in their respective rôles. Another famous Willmore was Will Mountford, of whom Dibdin relates, 'When he played Mrs. Behn's dissolute character of The Rover, it was remarked by many, and particularly by Queen Mary, that it was dangerous to see him act, he made vice so alluring.'

Amongst the more notable representations of the eighteenth century we find:—*Drury Lane; 18 February, 1703.* Willmore by Wilks; Hellena, Mrs. Oldfield; repeated on 15 October of the same year. *Haymarket; 20 January, 1707.* Willmore by Verbruggen; Blunt, Underhill; Hellena, Mrs. Bracegirdle; Angelica, Mrs. Barry; Florinda, Mrs. Bowman. *Drury Lane; 22 April, 1708.* Willmore by Wilks; Blunt, Estcourt; Frederick, Cibber; Hellena, Mrs. Oldfield; Angelica, Mrs. Barry; Florinda, Mrs. Porter. *Drury Lane; 30 December, 1715.* Willmore, Wilks; Blunt, Johnson; Hellena, Mrs. Mountfort; Angelica, Mrs. Porter. *Drury Lane; 6 March, 1716.* Don Pedro, Quin; Frederick, Ryan; Florinda, Mrs. Horton. *Lincoln's Inn Fields; 5 April, 1725.* 'Never acted there.' Performed for Ryan's benefit. Willmore, Ryan; Belvile, Quin; Blunt, Spiller; Hellena, Mrs. Bullock; Angelica, Mrs. Parker. *Covent Garden; 9 November, 1748.* Willmore, Ryan; Blunt, Bridgewater; Hellena, Mrs. Woffington; Angelica, Mrs. Horton. To make this performance more attractive there was also presented 'a musical entertainment', entitled, *Apollo and Daphne*, which had been originally produced at Lincoln's Inn Fields in 1726. *Covent Garden; 19 February, 1757.* 'Not acted twenty years.' Willmore, Smith; Belvile, Ridout; Frederick, Clarke; Don Antonio, Dyer; Blunt, Shuter; Hellena, Mrs. Woffington; Angelica, Mrs. Hamilton; Florinda, Mrs. Elmy. This, the latest revival, was performed with considerable expense, and proved successful, being repeated no less than ten times during the season. Wilkinson says that Shuter acted Blunt very realistically, and, as the stage directions of Act iii require, stripped to his very drawers.

On 8 March, 1790, J. P. Kemble presented at Drury Lane a pudibond alteration of *The Rover*, which he dubbed *Love in Many Masks* (8vo, 1790). It was well received, and acted eight times; in the following season once. Willmore was played by Kemble himself; Belvile, Wroughton; Blunt, Jack Bannister; Stephano, Suett; Hellena, Mrs. Jordan; Angelica, Mrs. Ward; Florinda, Mrs. Powell; Valeria, Mrs. Kemble; Lucetta, Miss Tidswell. It is not entirely worthless from a purely technical point of view, but yet very modest and mediocre. As might well be surmised, the raciness and spirit of *The Rover* entirely evaporate in the insipidity of emasculation. This is the last recorded performance of Mrs. Behn's brilliant comedy in any shape.

THE ROVER;
or, the Banish'd Cavaliers.

PART I.

PROLOGUE,
Written by a Person of Quality.

WITS, like Physicians, never can agree,
When of a different Society;
And Rabel's Drops [p. 7] * were never more cry'd down
By all the Learned Doctors of the Town,
Than a new Play, whose Author is unknown:
Nor can those Doctors with more Malice sue
(And powerful Purses) the dissenting Few,
Than those with an insulting Pride do rail
At all who are not of their own Cabal.
   If a Young Poet hit your Humor right,
You judge him then out of Revenge and Spite;
So amongst Men there are ridiculous Elves,
Who Monkeys hate for being too like themselves:
So that the Reason of the Grand Debate,
Why Wit so oft is damn'd, when good Plays take,
Is, that you censure as you love or hate.
Thus, like a learned Conclave, Poets sit
Catholic Judges both of Sense and Wit,
And damn or save, as they themselves think fit.
Yet those who to others Faults are so severe,
Are not so perfect, but themselves may err.
Some write correct indeed, but then the whole
(Bating their own dull Stuff i'th' Play) is stole:
As Bees do suck from Flowers their Honey-dew,
So they rob others, striving to please you.
Some write their Characters genteel and fine,
But then they do so toil for every Line,
That what to you does easy seem, and plain,
Is the hard issue of their laboring Brain.
And some th' Effects of all their Pains we see,
Is but to mimic good Extempore.
Others by long Converse about the Town,
Have Wit enough to write a leud Lampoon,
But their chief Skill lies in a Baudy Song.
In short, the only Wit that's now in Fashion
Is but the Gleanings of good Conversation.
As for the Author of this coming Play,
I ask'd him what he thought fit I should say,
In thanks for your good Company today:

He call'd me Fool, and said it was well known,
You came not here for our sakes, but your own.
New Plays are stuff'd with Wits, and with Debauches,
That croud and sweat like Cits in May-day Coaches. [p. 8]

* The page numbers referenced here refer to the page numbers of the original edition from which this text is drawn. The numbers have been retained here and in the corresponding note section at the end of the text.

DRAMATIS PERSONÆ.

MEN.

Don *Antonio*, the Vice-Roy's Son,
Don *Pedro*, a Noble *Spaniard*, his Friend,
Belvile, an English Colonel in love with Florinda,
Willmore, the ROVER,
Frederick, an *English* Gentleman, and Friend to *Belvile* and *Blunt*,
Blunt, an *English* Country Gentleman,
Stephano, Servant to Don *Pedro*,
Philippo, *Lucetta's* Gallant,
Sancho, Pimp to *Lucetta*,
Bisky and *Sebastian*, two Bravoes to *Angelica*.
Diego, Page to Don *Antonio*. [2] [p. 9]
Page to *Hellena*.
Boy, Page to *Belvile*.
Blunt's Man.
Officers and Soldiers.

WOMEN.

Florinda, Sister to Don *Pedro*,
Hellena, a gay young Woman design'd for a Nun, and Sister to *Florinda*,
Valeria, a Kinswoman to *Florinda*,
Angelica, [3] Bianca, a famous *Courtesan*,
Moretta, her Woman,
Callis, Governess to *Florinda* and *Hellena*,
Lucetta, a jilting Wench,
Servants, other Maskraders, Men and Women.

SCENE *Naples*, in Carnival-time.

ACT I.

Scene I. *A chamber.*

[*Enter* Florinda *and* Hellena.]

Flor. What an impertinent thing is a young Girl bred in a Nunnery! How full of Questions! Prithee no more, *Hellena*; I have told thee more than thou understand'st already.

Hell. The more's my Grief; I wou'd fain know as much as you, which makes me so inquisitive; nor is't enough to know you're a Lover, unless you tell me too, who 'tis you sigh for.

Flor. When you are a Lover, I'll think you fit for a Secret of that nature.

Hell. 'Tis true, I was never a Lover yet—but I begin to have a shrewd Guess, what 'tis to be so, and fancy it very pretty to sigh, and sing, and blush and wish, and dream and wish, and long and wish to see the Man; and when I do, look pale and tremble; just as you did when my Brother brought home the fine *English* Colonel to see you—what do you call him? Don *Belvile.*

Flor. Fie, *Hellena.*

Hell. That Blush betrays you—I am sure 'tis so—or is it Don *Antonio* the Vice-Roy's Son?—or perhaps the rich old Don *Vincentio*, whom my father designs for your Husband?—Why do you blush again?

Flor. With Indignation; and how near soever my Father thinks I am to marrying that hated Object, I shall let him see I understand better what's due to my Beauty, Birth and Fortune, and more to my Soul, than to obey those unjust Commands.

Hell. Now hang me, if I don't love thee for that dear Disobedience. I love Mischief strangely, as most of our Sex do, who are come to love nothing else—But tell me, dear *Florinda*, don't you love that fine *Anglese?*—for I vow next to loving him myself, 'twill please me most that you do so, for he is so gay and so handsome.

Flor. Hellena, a Maid design'd for a Nun ought not to be so curious in a Discourse of Love.

Hell. And dost thou think that ever I'll be a Nun? Or at least till I'm so old, I'm fit for nothing else. Faith no, Sister; and that which makes me long to know whether you love *Belvile*, is because I hope he has some mad Companion or other, that will spoil my Devotion; nay I'm resolv'd to provide myself this Carnival, if there be e'er a handsome Fellow of my Humor above Ground, tho I ask first.

Flor. Prithee be not so wild.

Hell. Now you have provided yourself with a Man, you take no Care for poor me—Prithee tell me, what dost thou see about me that is unfit for Love—have not I a world of Youth? a Humor gay? a Beauty passable? a Vigour desirable? well shap'd? clean limb'd? sweet breath'd? and Sense enough to know how all these ought to be employ'd to the best Advantage: yes, I do and Willmore Therefore lay aside your Hopes of my Fortune, by my being a Devotee, and tell me how you came acquainted with this *Belvile*; for I perceive you knew him before he came to *Naples.*

Flor. Yes, I knew him at the Siege of *Pampelona*, [p. 11] he was then a Colonel of *French* Horse, who when the Town was ransack'd, nobly treated my Brother and myself, preserving us from all Insolencies; and I must own, (besides great Obligations) I have I know not what, that pleads kindly for him about my Heart, and will suffer no other to enter—But see my Brother.

[*Enter* Don Pedro, Stephano, *with a Masquing Habit, and* Callis.]

Pedro. Good morrow, Sister. Pray, when saw you your Lover Don *Vincentio?*

Flor. I know not, Sir—*Callis*, when was he here? for I consider it so little, I know not when it was.

Pedro. I have a Command from my Father here to tell you, you ought not to despise him, a Man of so vast a Fortune, and such a Passion for you—*Stephano*, my things [4]—

[*Puts on his Masking Habit.*]

Flor. A Passion for me! 'tis more than e'er I saw, or had a desire should be known—I hate *Vincentio*, and I would not have a Man so dear to me as my Brother follow the ill Customs of our Country, and make a Slave of his Sister—And Sir, my Father's Will, I'm sure, you may divert.

Pedro. I know not how dear I am to you, but I wish only to be rank'd in your Esteem, equal with the *English* Colonel *Belvile*—Why do you frown and blush? Is there any Guilt belongs to the Name of that Cavalier?

Flor. I'll not deny I value *Belvile*: when I was expos'd to such Dangers as the licens'd Lust of common Soldiers threatened, when Rage and Conquest flew thro the City—then *Belvile*, this Criminal for my sake, threw himself into all Dangers to save my Honor, and will you not allow him my Esteem?

Pedro. Yes, pay him what you will in Honor—but you must consider Don *Vincentio's* Fortune, and the Jointure he'll make you.

Flor. Let him consider my Youth, Beauty and Fortune; which ought not to be thrown away on his Age and Jointure.

Pedro. 'Tis true, he's not so young and fine a Gentleman as that *Belvile*—but what Jewels will that Cavalier present you with? those of his Eyes and Heart?

Hell. And are not those better than any Don *Vincentio* has brought from the *Indies?*

Pedro. Why how now! Has your Nunnery-breeding taught you to understand the Value of Hearts and Eyes?

Hell. Better than to believe *Vincentio* deserves Value from any woman—He may perhaps increase her Bags, but not her Family.

Pedro. This is fine—Go up to your Devotion, you are not design'd for the Conversation of Lovers.

Hell. Nor Saints yet a while I hope. [*Aside.*] Is't not enough you make a Nun of me, but you must cast my Sister away too, exposing her to a worse confinement than a religious Life?

Pedro. The Girl's mad—Is it a Confinement to be carry'd into the Country, to an ancient Villa belonging to the Family of the *Vincentio's* these five hundred Years, and have no other Prospect than that pleasing one of seeing all her own that meets her Eyes—a fine Air, large Fields and Gardens, where she may walk and gather Flowers?

Hell. When? By Moon-Light? For I'm sure she dares not encounter with the heat of the Sun; that were a Task only for Don *Vincentio* and his *Indian* Breeding, who loves it in the Dog-days—And if these be her daily Divertissements, what are those of the Night? to lie in a wide Moth-eaten Bed-Chamber with Furniture in Fashion in the Reign of King *Sancho* the First; [p. 13] the Bed that which his Forefathers liv'd and dy'd in.

Pedro. Very well.

Hell. This Apartment (new furbished and fitted out for the young Wife) he (out of Freedom) makes his Dressing-room; and being a frugal and a jealous Coxcomb, instead of a Valet to uncase his feeble Carcass, he desires you to do that Office—Signs of Favor, I'll assure you, and such as you must not hope for, unless your Woman be out of the way.

Pedro. Have you done yet?

Hell. That Honor being past, the Giant stretches itself, yawns and sighs a Belch or two as loud as a Musket, throws himself into Bed, and expects you in his foul Sheets, and e'er you can get yourself undressed, calls you with a Snore or two—And are not these fine Blessings to a young Lady?

Pedro. Have you done yet?

Hell. And this man you must kiss, nay, you must kiss none but him too—and nuzle thro his Beard to find his Lips—and this you must submit to for threescore Years, and all for a Jointure.

Pedro. For all your Character of Don *Vincentio*, she is as like to marry him as she was before.

Hell. Marry Don *Vincentio!* hang me, such a Wedlock would be worse than Adultery with another Man: I had rather see her in the *Hostel de Dieu*, [p. 14] to waste her Youth there in Vows, and be a Handmaid to Lazers and Cripples, than to lose it in such a Marriage.

Pedro. You have consider'd, Sister, that *Belvile* has no Fortune to bring you to, is banished his Country, despis'd at home, and pity'd abroad.

Hell. What then? the Vice-Roy's Son is better than that Old Sir Fisty. Don *Vincentio!* Don *Indian!* he thinks he's trading to *Gambo* [p. 14] still, and wou'd barter himself (that Bell and Bawble) for your Youth and Fortune.

Pedro. *Callis*, take her hence, and lock her up all this Carnival, and at Lent she shall begin her everlasting Penance in a Monastery.

Hell. I care not, I had rather be a Nun, than be oblig'd to marry as you wou'd have me, if I were design'd for't.

Pedro. Do not fear the Blessing of that Choice—you shall be a Nun.

Hell. Shall I so? you may chance to be mistaken in my way of Devotion—A Nun! yes I am like to make a fine Nun! I have an excellent Humor for a Grate: No, I'll have a Saint of my own to pray to shortly, if I like any that dares venture on me. [*Aside.*]

Pedro. *Callis*, make it your Business to watch this wild Cat. As for you, *Florinda*, I've only try'd you all this while, and urg'd my Father's Will; but mine is, that you would love *Antonio*, he is brave and young, and all that can compleat the Happiness of a gallant Maid—This Absence of my Father will give us opportunity to free you from *Vincentio*, by marrying here, which you must do tomorrow.

Flor. Tomorrow!

Pedro. Tomorrow, or 'twill be too late—'tis not my Friendship to *Antonio*, which makes me urge this, but Love to thee, and Hatred to *Vincentio*—therefore resolve upon't tomorrow.

Flor. Sir, I shall strive to do, as shall become your Sister.

Pedro. I'll both believe and trust you—Adieu. [*Exit* Pedro *and* Stephano]

Hell. As become his Sister!—That is, to be as resolved your way, as he is his— [Hellena *goes to* Callis.]

Flor. I ne'er till now perceiv'd my Ruin near,
I've no Defence against *Antonio's* Love,
For he has all the Advantages of Nature,
The moving Arguments of Youth and Fortune.

Hell. But hark you, *Callis*, you will not be so cruel to lock me up indeed: will you?

Call. I must obey the Commands I hate—besides, do you consider what a Life you are going to lead?

Hell. Yes, *Callis*, that of a Nun: and till then I'll be indebted a World of Prayers to you, if you let me now see, what I never did, the Divertissements of a Carnival.

Call. What, go in Maskrade? 'twill be a fine farewell to the World I take it—pray what wou'd you do there?

Hell. That which all the World does, as I am told, be as mad as the rest, and take all innocent Freedom—Sister, you'll go too, will you not? come prithee be not sad—We'll out-wit twenty Brothers, if you'll be ruled by me—Come put off this dull Humor with your Clothes, and assume one as gay, and as fantastic as the Dress my Cousin *Valeria* and I have provided, and let's ramble.

Flor. Callis, will you give us leave to go?

Call. I have a youthful Itch of going myself. [*Aside.*]—Madam, if I thought your Brother might not know it, and I might wait on you, for by my troth I'll not trust young Girls alone.

Flor. Thou see'st my Brother's gone already, and thou shalt attend and watch us.

[*Enter* Stephano.]

Steph. Madam, the Habits are come, and your Cousin Valeria is dressed, and stays for you.

Flor. 'Tis well—I'll write a Note, and if I chance to see *Belvile*, and want an opportunity to speak to him, that shall let him know what I've resolv'd in favor of him.

Hell. Come, let's in and dress us. [*Exeunt.*]

Scene II. *A Long Street.*

[*Enter* Belvile*, melancholy,* Blunt *and* Frederick.]

Fred. Why, what the Devil ails the Colonel, in a time when all the World is gay, to look like mere Lent thus? Hadst thou been long enough in *Naples* to have been in love, I should have sworn some such Judgment had befall'n thee.

Belv. No, I have made no new Amours since I came to Naples.

Fred. You have left none behind you in Paris.

Belv. Neither.

Fred. I can't divine the Cause then; unless the old Cause, the want of Money.

Blunt. And another old Cause, the want of a Wench—Wou'd not that revive you?

Belv. You're mistaken, *Ned.*

Blunt. Nay, 'Sheartlikins, then thou art past Cure.

Fred. I have found it out; thou hast renew'd thy Acquaintance with the Lady that cost thee so many Sighs at the Siege of *Pampelona*—pox on't, what d'ye call her—her Brother's a noble *Spaniard*—Nephew to the dead General—*Florinda*—ay, *Florinda*—And will nothing serve thy turn but that damn'd virtuous Woman, whom on my

Conscience thou lov'st in spite too, because thou seest little or no possibility of gaining her?

Belv. Thou art mistaken, I have Interest enough in that lovely Virgin's Heart, to make me proud and vain, were it not abated by the Severity of a Brother, who perceiving my Happiness—

Fred. Has civilly forbid thee the House?

Belv. 'Tis so, to make way for a powerful Rival, the Vice-Roy's Son, who has the advantage of me, in being a Man of Fortune, a *Spaniard*, and her Brother's Friend; which gives him liberty to make his Court, whilst I have recourse only to Letters, and distant Looks from her Window, which are as soft and kind as those which Heav'n sends down on Penitents. [5]

Blunt. Hey day! 'Sheartlikins, Simile! by this Light the Man is quite spoil'd—*Frederick*, what the Devil are we made of, that we cannot be thus concern'd for a Wench?—'Sheartlikins, our *Cupids* are like the Cooks of the Camp, they can roast or boil a Woman, but they have none of the fine Tricks to set 'em off, no Hogoes [p. 17] to make the Sauce pleasant, and the Stomach sharp.

Fred. I dare swear I have had a hundred as young, kind and handsome as this *Florinda*; and Dogs eat me, if they were not as troublesome to me i'th' Morning as they were welcome o'er night.

Blunt. And yet, I warrant, he wou'd not touch another Woman, if he might have her for nothing.

Belv. That's thy Joy, a cheap Whore.

Blunt. Why, 'dsheartlikins, I love a frank Soul—When did you ever hear of an honest Woman that took a Man's Money? I warrant 'em good ones—But, Gentlemen, you may be free, you have been kept so poor with Parliaments and Protectors, that the little Stock you have is not worth preserving—but I thank my Stars, I have more Grace than to forfeit my Estate by Cavaliering.

Belv. Methinks only following the Court should be sufficient to entitle 'em to that.

Blunt. 'Sheartlikins, they know I follow it to do it no good, unless they pick a hole in my Coat for lending you Money now and then; which is a greater Crime to my Conscience, Gentlemen, than to the Common-wealth.

[*Enter* Willmore.]

Will. Ha! dear *Belvile!* noble Colonel!

Belv. Willmore! welcome ashore, my dear Rover!—what happy Wind blew us this good Fortune?

Will. Let me salute you my dear *Frederick*, and then command me—How is't honest Lad?

Fred. Faith, Sir, the old Complement, infinitely the better to see my dear mad *Willmore* again—Prithee why camest thou ashore? and where's the Prince?

Will. He's well, and reigns still Lord of the watery Element—I must aboard again within a Day or two, and my Business ashore was only to enjoy myself a little this Carnival.

Belv. Pray know our new Friend, Sir, he's but bashful, a raw Traveller, but honest, stout, and one of us. [Embraces *Blunt.*

Will. That you esteem him, gives him an Interest here.

Blunt. Your Servant, Sir.

Will. But well—Faith I'm glad to meet you again in a warm Climate, where the kind Sun has its god-like Power still over the Wine and Woman.—Love and Mirth are my Business in *Naples*; and if I mistake not the Place, here's an excellent Market for Chapmen of my Humor.

Belv. See here be those kind Merchants of Love you look for.

[*Enter several Men in masquing Habits, some playing on Music, others dancing after; Women dressed like Courtesans, with Papers pinn'd to their Breasts, and Baskets of Flowers in their Hands.*]

Blunt. 'Sheartlikins, what have we here!

Fred. Now the Game begins.

Will. Fine pretty Creatures! may a stranger have leave to look and love?—What's here—*Roses for every Month!* [*Reads the Paper.*]

Blunt. Roses for every Month! what means that?

Belv. They are, or wou'd have you think they're Courtesans, who herein *Naples* are to be hir'd by the Month.

Will. Kind and obliging to inform us—Pray where do these Roses grow? I would fain plant some of 'em in a Bed of mine.

Woman. Beware such Roses, Sir.

Will. A Pox of fear: I'll be bak'd with thee between a pair of Sheets, and that's thy proper Still, so I might but strow such Roses over me and under me—Fair one, wou'd you wou'd give me leave to gather at your Bush this idle Month, I wou'd go near to make some Body smell of it all the Year after.

Belv. And thou hast need of such a Remedy, for thou stinkest of Tar and Rope-ends, like a Dock or Pesthouse.

[*The Woman puts herself into the Hands of a Man, and Exit.*]

Will. Nay, nay, you shall not leave me so.

Belv. By all means use no Violence here.

Will. Death! just as I was going to be damnably in love, to have her led off! I could pluck that Rose out-of his Hand, and even kiss the Bed, the Bush it grew in.

Fred. No Friend to Love like a long Voyage at Sea.

Blunt. Except a Nunnery, *Frederick*

Will. Death! but will they not be kind, quickly be kind? Thou know'st I'm no tame Sigher, but a rampant Lion of the Forest.

[*Two Men dressed all over with Horns of several sorts, making Grimaces at one another, with Papers pinn'd on their Backs, advance from the farther end of the Scene.*]

Belv. Oh the fantastical Rogues, how they are dress'd! 'tis a Satir against the whole Sex.

Will. Is this a Fruit that grows in this warm Country?

Belv. Yes: 'Tis pretty to see these *Italian* start, swell, and stab at the Word *Cuckold*, and yet stumble at Horns on every Threshold.

Will. See what's on their Back—*Flowers for every Night.* [*Reads.*]—Ah Rogue! And more sweet than Roses of ev'ry Month! This is a Gardiner of *Adam's* own breeding. [*They dance.*]

Belv. What think you of those grave People?—is a Wake in *Essex* half so mad or extravagant?

Will. I like their sober grave way, 'tis a kind of legal authoriz'd Fornication, where the Men are not chid for't, nor the Women despis'd, as amongst our dull *English*; even the Monsieurs want that part of good Manners.

Belv. But here in *Italy* a Monsieur is the humblest best-bred Gentleman—Duels are so baffled by Bravo's that an age shows not one, but between a *Frenchman* and a Hangman, who is as much too hard for him on the Piazza, as they are for a *Dutchman* on the new Bridge—But see another Crew.

[*Enter* Florinda, Hellena, *and* Valeria, *dressed like Gypsies;* Callis *and* Stephano, Lucetta, Philippo *and* Sancho *in Maskrade.*]

Hell. Sister, there's your *Englishman*, and with him a handsome proper Fellow—I'll to him, and instead of telling him his Fortune, try my own.

Will. Gypsies, on my Life—Sure these will prattle if a Man cross their Hands. [*Goes to* Hellena]—Dear pretty (and I hope) young Devil, will you tell an amorous Stranger what Luck he's like to have?

Hell. Have a care how you venture with me, Sir, lest I pick your Pocket, which will more vex your *English* Humor, than an *Italian* Fortune will please you.

Will. How the Devil cam'st thou to know my Country and Humor?

Hell. The first I guess by a certain forward Impudence, which does not displease me at this time; and the Loss of your Money will vex you, because I hope you have but very little to lose.

Will. Egad Child, thou'rt i'th' right; it is so little, I dare not offer it thee for a Kindness—But cannot you divine what other things of more value I have about me, that I would more willingly part with?

Hell. Indeed no, that's the Business of a Witch, and I am but a Gipsy yet—Yet, without looking in your Hand, I have a parlous Guess, 'tis some foolish Heart you mean, an inconstant *English* Heart, as little worth stealing as your Purse.

Will. Nay, then thou dost deal with the Devil, that's certain—Thou hast guess'd as right as if thou hadst been one of that Number it has languished for—I find you'll be better acquainted with it; nor can you take it in a better time, for I am come from Sea, Child; and *Venus* not being propitious to me in her own Element, I have a world of Love in store—Wou'd you would be good-natur'd, and take some on't off my Hands.

Hell. Why—I could be inclin'd that way—but for a foolish Vow I am going to make—to die a Maid.

Will. Then thou art damn'd without Redemption; and as I am a good Christian, I ought in charity to divert so wicked a design—therefore prithee, dear Creature, let me know quickly when and where I shall begin to set a helping hand to so good a Work.

Hell. If you should prevail with my tender Heart (as I begin to fear you will, for you have horrible loving Eyes) there will be difficulty in't that you'll hardly undergo for my sake.

Will. Faith, Child, I have been bred in Dangers, and wear a Sword that has been employ'd in a worse Cause, than for a handsome kind Woman—Name the Danger—let it be anything but a long Siege, and I'll undertake it.

Hell. Can you storm?

Will. Oh, most furiously.

Hell. What think you of a Nunnery-wall? for he that wins me, must gain that first.

Will. A Nun! Oh how I love thee for't! there's no Sinner like a young Saint—Nay, now there's no denying me: the old Law had no Curse (to a Woman) like dying a Maid; witness *Jephtha's* Daughter.

Hell. A very good Text this, if well handled; and I perceive, Father Captain, you would impose no severe Penance on her who was inclin'd to console herself before she took Orders.

Will. If she be young and handsome.

Hell. Ay, there's it—but if she be not—

Will. By this Hand, Child, I have an implicit Faith, and dare venture on thee with all Faults—besides, 'tis more meritorious to leave the World when thou hast tasted and prov'd the Pleasure on't; then 'twill be a Virtue in thee, which now will be pure Ignorance.

Hell. I perceive, good Father Captain, you design only to make me fit for Heaven—but if on the contrary you should quite divert me from it, and bring me back to the World again, I should have a new Man to seek I find; and what a grief that will be—for when I begin, I fancy I shall love like any thing: I never try'd yet.

Will. Egad, and that's kind—Prithee, dear Creature, give me Credit for a Heart, for faith, I'm a very honest Fellow—Oh, I long to come first to the Banquet of Love; and such a swinging Appetite I bring—Oh, I'm impatient. Thy Lodging, Sweetheart, thy Lodging, or I'm a dead man.

Hell. Why must we be either guilty of Fornication or Murder, if we converse with you Men?—And is there no difference between leave to love me, and leave to lie with me?

Will. Faith, Child, they were made to go together.

Luc. Are you sure this is the Man? [*Pointing to* Blunt.]

Sancho. When did I mistake your Game?

Luc. This is a stranger, I know by his gazing; if he be brisk he'll venture to follow me; and then, if I understand my Trade, he's mine: he's *English* too, and they say that's a sort of good natur'd loving People, and have generally so kind an opinion of themselves, that a Woman with any Wit may flatter 'em into any sort of Fool she pleases.

Blunt. 'Tis so—she is taken—I have Beauties which my false Glass at home did not discover.

[*She often passes by* Blunt *and gazes on him; he struts, and cocks, and walks, and gazes on her.*] [6]

Flor. This Woman watches me so, I shall get no Opportunity to discover myself to him, and so miss the intent of my coming—But as I was saying, Sir—by this Line you should be a Lover. [*Looking in his Hand.*]

Belv. I thought how right you guess'd, all Men are in love, or pretend to be so—Come, let me go, I'm weary of this fooling. [*Walks away.*]

Flor. I will not, till you have confess'd whether the Passion that you have vow'd *Florinda* be true or false. [*She holds him, he strives to get from her.*]

Belv. Florinda! [*Turns quick towards her.*]

Flor. Softly.

Belv. Thou hast nam'd one will fix me here forever.

Flor. She'll be disappointed then, who expects you this Night at the Garden-gate, and if you'll fail not—as let me see the other Hand—you will go near to do—she vows to die or make you happy. [*Looks on* Callis, *who observes 'em.*]

Belv. What canst thou mean?

Flor. That which I say—Farewell. [*Offers to go.*]

Belv. Oh charming Sybil, stay, complete that Joy, which, as it is, will turn into Distraction!—Where must I be? at the Garden-gate? I know it—at night you say—I'll sooner forfeit Heaven than disobey.

[*Enter* Don Pedro *and other Maskers, and pass over the Stage.*]

Call. Madam, your Brother's here.

Flor. Take this to instruct you farther. [*Gives him a Letter, and goes off.*]

Fred. Have a care, Sir, what you promise; this may be a Trap laid by her Brother to ruin you.

Belv. Do not disturb my Happiness with Doubts. [*Opens the Letter.*]

Will. My dear pretty Creature, a Thousand Blessings on thee; still in this Habit, you say, and after Dinner at this Place.

Hell. Yes, if you will swear to keep your Heart, and not bestow it between this time and that.

Will. By all the little Gods of Love I swear, I'll leave it with you; and if you run away with it, those Deities of Justice will revenge me. [*Exit all the Women except* Lucetta.] [7]

Fred. Do you know the Hand?

Belv. 'Tis *Florinda's*. All Blessings fall upon the virtuous Maid.

Fred. Nay, no Idolatry, a sober Sacrifice I'll allow you.

Belv. Oh Friends! the welcom'st News, the softest Letter!—nay, you shall see it; and could you now be serious, I might be made the happiest Man the Sun shines on.

Will. The Reason of this mighty Joy.

Belv. See how kindly she invites me to deliver her from the threaten'd Violence of her Brother—will you not assist me?

Will. I know not what thou mean'st, but I'll make one at any Mischief where a Woman's concerned—but she'll be grateful to us for the Favor, will she not?

Belv. How mean you?

Will. How should I mean? Thou know'st there's but one way for a Woman to oblige me.

Belv. Don't prophane—the Maid is nicely virtuous.

Will. Who pox, then she's fit for nothing but a Husband; let her e'en go, Colonel.

Fred. Peace, she's the Colonel's Mistress, Sir.

Will. Let her be the Devil; if she be thy Mistress, I'll serve her—name the way.

Belv. Read here this Postscript. [*Gives him a Letter.*

Will. [*Reads.*] *At Ten at night—at the Garden-Gate—of which, if I cannot get the Key, I will contrive a way over the Wall—come attended with a Friend or two.*—Kind heart, if we three cannot weave a String to let her down a Garden-Wall, 'twere pity but the Hangman wove one for us all.

Fred. Let her alone for that: your Woman's Wit, your fair kind Woman, will out-trick a Brother or a Jew, and contrive like a Jesuit in Chains—but see, *Ned Blunt* is stolen out after the Lure of a Damsel. [*Exit* Blunt *and* Lucetta]

Belv. So he'll scarce find his way home again, unless we get him cry'd by the Bell-man in the Market-place, and 'twou'd sound prettily—a lost *English* Boy of Thirty.

Fred. I hope 'tis some common crafty Sinner, one that will fit him; it may be she'll sell him for *Peru*, the Rogue's sturdy and would work well in a Mine; at least I hope she'll dress him for our Mirth; cheat him of all, then have him well-favor'dly bang'd, and turn'd out naked at Midnight.

Will. Prithee what Humor is he of, that you wish him so well?

Belv. Why, of an *English* Elder Brother's Humor, educated in a Nursery, with a Maid to tend him till Fifteen, and lies with his Grand-mother till he's of Age; one that knows no Pleasure beyond riding to the next Fair, or going up to *London* with his right Worshipful Father in Parliament-time; wearing gay Clothes, or making honorable Love to his Lady Mother's Landry-Maid; gets drunk at a Hunting-Match, and ten to one then gives some Proofs of his Prowess—A pox upon him, he's our Banker, and has all our Cash about him, and if he fail we are all broke.

Fred. Oh let him alone for that matter, he's of a damn'd stingy Quality, that will secure our Stock. I know not in what Danger it were indeed, if the Jilt should pretend she's in love with him, for 'tis a kind believing Coxcomb; otherwise if he part with more than a Piece of Eight [p. 26]—geld him: for which offer he may chance to be beaten, if she be a Whore of the first Rank.

Belv. Nay the Rogue will not be easily beaten, he's stout enough; perhaps if they talk beyond his Capacity, he may chance to exercise his Courage upon some of them; else I'm sure they'll find it as difficult to beat as to please him.

Will. 'Tis a lucky Devil to light upon so kind a Wench!

Fred. Thou hadst a great deal of talk with thy little Gipsy, coud'st thou do no good upon her? for mine was hard-hearted.

Will. Hang her, she was some damn'd honest Person of Quality, I'm sure, she was so very free and witty. If her Face be but answerable to her Wit and Humor, I would be bound to Constancy this Month to gain her. In the mean time, have you made no kind Acquaintance since you came to Town?—You do not use to be honest so long, Gentlemen.

Fred. Faith Love has kept us honest, we have been all fir'd with a Beauty newly come to Town, the famous *Paduana Angelica Bianca.*

Will. What, the Mistress of the dead *Spanish* General?

Belv. Yes, she's now the only ador'd Beauty of all the Youth in *Naples*, who put on all their Charms to appear lovely in her sight, their Coaches, Liveries, and themselves, all gay, as on a Monarch's Birth-Day, to attract the Eyes of this fair Charmer, while she has the Pleasure to behold all languish for her that see her.

Fred. 'Tis pretty to see with how much Love the Men regard her, and how much Envy the Women.

Will. What Gallant has she?

Belv. None, she's exposed to Sale, and four Days in the Week she's yours—for so much a Month.

Will. The very Thought of it quenches all manner of Fire in me—yet prithee let's see her.

Belv. Let's first to Dinner, and after that we'll pass the Day as you please—but at Night ye must all be at my Devotion.

Will. I will not fail you. [*Exeunt.*]

ACT II.

Scene I. *The Long Street.*

[*Enter* Belvile *and* Frederick *in Masquing-Habits, and* Willmore *in his own Clothes, with a Vizard in his Hand.*]

Will. But why thus disguis'd and muzzl'd?

Belv. Because whatever Extravagances we commit in these Faces, our own may not be oblig'd to answer 'em.

Will. I should have chang'd my Eternal Buff too: but no matter, my little Gipsy wou'd not have found me out then: for if she should change hers, it is impossible I should know her, unless I should hear her prattle—A Pox on't, I cannot get her out of my Head: Pray Heaven, if ever I do see her again, she prove damnable ugly, that I may fortify myself against her Tongue.

Belv. Have a care of Love, for o' my conscience she was not of a Quality to give thee any hopes.

Will. Pox on 'em, why do they draw a Man in then? She has play'd with my Heart so, that 'twill never lie still till I have met with some kind Wench, that will play the Game out with me—Oh for my Arms full of soft, white, kind—Woman! such as I fancy *Angelica*.

Belv. This is her House, if you were but in stock to get admittance; they have not din'd yet; I perceive the Picture is not out.

[*Enter* Blunt.]

Will. I long to see the Shadow of the fair Substance, a Man may gaze on that for nothing.

Blunt. Colonel, thy Hand—and thine, *Frederick* I have been an Ass, a deluded Fool, a very Coxcomb from my Birth till this Hour, and heartily repent my little Faith.

Belv. What the Devil's the matter with thee *Ned?*

Blunt. Oh such a Mistress, *Frederick*, such a Girl!

Will. Ha! where?

Fred. Ay where!

Blunt. So fond, so amorous, so toying and fine! and all for sheer Love, ye Rogue! Oh how she looked and kiss'd! and sooth'd my Heart from my Bosom. I cannot think I was awake, and yet methinks I see and feel her Charms still—*Frederick*—Try if she have not left the Taste of her balmy Kisses upon my Lips—[*Kisses him.*]

Belv. Ha, ha, ha!

Will. Death Man, where is she?

Blunt. What a Dog was I to stay in dull *England* so long—How have I laughed at the Colonel when he sigh'd for Love! but now the little Archer has reveng'd him, and by his own Dart, I can guess at all his Joys, which then I took for Fancies, mere Dreams and Fables—Well, I'm resolved to sell all in *Essex*, and plant here forever.

50

Belv. What a Blessing 'tis, thou hast a Mistress thou dar'st boast of; for I know thy Humor is rather to have a proclaim'd Clap, than a secret Amour.

Will. Dost know her Name?

Blunt. Her Name? No, 'sheartlikins: what care I for Names?—She's fair, young, brisk and kind, even to ravishment: and what a Pox care I for knowing her by another Title?

Will. Didst give her anything?

Blunt. Give her!—Ha, ha, ha! why, she's a Person of Quality—That's a good one, give her! 'sheartlikins dost think such Creatures are to be bought? Or are we provided for such a Purchase? Give her, quoth ye? Why she presented me with this Bracelet, for the Toy of a Diamond I us'd to wear: No, Gentlemen, *Ned Blunt* is not every Body—She expects me again tonight.

Will. Egad that's well; we'll all go.

Blunt. Not a Soul: No, Gentlemen, you are Wits; I am a dull Country Rogue, I.

Fred. Well, Sir, for all your Person of Quality, I shall be very glad to understand your Purse be secure; 'tis our whole Estate at present, which we are loth to hazard in one Bottom: come, Sir, unload.

Blunt. Take the necessary Trifle, useless now to me, that am belov'd by such a Gentlewoman—'sheartlikins Money! Here take mine too.

Fred. No, keep that to be cozen'd, that we may laugh.

Will. Cozen'd!—Death! wou'd I cou'd meet with one, that wou'd cozen me of all the Love I cou'd spare tonight.

Fred. Pox 'tis some common Whore upon my Life.

Blunt. A Whore! yes with such Clothes! such Jewels! such a House! such Furniture, and so attended! a Whore!

Belv. Why yes, Sir, they are Whores, tho they'll neither entertain you with Drinking, Swearing, or Baudy; are Whores in all those gay Clothes, and right Jewels; are Whores with great Houses richly furnished with Velvet Beds, Store of Plate, handsome Attendance, and fine Coaches, are Whores and errant ones.

Will. Pox on't, where do these fine Whores live?

Belv. Where no Rogue in Office yclep'd Constables dare give 'em laws, nor the Wine-inspired Bullies of the Town break their Windows; yet they are Whores, tho this *Essex* Calf believe them Persons of Quality.

Blunt. 'Sheartlikins, y'are all Fools, there are things about this *Essex* Calf, that shall take with the Ladies, beyond all your Wits and Parts—This Shape and Size, Gentlemen, are not to be despis'd; my Waste tolerably long, with other inviting Signs, that shall be nameless.

Will. Egad I believe he may have met with some Person of Quality that may be kind to him.

Belv. Dost thou perceive any such tempting things about him, should make a fine Woman, and of Quality, pick him out from all Mankind, to throw away her Youth and Beauty upon, nay, and her dear Heart too?—no, no, *Angelica* has rais'd the Price too high.

Will. May she languish for Mankind till she die, and be damn'd for that one Sin alone.

[*Enter two Bravoes, and hang up a great Picture of* Angelica's, *against the Balcony, and two little ones at each side of the Door.*] [p. 30]

Belv. See there the fair Sign to the Inn, where a Man may lodge that's Fool enough to give her Price. [Willmore *gazes on the Picture.*]

Blunt. 'Sheartlikins, Gentlemen, what's this?

Belv. A famous Courtesan that's to be sold.

Blunt. How! to be sold! nay then I have nothing to say to her—sold! what Impudence is practis'd in this Country?—With Order and Decency Whoring's established here by virtue of the Inquisition—Come let's be gone, I'm sure we're no Chapmen for this Commodity.

Fred. Thou art none, I'm sure, unless thou could'st have her in thy Bed at the Price of a Coach in the Street.

Will. How wondrous fair she is—a Thousand Crowns a Month—by Heaven as many Kingdoms were too little. A plague of this Poverty—of which I ne'er complain, but when it hinders my Approach to Beauty, which Virtue ne'er could purchase. [*Turns from the Picture.*]

Blunt. What's this?—[*Reads*] *A Thousand Crowns a Month!*—'Sheartlikins, here's a Sum! sure 'tis a mistake.—Hark you, Friend, does she take or give so much by the Month!

Fred. A Thousand Crowns! Why, 'tis a Portion for the *Infanta.*

Blunt. Hark ye, Friends, won't she trust?

Brav. This is a Trade, Sir, that cannot live by Credit.

[*Enter* Don Pedro *in Maskrade, follow'd by* Stephano.]

Belv. See, here's more Company, let's walk off a while.

[Pedro *Reads.*] [*Exeunt* English.]
[*Enter* Angelica *and* Moretta *in the Balcony, and draw a Silk Curtain.*]

Pedro. Fetch me a Thousand Crowns, I never wish to buy this Beauty at an easier Rate. [*Passes off.*]

Ang. Prithee what said those Fellows to thee?

Brav. Madam, the first were Admirers of Beauty only, but no purchasers; they were merry with your Price and Picture, laughed at the Sum, and so past off.

Ang. No matter, I'm not displeas'd with their rallying; their Wonder feeds my Vanity, and he that wishes to buy, gives me more Pride, than he that gives my Price can make me Pleasure.

Brav. Madam, the last I knew thro all his disguises to be Don *Pedro*, Nephew to the General, and who was with him in *Pampelona.*

Ang. Don *Pedro!* my old Gallant's Nephew! When his Uncle dy'd, he left him a vast Sum of Money; it is he who was so in love with me at *Padua*, and who us'd to make the General so jealous.

Moret. Is this he that us'd to prance before our Window and take such care to show himself an amorous Ass? if I am not mistaken, he is the likeliest Man to give your Price.

Ang. The Man is brave and generous, but of an Humor so uneasy and inconstant, that the victory over his Heart is as soon lost as won; a Slave that can add little to the Triumph of the Conqueror: but inconstancy's the Sin of all Mankind, therefore I'm resolv'd that nothing but Gold shall charm my Heart.

Moret. I'm glad on't; 'tis only interest that Women of our Profession ought to consider: tho I wonder what has kept you from that general Disease of our Sex so long, I mean that of being in love.

Ang. A kind, but sullen Star, under which I had the Happiness to be born; yet I have had no time for Love; the bravest and noblest of Mankind have purchas'd my Favors at so dear a Rate, as if no Coin but Gold were current with our Trade—But here's Don *Pedro* again, fetch me my Lute—for 'tis for him or Don *Antonio* the Vice-Roy's Son, that I have spread my Nets.

[*Enter at one Door Don* Pedro, *and* Stephano; *Don* Antonio *and* Diego [*his page*] , *at the other Door, with People following him in Maskrade, antickly attir'd, some with Music: they both go up to the Picture.*]

Ant. A thousand Crowns! had not the Painter flatter'd her, I should not think it dear.

Pedro. Flatter'd her! by Heaven he cannot. I have seen the Original, nor is there one Charm here more than adorns her Face and Eyes; all this soft and sweet, with a certain languishing Air, that no Artist can represent.

Ant. What I heard of her Beauty before had fir'd my Soul, but this confirmation of it has blown it into a flame.

Pedro. Ha! [8]

Page. Sir, I have known you throw away a Thousand Crowns on a worse Face, and tho y' are near your Marriage, you may venture a little Love here; *Florinda*—will not miss it.

Pedro. Ha! *Florinda!* Sure 'tis *Antonio.* [*Aside.*] [9]

Ant. Florinda! name not those distant Joys, there's not one thought of her will check my Passion here.

Pedro. Florinda scorn'd! and all my Hopes defeated of the Possession of *Angelica!* [*A noise of a Lute above.* Antonio *gazes up.*] Her Injuries by Heaven he shall not boast of. [*Song to a Lute above.*]

SONG.

When Damon *first began to love,*
He languished in a soft Desire,
And knew not how the Gods to move,
To lessen or increase his Fire,
For Cælia *in her charming Eyes*
Wore all Love's Sweet, and all his Cruelties.

II.

But as beneath a Shade he lay,
Weaving of Flow'rs for Cælia's *Hair,*
She chanc'd to lead her Flock that way,
And saw the am'rous Shepherd there.
She gaz'd around upon the Place,
And saw the Grove (resembling Night)
To all the Joys of Love invite,

Whilst guilty Smiles and Blushes dressed her Face.
At this the bashful Youth all Transport grew,
And with kind Force he taught the Virgin how
To yield what all his Sighs cou'd never do.

Ant. By Heav'n she's charming fair!

[Angelica *throws open the Curtains, and bows to* Antonio, *who pulls off his Vizard, and bows and blows up Kisses.* Pedro *unseen looks in his Face.*]

Pedro. 'Tis he, the false *Antonio!*
Ant. Friend, where must I pay my offering of Love? [*To the* Bravo.] My Thousand Crowns I mean.
Pedro. That Offering I have design'd to make,
And yours will come too late.
Ant. Prithee be gone, I shall grow angry else,
And then thou art not safe.
Pedro. My Anger may be fatal, Sir, as yours;
And he that enters here may prove this Truth.
Ant. I know not who thou art, but I am sure thou'rt worth my killing, and aiming at *Angelica.* [*They draw and fight.*]

[*Enter* Willmore *and* Blunt, *who draw and part 'em.*]

Blunt. 'Sheartlikins, here's fine doings.
Will. Tilting for the Wench I'm sure—nay gad, if that wou'd win her, I have as good a Sword as the best of ye—Put up—put up, and take another time and place, for this is design'd for Lovers only. [*They all put up.*]
Pedro. We are prevented; dare you meet me tomorrow on the *Molo?*
For I've a Title to a better quarrel,
That of *Florinda*, in whose credulous Heart
Thou'st made an Int'rest, and destroy'd my Hopes.
Ant. Dare?
I'll meet thee there as early as the Day.
Pedro. We will come thus disguis'd, that whosoever chance to get the better, he may escape unknown.
Ant. It shall be so. [*Exit* Pedro *and* Stephano.] Who shou'd this Rival be? unless the *English* Colonel, of whom I've often heard Don *Pedro* speak; it must be he, and time he were removed, who lays a Claim to all my Happiness.

[Willmore *having gaz'd all this while on the Picture, pulls down a little one.*]

Will. This posture's loose and negligent,
The sight on't wou'd beget a warm desire
In Souls, whom Impotence and Age had chill'd.
—This must along with me.
Brav. What means this rudeness, Sir?—restore the Picture.
Ant. Ha! Rudeness committed to the fair *Angelica!*—Restore the Picture, Sir.

Will. Indeed I will not, Sir.

Ant. By Heav'n but you shall.

Will. Nay, do not show your Sword; if you do, by this dear Beauty—I will show mine too.

Ant. What right can you pretend to't?

Will. That of Possession which I will maintain—you perhaps have 1000 Crowns to give for the Original.

Ant. No matter, Sir, you shall restore the Picture.

Ang. Oh, *Moretta!* what's the matter? [Angelica *and* Moretta *above.*]

Ant. Or leave your Life behind.

Will. Death! you lye—I will do neither.

Ang. Hold, I command you, if for me you fight.

[*They fight, the Spaniards join with* Antonio, Blunt *laying on like mad. They leave off and bow.*]

Will. How heavenly fair she is!—ah Plague of her Price.

Ang. You Sir in Buff, you that appear a Soldier, that first began this Insolence.

Will. 'Tis true, I did so, if you call it Insolence for a Man to preserve himself; I saw your charming Picture, and was wounded: quite thro my Soul each pointed Beauty ran; and wanting a Thousand Crowns to procure my Remedy, I laid this little Picture to my Bosom—which if you cannot allow me, I'll resign.

Ang. No, you may keep the Trifle.

Ant. You shall first ask my leave, and this. [*Fight again as before.*]

[*Enter* Belvile *and* Frederick *who join with the English.*]

Ang. Hold; will you ruin me?—*Biskey, Sebastian,* part them. [*The* Spaniards *are beaten off.*]

Moret. Oh Madam, we're undone, a pox upon that rude Fellow, he's set on to ruin us: we shall never see good days, till all these fighting poor Rogues are sent to the Gallies.

[*Enter* Belvile, Blunt *and* Willmore, *with his shirt bloody.*] [10]

Blunt. 'Sheartlikins, beat me at this Sport, and I'll ne'er wear Sword more.

Belv. The Devil's in thee for a mad Fellow, thou art always one at an unlucky Adventure.—Come, let's be gone whilst we're safe, and remember these are *Spaniards,* a sort of People that know how to revenge an Affront.

Fred. You bleed; I hope you are not wounded. [*To* Willmore.]

Will. Not much:—a plague upon your Dons, if they fight no better they'll ne'er recover *Flanders.*—What the Devil was't to them that I took down the Picture?

Blunt. Took it! 'Sheartlikins, we'll have the great one too; 'tis ours by Conquest.—Prithee, help me up, and I'll pull it down.—

Ang. Stay, Sir, and e'er you affront me further, let me know how you durst commit this Outrage—To you I speak, Sir, for you appear like a Gentleman.

Will. To me, Madam?—Gentlemen, your Servant. [*Belvile stays him.*

Belv. Is the Devil in thee? Do'st know the danger of entering the house of an incens'd Courtesan?

Will. I thank you for your care—but there are other matters in hand, there are, tho we have no great Temptation.—Death! let me go.

Fred. Yes, to your Lodging, if you will, but not in here.—Damn these gay Harlots— by this Hand I'll have as sound and handsome a Whore for a Patacoone. [p. 36]—Death, Man, she'll murder thee.

Will. Oh! fear me not, shall I not venture where a Beauty calls? a lovely charming Beauty? for fear of danger! when by Heaven there's none so great as to long for her, whilst I want Money to purchase her.

Fred. Therefore 'tis loss of time, unless you had the thousand Crowns to pay.

Will. It may be she may give a Favor, at least I shall have the pleasure of saluting her when I enter, and when I depart.

Belv. Pox, she'll as soon lie with thee, as kiss thee, and sooner stab than do either— you shall not go.

Ang. Fear not, Sir, all I have to wound with, is my Eyes.

Blunt. Let him go, 'Sheartlikins, I believe the Gentle-woman means well.

Belv. Well, take thy Fortune, we'll expect you in the next Street.—Farewell Fool,— farewell—

Will. B'ye Colonel—[*Goes in.*]

Fred. The Rogue's stark mad for a Wench. [*Exeunt.*]

Scene II. *A Fine Chamber.*

[*Enter* Willmore, Angelica, *and* Moretta.]

Ang. Insolent Sir, how durst you pull down my Picture?

Will. Rather, how durst you set it up, to tempt poor amorous Mortals with so much Excellence? which I find you have but too well consulted by the unmerciful price you set upon't.—Is all this Heaven of Beauty shown to move Despair in those that cannot buy? and can you think the effects of that Despair shou'd be less extravagant than I have shown?

Ang. I sent for you to ask my Pardon, Sir, not to aggravate your Crime.—I thought I shou'd have seen you at my Feet imploring it.

Will. You are deceived, I came to rail at you, and talk such Truths, too, as shall let you see the Vanity of that Pride, which taught you how to set such a Price on Sin. For such it is, whilst that which is Love's due is meanly barter'd for.

Ang. Ha, ha, ha, alas, good Captain, what pity 'tis your edifying Doctrine will do no good upon me—*Moretta,* fetch the Gentleman a Glass, and let him survey himself, to see what Charms he has,—and guess my Business. [*Aside in a soft tone.*]

Moret. He knows himself of old, I believe those Breeches and he have been acquainted ever since he was beaten at *Worcester.*

Ang. Nay, do not abuse the poor Creature.—

Moret. Good Weather-beaten Corporal, will you march off? we have no need of your Doctrine, tho you have of our Charity; but at present we have no Scraps, we can afford no kindness for God's sake; in fine, Sirrah, the Price is too high i'th' Mouth [11] for you, therefore troop, I say.

Will. Here, good Fore-Woman of the Shop, serve me, and I'll be gone.

Moret. Keep it to pay your Landress, your Linen stinks of the Gun-Room; for here's no selling by Retail.

Will. Thou hast sold plenty of thy stale Ware at a cheap Rate.

Moret. Ay, the more silly kind Heart I, but this is an Age wherein Beauty is at higher Rates.—In fine, you know the price of this.

Will. I grant you 'tis here set down a thousand Crowns a Month—Baud, take your black Lead and sum it up, that I may have a Pistole-worth [p. 38] of these vain gay things, and I'll trouble you no more.

Moret. Pox on him, he'll fret me to Death:—abominable Fellow, I tell thee, we only sell by the whole Piece.

Will. 'Tis very hard, the whole Cargo or nothing—Faith, Madam, my Stock will not reach it, I cannot be your Chapman.—Yet I have Countrymen, in Town, Merchants of Love, like me; I'll see if they'll put for a share, we cannot lose much by it, and what we have no use for, we'll sell upon the *Friday's* Mart, at—*Who gives more?* I am studying, Madam, how to purchase you, tho at present I am unprovided of Money.

Ang. Sure, this from any other Man would anger me—nor shall he know the Conquest he has made—Poor angry Man, how I despise this railing.

Will. Yes, I am poor—but I'm a Gentleman,
And one that scorns this Baseness which you practise.
Poor as I am, I would not sell myself,
No, not to gain your charming high-priz'd Person.
Tho I admire you strangely for your Beauty,
Yet I contemn your Mind.
—And yet I wou'd at any rate enjoy you;
At your own rate—but cannot—See here
The only Sum I can command on Earth;
I know not where to eat when this is gone:
Yet such a Slave I am to Love and Beauty,
This last reserve [12] I'll sacrifice to enjoy you.
—Nay, do not frown, I know you are to be bought,
And wou'd be bought by me, by me, [13]
For a mean trifling Sum, if I could pay it down.
Which happy knowledge I will still repeat,
And lay it to my Heart, it has a Virtue in't,
And soon will cure [14] those Wounds your Eyes have made.
—And yet—there's something so divinely powerful there—
Nay, I will gaze—to let you see my Strength.

[*Holds her, looks on her, and pauses and sighs.*]

By Heaven, bright Creature—I would not for the World
Thy Fame were half so fair as is thy Face. [*Turns her away from him.*]

Ang. His words go thro me to the very Soul. [*Aside.*]—If you have nothing else to say to me.

Will. Yes, you shall hear how infamous you are—
For which I do not hate thee:
But that secures my Heart, and all the Flames it feels
Are but so many Lusts,
I know it by their sudden bold intrusion.
The Fire's impatient and betrays, 'tis false—

For had it been the purer Flame of Love,
I should have pin'd and languished at your Feet,
E'er found the Impudence to have discover'd it.
I now dare stand your Scorn, and your Denial.

Moret. Sure she's bewitched, that she can stand thus tamely, and hear his saucy railing.—Sirrah, will you be gone?

Ang. How dare you take this liberty?—Withdraw. [*To* Moretta]—Pray, tell me, Sir, are not you guilty of the same mercenary Crime? When a Lady is proposed to you for a Wife, you never ask, how fair, discreet, or virtuous she is; but what's her Fortune—which if but small, you cry—She will not do my business—and basely leave her, tho she languish for you.—Say, is not this as poor?

Will. It is a barbarous Custom, which I will scorn to defend in our Sex, and do despise in yours.

Ang. Thou art a brave Fellow! [15] put up thy Gold, and know,
That were thy Fortune large, as is thy Soul,
Thou shouldst not buy my Love,
Couldst thou forget those mean Effects of Vanity,
Which set me out to sale; and as a Lover, prize
My yielding Joys.
Canst thou believe they'll be entirely thine,
Without considering they were mercenary?

Will. I cannot tell, I must bethink me first—ha, Death, I'm going to believe her. [*Aside.*]

Ang. Prithee, confirm that Faith—or if thou canst not—flatter me a little, 'twill please me from thy Mouth.

Will. Curse on thy charming Tongue! dost thou return
My feign'd Contempt with so much subtlety? [*Aside.*]
Thou'st found the easiest way into my Heart,
Tho I yet know that all thou say'st is false. [*Turning from her in a Rage.*]

Ang. By all that's good 'tis real,
I never lov'd before, tho oft a Mistress.
—Shall my first Vows be slighted?

Will. What can she mean? [*Aside.*]

Ang. I find you cannot credit me. [*In an angry tone.*]

Will. I know you take me for an errant Ass,
An Ass that may be sooth'd into Belief,
And then be us'd at pleasure.
—But, Madam I have been so often cheated
By perjur'd, soft, deluding Hypocrites,
That I've no Faith left for the cozening Sex,
Especially for Women of your Trade.

Ang. The low esteem you have of me, perhaps
May bring my Heart again:
For I have Pride that yet surmounts my Love. [*She turns with Pride, he holds her.*]

Will. Throw off this Pride, this Enemy to Bliss,
And show the Power of Love: 'tis with those Arms
I can be only vanquished, made a Slave.

Ang. Is all my mighty Expectation vanished?

—No, I will not hear thee talk,—thou hast a Charm
In every word, that draws my Heart away.
And all the thousand Trophies I design'd,
Thou hast undone—Why art thou soft?
Thy Looks are bravely rough, and meant for War.
Could thou not storm on still?
I then perhaps had been as free as thou.
    Will. Death! how she throws her Fire about my Soul! [*Aside.*]
—Take heed, fair Creature, how you raise my Hopes,
Which once assum'd pretend to all Dominion.
There's not a Joy thou hast in store
I shall not then command:
For which I'll pay thee back my Soul, my Life.
Come, let's begin th' account this happy minute.
    Ang. And will you pay me then the Price I ask?
    Will. Oh, why dost thou draw me from an awful Worship,
By showing thou art no Divinity?
Conceal the Fiend, and show me all the Angel;
Keep me but ignorant, and I'll be devout,
And pay my Vows for ever at this Shrine. [*Kneels, and kisses her Hand.*]
    Ang. The Pay I mean is but thy Love for mine.—Can you give that?
    Will. Entirely—come, let's withdraw: where I'll renew my Vows,—and breathe 'em with such Ardour, thou shall not doubt my Zeal.
    Ang. Thou hast a Power too strong to be resisted. [Exit *Willmore* and *Angelica.*]
    Moret. Now my Curse go with you—Is all our Project fallen to this? to love the only Enemy to our Trade? Nay, to love such a Shameroon, [p. 42] a very Beggar; nay, a Pirate-Beggar, whose Business is to rifle and be gone, a No-Purchase, No-Pay Tatterdemalion, an *English* Piccaroon; a Rogue that fights for daily Drink, and takes a Pride in being loyally lousy—Oh, I could curse now, if I durst—This is the Fate of most Whores.

> *Trophies, which from believing Fops we win,*
> *Are Spoils to those who cozen us again.*

ACT III.

Scene I. *A Street.*

[*Enter* Florinda, Valeria, Hellena, *in Antique different Dresses from what they were in before,* Callis *attending.*]

    Flor. I wonder what should make my Brother in so ill a Humor: I hope he has not found out our Ramble this Morning.
    Hell. No, if he had, we should have heard on't at both Ears, and have been mew'd up this Afternoon; which I would not for the World should have happen'd—Hey ho! I'm sad as a Lover's Lute.
    Val. Well, methinks we have learnt this Trade of Gypsies as readily as if we had been bred upon the Road to *Loretto*: and yet I did so fumble, when I told the Stranger his

Fortune, that I was afraid I should have told my own and yours by mistake—But methinks *Hellena* has been very serious ever since.

Flor. I would give my Garters she were in love, to be reveng'd upon her, for abusing me—How is't, *Hellena?*

Hell. Ah!—would I had never seen my mad Monsieur—and yet for all your laughing I am not in love—and yet this small Acquaintance, o my Conscience, will never out of my Head.

Val. Ha, ha, ha—I laugh to think how thou art fitted with a Lover, a Fellow that, I warrant, loves every new Face he sees.

Hell. Hum—he has not kept his Word with me here—and may be taken up—that thought is not very pleasant to me—what the Duce should this be now that I feel?

Val. What is't like?

Hell. Nay, the Lord knows—but if I should be hanged, I cannot chose but be angry and afraid, when I think that mad Fellow should be in love with any Body but me—What to think of myself I know not—Would I could meet with some true damn'd Gipsy, that I might know my Fortune.

Val. Know it! why there's nothing so easy; thou wilt love this wandering Inconstant till thou find'st thy self hanged about his Neck, and then be as mad to get free again.

Flor. Yes, *Valeria*; we shall see her bestride his Baggage-horse, and follow him to the Campaign.

Hell. So, so; now you are provided for, there's no care taken of poor me—But since you have set my Heart a wishing, I am resolv'd to know for what. I will not die of the Pip, so I will not.

Flor. Art thou mad to talk so? Who will like thee well enough to have thee, that hears what a mad Wench thou art?

Hell. Like me! I don't intend, every he that likes me shall have me, but he that I like: I shou'd have stayed in the Nunnery still, if I had lik'd my Lady Abbess as well as she lik'd me. No, I came thence, not (as my wise Brother imagines) to take an eternal Farewell of the World, but to love and to be belov'd; and I will be belov'd or I'll get one of your Men, so I Willmore

Val. Am I put into the Number of Lovers?

Hell. You! my Couz, I know thou art too good natur'd to leave us in any Design: Thou wou't [16] venture a Cast, tho thou comest off a Loser, especially with such a Gamester—I observ'd your Man, and your willing Ears incline that way; and if you are not a Lover, 'tis an Art soon learnt—that I find. [*Sighs.*]

Flor. I wonder how you learnt to love so easily, I had a thousand Charms to meet my Eyes and Ears, e'er I cou'd yield; and 'twas the knowledge of *Belvile's* Merit, not the surprising Person, took my Soul—Thou art too rash to give a Heart at first sight.

Hell. Hang your considering Lover; I ne'er thought beyond the Fancy, that 'twas a very pretty, idle, silly kind of Pleasure to pass ones time with, to write little, soft, nonsensical Billets, and with great difficulty and danger receive Answers; in which I shall have my Beauty prais'd, my Wit admir'd (tho little or none) and have the Vanity and Power to know I am desirable; then I have the more Inclination that way, because I am to be a Nun, and so shall not be suspected to have any such earthly Thoughts about me—But when I walk thus—and sigh thus—they'll think my Mind's upon my Monastery, and cry, how happy 'tis she's so resolv'd!—But not a Word of Man.

Flor. What a mad Creature's this!

Hell. I'll warrant, if my Brother hears either of you sigh, he cries (gravely)—I fear you have the Indiscretion to be in love, but take heed of the Honor of our House, and your own unspotted Fame; and so he conjures on till he has laid the soft-wing'd God in your Hearts, or broke the Birds-nest—But see here comes your Lover: but where's my inconstant? let's step aside, and we may learn something. [*Go aside.*]

[*Enter* Belvile, Frederick *and* Blunt.]

Belv. What means this? the Picture's taken in.

Blunt. It may be the Wench is good natur'd, and will be kind *gratis*. Your Friend's a proper handsome Fellow.

Belv. I rather think she has cut his Throat and is fled: I am mad he should throw himself into Dangers—Pox on't, I shall want him tonight—let's knock and ask for him.

Hell. My heart goes a-pit a-pat, for fear 'tis my Man they talk of. [*Knock,* Moretta *above.*]

Moret. What would you have?

Belv. Tell the Stranger that enter'd here about two Hours ago, [17] that his Friends stay here for him.

Moret. A Curse upon him for *Moretta*, would he were at the Devil—but he's coming to you. [*Enter* Wilmore.]

Hell. I, I, 'tis he. Oh how this vexes me.

Belv. And how, and how, dear Lad, has Fortune smil'd? Are we to break her Windows, or raise up Altars to her! hah!

Will. Does not my Fortune sit triumphant on my Brow? dost not see the little wanton God there all gay and smiling? have I not an Air about my Face and Eyes, that distinguish me from the Croud of common Lovers? By Heav'n, *Cupid's* Quiver has not half so many Darts as her Eyes—Oh such a *Bona Rota*, to sleep in her Arms is lying in Fresco, all perfum'd Air about me.

Hell. Here's fine encouragement for me to fool on. [*Aside.*]

Will. Hark ye, where didst thou purchase that rich Canary we drank to-day? Tell me, that I may adore the Spigot, and sacrifice to the Butt: the Juice was divine, into which I must dip my Rosary, and then bless all things that I would have bold or fortunate.

Belv. Well, Sir, let's go take a Bottle, and hear the Story of your Success.

Fred. Would not *French* Wine do better?

Will. Damn the hungry Balderdash; cheerful Sack has a generous Virtue in't, inspiring a successful Confidence, gives Eloquence to the Tongue, and Vigour to the Soul; and has in a few Hours completed all my Hopes and Wishes. There's nothing left to raise a new Desire in me—Come let's be gay and wanton—and, Gentlemen, study, study what you want, for here are Friends,—that will supply, Gentlemen,—hark! what a charming sound they make—'tis he and she Gold whilst here, shall beget new Pleasures every moment.

Blunt. But hark ye, Sir, you are not married, are you?

Will. All the Honey of Matrimony, but none of the Sting, Friend.

Blunt. 'Sheartlikins, thou'rt a fortunate Rogue.

Will. I am so, Sir, let these inform you.—Ha, how sweetly they chime! Pox of Poverty, it makes a Man a Slave, makes Wit and Honor sneak, my Soul grew lean and rusty for want of Credit.

Blunt. 'Sheartlikins, this I like well, it looks like my lucky Bargain! Oh how I long for the Approach of my Squire, that is to conduct me to her House again. Why! here's two provided for.

Fred. By this light y're happy Men.

Blunt. Fortune is pleased to smile on us, Gentlemen,—to smile on us.

[*Enter* Sancho, *and pulls* Blunt *by the Sleeve. They go aside.*]

Sancho. Sir, my Lady expects you—she has remov'd all that might oppose your Will and Pleasure—and is impatient till you come.

Blunt. Sir, I'll attend you—Oh the happiest Rogue! I'll take no leave, lest they either dog me, or stay me. [*Exit with* Sancho.]

Belv. But then the little Gipsy is forgot?

Will. A Mischief on thee for putting her into my thoughts; I had quite forgot her else, and this Night's Debauch had drunk her quite down.

Hell. Had it so, good Captain? [*Claps him on the Back.*]

Will. Ha! I hope she did not hear.

Hell. What, afraid of such a Champion!

Will. Oh! you're a fine Lady of your word, are you not? to make a Man languish a whole day—

Hell. In tedious search of me.

Will. Egad, Child, thou'rt in the right, hadst thou seen what a melancholy Dog I have been ever since I was a Lover, how I have walked the Streets like a *Capuchin*, with my Hands in my Sleeves—Faith, Sweetheart, thou wouldst pity me.

Hell. Now, if I should be hang'd, I can't be angry with him, he dissembles so heartily—Alas, good Captain, what pains you have taken—Now were I ungrateful not to reward so true a Servant.

Will. Poor Soul! that's kindly said, I see thou bearest a Conscience—come then for a beginning show me thy dear Face.

Hell. I'm afraid, my small Acquaintance, you have been staying that swinging stomach you boasted of this morning; I remember then my little Collation would have gone down with you, without the Sauce of a handsome Face—Is your Stomach so queasy now?

Will. Faith long fasting, Child, spoils a Man's Appetite—yet if you durst treat, I could so lay about me still.

Hell. And would you fall to, before a Priest says Grace?

Will. Oh fie, fie, what an old out-of-fashion'd thing hast thou nam'd? Thou could'st not dash me more out of Countenance, shouldst thou show me an ugly Face.

[*Whilst he is seemingly courting* Hellena, *enter* Angelica, Moretta, Biskey, *and* Sebastian, *all in Masquerade:* Angelica *sees* Willmore *and starts.*] [18]

Ang. Heavens, is't he? and passionately fond to see another Woman?

Moret. What cou'd you expect less from such a Swaggerer?

Ang. Expect! as much as I paid him, [19] a Heart entire,
Which I had pride enough to think when e'er I gave
It would have rais'd the Man above the Vulgar,
Made him all Soul, and that all soft and constant.

Hell. You see, Captain, how willing I am to be Friends with you, till Time and Ill-luck make us Lovers; and ask you the Question first, rather than put your Modesty to the blush, by asking me: for alas, I know you Captains are such strict Men, severe Observers of your Vows to Chastity, that 'twill be hard to prevail with your tender Conscience to marry a young willing Maid.

Will. Do not abuse me, for fear I should take thee at thy word, and marry thee indeed, which I'm sure will be Revenge sufficient.

Hell. O' my Conscience, that will be our Destiny, because we are both of one humor; I am as inconstant as you, for I have considered, Captain, that a handsome Woman has a great deal to do whilst her Face is good, for then is our Harvest-time to gather Friends; and should I in these days of my Youth, catch a fit of foolish Constancy, I were undone; 'tis loitering by day-light in our great Journey: therefore declare, I'll allow but one year for Love, one year for Indifference, and one year for Hate—and then—go hang your self—for I profess myself the gay, the kind, and the inconstant—the Devil's in't if this won't please you.

Will. Oh most damnably!—I have a Heart with a hole quite thro it too, no Prison like mine to keep a Mistress in.

Ang. Perjur'd Man! how I believe thee now! [*Aside.*]

Hell. Well, I see our Business as well as Humors are alike, yours to cozen as many Maids as will trust you, and I as many Men as have Faith—See if I have not as desperate a lying look, as you can have for the heart of you. [*Pulls off her Vizard; he starts.*]—How do you like it, Captain?

Will. Like it! by Heav'n, I never saw so much Beauty. Oh the Charms of those sprightly black Eyes, that strangely fair Face, full of Smiles and Dimples! those soft round melting cherry Lips! and small even white Teeth! not to be expressed, but silently adored!—Oh one Look more, and strike me dumb, or I shall repeat nothing else till I am mad. [*He seems to court her to pull off her Vizard: she refuses.*]

Ang. I can endure no more—nor is it fit to interrupt him; for if I do, my Jealousy has so destroy'd my Reason,—I shall undo him—Therefore I'll retire. And you *Sebastian* [*To one of her Bravoes*] follow that Woman, and learn who 'tis; while you tell the Fugitive, I would speak to him instantly. [*To the other Bravo.*] [*Exit.*]

[*This while* Florinda *is talking to* Belvile, *who stands sullenly.* Frederick *courting* Valeria.]

Val. Prithee, dear Stranger, be not so sullen; for tho you have lost your Love, you see my Friend frankly offers you hers, to play with in the mean time.

Belv. Faith, Madam, I am sorry I can't play at her Game.

Fred. Pray leave your Intercession, and mind your own Affair, they'll better agree apart; he's a model Sigher in Company, but alone no Woman escapes him.

Flor. Sure he does but rally [20]—yet if it should be true—I'll tempt him farther—Believe me, noble Stranger, I'm no common Mistress—and for a little proof on't—wear this Jewel—nay, take it, Sir, 'tis right, and Bills of Exchange may sometimes miscarry.

Belv. Madam, why am I chose out of all Mankind to be the Object of your Bounty?

Val. There's another civil Question asked.

Fred. Pox of's Modesty, it spoils his own Markets, and hinders mine.

Flor. Sir, from my Window I have often seen you; and Women of Quality have so few opportunities for Love, that we ought to lose none.

Fred. Ay, this is something! here's a Woman!—When shall I be blest with so much kindness from your fair Mouth?—Take the Jewel, Fool. [Aside to *Belvile*

Belv. You tempt me strangely, Madam, every way.

Flor. So, if I find him false, my whole Repose is gone. [*Aside.*]

Belv. And but for a Vow I've made to a very fine Lady, this Goodness had subdu'd me.

Fred. Pox on't be kind, in pity to me be kind, for I am to thrive here but as you treat her Friend.

Hell. Tell me what did you in yonder House, and I'll unmask.

Will. Yonder House—oh—I went to—a—to—why, there's a Friend of mine lives there.

Hell. What a she, or a he Friend?

Will. A Man upon my Honor! a Man—A She Friend! no, no, Madam, you have done my Business, I thank you.

Hell. And was't your Man Friend, that had more Darts in's Eyes than *Cupid* carries in a whole Budget of Arrows?

Will. So—

Hell. Ah such a *Bona Roba*: to be in her Arms is lying in *Fresco*, all perfumed Air about me—Was this your Man Friend too?

Will. So—

Hell. That gave you the He, and the She—Gold, that begets young Pleasures.

Will. Well, well, Madam, then you see there are Ladies in the World, that will not be cruel—there are, Madam, there are—

Hell. And there be Men too as fine, wild, inconstant Fellows as yourself, there be, Captain, there be, if you go to that now—therefore I'm resolv'd—

Will. Oh!

Hell. To see your Face no more—

Will. Oh!

Hell. Till tomorrow.

Will. Egad you frighted me.

Hell. Nor then neither, unless you'l swear never to see that Lady more.

Will. See her!—why! never to think of Womankind again?

Hell. Kneel, and swear. [*Kneels, she gives him her hand.*]

Hell. I do, never to think—to see—to love—nor lie with any but thy self.

Hell. Kiss the Book.

Will. Oh, most religiously. [*Kisses her Hand.*]

Hell. Now what a wicked Creature am I, to damn a proper Fellow.

Call. Madam, I'll stay no longer, 'tis e'en dark. [*To* Florinda.]

Flor. However, Sir, I'll leave this with you—that when I'm gone, you may repent the opportunity you have lost by your modesty. [*Gives him the Jewel, which is her Picture, and Exit He gazes after her.*]

Will. 'Twill be an Age till tomorrow,—and till then I will most impatiently expect you—Adieu, my dear pretty Angel. [*Exit all the Women.*]

Belv. Ha! *Florinda's* Picture! 'twas she her self—what a dull Dog was I? I would have given the World for one minute's discourse with her.—

Fred. This comes of your Modesty,—ah pox on your Vow, 'twas ten to one but we had lost the Jewel by't.

Belv. Willmore! the blessed'st Opportunity lost!—*Florinda*, Friends, *Florinda!*

Will. Ah Rogue! such black Eyes, such a Face, such a Mouth, such Teeth,—and so much Wit!

Belv. All, all, and a thousand Charms besides.

Will. Why, dost thou know her?

Belv. Know her! ay, ay, and a Pox take me with all my Heart for being modest.

Will. But hark ye, Friend of mine, are you my Rival? and have I been only beating the Bush all this while?

Belv. I understand thee not—I'm mad—see here—[*Shows the Picture.*]

Will. Ha! whose Picture is this?—'tis a fine Wench.

Fred. The Colonel's Mistress, Sir.

Will. Oh, oh, here—I thought it had been another Prize—come, come, a Bottle will set thee right again. [*Gives the Picture back.*]

Belv. I am content to try, and by that time 'twill be late enough for our Design.

Will. Agreed.

> Love does all day the Soul's great Empire keep,
> But Wine at night lulls the soft God asleep. [*Exeunt.*] [21]

Scene II. *Lucetta's* House.

[*Enter* Blunt *and* Lucetta *with a Light.*]

Luc. Now we are safe and free, no fears of the coming home of my old jealous Husband, which made me a little thoughtful when you came in first—but now Love is all the business of my Soul.

Blunt. I am transported—Pox on't, that I had but some fine things to say to her, such as Lovers use—I was a Fool not to learn of *Frederick*, a little by Heart before I came—something I must say.—[*Aside.*] 'Sheartlikins, sweet Soul, I am not us'd to complement, but I'm an honest Gentleman, and thy humble Servant.

Luc. I have nothing to pay for so great a Favor, but such a Love as cannot but be great, since at first sight of that sweet Face and Shape it made me your absolute Captive.

Blunt. Kind heart, how prettily she talks! Egad I'll show her Husband a *Spanish* Trick; send him out of the World, and marry her: she's damnably in love with me, and will ne'er mind Settlements, and so there's that say'd. [*Aside.*]

Luc. Well, Sir, I'll go and undress me, and be with you instantly.

Blunt. Make haste then, for 'dsheartlikins, dear Soul, thou canst not guess at the pain of a longing Lover, when his Joys are drawn within the compass of a few minutes.

Luc. You speak my Sense, and I'll make haste to provide it. [*Exit.*] [22]

Blunt. 'Tis a rare Girl, and this one night's enjoyment with her will be worth all the days I ever past in Essex—Would she'd go with me into *England*, tho to say truth, there's plenty of Whores there already.—But a pox on 'em they are such mercenary prodigal Whores, that they want such a one as this, that's free and generous, to give 'em good Examples:—Why, what a House she has! how rich and fine!

[*Enter* Sancho.] [23]

Sancho. Sir, my Lady has sent me to conduct you to her Chamber.

Blunt. Sir, I shall be proud to follow—Here's one of her Servants too: 'dsheartlikins, by his Garb and Gravity he might be a Justice of Peace in *Essex*, and is but a Pimp here. [*Exeunt.*]

[*The Scene changes to a Chamber with an Alcove-Bed in it, a Table, &c.* Lucetta *in Bed. Enter* Sancho *and* Blunt, *who takes the Candle of* Sancho *at the Door.*]

Sancho. Sir, my Commission reaches no farther.
Blunt. Sir, I'll excuse your Complement:—what, in Bed, my sweet Mistress?
Luc. You see, I still out-do you in kindness.
Blunt. And thou shall see what haste I'll make to quit scores—oh the luckiest Rogue! [*Undresses himself.*]
Luc. Shou'd you be false or cruel now!
Blunt. False, 'Sheartlikins, what dost thou take me for a *Jew?* an insensible Heathen,—A Pox of thy old jealous Husband: and he were dead, egad, sweet Soul, it shou'd be none of my fault, if I did not marry thee.
Luc. It never shou'd be mine.
Blunt. Good Soul, I'm the fortunatest Dog!
Luc. Are you not undressed yet?
Blunt. As much as my Impatience will permit. [*Goes towards the Bed in his Shirt and Drawers.*]
Luc. Hold, Sir, put out the Light, it may betray us else.
Blunt. Anything, I need no other Light but that of thine Eyes!—'sheartlikins, there I think I had it. [*Aside.*]

[*Puts out the Candle, the Bed descends, he gropes about to find it.*]

—Why—why—where am I got? what, not yet?—where are you sweetest?—ah, the Rogue's silent now—a pretty Love-trick this—how she'll laugh at me anon!—you need not, my dear Rogue! you need not! I'm all on a fire already—come, come, now call me in for pity—Sure I'm enchanted! I have been round the Chamber, and can find neither Woman, nor Bed—I locked the Door, I'm sure she cannot go that way; or if she cou'd, the Bed cou'd not—Enough, enough, my pretty Wanton, do not carry the Jest too far—Ha, betray'd! Dogs! Rogues! Pimps! [24] help! help! [*Lights on a Trap, and is let down.*]

[*Enter* Lucetta, Philippo, *and* Sancho *with a Light.*]

Phil. Ha, ha, ha, he's dispatched finely.
Luc. Now, Sir, had I been coy, we had mist of this Booty.
Phil. Nay when I saw 'twas a substantial Fool, I was mollified; but when you dote upon a
 Serenading Coxcomb, upon a Face, fine Clothes, and a Lute, it makes me rage.
Luc. You know I never was guilty of that Folly, my dear *Philippo*, but with your self—
 But come let's see what we have got by this.
Phil. A rich Coat!—Sword and Hat!—these Breeches too—are well lin'd!—see here a
 Gold Watch!—a Purse—ha! Gold!—at least two hundred Pistoles! a bunch of
 Diamond Rings; and one with the Family Arms!—a Gold Box!—with a Medal of his
 King! and his Lady Mother's Picture!—these were sacred Reliques, believe me!—
 see, the Waistband of his Breeches have a Mine of Gold!—Old Queen *Bess's.* We

have a Quarrel to her ever since *Eighty Eight*, and may therefore justify the Theft, the Inquisition might have committed it.

Luc. See, a Bracelet of bow'd Gold, [p. 54] these his Sister ty'd about his Arm at parting—but well—for all this, I fear his being a Stranger may make a noise, and hinder our Trade with them hereafter.

Phil. That's our security; he is not only a Stranger to us, but to the Country too—the Common-Shore into which he is descended, thou know'st, conducts him into another Street, which this Light will hinder him from ever finding again—he knows neither your Name, nor the Street where your House is, nay, nor the way to his own Lodgings.

Luc. And art not thou an unmerciful Rogue, not to afford him one Night for all this?—I should not have been such a *Jew*.

Phil. Blame me not, *Lucetta*, to keep as much of thee as I can to my self—come, that thought makes me wanton,—let's to Bed,—Sancho, lock up these.
> This is the Fleece which Fools do bear,
> Design'd for witty Men to sheer. [25] [*Exeunt.*]

[*The Scene changes, and discovers* Blunt, *creeping out of a Common Shore, his Face, &c., all dirty.*]

Blunt. Oh Lord! [*Climbing up.*] I am got out at last, and (which is a Miracle) without a Clue—and now to Damning and Cursing,—but if that would ease me, where shall I begin? with my Fortune, myself, or the Quean that cozen'd me—What a dog was I to believe in Women! Oh Coxcomb—ignorant conceited Coxcomb! to fancy she cou'd be enamor'd with my Person, at the first sight enamor'd—Oh, I'm a cursed Puppy, 'tis plain, Fool was writ upon my Forehead, she perceiv'd it,—saw the *Essex* Calf there—for what Allurements could there be in this Countenance? which I can endure, because I'm acquainted with it—Oh, dull silly Dog! to be thus sooth'd into a Cozening! Had I been drunk, I might fondly have credited the young Quean! but as I was in my right Wits, to be thus cheated, confirms I am a dull believing *English* Country Fop.—But my Comrades! Death and the Devil, there's the worst of all—then a Ballad will be sung tomorrow on the *Prado*, to a lousy Tune of the enchanted Squire, and the annihilated Damsel—But *Frederick*, that Rogue, and the Colonel, will abuse me beyond all Christian patience—had she left me my Clothes, I have a Bill of Exchange at home wou'd have sav'd my Credit—but now all hope is taken from me—Well, I'll home (if I can find the way) with this Consolation, that I am not the first kind believing Coxcomb; but there are, Gallants, many such good Natures amongst ye.
> And tho you've better Arts to hide your Follies,
> Adsheartlikins y'are all as errant Cullies.

Scene III. The Garden, in the Night.

[*Enter* Florinda *undres'd, with a Key, and a little Box.*]

Flor. Well, thus far I'm in my way to Happiness; I have got my self free from *Callis*; my Brother too, I find by yonder light, is gone into his Cabinet, and thinks not of me: I have by good Fortune got the Key of the Garden Back-door,—I'll open it, to prevent *Belvile's* knocking,—a little noise will now alarm my Brother. Now am I as fearful as a young Thief. [*Unlocks the Door.*]—Hark,—what noise is that?—Oh, 'twas the Wind that plaid amongst the Boughs.—*Belvile* stays long, methinks—it's time—stay—for fear of a surprise, I'll hide these Jewels in yonder Jessamin. [*She goes to lay down the Box.*]

[*Enter* Willmore *drunk.*]

Will. What the Devil is become of these Fellows, *Belvile* and *Frederick?* They promis'd to stay at the next corner for me, but who the Devil knows the corner of a full Moon?—Now—whereabouts am I?—hah—what have we here? a Garden!—a very convenient place to sleep in—hah—what has God sent us here?—a Female—by this light, a Woman; I'm a Dog if it be not a very Wench.—

Flor. He's come!—hah—who's there?

Will. Sweet Soul, let me salute thy Shoe-string.

Flor. 'Tis not my *Belvile*—good Heavens, I know him not.—Who are you, and from whence come you?

Will. Prithee—prithee, Child—not so many hard Questions—let it suffice I am here, Child—Come, come kiss me.

Flor. Good Gods! what luck is mine?

Will. Only good luck, Child, parlous good luck—Come hither,—'tis a delicate shining Wench,—by this Hand she's perfum'd, and smells like any Nosegay.—Prithee, dear Soul, let's not play the Fool, and lose time,—precious time—for as Gad shall save me, I'm as honest a Fellow as breathes, tho I am a little disguis'd [p. 57] at present.— Come, I say,—why, thou may'st be free with me, I'll be very secret. I'll not boast who 'twas oblig'd me, not I—for hang me if I know thy Name.

Flor. Heavens! what a filthy beast is this!

Will. I am so, and thou oughtst the sooner to lie with me for that reason,—for look you, Child, there will be no Sin in't, because 'twas neither design'd nor premeditated; 'tis pure Accident on both sides—that's a certain thing now—Indeed should I make love to you, and you vow Fidelity—and swear and lye till you believ'd and yielded—Thou art therefore (as thou art a good Christian) oblig'd in Conscience to deny me nothing. Now— come, be kind, without any more idle prating.

Flor. Oh, I am ruin'd—wicked Man, unhand me.

Will. Wicked! Egad, Child, a Judge, were he young and vigorous, and saw those Eyes of thine, would know 'twas they gave the first blow—the first provocation.—Come, prithee let's lose no time, I say—this is a fine convenient place.

Flor. Sir, let me go, I conjure you, or I'll call out.

Will. Ay, ay, you were best to call Witness to see how finely you treat me—do.—

Flor. I'll cry Murder, Rape, or anything, if you do not instantly let me go.

Will. A Rape! Come, come, you lie, you Baggage, you lie: What, I'll warrant you would fain have the World believe now that you are not so forward as I. No, not you,— why at this time of Night was your Cobweb-door set open, dear Spider—but to catch Flies?—Hah come—or I shall be damnably angry.—Why what a Coil is here.—

Flor. Sir, can you think—

Will. That you'd do it for nothing? oh, oh, I find what you'd be at—look here, here's a Pistole for you—here's a work indeed—here—take it, I say.—

Flor. For Heaven's sake, Sir, as you're a Gentleman—

Will. So—now—she would be wheedling me for more—what, you will not take it then—you're resolv'd you will not.—Come, come, take it, or I'll put it up again; for, look ye, I never give more.—Why, how now, Mistress, are you so high i'th' Mouth, a Pistole won't down with you?—hah—why, what a work's here—in good time—come, no struggling, be gone—But an y'are good at a dumb Wrestle, I'm for ye,—look ye,—I'm for ye.—[*She struggles with him.*]

[*Enter* Belvile *and* Frederick.]

Belv. The Door is open, a Pox of this mad Fellow, I'm angry that we've lost him, I durst have sworn he had follow'd us.
Fred. But you were so hasty, Colonel, to be gone.
Flor. Help, help,—Murder!—help—oh, I'm ruin'd.
Belv. Ha, sure that's *Florinda's* Voice. [*Comes up to them.*]—A Man! Villain, let go that Lady. [*A noise.*]

[Willmore *turns and draws,* Frederick *interposes.*]

Flor. Belvile! Heavens! my Brother too is coming, and 'twill be impossible to escape.—*Belvile*, I conjure you to walk under my Chamber-window, from whence I'll give you some instructions what to do—This rude Man has undone us. [*Exit.*]
Will. Belvile!

[*Enter* Pedro, Stephano, *and other Servants with Lights.*]

Pedro. I'm betray'd; run, *Stephano*, and see if *Florinda* be safe. [*Exit* Stephano.] So whoe'er they be, all is not well, I'll to *Florinda's* Chamber. [*They fight, and* Pedro's *Party beats 'em out; going out, meets* Stephano.]
Steph. You need not, Sir, the poor Lady's fast asleep, and thinks no harm: I wou'd not wake her, Sir, for fear of frightening her with your danger.
Pedro. I'm glad she's there—Rascals, how came the Garden-Door open?
Steph. That Question comes too late, Sir: some of my Fellow-Servants Masquerading I'll warrant.
Pedro. Masquerading! a leud Custom to debauch our Youth—there's something more in this than I imagine. [*Exeunt.*]

Scene IV. *Changes to the Street.*

[*Enter* Belvile *in Rage,* Frederick *holding him, and* Willmore *melancholy.*]

Will. Why, how the Devil shou'd I know *Florinda?*
Belv. Ah plague of your ignorance! if it had not been *Florinda*, must you be a Beast?—a Brute, a senseless Swine?
Will. Well, Sir, you see I am endu'd with Patience—I can bear—tho egad y're very free with me methinks,—I was in good hopes the Quarrel wou'd have been on my side, for so uncivilly interrupting me.
Belv. Peace, Brute, whilst thou'rt safe—oh, I'm distracted.
Will. Nay, nay, I'm an unlucky Dog, that's certain.
Belv. Ah curse upon the Star that rul'd my Birth! or whatsoever other Influence that makes me still so wretched.

Will. Thou break'st my Heart with these Complaints; there is no Star in fault, no Influence but Sack, the cursed Sack I drank.

Fred. Why, how the Devil came you so drunk?

Will. Why, how the Devil came you so sober?

Belv. A curse upon his thin Skull, he was always before-hand that way.

Fred. Prithee, dear Colonel, forgive him, he's sorry for his fault.

Belv. He's always so after he has done a mischief—a plague on all such Brutes.

Will. By this Light I took her for an errant Harlot.

Belv. Damn your debauched Opinion: tell me, Sot, hadst thou so much sense and light about thee to distinguish her to be a Woman, and could'st not see something about her Face and Person, to strike an awful Reverence into thy Soul?

Will. Faith no, I consider'd her as mere a Woman as I could wish.

Belv. 'Sdeath I have no patience—draw, or I'll kill you.

Will. Let that alone till tomorrow, and if I set not all right again, use your Pleasure.

Belv. Tomorrow, damn it.
The spiteful Light will lead me to no happiness.
Tomorrow is *Antonio's*, and perhaps
Guides him to my undoing;—oh that I could meet
This Rival, this powerful Fortunate.

Will. What then?

Belv. Let thy own Reason, or my Rage instruct thee.

Will. I shall be finely inform'd then, no doubt; hear me, Colonel—hear me—show me the Man and I'll do his Business.

Belv. I know him no more than thou, or if I did, I should not need thy aid.

Will. This you say is *Angelica's* House, I promis'd the kind Baggage to lie with her tonight. [*Offers to go in.*]

[*Enter* Antonio *and his Page.* Antonio *knocks on the Hilt of his Sword.*]

Ant. You paid the thousand Crowns I directed?

Page. To the Lady's old Woman, Sir, I did.

Will. Who the Devil have we here?

Belv. I'll now plant myself under *Florinda's* Window, and if I find no comfort there, I'll die. [*Exit Belvile and* Frederick.]

[*Enter* Moretta.]

Moret. Page!

Page. Here's my Lord.

Will. How is this, a Piccaroon going to board my Frigate! here's one Chase-Gun for you. [*Drawing his Sword, jostles* Antonio *who turns and draws. They fight,* Antonio *falls.*]

Moret. Oh, bless us, we are all undone! [*Runs in, and shuts the Door.*]

Page. Help, Murder! [Belvile *returns at the noise of fighting.*]

Belv. Ha, the mad Rogue's engag'd in some unlucky Adventure again.

[*Enter two or three Masqueraders.*]

Masq. Ha, a Man kill'd!

Will. How! a Man kill'd! then I'll go home to sleep. [*Puts up, and reels out.* Exit *Masqueraders another way.*]

Belv. Who shou'd it be! pray Heaven the Rogue is safe, for all my Quarrel to him. [*As* Belvile *is groping about, enter an Officer and six Soldiers.*]

Sold. Who's there?

Offic. So, here's one dispatched—secure the Murderer.

Belv. Do not mistake my Charity for Murder:
I came to his Assistance. [*Soldiers seize on* Belvile.]

Offic. That shall be tried, Sir.—St. *Jago*, Swords drawn in the Carnival time! [*Goes to* Antonio.]

Ant. Thy Hand prithee.

Offic. Ha, Don *Antonio!* look well to the Villain there.—How is't, Sir?

Ant. I'm hurt.

Belv. Has my Humanity made me a Criminal?

Offic. Away with him.

Belv. What a curst Chance is this! [*Exit Soldiers with* Belvile.]

Ant. This is the Man that has set upon me twice—carry him to my Apartment till you have further Orders from me. [*To the Officer. Exit* Antonio *led.*]

ACT IV.

Scene I. *A fine Room.*

[*Discovers* Belvile, *as by Dark alone.*]

Belv. When shall I be weary of railing on Fortune, who is resolv'd never to turn with Smiles upon me?—Two such Defeats in one Night—none but the Devil and that mad Rogue could have contriv'd to have plagued me with—I am here a Prisoner—but where?—Heaven knows—and if there be Murder done, I can soon decide the Fate of a Stranger in a Nation without Mercy—Yet this is nothing to the Torture my Soul bows with, when I think of losing my fair, my dear *Florinda.*—Hark—my Door opens—a Light—a Man—and seems of Quality—arm'd too.—Now shall I die like a Dog without defence.

[*Enter* Antonio *in a Night-Gown, with a Light; his Arm in a Scarf, and a Sword under his Arm: He sets the Candle on the Table.*]

Ant. Sir, I come to know what Injuries I have done you, that could provoke you to so mean an Action, as to attack me basely, without allowing time for my Defence.

Belv. Sir, for a Man in my Circumstances to plead Innocence, would look like Fear— but view me well, and you will find no marks of a Coward on me, nor any thing that betrays that Brutality you accuse me of.

Ant. In vain, Sir, you impose upon my Sense,
You are not only he who drew on me last Night,
But yesterday before the same House, that of *Angelica.*
Yet there is something in your Face and Mein—

Belv. I own I fought today in the defence of a Friend of mine, with whom you (if you're the same) and your Party were first engag'd.
Perhaps you think this Crime enough to kill me,
But if you do, I cannot fear you'll do it basely.

Ant. No, Sir, I'll make you fit for a Defence with this. [*Gives him the Sword.*]

Belv. This Gallantry surprises me—nor know I how to use this Present, Sir, against a Man so brave.

Ant. You shall not need;
For know, I come to snatch you from a Danger
That is decreed against you;
Perhaps your Life, or long Imprisonment:
And 'twas with so much Courage you offended,
I cannot see you punished.

Belv. How shall I pay this Generosity?

Ant. It had been safer to have kill'd another,
Than have attempted me:
To show your Danger, Sir, I'll let you know my Quality;
And 'tis the Vice-Roy's Son whom you have wounded.

Belv. The Vice-Roy's Son!
Death and Confusion! was this Plague reserved
To complete all the rest?—oblig'd by him!
The Man of all the World I would destroy. [*Aside.*]

Ant. You seem disorder'd, Sir.

Belv. Yes, trust me, Sir, I am, and 'tis with pain
That Man receives such Bounties,
Who wants the pow'r to pay 'em back again.

Ant. To gallant Spirits 'tis indeed uneasy;
—But you may quickly over-pay me, Sir.

Belv. Then I am well—kind Heaven! but set us even,
That I may fight with him, and keep my Honor safe. [*Aside.*]
—Oh, I'm impatient, Sir, to be discounting
The mighty Debt I owe you; command me quickly—

Ant. I have a Quarrel with a Rival, Sir,
About the Maid we love.

Belv. Death, 'tis *Florinda* he means—
That Thought destroys my Reason, and I shall kill him—[*Aside.*]

Ant. My Rival, Sir.
Is one has all the Virtues Man can boast of.

Belv. Death! who shou'd this be? [*Aside.*]

Ant. [26] He challeng'd me to meet him on the *Molo*,
As soon as Day appear'd; but last Night's quarrel
Has made my Arm unfit to guide a Sword.

Belv. I apprehend you, Sir, you'd have me kill the Man
That lays a claim to the Maid you speak of.
—I'll do't—I'll fly to do it.

Ant. Sir, do you know her?

Belv.—No, Sir, but 'tis enough she is admired by you.

Ant. Sir, I shall rob you of the Glory on't,

For you must fight under my Name and Dress.

Belv. That Opinion [27] must be strangely obliging that makes
You think I can personate the brave *Antonio*,
Whom I can but strive to imitate.

Ant. You say too much to my Advantage.
Come, Sir, the Day appears that calls you forth.
Within, Sir, is the Habit. [*Exit* Antonio.]

Belv. Fantastic Fortune, thou deceitful Light,
That cheats the wearied Traveller by Night,
Tho on a Precipice each step you tread,
I am resolv'd to follow where you lead. [*Exit.*]

Scene II. *The Molo.*

[*Enter* Florinda *and* Callis *in Masks, with* Stephano.]

Flor. I'm dying with my fears; *Belvile's* not coming,
As I expected, underneath my Window,
Makes me believe that all those Fears are true. [*Aside.*]
—Canst thou not tell with whom my Brother fights?

Steph. No, Madam, they were both in Masquerade, I was by when they challeng'd one another, and they had decided the Quarrel then, but were prevented by some Cavaliers; which made 'em put it off till now—but I am sure 'tis about you they fight.

Flor. Nay then 'tis with *Belvile,* for what other Lover have I that dares fight for me, except *Antonio?* and he is too much in favor with my Brother—If it be he, for whom shall I direct my Prayers to Heaven? [*Aside.*] [28]

Steph. Madam, I must leave you; for if my Master see me, I shall be hang'd for being your Conductor.—I escap'd narrowly for the Excuse I made for you last night i'th' Garden.

Flor. And I'll reward thee for't—prithee no more. [*Exit Stephano.*]

[*Enter* Don Pedro *in his Masking Habit.*] [29]

Pedro. Antonio's late today, the place will fill, and we may be prevented. [*Walk about.*]

Flor. Antonio! sure I heard amiss. [*Aside.*]

Pedro. But who would not excuse a happy Lover.
When soft fair Arms confine the yielding Neck;
And the kind Whisper languishingly breathes,
Must you be gone so soon?
Sure I had dwelt for ever on her Bosom.
—But stay, he's here.

[*Enter* Belvile *dressed in* Antonio's *Clothes.*]

Flor. 'Tis not *Belvile,* half my Fears are vanished.
Pedro. Antonio!—

Belv. This must be he. [*Aside.*] You're early, Sir,—I do not use to be out-done this way.

Pedro. The wretched, Sir, are watchful, and 'tis enough
You have the advantage of me in *Angelica.*

Belv. Angelica!
Or I've mistook my Man! Or else *Antonio,*
Can he forget his Interest in *Florinda,*
And fight for common Prize? [*Aside.*]

Pedro. Come, Sir, you know our terms—

Belv. By Heaven, not I. [*Aside.*]—No talking, I am ready, Sir.

[*Offers to fight.* Florinda *runs in.*]

Flor. Oh, hold! whoe'er you be, I do conjure you hold.
If you strike here—I die—[30] [*To* Belvile.]

Pedro. Florinda!

Belv. Florinda imploring for my Rival!

Pedro. Away, this Kindness is unseasonable. [*Puts her by, they fight; she runs in just as* Belvile *disarms* Pedro.]

Flor. Who are you, Sir, that dare deny my Prayers?

Belv. Thy Prayers destroy him; if thou wouldst preserve him.
Do that thou'rt unacquainted with, and curse him. [*She holds him.*]

Flor. By all you hold most dear, by her you love,
I do conjure you, touch him not.

Belv. By her I love!
See—I obey—and at your Feet resign
The useless Trophy of my Victory. [*Lays his sword at her Feet.*]

Pedro. Antonio, you've done enough to prove you love *Florinda.*

Belv. Love *Florinda!* [31]
Does Heaven love Adoration, Pray'r, or Penitence?
Love her! here Sir,—your Sword again. [*Snatches up the Sword, and gives it him.*]
Upon this Truth I'll fight my Life away.

Pedro. No, you've redeem'd my Sister, and my Friendship.

Belv. Don *Pedro!*

[*He gives him* Florinda *and pulls off his Vizard to show his Face, and puts it on again.*]

Pedro. Can you resign your Claims to other Women,
And give your Heart entirely to *Florinda?*

Belv. Entire, as dying Saints Confessions are.
I can delay my happiness no longer.
This minute let me make *Florinda* mine:

Pedro. This minute let it be—no time so proper,
This Night my Father will arrive from *Rome,*
And possibly may hinder what we propose.

Flor. Oh Heavens! this Minute! [*Enter Masqueraders, and pass over.*]

Belv. Oh, do not ruin me!

74

Pedro. The place begins to fill; and that we may not be observ'd, do you walk off to St. *Peter's* Church, where I will meet you, and conclude your Happiness.

Belv. I'll meet you there—if there be no more Saints Churches in *Naples*. [*Aside.*]

Flor. Oh stay, Sir, and recall your hasty Doom:
Alas I have not yet prepar'd my Heart
To entertain so strange a Guest.

Pedro. Away, this silly Modesty is assum'd too late.

Belv. Heaven, Madam! what do you do?

Flor. Do! despise the Man that lays a Tyrant's Claim
To what he ought to conquer by Submission.

Belv. You do not know me—move a little this way. [*Draws her aside.*]

Flor. Yes, you may even force me to the Altar,
But not the holy Man that offers there
Shall force me to be thine. [Pedro *talks to* Callis *this while.*]

Belv. Oh do not lose so blest an opportunity!
See—'tis your *Belvile*—not *Antonio*,
Whom your mistaken Scorn and Anger ruins. [*Pulls off his Vizard.*]

Flor. Belvile!
Where was my Soul it cou'd not meet thy Voice,
And take this knowledge in?

[*As they are talking, enter* Willmore *finely dressed, and* Frederick.]

Will. No Intelligence! no News of *Belvile* yet—well I am the most unlucky Rascal in Nature—ha!—am I deceiv'd—or is it he—look, *Frederick*—'tis he [32]—my dear *Belvile*.

[*Runs and embraces him.* Belvile *Vizard falls out on's Hand.*] [33]

Belv. Hell and Confusion seize thee!

Pedro. Ha! *Belvile!* I beg your Pardon, Sir. [*Takes* Florinda *from him.*]

Belv. Nay, touch her not, she's mine by Conquest, Sir. I won her by my Sword.

Will. Did'st thou so—and egad, Child, we'll keep her by the Sword. [*Draws on* Pedro, Belvile *goes between.*]

Belv. Standoff.
Thou'rt so profanely leud, so curst by Heaven,
All Quarrels thou espousest must be fatal.

Will. Nay, an you be so hot, [34] my Valor's coy,
And shall be courted when you want it next. [*Puts up his Sword.*]

Belv. You know I ought to claim a Victor's Right, [*To* Pedro.]
But you're the Brother to divine *Florinda*,
To whom I'm such a Slave—to purchase her,
I durst not hurt the Man she holds so dear.

Pedro. 'Twas by *Antonio's*, not by *Belvile's* Sword,
This Question should have been decided, Sir:
I must confess much to your Bravery's due,
Both now, and when I met you last in Arms.
But I am nicely punctual in my word,

As Men of Honor ought, and beg your Pardon.
—For this Mistake another Time shall clear.
—This was some Plot between you and Belvile:
But I'll prevent you. [*Aside to* Florinda *as they are going out.*]

[Belvile *looks after her, and begins to walk up and down in a Rage.*]

Will. Do not be modest now, and lose the Woman: but if we shall fetch her back, so—

Belv. Do not speak to me.

Will. Not speak to you!—Egad, I'll speak to you, and will be answered too.

Belv. Will you, Sir?

Will. I know I've done some mischief, but I'm so dull a Puppy, that I am the Son of a Whore, if I know how, or where—prithee inform my Understanding.—

Belv. Leave me I say, and leave me instantly.

Will. I will not leave you in this humor, nor till I know my Crime.

Belv. Death, I'll tell you, Sir—

[*Draws and runs at* Willmore *he runs out;* Belvile *after him,* Frederick *interposes.*]

[Enter *Angelica, Moretta,* and *Sebastian.*]

Ang. Ha—Sebastian—Is not that *Willmore?* haste, haste, and bring him back.

Fred. The Colonel's mad—I never saw him thus before; I'll after 'em, lest he do some mischief, for I am sure *Willmore* will not draw on him. [*Exit.*]

Ang. I am all Rage! [35] my first desires defeated
For one, for ought he knows, that has no
Other Merit than her Quality,—
Her being Don *Pedro's* Sister—He loves her:
I know 'tis so—dull, dull, insensible—
He will not see me now tho oft invited;
And broke his Word last night—false perjur'd Man!
—He that but yesterday fought for my Favors,
And would have made his Life a Sacrifice
To've gain'd one Night with me,
Must now be hired and courted to my Arms.

Moret. I told you what wou'd come on't, but *Moretta's* an old doting Fool—Why did you give him five hundred Crowns, but to set himself out for other Lovers? You shou'd have kept him poor, if you had meant to have had any good from him.

Ang. Oh, name not such mean Trifles.—Had I given him all
My Youth has earn'd from Sin,
I had not lost a Thought nor Sigh upon't.
But I have given him my eternal Rest,
My whole Repose, my future Joys, my Heart;
My Virgin Heart. *Moretta!* oh 'tis gone!

Moret. Curse on him, here he comes;
How fine she has made him too!

[*Enter* Willmore *and* Sebastian. Angelica *turns and walks away.*]

Will. How now, turn'd Shadow?
Fly when I pursue, and follow when I fly!

    Stay gentle Shadow of my Dove, [*Sings.*]
      And tell me e'er I go,
    Whether the Substance may not prove
    A fleeting Thing like you.

There's a soft kind Look remaining yet. [*As she turns she looks on him.*]

    Ang. Well, Sir, you may be gay; all Happiness, all Joys pursue you still, Fortune's your Slave, and gives you every hour choice of new Hearts and Beauties, till you are cloy'd with the repeated Bliss, which others vainly languish for—But know, false Man, that I shall be reveng'd. [*Turns away in a Rage.*]

    Will. So, 'gad, there are of those faint-hearted Lovers, whom such a sharp Lesson next their Hearts would make as impotent as Fourscore—pox o' this whining—my Bus'ness is to laugh and love—a pox on't; I hate your sullen Lover, a Man shall lose as much time to put you in Humor now, as would serve to gain a new Woman.

    Ang. I scorn to cool that Fire I cannot raise, Or do the Drudgery of your virtuous Mistress.

    Will. A virtuous Mistress! Death, what a thing thou hast found out for me! why what the Devil should I do with a virtuous Woman?—a fort of ill-natur'd Creatures, that take a Pride to torment a Lover. Virtue is but an Infirmity in Women, a Disease that renders even the handsome ungrateful; whilst the ill-favor'd, for want of Solicitations and Address, only fancy themselves so.—I have lain with a Woman of Quality, who has all the while been railing at Whores.

    Ang. I will not answer for your Mistress's Virtue,
Tho she be young enough to know no Guilt:
And I could wish you would persuade my Heart,
'Twas the two hundred thousand Crowns you courted.

    Will. Two hundred thousand Crowns! what Story's this?—what Trick?—what Woman?—ha.

    Ang. How strange you make it! have you forgot the Creature you entertain'd on the Piazza last night?

    Will. Ha, my Gipsy worth two hundred thousand Crowns!—oh how I long to be with her—pox, I knew she was of Quality. [*Aside.*]

    Ang. False Man, I see my Ruin in thy Face.
How many vows you breath'd upon my Bosom,
Never to be unjust—have you forgot so soon?

    Will. Faith no, I was just coming to repeat 'em—but here's a Humor indeed—would make a Man a Saint—Wou'd she'd be angry enough to leave me, and command me not to wait on her. [*Aside.*]

[*Enter* Hellena, *dressed in Man's Clothes.*]

Hell. This must be *Angelica*, I know it by her mumping Matron here—Ay, ay, 'tis she: my mad Captain's with her too, for all his swearing—how this unconstant [36] Humor makes me love him:—pray, good grave Gentlewoman, is not this *Angelica?*

Moret. My too young Sir, it is—I hope 'tis one from Don *Antonio.* [*Goes to* Angelica.]

Hell. Well, something I'll do to vex him for this. [*Aside.*]

Ang. I will not speak with him; am I in humor to receive a Lover?

Will. Not speak with him! why I'll be gone—and wait your idler minutes—Can I show less Obedience to the thing I love so fondly? [*Offers to go.*]

Ang. A fine Excuse this—stay—

Will. And hinder your Advantage: should I repay your Bounties so ungratefully?

Ang. Come hither, Boy,—that I may let you see
How much above the Advantages you name
I prize one Minute's Joy with you.

Will. Oh, you destroy me with this Endearment. [*Impatient to be gone.*]—Death, how shall I get away?—Madam, 'twill not be fit I should be seen with you—besides, it will not be convenient—and I've a Friend—that's dangerously sick.

Ang. I see you're impatient—yet you shall stay.

Will. And miss my Assignation with my Gipsy. [*Aside, and walks about impatiently.*]

Hell. Madam, [Moretta *brings* Hellena, *who addresses herself to* Angelica.]
You'll hardly pardon my Intrusion,
When you shall know my Business;
And I'm too young to tell my Tale with Art:
But there must be a wondrous store of Goodness
Where so much Beauty dwells.

Ang. A pretty Advocate, whoever sent thee,—Prithee proceed—Nay, Sir, you shall not go. [*To* Willmore *who is stealing off.*]

Will. Then shall I lose my dear Gipsy forever.—Pox on't, she stays me out of spite. [*Aside.*]

Hell. I am related to a Lady, Madam,
Young, rich, and nobly born, but has the fate
To be in love with a young *English* Gentleman.
Strangely she loves him, at first sight she lov'd him,
But did adore him when she heard him speak;
For he, she said, had Charms in every word,
That fail'd not to surprise, to wound, and conquer—

Will. Ha, Egad I hope this concerns me. [*Aside.*]

Ang. 'Tis my false Man, he means—wou'd he were gone.
This Praise will raise his Pride and ruin me—Well,
Since you are so impatient to be gone,
I will release you, Sir. [*To* Willmore.]

Will. Nay, then I'm sure 'twas me he spoke of,
this cannot be the Effects of Kindness in her. [*Aside.*]
—No, Madam, I've consider'd better on't,
And will not give you cause of Jealousy.

Ang. But, Sir, I've—business, that—

Will. This shall not do, I know 'tis but to try me.

Ang. Well, to your Story, Boy,—tho 'twill undo me. [*Aside.*]

Hell. With this Addition to his other Beauties,
He won her unresisting tender Heart,
He vow'd and sigh'd, and swore he lov'd her dearly;
And she believ'd the cunning Flatterer,
And thought herself the happiest Maid alive:
Today was the appointed time by both,
To consummate their Bliss;
The Virgin, Altar, and the Priest were dressed,
And whilst she languished for the expected Bridegroom,
She heard, he paid his broken Vows to you.

 Will. So, this is some dear Rogue that's in love with me, and this way lets me know it; or if it be not me, she means some one whose place I may supply. [*Aside.*] [37]

 Ang. Now I perceive [38]
The cause of thy Impatience to be gone,
And all the business of this glorious Dress.

 Will. Damn the young Prater, I know not what he means.

 Hell. Madam,
In your fair Eyes I read too much concern
To tell my farther Business.

 Ang. Prithee, sweet Youth, talk on, thou may'st perhaps
Raise here a Storm that may undo my Passion,
And then I'll grant thee anything.

 Hell. Madam, 'tis to intreat you, (oh unreasonable!)
You wou'd not see this Stranger;
For if you do, she vows you are undone,
Tho Nature never made a Man so excellent;
And sure he'ad been a God, but for Inconstancy.

 Will. Ah, Rogue, how finely he's instructed! [*Aside.*]—'Tis plain some Woman that has seen me *en passant.*

 Ang. Oh, I shall burst with Jealousy! do you know the Man you speak of?—

 Hell. Yes, Madam, he us'd to be in Buff and Scarlet.

 Ang. Thou, false as Hell, what canst thou say to this? [*To* Willmore.]

 Will. By Heaven—

 Ang. Hold, do not damn thy self—

 Hell. Nor hope to be believ'd. [*He walks about, they follow.*]

 Ang. Oh, perjur'd Man!
Is't thus you pay my generous Passion back?

 Hell. Why wou'd you, Sir, abuse my Lady's Faith?

 Ang. And use me so inhumanly?

 Hell. A Maid so young, so innocent—

 Will. Ah, young Devil!

 Ang. Dost thou not know thy Life is in my Power?

 Hell. Or think my Lady cannot be reveng'd?

 Will. So, so, the Storm comes finely on. [*Aside.*]

 Ang. Now thou art silent, Guilt has struck thee dumb.
Oh, hadst thou still been so, I'd liv'd in safety. [She turns away and weeps.]

Will. Sweetheart, the Lady's Name and House—quickly: I'm impatient to be with her.—[*Aside to* Hellena, *looks towards* Angelica *to watch her turning; and as she comes towards them, he meets her.*]

Hell. So now is he for another Woman. [*Aside.*]

Will. The impudent'st young thing in Nature!
I cannot persuade him out of his Error, Madam.

Ang. I know he's in the right,—yet thou'st a Tongue
That wou'd persuade him to deny his Faith. [*In Rage walks away.*]

Will. Her Name, her Name, dear Boy—[*Said softly to* Hellena.]

Hell. Have you forgot it, Sir?

Will. Oh, I perceive he's not to know I am a Stranger to his Lady. [*Aside.*]—Yes, yes, I do know—but—I have forgot the—[Angel *turns.*]—By Heaven, such early confidence I never saw.

Ang. Did I not charge you with this Mistress, Sir?
Which you denied, tho I beheld your Perjury.
This little Generosity of thine has render'd back my Heart. [*Walks away.*]

Will. So, you have made sweet work here, [39] my little mischief;
Look your Lady be kind and good-natur'd now, or
I shall have but a cursed Bargain on't. [Angelica *turns towards them.*]
—The Rogue's bred up to Mischief,
Art thou so great a Fool to credit him?

Ang. Yes, I do; and you in vain impose upon me.—Come hither, Boy—Is not this he you speak of?

Hell. I think—it is; I cannot swear, but I vow he has just such another lying Lover's look. [Hellena *looks in his Face, he gazes on her.*]

Will. Hah! do not I know that Face?—
By Heaven, my little Gipsy! what a dull Dog was I?
Had I but looked that way, I'd known her.
Are all my hopes of a new Woman banished? [*Aside.*]
—Egad, if I don't fit thee for this, hang me.
—Madam, I have found out the Plot.

Hell. Oh Lord, what does he say? am I discover'd now?

Will. Do you see this young Spark here?

Hell. He'll tell her who I am.

Will. Who do you think this is?

Hell. Ay, ay, he does know me.—Nay, dear Captain, I'm undone if you discover me.

Will. Nay, nay, no cogging; [p. 75] she shall know what a precious Mistress I have.

Hell. Will you be such a Devil?

Will. Nay, nay, I'll teach you to spoil sport you will not make.—This small Ambassador comes not from a Person of Quality, as you imagine, and he says; but from a very errant Gipsy, the talkingst, pratingst, cantingst little Animal thou ever saw'st.

Ang. What news you tell me! that's the thing I mean.

Hell. Wou'd I were well off the place.—If ever I go a Captain-hunting again.— [*Aside.*]

Will. Mean that thing? that Gipsy thing? thou may'st as well be jealous of thy Monkey, or Parrot as her: a German Motion were worth a dozen of her, and a Dream were a better Enjoyment, a Creature of Constitution fitter for Heaven than Man.

Hell. Tho I'm sure he lies, yet this vexes me. [*Aside.*]

Ang. You are mistaken, [40] she's a Spanish Woman Made up of no such dull Materials.

Will. Materials! Egad, and she be made of any that will either dispense, or admit of Love, I'll be bound to continence. [41]

Hell. Unreasonable Man, do you think so? [*Aside to him.*]

Will. [42] You may Return, my little Brazen Head, and tell your Lady, that till she be handsome enough to be belov'd, or I dull enough to be religious, there will be small hopes of me.

Ang. Did you not promise then to marry her?

Will. Not I, by Heaven.

Ang. You cannot undeceive my fears and torments, till you have vow'd you will not marry her.

Hell. If he swears that, he'll be reveng'd on me indeed for all my Rogueries.

Ang. I know what Arguments you'll bring against me, Fortune and Honor.

Will. Honor! I tell you, I hate it in your Sex; and those that fancy themselves possessed of that Foppery, are the most impertinently troublesome of all Woman-kind, and will transgress nine Commandments to keep one: and to satisfy your Jealousy I swear—

Hell. Oh, no swearing, dear Captain—[*Aside to him.*]

Will. If it were possible I should ever be inclin'd to marry, it should be some kind young Sinner, one that has Generosity enough to give a favor handsomely to one that can ask it discreetly, one that has Wit [43] enough to manage an Intrigue of Love—oh, how civil such a Wench is, to a Man than does her the Honor to marry her.

Ang. By Heaven, there's no Faith in anything he says.

[*Enter* Sebastian.]

Sebast. Madam, *Don Antonio*—

Ang. Come hither.

Hell. Ha, *Antonio!* he may be coming hither, and he'll certainly discover me, I'll therefore retire without a Ceremony. [*Exit* Hellena.]

Ang. I'll see him, get my Coach ready.

Sebast. It waits you, Madam.

Will. This is lucky: what, Madam, now I may be gone and leave you to the enjoyment of my Rival?

Ang. Dull Man, that canst not see how ill, how poor
That false dissimulation looks—Be gone,
And never let me see thy cozening Face again,
Lest I relapse and kill thee.

Will. Yes, you can spare me now,—farewell till you are in a better Humor—I'm glad of this release—Now for my Gipsy:
For tho to worse we change, yet still we find
New Joys, New Charms, in a new Miss that's kind. [*Exit* Willmore.]

Ang. He's gone, and in this Ague of My Soul
The shivering Fit returns;
Oh with what willing haste he took his leave,
As if the long'd for Minute were arriv'd,
Of some blest Assignation.

In vain I have consulted all my Charms,
In vain this Beauty priz'd, in vain believ'd
My eyes cou'd kindle any lasting Fires.
I had forgot my Name, my Infamy,
And the Reproach that Honor lays on those
That dare pretend a sober passion here.
Nice Reputation, tho it leave behind
More Virtues than inhabit where that dwells,
Yet that once gone, those virtues shine no more.
—Then since I am not fit to belov'd,
I am resolv'd to think on a Revenge
On him that sooth'd me thus to my undoing. [*Exeunt.*]

Scene III. *A Street.*

[*Enter* Florinda *and* Valeria *in Habits different from what they have been seen in.*]

Flor. We're happily escap'd, yet I tremble still.

Val. A Lover and fear! why, I am but half a one, and yet I have Courage for any Attempt. Would *Hellena* were here. I wou'd fain have had her as deep in this Mischief as we, she'll fare but ill else I doubt.

Flor. She pretended a Visit to the Augustine Nuns, but I believe some other design carried her out, pray Heavens we light on her.—Prithee what didst do with Callis?

Val. When I saw no Reason wou'd do good on her, I follow'd her into the Wardrobe, and as she was looking for something in a great Chest, I tumbled her in by the Heels, snatched the Key of the Apartment where you were confin'd, locked her in, and left her bawling for help.

Flor. 'Tis well you resolve to follow my Fortunes, for thou darest never appear at home again after such an Action.

Val. That's according as the young Stranger and I shall agree—But to our business—I deliver'd your Letter, your Note to *Belvile*, when I got out under pretence of going to Mass, I found him at his Lodging, and believe me it came seasonably; for never was Man in so desperate a Condition. I told him of your Resolution of making your escape today, if your Brother would be absent long enough to permit you; if not, die rather than be *Antonio's*.

Flor. Thou shou'dst have told him I was confin'd to my Chamber upon my Brother's suspicion, that the Business on the *Molo* was a Plot laid between him and I.

Val. I said all this, and told him your Brother was now gone to his Devotion, and he resolves to visit every Church till he find him; and not only undeceive him in that, but caress him so as shall delay his return home.

Flor. Oh Heavens! he's here, and *Belvile* with him too. [They put on their Vizards.]

[*Enter* Don Pedro, Belvile, Willmore; Belvile
and Don Pedro *seeming in serious Discourse.*]

Val. Walk boldly by them, I'll come at a distance, lest he suspect us. [*She walks by them, and looks back on them.*]

Will. Ha! A Woman! [44] and of an excellent Mien!

Pedro. She throws a kind look back on you.

Will. Death, 'tis a likely Wench, and that kind look shall not be cast away—I'll follow her.

Belv. Prithee do not.

Will. Do not! By Heavens to the Antipodes, with such an Invitation. [*She goes out, and* Willmore *follows her.*]

Belv. 'Tis a mad Fellow for a Wench.

[*Enter* Frederick.]

Fred. Oh Colonel, such News.

Belv. Prithee what?

Fred. News that will make you laugh in spite of Fortune.

Belv. What, *Blunt* has had some damn'd Trick put upon him, cheated, bang'd, or clapped?

Fred. Cheated, Sir, rarely cheated of all but his Shirt and Drawers; the unconscionable Whore too turn'd him out before Consummation, so that traversing the Streets at Midnight, the Watch found him in this *Fresco,* and conducted him home: By Heaven 'tis such a slight, and yet I durst as well have been hang'd as laugh at him, or pity him; he beats all that do but ask him a Question, and is in such an Humor—

Pedro. Who is't has met with this ill usage, Sir?

Belv. A Friend of ours, whom you must see for Mirth's sake. I'll employ him to give *Florinda* time for an escape. [*Aside.*]

Pedro. Who is he?

Belv. A young Countryman of ours, one that has been educated at so plentiful a rate, he yet ne'er knew the want of Money, and 'twill be a great Jest to see how simply he'll look without it. For my part I'll lend him none, and the Rogue [45] knows not how to put on a borrowing Face, and ask first. I'll let him see how good 'tis to play our parts whilst I play his—Prithee, *Frederick* do go home and keep him in that posture till we come. [*Exeunt.*]

[*Enter* Florinda *from the farther end of the Scene, looking behind her.*]

Flor. I am follow'd still—hah—my Brother too advancing this way, good Heavens defend me from being seen by him. [*She goes off.*]

[*Enter* Willmore, *and after him* Valeria, *at a little distance.*]

Will. Ah! There she sails, she looks back as she were willing to be boarded, I'll warrant her Prize. [*He goes out,* Valeria *following.*]

[*Enter* Hellena, *just as he goes out, with a Page.*]

Hell. Hah, is not that my Captain that has a Woman in chase?—'tis not *Angelica.* Boy, follow those People at a distance, and bring me an Account where they go in.—I'll find his Haunts, and plague him everywhere.—ha—my Brother! [*Exit Page.*]

[Belvile, Willmore, Pedro *cross the Stage:* Hellena *runs off.*]

[*Scene changes to another Street. Enter* Florinda.]

Flor. What shall I do, my Brother now pursues me. Will no kind Power protect me from his Tyranny?—Hah, here's a Door open, I'll venture in, since nothing can be worse than to fall into his Hands, my Life and Honor are at stake, and my Necessity has no choice. [*She goes in.*]

[*Enter* Valeria, *and* Hellena's *Page peeping after* Florinda.]

Page. Here she went in, I shall remember this House. [*Exit* Boy.]
Val. This is *Belvile's* Lodgings; she's gone in as readily as if she knew it—hah—here's that mad Fellow again, I dare not venture in—I'll watch my Opportunity. [*Goes aside.*]

[*Enter* Willmore, *gazing about him.*]

Will. I have lost her hereabouts—Pox on't she must not scape me so. [*Goes out.*]

[*Scene changes to* Blunt's *Chamber, discovers him sitting on a Couch in his Shirt and Drawers, reading.*]

Blunt. So, now my Mind's a little at Peace, since I have resolv'd Revenge—A Pox on this Taylor tho, for not bringing home the Clothes I bespoke; and a Pox of all poor Cavaliers, a Man can never keep a spare Suit for 'em; and I shall have these Rogues come in and find me naked; and then I'm undone; but I'm resolv'd to arm my self—the Rascals shall not insult over me too much. [*Puts on an old rusty Sword and Buff-Belt.*]—Now, how like a Morrice-Dancer I am equipped—a fine Lady-like Whore to cheat me thus, without affording me a Kindness for my Money, a Pox light on her, I shall never be reconciled to the Sex more, she has made me as faithless as a Physician, as uncharitable as a Churchman, and as ill-natur'd as a Poet. O how I'll use all Women-kind hereafter! what wou'd I give to have one of 'em within my reach now! any Mortal thing in Petticoats, kind Fortune, send me; and I'll forgive thy last Night's Malice—Here's a cursed Book too, (a Warning to all young Travellers) that can instruct me how to prevent such Mischiefs now 'tis too late. Well 'tis a rare convenient thing to read a little now and then, as well as hawk and hunt. [*Sits down again and reads.*]

[*Enter to him* Florinda.]

Flor. This House is haunted sure, 'tis well furnished and no living thing inhabits it—hah—a Man! Heavens how he's attir'd! sure 'tis some Rope-dancer, or Fencing-Master; I tremble now for fear, and yet I must venture now to speak to him—Sir, if I may not interrupt your Meditations—[*He starts up and gazes.*] [46]
Blunt. Hah—what's here? Are my wishes granted? and is not that a she Creature? Adsheartlikins 'tis! what wretched thing art thou—hah!
Flor. Charitable Sir, you've told your self already what I am; a very wretched Maid, forc'd by a strange unlucky Accident, to seek a safety here, and must be ruin'd, if you do not grant it.

Blunt. Ruin'd! Is there any Ruin so inevitable as that which now threatens thee? Dost thou know, miserable Woman, into what Den of Mischiefs thou art fall'n? what a Bliss of Confusion?—hah—dost not see something in my looks that frights thy guilty Soul, and makes thee wish to change that Shape of Woman for any humble Animal, or Devil? for those were safer for thee, and less mischievous.

Flor. Alas, what mean you, Sir? I must confess your Looks have something in 'em makes me fear; but I beseech you, as you seem a Gentleman, pity a harmless Virgin, that takes your House for Sanctuary.

Blunt. Talk on, talk on, and weep too, till my faith return. Do, flatter me out of my Senses again—a harmless Virgin with a Pox, as much one as t'other, adsheartlikins. Why, what the Devil can I not be safe in my House for you? not in my Chamber? nay, even being naked too cannot secure me. This is an Impudence greater than has invaded me yet.—Come, no Resistance. [*Pulls her rudely.*]

Flor. Dare you be so cruel?

Blunt. Cruel, adsheartlikins as a Galley-slave, or a *Spanish* Whore: Cruel, yes, I will kiss and beat thee all over; kiss, and see thee all over; thou shalt lie with me too, not that I care for the Enjoyment, but to let you see I have ta'en deliberated Malice to thee, and will be revenged on one Whore for the Sins of another; I will smile and deceive thee, flatter thee, and beat thee, kiss and swear, and lye to thee, embrace thee and rob thee, as she did me, fawn on thee, and strip thee stark naked, then hang thee out at my Window by the Heels, with a Paper of scurvey Verses fasten'd to thy Breast, in praise of damnable Women—Come, come along.

Flor. Alas, Sir, must I be sacrific'd for the Crimes of the most infamous of my Sex? I never understood the Sins you name.

Blunt. Do, persuade the Fool you love him, or that one of you can be just or honest; tell me I was not an easy Coxcomb, or any strange impossible Tale: it will be believ'd sooner than thy false Showers or Protestations. A Generation of damn'd Hypocrites, to flatter my very Clothes from my back! dissembling Witches! are these the Returns you make an honest Gentleman that trusts, believes, and loves you?—But if I be not even with you—Come along, or I shall—[*Pulls her again.*]

[*Enter* Frederick.]

Fred. Hah, what's here to do?

Blunt. Adsheartlikins, *Frederick* I am glad thou art come, to be a Witness of my dire Revenge.

Fred. What's this, a Person of Quality too, who is upon the Ramble to supply the Defects of some grave impotent Husband?

Blunt. No, this has another Pretence, some very unfortunate Accident brought her hither, to save a Life pursued by I know not who, or why, and forc'd to take Sanctuary here at Fools Haven. Adsheartlikins to me of all Mankind for Protection? Is the Ass to be cajol'd again, think ye? No, young one, no Prayers or Tears shall mitigate my Rage; therefore prepare for both my Pleasure of Enjoyment and Revenge, for I am resolved to make up my Loss here on thy Body, I'll take it out in kindness and in beating.

Fred. Now, Mistress of mine, what do you think of this?

Flor. I think he will not—dares not be so barbarous.

Fred. Have a care, *Blunt*, she fetch'd a deep Sigh, she is enamor'd with thy Shirt and Drawers, she'll strip thee even of that. There are of her Calling such unconscionable

Baggages, and such dexterous. [47] Thieves, they'll flea a Man, and he shall ne'er miss his Skin, till he feels the Cold. There was a Country-man of ours robb'd of a Row of Teeth whilst he was sleeping, which the Jilt made him buy again when he wak'd—You see, Lady, how little Reason we have to trust you.

Blunt. 'Dsheartlikins, why, this is most abominable.

Flor. Some such Devils there may be, but by all that's holy I am none such, I entered here to save a Life in danger.

Blunt. For no goodness I'll warrant her.

Fred. Faith, Damsel, you had e'en confess the plain Truth, for we are Fellows not to be caught twice in the same Trap: Look on that Wreck, a tight Vessel when he set out of Haven, well trim'd and laden, and see how a Female Piccaroon of this Island of Rogues has shatter'd him, and canst thou hope for any Mercy?

Blunt. No, no, Gentlewoman, come along, adsheartlikins we must be better acquainted—we'll both lie with her, and then let me alone to bang her.

Fred. I am ready to serve you in matters of Revenge, that has a double Pleasure in't.

Blunt. Well said. You hear, little one, how you are condemn'd by public Vote to the Bed within, there's no resisting your Destiny, Sweetheart. [*Pulls her.*]

Flor. Stay, Sir, I have seen you with *Belvile*, an *English* Cavalier, for his sake use me kindly; you know how, Sir.

Blunt. Belvile! why, yes, Sweeting, we do know *Belvile*, and wish he were with us now, he's a Cormorant at Whore and Bacon, he'd have a Limb or two of thee, my Virgin Pullet: but 'tis no matter, we'll leave him the Bones to pick.

Flor. Sir, if you have any Esteem for that *Belvile*, I conjure you to treat me with more Gentleness; he'll thank you for the Justice.

Fred. Hark ye, *Blunt*, I doubt we are mistaken in this matter.

Flor. Sir, If you find me not worth *Belvile's* Care, use me as you please; and that you may think I merit better treatment than you threaten—pray take this Present—[*Gives him a Ring: He looks on it.*]

Blunt. Hum—A Diamond! why, 'tis a wonderful Virtue now that lies in this Ring, a mollifying Virtue; adsheartlikins there's more persuasive Rhetoric in't, than all her Sex can utter.

Fred. I begin to suspect something; and 'twou'd anger us vilely to be truss'd up for a Rape upon a Maid of Quality, when we only believe we ruffle a Harlot.

Blunt. Thou art a credulous Fellow, but adsheartlikins I have no Faith yet; why, my Saint prattled as parlously as this does, she gave me a Bracelet too, a Devil on her: but I sent my Man to sell it today for Necessaries, and it prov'd as counterfeit as her Vows of Love.

Fred. However let it reprieve her till we see *Belvile*.

Blunt. That's hard, yet I will grant it.

[*Enter a Servant.*]

Serv. Oh, Sir, the Colonel is just come with his new Friend and a *Spaniard* of Quality, and talks of having you to Dinner with 'em.

Blunt. 'Dsheartlikins, I'm undone—I would not see 'em for the World: Harkye, *Frederick*, lock up the Wench in your Chamber.

Fred. Fear nothing, Madam, whate'er he threatens, you're safe whilst in my Hands. [*Exit* Frederick *and* Florinda.]

Blunt. And, Sirrah—upon your Life, say—I am not at home—or that I am asleep—or—or anything—away—I'll, prevent them coming this way. [*Locks the Door and Exeunt.*] [48]

ACT V.

Scene I. *Blunt's Chamber.* [49]

[*After a great knocking as at his Chamber-door,* [50] *enter* Blunt *softly, crossing the Stage in his Shirt and Drawers, as before.*]

Ned, Ned Blunt, Ned Blunt. [*Call within.*]
Blunt. The Rogues are up in Arms, 'dsheartlikins, this villainous *Frederick* has betray'd me, they have heard of my blessed Fortune.
Ned Blunt, Ned, Ned—[*and knocking within.*]
Belv. Why, he's dead, Sir, without dispute dead, he has not been seen today; let's break open the Door—here—Boy—
Blunt. Ha, break open the Door! 'dsheartlikins that mad Fellow will be as good as his word.
Belv. Boy, bring something to force the Door. [*A great noise within at the Door again.*]
Blunt. So, now must I speak in my own Defence, I'll try what Rhetoric will do—hold—hold, what do you mean, Gentlemen, what do you mean?
Belv. Oh Rogue, art alive? prithee open the Door, and convince us.
Blunt. Yes, I am alive, Gentlemen—but at present a little busy.
Belv. How! *Blunt* grown a man of Business! come, come, open, and let's see this Miracle. [*within.*]
Blunt. No, no, no, no, Gentlemen, 'tis no great Business—but—I am—at—my Devotion,—'dsheartlikins, will you not allow a man time to pray?
Belv. Turn'd religious! a greater Wonder than the first, therefore open quickly, or we shall unhinge, we shall. [*within.*]
Blunt. This won't do—Why, hark ye, Colonel; to tell you the plain Truth, I am about a necessary Affair of Life.—I have a Wench with me—you apprehend me? the Devil's in't if they be so uncivil as to disturb me now.
Will. How, a Wench! Nay, then we must enter and partake; no Resistance,—unless it be your Lady of Quality, and then we'll keep our distance.
Blunt. So, the Business is out.
Will. Come, come, lend more hands to the Door,—now heave altogether—so, well done, my Boys—[*Breaks open the Door.*]

[*Enter* Belvile, Willmore, Frederick Pedro *and* Belvile's *Page:* [51] Blunt *looks simply, they all laugh at him, he lays his hand on his Sword, and conies up to* Willmore.]

Blunt. Hark ye, Sir, laugh out your laugh quickly, d'ye hear, and be gone, I shall spoil your sport else; 'dsheartlikins, Sir, I shall—the Jest has been carried on too long,—a Plague upon my Taylor—[*Aside.*]
Will. 'Sdeath, how the Whore has dressed him! Faith, Sir, I'm sorry.

Blunt. Are you so, Sir? keep't to yourself then, Sir, I advise you, d'ye hear? for I can as little endure your Pity as his Mirth. [*Lays his Hand on's Sword.*]

Belv. Indeed, *Willmore*, thou wert a little too rough with *Ned Blunt's* Mistress; call a Person of Quality Whore, and one so young, so handsome, and so eloquent!—ha, ha, ha.

Blunt. Hark ye, Sir, you know me, and know I can be angry; have a care—for 'dsheartlikins I can fight too—I can, Sir,—do you mark me—no more.

Belv. Why so peevish, good *Ned?* some Disappointments, I'll warrant—What! did the jealous Count her Husband return just in the nick?

Blunt. Or the Devil, Sir,—d'ye laugh? [*They laugh.*] Look ye, settle me a good sober Countenance, and that quickly too, or you shall know *Ned Blunt* is not—

Belv. Not every Body, we know that.

Blunt. Not an Ass, to be laughed at, Sir.

Will. Unconscionable Sinner, to bring a Lover so near his Happiness, a vigorous passionate Lover, and then not only cheat him of his Moveables, but his Desires too.

Belv. Ah, Sir, a Mistress is a Trifle with *Blunt*, he'll have a dozen the next time he looks abroad; his Eyes have Charms not to be resisted: There needs no more than to expose that taking Person to the view of the Fair, and he leads 'em all in Triumph.

Pedro. Sir, tho I'm a stranger to you, I'm ashamed at the rudeness of my Nation; and could you learn who did it, would assist you to make an Example of 'em.

Blunt. Why, ay, there's one speaks sense now, and handsomely; and let me tell you Gentlemen, I should not have show'd myself like a Jack-Pudding, thus to have made you Mirth, but that I have revenge within my power; for know, I have got into my possession a Female, who had better have fallen under any Curse, than the Ruin I design her: 'dsheartlikins, she assaulted me here in my own Lodgings, and had doubtless committed a Rape upon me, had not this Sword defended me.

Fred. I knew not that, but o' my Conscience thou hadst ravished her, had she not redeem'd herself with a Ring—let's see't, *Blunt.* [Blunt *shows the Ring.*]

Belv. Hah!—the Ring I gave *Florinda* when we exchang'd our Vows!—hark ye, *Blunt*—[*Goes to whisper to him.*]

Will. No whispering, good Colonel, there's a Woman in the case, no whispering.

Belv. Hark ye, Fool, be advis'd, and conceal both the Ring and the Story, for your Reputation's sake; don't let People know what despis'd Cullies we *English* are: to be cheated and abus'd by one Whore, and another rather bribe thee than be kind to thee, is an Infamy to our Nation.

Will. Come, come, where's the Wench? we'll see her, let her be what she will, we'll see her.

Pedro. Ay, ay, let us see her, I can soon discover whether she be of Quality, or for your Diversion.

Blunt. She's in *Frederick's* Custody.

Will. Come, come, the Key. [*To* Frederick *who gives him the Key, they are going.*]

Belv. Death! what shall I do?—stay, Gentlemen—yet if I hinder 'em, I shall discover all—hold, let's go one at once—give me the Key.

Will. Nay, hold there, Colonel, I'll go first.

Fred. Nay, no Dispute, *Ned* and I have the property of her.

Will. Damn Property—then we'll draw Cuts. [Belvile *goes to whisper* Willmore] Nay, no Corruption, good Colonel: come, the longest Sword carries her.—[*They all draw, forgetting* Don Pedro, *being a Spaniard, had the longest.*]

Blunt. I yield up my Interest to you Gentlemen, and that will be Revenge sufficient.

Will. The Wench is yours—[To *Pedro*] Pox of his *Toledo*, I had forgot that.

Fred. Come, Sir, I'll conduct you to the Lady. [*Exit* Frederick *and* Pedro.]

Belv. To hinder him will certainly discover—[*Aside.*] Dost know, dull Beast, what Mischief thou hast done? [Willmore *walking up and down out of Humor.*]

Will. Ay, ay, to trust our Fortune to Lots, a Devil on't, 'twas madness, that's the Truth on't.

Belv. Oh intolerable Sot!

[*Enter* Florinda, *running mask'd,* Pedro *after her,* Willmore *gazing round her.*]

Flor. Good Heaven, defend me from discovery. [*Aside.*]

Pedro. 'Tis but in vain to fly me, you are fallen to my Lot.

Belv. Sure she is undiscover'd yet, but now I fear there is no way to bring her off.

Will. Why, what a Pox is not this my Woman, the same I follow'd but now?

[Pedro *talking to* Florinda, *who walks up and down.*]

Pedro. As if I did not know ye, and your Business here.

Flor. Good Heaven! I fear he does indeed—[*Aside.*]

Pedro. Come, pray be kind, I know you meant to be so when you enter'd here, for these are proper Gentlemen.

Will. But, Sir—perhaps the Lady will not be impos'd upon, she'll chose her Man.

Pedro. I am better bred, than not to leave her Choice free.

[*Enter* Valeria, *and is surprized at the Sight of* Don Pedro.]

Val. Don *Pedro* here! there's no avoiding him. [*Aside.*]

Flor. Valeria! then I'm undone—[*Aside.*]

Val. Oh! have I found you, Sir—[*To* Pedro, *running to him.*]—The strangest Accident—if I had breath—to tell it.

Pedro. Speak—is *Florinda* safe? *Hellena* well?

Val. Ay, ay, Sir—*Florinda*—is safe—from any fears of you.

Pedro. Why, where's *Florinda?*—speak.

Val. Ay, where indeed, Sir? I wish I could inform you,—But to hold you no longer in doubt—

Flor. Oh, what will she say! [*Aside.*]

Val. She's fled away in the Habit of one of her Pages, Sir—but *Callis* thinks you may retrieve her yet, if you make haste away; she'll tell you, Sir, the rest—if you can find her out. [*Aside.*]

Pedro. Dishonorable Girl, she has undone my Aim—Sir—you see my necessity of leaving you, and I hope you'll pardon it: my Sister, I know, will make her flight to you; and if she do, I shall expect she should be render'd back.

Belv. I shall consult my Love and Honor, Sir. [*Exit* Pedro.]

Flor. My dear Preserver, let me embrace thee. [*To* Valeria.]

Will. What the Devil's all this?

Blunt. Mystery by this Light.

Val. Come, come, make haste and get your selves married quickly, for your Brother will return again.

Belv. I am so surpriz'd with Fears and Joys, so amaz'd to find you here in safety, I can scarce persuade my Heart into a Faith of what I see—

Will. Harkye, Colonel, is this that Mistress who has cost you so many Sighs, and me so many Quarrels with you?

Belv. It is—Pray give him the Honor of your Hand. [*To* Florinda.]

Will. Thus it must be receiv'd then. [Kneels and kisses her Hand.] And with it give your Pardon too.

Flor. The Friend to *Belvile* may command me anything.

Will. Death, wou'd I might, 'tis a surprising Beauty. [*Aside.*]

Belv. Boy, run and fetch a Father instantly. [*Exit* Boy.]

Fred. So, now do I stand like a Dog, and have not a Syllable to plead my own Cause with: by this Hand, Madam, I was never thoroughly confounded before, nor shall I ever more dare look up with Confidence, till you are pleased to pardon me.

Flor. Sir, I'll be reconcil'd to you on one Condition, that you'll follow the Example of your Friend, in marrying a Maid that does not hate you, and whose Fortune (I believe) will not be unwelcome to you.

Fred. Madam, had I no Inclinations that way, I shou'd obey your kind Commands.

Belv. Who, *Frederick* marry; he has so few Inclinations for Womankind, that had he been possessed of Paradise, he might have continu'd there to this Day, if no Crime but Love cou'd have disinherited him.

Fred. Oh, I do not use to boast of my Intrigues.

Belv. Boast! why thou do'st nothing but boast; and I dare swear, wer't thou as innocent from the Sin of the Grape, as thou art from the Apple, thou might'st yet claim that right in *Eden* which our first Parents lost by too much loving.

Fred. I wish this Lady would think me so modest a Man.

Val. She shou'd be sorry then, and not like you half so well, and I shou'd be loth to break my Word with you; which was, That if your Friend and mine are agreed, it shou'd be a Match between you and I. [*She gives him her Hand.*]

Fred. Bear witness, Colonel, 'tis a Bargain. [*Kisses her Hand.*]

Blunt. I have a Pardon to beg too; but adsheartlikins I am so out of Countenance, that I am a Dog if I can say anything to purpose. [*To* Florinda.]

Flor. Sir, I heartily forgive you all.

Blunt. That's nobly said, sweet Lady—*Belvile*, prithee present her her Ring again, for I find I have not Courage to approach her myself. [*Gives him the Ring, he gives it to* Florinda.]

[*Enter* Boy.]

Boy. Sir, I have brought the Father that you sent for.

Belv. 'Tis well, and now my dear *Florinda*, let's fly to complete that mighty Joy we have so long wish'd and sigh'd for.—Come, *Frederick* you'll follow?

Fred. Your Example, Sir, 'twas ever my Ambition in War, and must be so in Love.

Will. And must not I see this juggling Knot ty'd?

Belv. No, thou shalt do us better Service, and be our Guard, lest Don *Pedro's* sudden Return interrupt the Ceremony.

Will. Content; I'll secure this Pass. [*Exit* Belvile, Florinda, Frederick *and* Valeria.]

[*Enter* Boy.]

Boy. Sir, there's a Lady without wou'd speak to you. [*To* Willmore.]

Will. Conduct her in, I dare not quit my Post.

Boy. And, Sir, your Taylor waits you in your Chamber.

Blunt. Some comfort yet, I shall not dance naked at the Wedding. [*Exit* Blunt *and* Boy.]

[*Enter again the* Boy, *conducting in* Angelica *in a masking Habit and a Vizard,* Willmore *runs to her.*]

Will. This can be none but my pretty Gipsy—Oh, I see you can follow as well as fly—Come, confess thy self the most malicious Devil in Nature, you think you have done my Bus'ness with *Angelica*—

Ang. Stand off, base Villain—[*She draws a Pistol and holds to his Breast.*]

Will. Hah, 'tis not she: who art thou? and what's thy Business?

Ang. One thou hast injur'd, and who comes to kill thee for't.

Will. What the Devil canst thou mean?

Ang. By all my Hopes to kill thee—[*Holds still the Pistol to his Breast, he going back, she following still.*]

Will. Prithee on what Acquaintance? for I know thee not.

Ang. Behold this Face!—so lost to thy Remembrance!
And then call all thy Sins about thy Soul,
And let them die with thee. [*Pulls off her Vizard.*]

Will. Angelica!

Ang. Yes, Traitor.
Does not thy guilty Blood run shivering thro thy Veins?
Hast thou no Horror at this Sight, that tells thee,
Thou hast not long to boast thy shameful Conquest?

Will. Faith, no Child, my Blood keeps its old Ebbs and Flows still, and that usual Heat too, that cou'd oblige thee with a Kindness, had I but opportunity.

Ang. Devil! dost wanton with my Pain—have at thy Heart.

Will. Hold, dear Virago! hold thy Hand a little, I am not now at leisure to be kill'd—hold and hear me—Death, I think she's in earnest. [*Aside.*]

Ang. Oh if I take not heed, My coward Heart will leave me to his Mercy. [*Aside, turning from him.*]—What have you, Sir, to say?—but should I hear thee,
Thoud'st talk away all that is brave about me: [*Follows him with the Pistol to his Breast.*] And I have vow'd thy Death, by all that's sacred.

Will. Why, then there's an end of a proper handsome Fellow, that might have liv'd to have done good good Service yet:—That's all I can say to't.

Ang. Yet—I wou'd give thee—time for Penitence. [*Pausingly.*]

Will. Faith, Child, I thank God, I have ever took care to lead a good, sober, hopeful Life, and am of a Religion that teaches me to believe, I shall depart in Peace.

Ang. So will the Devil: tell me
How many poor believing Fools thou hast undone;
How many Hearts thou hast betray'd to ruin!
—Yet these are little Mischiefs to the Ills
Thou'st taught mine to commit: thou'st taught it Love.

Will. Egad, 'twas shrewdly hurt the while.

Ang.—Love, that has robb'd it of its Unconcern,
Of all that Pride that taught me how to value it,
And in its room a mean submissive Passion was convey'd,
That made me humbly bow, which I ne'er did
To anything but Heaven.
—Thou, perjur'd Man, didst this, and with thy Oaths,
Which on thy Knees thou didst devoutly make,
Soften'd my yielding Heart—And then, I was a Slave—
Yet still had been content to've worn my Chains,
Worn 'em with Vanity and Joy forever,
Hadst thou not broke those Vows that put them on.
—'Twas then I was undone. [*All this while follows him with a Pistol to his Breast.*]
 Will. Broke my Vows! why, where hast thou lived?
Amongst the Gods! For I never heard of mortal Man,
That has not broke a thousand Vows.
 Ang. Oh, Impudence!
 Will. Angelica! that Beauty has been too long tempting,
Not to have made a thousand Lovers languish,
Who in the amorous Favor, no doubt have sworn
Like me; did they all die in that Faith? still adoring?
I do not think they did.
 Ang. No, faithless Man: had I repaid their Vows, as I did thine, I wou'd have kill'd the ungrateful that had abandon'd me.
 Will. This old General has quite spoil'd thee, nothing makes a Woman so vain, as being flatter'd; your old Lover ever supplies the Defects of Age, with intolerable Dotage, vast Charge, and that which you call Constancy; and attributing all this to your own Merits, you domineer, and throw your Favors in's Teeth, upbraiding him still with the Defects of Age, and cuckold him as often as he deceives your Expectations. But the gay, young, brisk Lover, that brings his equal Fires, and can give you Dart for Dart, he'll be as nice as you sometimes.
 Ang. All this thou'st made me know, for which I hate thee.
Had I remain'd in innocent Security,
I shou'd have thought all Men were born my Slaves;
And worn my Pow'r like Lightning in my Eyes,
To have destroy'd at Pleasure when offended.
—But when Love held the Mirror, the undeceiving Glass
Reflected all the Weakness of my Soul, and made me know,
My richest Treasure being lost, my Honor,
All the remaining Spoil cou'd not be worth
The Conqueror's Care or Value.
—Oh how I fell like a long worship'd Idol,
Discovering all the Cheat!
Wou'd not the Incense and rich Sacrifice,
Which blind Devotion offer'd at my Altars,
Have fall'n to thee?
Why woud'st thou then destroy my fancy'd Power?
 Will. By Heaven thou art brave, and I admire thee strangely.
I wish I were that dull, that constant thing,

92

Which thou woud'st have, and Nature never meant me:
I must, like cheerful Birds, sing in all Groves,
And perch on every Bough,
Billing the next kind She that flies to meet me;
Yet after all cou'd build my Nest with thee,
Thither repairing when I'd lov'd my round,
And still reserve a tributary Flame.
—To gain your Credit, I'll pay you back your Charity,
And be oblig'd for nothing but for Love. [*Offers her a Purse of Gold.*]

Ang. Oh that thou wert in earnest!
So mean a Thought of me,
Wou'd turn my Rage to Scorn, and I shou'd pity thee,
And give thee leave to live;
Which for the public Safety of our Sex,
And my own private Injuries, I dare not do.
Prepare—[*Follows still, as before.*]
—I will no more be tempted with Replies.

Will. Sure—

Ang. Another Word will damn thee! I've heard thee talk too long. [*She follows him with a Pistol ready to shoot: he retires still amaz'd.*]

[*Enter* Don Antonio, *his Arm in a Scarf, and lays hold on the Pistol.*]

Ant. Hah! *Angelica!* [52]

Ang. Antonio! What Devil [53] brought thee hither?

Ant. Love and Curiosity, seeing your Coach at Door. Let me disarm you of this unbecoming Instrument of Death.—[*Takes away the Pistol.*] Amongst the Number of your Slaves, was there not one worthy the Honor to have fought your Quarrel?—Who are you, Sir, that are so very wretched To merit Death from her?

Will. One, Sir, that cou'd have made a better End of an amorous Quarrel without you, than with you.

Ant. Sure 'tis some Rival—hah—the very Man took down her Picture yesterday—the very same that set on me last night—Blest opportunity—[*Offers to shoot him.*]

Ang. Hold, you're mistaken, Sir.

Ant. By Heaven the very same!
—Sir, what pretensions have you to this Lady?

Will. Sir, I don't use to be examin'd, and am ill at all Disputes but this—[*Draws,* Antonio *offers to shoot.*]

Ang. Oh, hold! you see he's arm'd with certain Death: [*To* Willmore.]
—And you, *Antonio,* I command you hold,
By all the Passion you've so lately vow'd me.

[*Enter* Don Pedro, *sees* Antonio, *and stays.*]

Pedro. Hah, *Antonio!* and *Angelica!* [*Aside.*]

Ant. When I refuse Obedience to your Will,
May you destroy me with your mortal Hate.
By all that's Holy I adore you so,

That even my Rival, who has Charms enough
To make him fall a Victim to my Jealousy,
Shall live, nay, and have leave to love on still.

Pedro. What's this I hear? [*Aside.*]

Ang. Ah thus, 'twas thus he talk'd, and I believ'd. [*Pointing to* Willmore.]
—*Antonio*, yesterday,
I'd not have sold my Interest in his Heart,
For all the Sword has won and lost in Battle.
—But now to show my utmost of Contempt,
I give thee Life—which if thou would'st preserve,
Live where my Eyes may never see thee more,
Live to undo some one, whose Soul may prove
So bravely constant to revenge my Love.

[*Goes out,* Antonio *follows, but* Pedro *pulls him back.*]

Pedro. Antonio—stay.

Ant. Don *Pedro*—

Pedro. What Coward Fear was that prevented thee
From meeting me this Morning on the *Molo?*

Ant. Meet thee?

Pedro. Yes me; I was the Man that dar'd thee to't.

Ant. Hast thou so often seen me fight in War,
To find no better Cause to excuse my Absence?
—I sent my Sword and one to do thee Right,
Finding myself uncapable to use a Sword.

Pedro. But 'twas *Florinda's* Quarrel that we fought,
And you to show how little you esteem'd her,
Sent me your Rival, giving him your Interest.
—But I have found the Cause of this Affront,
But when I meet you fit for the Dispute,
—I'll tell you my Resentment.

Ant. I shall be ready, Sir, e'er long to do you Reason. [*Exit* Antonio.]

Pedro. If I cou'd find *Florinda*, now whilst my Anger's high, I think I shou'd be kind, and give her to *Belvile* in Revenge.

Will. Faith, Sir, I know not what you wou'd do, but I believe the Priest within has been so kind.

Pedro. How! my Sister married?

Will. I hope by this time she is, and bedded too, or he has not my longings about him.

Pedro. Dares he do thus? Does he not fear my Pow'r?

Will. Faith not at all. If you will go in, and thank him for the Favor he has done your Sister, so; if not, Sir, my Power's greater in this House than yours; I have a damn'd surly Crew here, that will keep you till the next Tide, and then clap you an board my Prize; my Ship lies but a League off the *Molo*, and we shall show your Donship a damn'd *Tramontana* [p. 99] Rover's Trick.

[*Enter* Belvile.]

Belv. This Rogue's in some new Mischief—hah, *Pedro* return'd!

Pedro. Colonel *Belvile*, I hear you have married my Sister.

Belv. You have heard truth then, Sir.

Pedro. Have I so? then, Sir, I wish you Joy.

Belv. How!

Pedro. By this Embrace I do, and I glad on't.

Belv. Are you in earnest?

Pedro. By our long Friendship and my Obligations to thee, I am. The sudden Change I'll give you Reasons for anon. Come lead me into my Sister, that she may know I now approve her Choice. [*Exit* Belvile *with* Pedro.]

[Willmore *goes to follow them. Enter* Hellena *as before in Boy's Clothes, and pulls him back.*]

Will. Ha! my Gipsy—Now a thousand Blessings on thee for this Kindness. Egad, Child, I was e'en in despair of ever seeing thee again; my Friends are all provided for within, each Man his kind Woman.

Hell. Hah! I thought they had serv'd me some such Trick.

Will. And I was e'en resolv'd to go aboard, condemn myself to my lone Cabin, and the Thoughts of thee.

Hell. And cou'd you have left me behind? wou'd you have been so ill-natur'd?

Will. Why, 'twou'd have broke my Heart, Child—but since we are met again, I defy foul Weather to part us.

Hell. And wou'd you be a faithful Friend now, if a Maid shou'd trust you?

Will. For a Friend I cannot promise, thou art of a Form so excellent, a Face and Humor too good for cold dull Friendship; I am parlously afraid of being in love, Child, and you have not forgot how severely you have us'd me.

Hell. That's all one, such Usage you must still look for, to find out all your Haunts, to rail at you to all that love you, till I have made you love only me in your own Defence, because nobody else will love.

Will. But hast thou no better Quality to recommend thy self by?

Hell. Faith none, Captain—Why, 'twill be the greater Charity to take me for thy Mistress, I am a lone Child, a kind of Orphan Lover; and why I shou'd die a Maid, and in a Captain's Hands too, I do not understand.

Will. Egad, I was never claw'd away with Broad-Sides from any Female before, thou hast one Virtue I adore, good-Nature; I hate a coy demure Mistress, she's as troublesome as a Colt, I'll break none; no, give me a mad Mistress when mew'd, and in flying on [e] I dare trust upon the Wing, that whilst she's kind will come to the Lure.

Hell. Nay, as kind as you will, good Captain, whilst it lasts, but let's lose no time.

Will. My time's as precious to me, as thine can be; therefore, dear Creature, since we are so well agreed, let's retire to my Chamber, and if ever thou were treated with such savory Love—Come—My Bed's prepar'd for such a Guest, all clean and sweet as thy fair self; I love to steal a Dish and a Bottle with a Friend, and hate long Graces—Come, let's retire and fall to.

Hell. 'Tis but getting my Consent, and the Business is soon done; let but old Gaffer *Hymen* and his Priest say Amen to't, and I dare lay my Mother's Daughter by as proper a Fellow as your Father's Son, without fear or blushing.

Will. Hold, hold, no Bugg Words, Child, Priest and *Hymen*: prithee add Hangman to 'em to make up the Consort—No, no, we'll have no Vows but Love, Child, nor Witness but the Lover; the kind Deity enjoins naught but love and enjoy. *Hymen* and Priest wait still upon Portion, and Jointure; Love and Beauty have their own Ceremonies. Marriage is as certain a Bane to Love, as lending Money is to Friendship: I'll neither ask nor give a Vow, tho I could be content to turn Gipsy, and become a Left-hand Bridegroom, to have the Pleasure of working that great Miracle of making a Maid a Mother, if you durst venture; 'tis upse Gipsy that, and if I miss, I'll lose my Labor.

Hell. And if you do not lose, what shall I get? A Cradle full of Noise and Mischief, with a Pack of Repentance at my Back? Can you teach me to weave Inkle [p. 101] to pass my time with? 'Tis upse [p. 101] Gipsy that too.

Will. I can teach thee to weave a true Love's Knot better.

Hell. So can my Dog.

Will. Well, I see we are both upon our Guard, and I see there's no way to conquer good Nature, but by yielding—here—give me thy Hand—one Kiss and I am thine—

Hell. One Kiss! How like my Page he speaks; I am resolv'd you shall have none, for asking such a sneaking Sum—He that will be satisfied with one Kiss, will never die of that Longing; good Friend single-Kiss, is all your talking come to this? A Kiss, a Caudle! farewell, Captain single-Kiss. [*Going out he stays her.*]

Will. Nay, if we part so, let me die like a Bird upon a Bough, at the Sheriff's Charge. By Heaven, both the *Indies* shall not buy thee from me. I adore thy Humor and will marry thee, and we are so of one Humor, it must be a Bargain—give me thy Hand—[*Kisses her hand.*] And now let the blind ones (Love and Fortune) do their worst.

Hell. Why, God-a-mercy, Captain!

Will. But harkye—The Bargain is now made; but is it not fit we should know each other's Names? That when we have Reason to curse one another hereafter, and People ask me who 'tis I give to the Devil, I may at least be able to tell what Family you came of.

Hell. Good reason, Captain; and where I have cause, (as I doubt not but I shall have plentiful) that I may know at whom to throw my—Blessings—I beseech ye your Name.

Will. I am call'd *Robert the Constant.*

Hell. A very fine Name! pray was it your Faulkner or Butler that christen'd you? Do they not use to whistle when then call you?

Will. I hope you have a better, that a Man may name without crossing himself, you are so merry with mine.

Hell. I am call'd *Hellena the Inconstant.*

[*Enter* Pedro, Belvile, Florinda, Frederick Valeria.]

Pedro. Hah! *Hellena!*

Flor. Hellena!

Hell. The very same—hah my Brother! now, Captain, show your Love and Courage; stand to your Arms, and defend me bravely, or I am lost forever.

Pedro. What's this I hear? false Girl, how came you hither, and what's your Business? Speak. [*Goes roughly to her.*]

Will. Hold off, Sir, you have leave to parley only. [*Puts himself between.*]

Hell. I had e'en as good tell it, as you guess it. Faith, Brother, my Business is the same with all living Creatures of my Age, to love, and be loved, and here's the Man.

Pedro. Perfidious Maid, hast thou deceiv'd me too, deceiv'd thy self and Heaven?

Hell. 'Tis time enough to make my Peace with that: Be you but kind, let me alone with Heaven.

Pedro. Belvile, I did not expect this false Play from you; was't not enough you'd gain *Florinda* (which I pardon'd) but your leud Friends too must be enrich'd with the Spoils of a noble Family?

Belv. Faith, Sir, I am as much surpriz'd at this as you can be: Yet, Sir, my Friends are Gentlemen, and ought to be esteem'd for their Misfortunes, since they have the Glory to suffer with the best of Men and Kings; 'tis true, he's a Rover of Fortune, yet a Prince aboard his little wooden World.

Pedro. What's this to the maintenance of a Woman or her Birth and Quality?

Will. Faith, Sir, I can boast of nothing but a Sword which does me Right where-e'er I come, and has defended a worse Cause than a Woman's: and since I lov'd her before I either knew her Birth or Name, I must pursue my Resolution, and marry her.

Pedro. And is all your holy Intent of becoming a Nun debauch'd into a Desire of Man?

Hell. Why—I have consider'd the matter, Brother, and find the Three hundred thousand Crowns my Uncle left me (and you cannot keep from me) will be better laid out in Love than in Religion, and turn to as good an Account—let most Voices carry it, for Heaven or the Captain? All cry, a Captain, a Captain.

Hell. Look ye, Sir, 'tis a clear Case.

Pedro. Oh I am mad—if I refuse, my Life's in Danger—[*Aside.*]—Come—There's one motive induces me—take her—I shall now be free from the fear of her Honor; guard it you now, if you can, I have been a Slave to't long enough. [*Gives her to him.*]

Will. Faith, Sir, I am of a Nation, that are of opinion a Woman's Honor is not worth guarding when she has a mind to part with it.

Hell. Well said, Captain.

Pedro. This was your Plot, Mistress, but I hope you have married one that will revenge my Quarrel to you—[*To* Valeria.]

Val. There's no altering Destiny, Sir.

Pedro. Sooner than a Woman's Will, therefore I forgive you all—and wish you may get my Father's Pardon as easily; which I fear.

[*Enter* Blunt *dressed in a Spanish Habit, looking very ridiculously; his Man adjusting his Band.*]

Man. 'Tis very well, Sir.

Blunt. Well, Sir, 'dsheartlikins I tell you 'tis damnable ill, Sir—a Spanish Habit, good Lord! cou'd the Devil and my Taylor devise no other Punishment for me, but the Mode of a Nation I abominate?

Belv. What's the matter, *Ned?*

Blunt. Pray view me round, and judge—[*Turns round.*]

Belv. I must confess thou art a kind of an odd Figure.

Blunt. In a Spanish Habit with a Vengeance! I had rather be in the Inquisition for Judaism, than in this Doublet and Breeches; a Pillory were an easy Collar to this, three Handfuls high; and these Shoes too are worse than the Stocks, with the Sole an Inch shorter than my Foot: In fine, Gentlemen, methinks I look altogether like a Bag of Bays stuff'd full of Fools Flesh.

Belv. Methinks 'tis well, and makes thee look *en Cavalier:* Come, Sir, settle your Face, and salute our Friends, Lady—

Blunt. Hah! Say'st thou so, my little Rover? [*To* Hellena] Lady—(if you be one) give me leave to kiss your Hand, and tell you, adsheartlikins, for all I look so, I am your humble Servant—A Pox of my *Spanish* Habit.

Will. Hark—what's this? [*Music is heard to Play.*]

[*Enter* Boy.]

Boy. Sir, as the Custom is, the gay People in Masquerade, who make every Man's House their own, are coming up.

[*Enter several Men and Women in masking Habits, with Music, they put themselves in order and dance.*]

Blunt. Adsheartlikins, wou'd 'twere lawful to pull off their false Faces, that I might see if my Doxy were not amongst 'em.

Belv. Ladies and Gentlemen, since you are come so *a propos*, you must take a small Collation with us. [*To the* Masqueraders.]

Will. Whilst we'll to the Good Man within, who stays to give us a Cast of his Office. [*To* Hellena.]—Have you no trembling at the near approach?

Hell. No more than you have in an Engagement or a Tempest.

Will. Egad, thou'rt a brave Girl, and I admire thy Love and Courage.
Lead on, no other Dangers they can dread,
Who venture in the Storms o'th' Marriage-Bed. [*Exeunt.*]

EPILOGUE

The banished Cavaliers! a Roving Blade!
A popish Carnival! a Masquerade!
The Devil's in't if this will please the Nation,
In these our blessed Times of Reformation,
When Conventicling is so much in Fashion.
And yet—
That mutinous Tribe less Factions do beget,
Than your continual differing in Wit;
Your Judgment's (as your Passions) a Disease:
Nor Muse nor Miss your Appetite can please;
You're grown as nice as queasy Consciences,
Whose each Convulsion, when the Spirit moves,
Damns everything that Maggot disapproves.
With canting Rule you wou'd the Stage refine,
And to dull Method all our Sense confine.
With th' Insolence of Common-wealths you rule,
Where each gay Fop, and politick brave Fool,
On Monarch Wit impose without controul.
As for the last who seldom sees a Play,
Unless it be the old Black-Fryers way,

Shaking his empty Noddle o'er Bamboo,
He crys—Good Faith, these Plays will never do.
—Ah, Sir, in my young days, what lofty Wit,
What high-strain'd Scenes of Fighting there were writ:
These are slight airy Toys. But tell me, pray,
What has the House of Commons *done today?*
Then shows his Politics, to let you see
Of State Affairs he'll judge as notably,
As he can do of Wit and Poetry.
    The younger Sparks, who hither do resort,
Cry—
Pox o' your gentle things, give us more Sport;
—Damn me, I'm sure 'twill never please the Court.
Such Fops are never pleas'd, unless the Play
Be stuff'd with Fools, as brisk and dull as they:
Such might the Half-Crown spare, and in a Glass
At home behold a more accomplished Ass,
Where they may set their Cravats, Wigs and Faces,
And practice all their Buffoonery Grimaces;
See how this—Huff becomes—this Dammy—flare—
Which they at home may act, because they dare,
But—must with prudent Caution do elsewhere.
Oh that our Nokes, *or* Tony Lee [p. 106] *could show*
A Fop but half so much to th' Life as you.

POST-SCRIPT [54]

This Play had been sooner in Print, but for a Report about the Town (made by some either very Malicious or very Ignorant) that 'twas Thomaso *altered; which made the Book-sellers fear some trouble from the Proprietor of that Admirable Play, which indeed has Wit enough to stock a Poet, and is not to be piec't or mended by any but the Excellent Author himself; That I have stol'n some hints from it may be a proof, that I valu'd it more than to pretend to alter it: had I had the Dexterity of some Poets who are not more expert in stealing than in the Art of Concealing, and who even that way out-do the Spartan-Boys I might have appropriated all to myself, but I, vainly proud of my Judgment hang out the Sign of* ANGELICA *(the only Stol'n Object) to give Notice where a great part of the Wit dwelt; though if the Play of the* Novella [p. 107] *were as well worth remembering as* Thomaso, *they might (bating the Name) have as well said, I took it from thence: I will only say the Plot and Bus'ness (not to boast on't) is my own: as for the Words and Characters, I leave the Reader to judge and compare 'em with* Thomaso, *to whom I recommend the great Entertainment of reading it, tho' had this succeeded ill, I shou'd have had no need of imploring that Justice from the Critics, who are naturally so kind to any that pretend to usurp their Dominion, they wou'd doubtless have given me the whole Honor on't. Therefore I will only say in* English *what the famous* Virgil [p. 107] *does in Latin: I make Verses and others have the Fame.*

THE ROVER; OR,
THE BANISH'D CAVALIERS.
PART II.

ARGUMENT.

The exiled cavaliers, Willmore the Rover, Shift and Hunt, two officers, Ned Blunt and Fetherfool, his friend, have arrived at Madrid, where they are welcomed by Beaumond, nephew to the English Ambassador. Both Willmore and Beaumond are enamored of La Nuche, a beautiful courtesan, whilst Shift and Hunt are respectively courting a Giantess and a Dwarf, two Mexican Jewesses of immense wealth, newly come to Madrid with an old Hebrew, their uncle and guardian. Beaumond is contracted to Ariadne, who loves Willmore. Whilst the Rover is complimenting La Nuche, some Spaniards, headed by Don Carlo, an aged admirer of the lady, attempt to separate the pair. During the scuffle the ladies enter a church, where they are followed by the gallants. A little later Fetherfool comes to terms with La Nuche's duenna, Petronella, whilst Willmore makes love to Ariadne. Shift next informs Willmore of the arrival of a celebrated mountebank, and the Rover resolves to take the quack's place, which he does in effective disguise. Fetherfool and Blunt visit the pseudo-doctor's house, where the Giantess and Dwarf are lodged to be converted to a reasonable size by his medicaments; covetous of their great fortunes, the coxcombs also begin to court the two Jewesses. La Nuche comes to consult the mountebank and meets Ariadne attired as a boy, and Willmore in his own dress. Ariadne, who has a rendezvous that evening with Willmore, is accidentally anticipated by La Nuche, who runs into the garden during a night brawl between Beaumond and the Rover, each of whom is ignorant of his opponent's personality. Both the combatants encounter the courtesan in the garden and are joined by Ariadne. The confusion and mistakes that ensue are augmented by the arrival of Beaumond's page and eventually all disperse in different directions. La Nuche returns to her house, where Fetherfool—led on by the Duenna—awaits her. Carlo, however, come thither for the same purpose, enters the chambers, and after they have fallen to fisticuffs, Fetherfool in a fright escapes through a window. Meanwhile La Nuche is engaged with Willmore; Beaumond interrupts, and both leave her in pretended disdain. Ariadne, purposing to meet the Rover, mistakes Beaumond for him in the dark and they hurry away to the quack's house. Here, however, Fetherfool has already arrived and, finding the Giantess asleep, robs her of a pearl necklace; but he is alarmed by Shift, who takes her off and promptly weds her, whilst Hunt does the same by the Dwarf. Blunt next appears leading Petronella, veiled, who, filching a casket of jewels, has just fled from La Nuche; but the hag is discovered and compelled to disgorge. The Jewish Guardian is reconciled to the marriages of his wards; Beaumond and Ariadne, Willmore and La Nuche arrive, and the various mistakes with regard to identity are rectified, Willmore incidentally revealing himself as the sham mountebank. Beaumond and Ariadne agree to marry, whilst La Nuche gives herself to the Rover.

SOURCE.

Induced by the extraordinary success of *The Rover* in 1677, Mrs. Behn, four years later, turned again to Killigrew's *Thomaso; or, The Wanderer*, and produced a sequel to her play. She had, however, already made good use of the best points of the old comedy, and the remaining material only being that which her judgment first rejected, it is not a matter of surprise to find the second part of *The Rover* somewhat inferior to the first. This is by no means to say that it is not an amusing comedy full of bustle and humor. The intrigue of Willmore and La Nuche, together with the jocantries of the inimitable Blunt, Nick Fetherfool, and the antique Petronella Elenora, are all alive with the genius of Astrea, although it may be possibly objected that some of the episodes with the two Monsters and the pranks of Harlequin are apt to trench a little too nearly on the realm of farce.

THEATRICAL HISTORY.

The Second Part of The Rover was produced at the Duke's Theatre, Dorset Gardens, in 1681. It is noticeable that Will Smith had so distinguished himself in Willmore, that Betterton, who appeared as Belvile in the first part, did not essay a character in the second. The cast was reinforced, however, by Mrs. Barry, who took the role of La Nuche.

The play was received with great applause; it suffered none the less the fate of most sequels and, being overshadowed by its predecessor, after a few decades disappeared from the boards.

TO HIS
ROYAL HIGHNESS
THE
DUKE, [p. 113] &c.

Great Sir,

I dread to appear in this Humble Dedication to Your Royal Highness, as one of those Insolent and Saucy Offenders who take occasion by Your absence to commit ill-mannered indecencies, unpardonable to a Prince of your Illustrious Birth and God-like Goodness, but that in spite of Seditious Scandal You can forgive; and all the World knows You can suffer with a Divine Patience: the proofs You have early and late given of this, have been such, as if Heaven design'd 'em only to give the World an undeniable Testimony of Your Noble Virtues, Your Loyalty and True Obedience (if I may presume to say so,) both to Your Sacred Brother, and the never satisfied People, when either one Commanded, or t'other repin'd, With how cheerful and entire a submission You Obey'd? And tho the Royal Son of a Glorious Father who was render'd unfortunate by the unexemplary ingratitude of his worst of Subjects; and sacrific'd to the insatiate and cruel Villany of a seeming sanctifi'd Faction, who cou'd never hope to expiate for the unparallell'd sin, but by an entire submission to the Gracious Off-spring of this Royal Martyr: yet You, Great Sir, denying Yourself the Rights and Privileges the meanest Subject Claims, with a Fortitude worthy Your Adorable Virtues, put Yourself upon a voluntary Exile to appease the causeless murmurs of this again gathering Faction, who make their needless and self-created fears, an occasion to Play the old Game o're again;

whil'st the Politick self-interested and malicious few betray the unconsidering Rest, with the delicious sounds of Liberty and Public Good; that lucky Cant which so few years since so miserably reduc'd all the Noble, Brave and Honest, to the Obedience of the ill-gotten Power, and worse-acted Greatness of the Rabble; so that whil'st they most unjustly cry'd down the oppression of one of the best of Monarchs, and all Kingly Government: all England found itself deplorably enslav'd by the Arbitrary Tyranny of many Pageant Kings. Oh that we shou'd so far forget with what greatness of mind You then shar'd the common Fate, as now and again to force Your Royal Person to new Perils, and new Exiles; but such ingratitude we are punished with, and You still suffer for, and still forgive it.

Some of Oliver's Commanders at Dunkirk. [p. 114] This more than Human Goodness, with the encouragement Your Royal Highness was pleas'd to give the Rover at his first appearance, and the concern You were pleas'd to have for his second, makes me presume to lay him at Your feet; he is a wanderer too, distressed; belov'd, the unfortunate, and ever consent to Loyalty; were he Legions he should follow and suffer still with so Excellent a Prince and Master. Your Infant worth he knew, and all Your growing Glories; has seen you like young Cesar in the Field, [p. 114] when yet a Youth, exchanging Death for Laurels, and wondered at a Bravery so early, which still made double Conquest, not only by Your Sword, but by Your Virtues, which taught even Your Enemies so entire an Obedience, that asham'd of their Rebel Gallantry, they have resign'd their guilty Commissions, and Vow'd never to Draw Sword more but in the Royal Cause; which Vow Religiously they kept: a noble Example for the busy and hot Mutineers of this Age misled by Youth, false Ambition and falser Council.

How careless since Your Glorious Restoration You have been, of Your Life for the service of Your mistaken Country, the whole World knows, and all brave men admire.

Pardon me then, Great Sir, if I presume to present my faithful Soldier, (which no Storms of Fate can ever draw from his Obedience) to so great a General: allow him, Royal Sir, a shelter and protection, who was driven from his Native Country with You, forc'd as You were, to fight for his Bread in a Strange Land, and suffer'd with You all the Ills of Poverty, War and Banishment; and still pursues Your Fortunes; and though he cannot serve Your Highness, he may possibly have the Honor of diverting You a few moments: which tho Your Highness cannot want in a place where all Hearts and Knees are justly bow'd in Adoration, where all conspire, as all the Earth (who have the blessing of Your presence) ought to entertain, serve and please You; yet this humble Tribute of a most Zealous and Devout Heart, may find amongst Your busier hours of greater moment, someone wherein it may have the Glory of Your regard, and be capable in some small degree of unbending Your great mind from Royal Cares, the weightiest Cares of all; which if it be so fortunate as to do, I have my end, and the Glory I design, a sufficient reward for her who does and will eternally pray for the Life, Health and Safety of Your Royal Highness, as in Duty all the World is bound to do, but more especially,

Illustrious Sir,

Your Highnesses most Humble,

most Faithful, and

most Obedient Servant,

A. BEHN.

PROLOGUE,

Spoken by Mr. *Smith*.

IN vain we labor to reform the Stage,
Poets have caught too the Disease o'th' Age,
That Pest, of not being quiet when they're well,
That restless Fever, in the Brethren, Zeal;
In public Spirits call'd, Good o' th' Commonweal.
Some for this Faction cry, others for that,
The pious Mobile fir they know not what:
So tho by different ways the Fever seize,
In all 'tis one and the same mad Disease.
Our Author too, as all new Zealots do,
Full of Conceit and Contradiction too,
'Cause the first Project took, is now so vain,
T'attempt to play the old Game o'er again:
The Scene is only changed; for who wou'd lay
A Plot, so hopeful, just the same dull way?
Poets, like Statesmen, with a little change,
Pass off old Politicks for new and strange;
Tho the few Men of Sense decry't aloud,
The Cheat will pass with the unthinking Crowd:
The Rabble 'tis we court, those powerful things,
Whose Voices can impose even Laws on Kings.
A Pox of Sense and Reason, or dull Rules,
Give us an Audience that declares for Fools;
Our Play will stand fair: we've Monsters too,
Which far exceed your City Pope [p. 115] *for Show.*
   Almighty Rabble, 'tis to you this Day
Our humble Author dedicates the Play,
From those who in our lofty Tire [p. 116] *sit,*
Down to the dull Stage-Cullies of the Pit,
Who have much Money, and but little Wit:
Whose useful Purses, and whose empty Skulls
To private Int'rest make ye Public Tools;
To work on Projects which the wiser frame,
And of fine Men of Business get the Name.
You who have left caballing here of late,
Employ'd in matters of a mightier weight;
To you we make our humble Application,
You'd spare some time from your dear new Vocation,
Of drinking deep, then settling the Nation,
To countenance us, whom Commonwealths of old
Did the most politick Diversion hold.
Plays were so useful thought to Government,
That Laws were made for their Establishment;

Howe'er in Schools differing Opinions jar,
Yet all agree i' th' crowded Theatre,
Which none forsook in any Change or War.
That, like their Gods, unviolated stood,
Equally needful to the public Good.
Throw then, Great Sirs, some vacant hours away,
And your Petitioners shall humbly pray. &c.

DRAMATIS PERSONÆ.

MEN.

Willmore, The Rover, in love with *La Nuche*.
Beaumond, the *English* Ambassador's Nephew, in love with La Nuche, contracted to *Ariadne*.
Ned Blunt, an *English* Country Gentleman.
Nicholas Fetherfool, an *English* Squire, his Friend.
Shift, an *English Lieutenant*, Friend and Officer to *Willmore*.
Hunt, an Ensign, Friend and Officer to *Willmore*.
Harlequin, Willmore's Man. [p. 117]
Abevile, Page to Beaumond.
Don *Carlo* an old Grandee, in love with *La Nuche*.
Sancho, Bravo to *La Nuche*.
An old *Jew*, Guardian to the two Monsters.
Porter at the English Ambassador's. [55]
Rag, Boy to Willmore. [55]
Scaramouche.

WOMEN.

Ariadne, the *English* Ambassador's Daughter-in-law, in love with *Willmore*.
Lucia, her Kinswoman, a Girl. [p. 117]
La Nuche, a *Spanish* Courtesan, in love with the *Rover*.
Petronella Elenora, her Baud.
Aurelia, her Woman.
A Woman Giant.
A Dwarf, her Sister.

Footmen, Servants, Musicians, Operators and Spectators.

SCENE, *Madrid*.

104

ACT I.

Scene I. *A Street.* [56]

[*Enter* Willmore, Blunt, Fetherfool, *and* Hunt, *two more in Campaign* [57] *Dresses, Rag the Captain's Boy.*]

Will. Stay, this is the *English* Ambassador's. I'll inquire if *Beaumond* be return'd from *Paris.*

Feth. Prithee, dear Captain, no more Delays, unless thou thinkest he will invite us to Dinner; for this fine thin sharp Air of *Madrid* has a most notable Faculty of provoking an Appetite: Prithee let's to the Ordinary.

Will. I will not stay—[*Knocks, enter a Porter.*]—Friend, is the Ambassador's Nephew, Mr. *Beaumond*, return'd to *Madrid* yet? If he be, I would speak with him.

Port. I'll let him know so much. [*Goes in, shuts the door.*]

Blunt. Why, how now, what's the Door shut upon us?

Feth. And reason, *Ned*, 'tis Dinner-time in the Ambassador's Kitchen, and should they let the savoury Steam out, what a world of *Castilians* would there be at the Door feeding upon't.—Oh there's no living in *Spain* when the Pot's uncover'd.

Blunt. Nay, 'tis a Nation of the finest clean Teeth—

Feth. Teeth! Gad an they use their Swords no oftner, a Scabbard will last an Age.

[*Enter* Shift *from the House.*]

Will. Honest Lieutenant—

Shift. My noble Captain—Welcome to Madrid. What Mr. *Blunt*, and my honored Friend *Nicholas Fetherfool* Esq.

Feth. Thy Hand, honest *Shift*—[*They embrace him.*]

Will. And how, Lieutenant, how stand Affairs in this unsanctify'd Town?—How does Love's great Artillery, the fair La Nuche, from whose bright Eyes the little wanton God throws Darts to wound Mankind?

Shift. Faith, she carries all before her still; undoes her Fellow-traders in Love's Art: and amongst the Number, old *Carlo de Minalta Segosa* pays high for two Nights in a Week.

Will. Hah—Carlo! Death, what a greeting's here! Carlo, the happy Man! a Dog! a Rascal, gain the bright La Nuche! Oh Fortune! Cursed blind mistaken Fortune! eternal Friend to Fools! Fortune! that takes the noble Rate from Man, to place it on her Idol Interest.

Shift. Why Faith, Captain, I should think her Heart might stand as fair for you as any, could you be less satirical—but by this Light, Captain, you return her Raillery a little too roughly.

Will. Her Raillery! By this Hand I had rather be handsomely abus'd than dully flatter'd; but when she touches on my Poverty, my honorable Poverty, she presses me too sensibly—for nothing is so nice as Poverty—But damn her, I'll think of her no more: for she's a Devil, tho her Form be Angel. Is Beaumond come from Paris yet?

Shift. He is, I came with him; he's impatient of your Return: I'll let him know you're here. [*Exit* Shift.]

Feth. Why, what a Pox ails the Captain o'th' sudden? He looks as sullenly as a routed General, or a Lover after hard Service.

Blunt. Oh—something the Lieutenant has told him about a Wench; and when *Cupid's* in his Breeches, the Devil's ever in's Head—how now—What a pox is the matter with you, you look so scurvily now?—What, is the Gentlewoman otherwise provided? has she cashier'd ye for want of Pay? or what other dire Mischance?—hah—

Will. Do not trouble me—

Blunt. Adsheartlikins, but I will, and beat thee too, but I'll know the Cause. I heard *Shift* tell thee something about *La Nuche*, a Damsel I have often heard thee Fool enough to sigh for.

Will. Confound the mercenary Jilt!

Blunt. Nay, adsheartlikins they are all so; tho I thought you had been Whore-proof; 'tis enough for us Fools, Country Gentlemen, Esquires, and Cullies, to miscarry in their amorous Adventures, you Men of Wit weather all Storms you.

Will. Oh, Sir, you're become a new Man, wise and wary, and can no more be cozen'd.

Blunt. Not by Woman-kind; and for Man I think my Sword will secure me. Pox, I thought a two Months absence and a Siege would have put such Trifles out of thy Head: You do not use to be such a Miracle of Constancy.

Will. That Absence makes me think of her so much; and all the Passions thou find'st about me are to the Sex alone. Give me a Woman, Ned, a fine young amorous Wanton, who would allay this Fire that makes me rave thus, and thou shouldst find me no longer particular, but cold [58] as Winter-Nights to this La Nuche: Yet since I lost my little charming Gypsy, nothing has gone so near my Heart as this.

Blunt. Ay, there was a Girl, the only she thing that could reconcile me to the Petticoats again after my Naples Adventure, when the Quean rob'd and stript me.

Will. Oh name not Hellena! She was a Saint to be ador'd on Holy-days.

[*Enter* Beaumond.]

Beau. Willmore! my careless wild inconstant—how is't, my lucky Rover? [*embracing.*] [59]

Will. My Life! my Soul! how glad am I to find thee in my Arms again—and well— When left you *Paris? Paris*, that City of Pottage and Crab-Wine, [p. 120] swarming with Lacquies and Philies, [60] whose Government is carried on by most Hands, not most Voices—And prithee how does *Belvile* and his Lady?

Beau. I left 'em both in Health at St. *Germains.*

Will. Faith, I have wished myself with ye at the old Temple of Bacchus at *St. Clou*, to sacrifice a Bottle and a Damsel to his Deity.

Beau. My constant Place of Worship whilst there, tho for want of new Saints my Zeal grew something cold, which I was ever fain to supply with a Bottle, the old Remedy when *Phyllis* is sullen and absent.

Will. Now thou talk'st of Phillis prithee, dear *Harry*, what Women hast in store?

Beau. I'll tell thee; but first inform me whom these two Sparks are.

Will. Egad, and so they are, Child: Salute 'em—They are my Friends—True Blades, *Hal.* highly guilty of the royal Crime, poor and brave, loyal Fugitives.

Beau. I love and honor 'em, Sir, as such [*Bowing to* Blunt.]

Blunt. Sir, there's neither Love nor Honor lost.

Feth. Sir, I scorn to be behind-hand in Civilities.

Beau. At first sight I find I am much yours, Sir. [To *Fetherfool.*]

Feth. Sir, I love and honor any Man that's a Friend to Captain *Willmore*—and therefore I am yours—

[*Enter* Shift.]

—Well, honest Lieutenant, how does thy Body?—When shall *Ned*, and thou and I, crack a Biscuit o'er a Glass of Wine, have a Slice of Treason and settle the Nation, hah?

Shift. You know, Squire, I am devotedly yours. [*They talk aside.*]

Beau. Prithee who are these?

Will. Why, the first you saluted is the same *Ned Blunt* you have often heard *Belvile* and I speak of: the other is a Rarity of another Nature, one Squire *Fetherfool* of *Croydon*, a tame Justice of Peace, who liv'd as innocently as Ale and Food could keep him, till for a mistaken Kindness to one of the Royal Party, he lost his Commission, and got the Reputation of a Sufferer: He's rich, but covetous as an Alderman.

Beau. What a Pox do'st keep 'em Company for, who have neither Wit enough to divert thee, nor Good-nature enough to serve thee?

Will. Faith, *Harry*, 'tis true, and if there were no more Charity than Profit in't, a Man would sooner keep a Cough o'th' Lungs than be troubled with 'em: but the Rascals have a blind side as all conceited Coxcombs have, which when I've nothing else to do, I shall expose to advance our Mirth; the Rogues must be cozen'd, because they're so positive they never can be so: but I am now for softer Joys, for Woman, for Woman in abundance—dear *Hal.* inform me where I may safely unlade my Heart.

Beau. The same Man still, wild and wanton!

Will. And would not change to be the Catholic King.

Beau. I perceive Marriage has not tam'd you, nor a Wife who had all the Charms of her Sex.

Will. Ay—she was too good for Mortals. [*With a sham Sadness.*]

Belv. I think thou hadst her but a Month, prithee how dy'd she?

Will. Faith, e'en with a fit of Kindness, poor Soul—she would to Sea with me, and in a Storm—far from Land, she gave up the Ghost—'twas a Loss, but I must bear it with a Christian Fortitude.

Beau. Short Happinesses vanish like to Dreams.

Will. Ay faith, and nothing remains with me but the sad Remembrance—not so much as the least Part of her hundred thousand Crowns; *Brussels* [61] that enchanted Court has eas'd me of that Grief, where our Heroes act *Tantalus* better than ever *Ovid* describ'd him, [p. 122] condemn'd daily to see an Apparition of Meat, Food in Vision only. Faith, I had Bowels, was good-natur'd, and lent upon the public Faith as far as 'twill go—But come, let's leave this mortifying Discourse, and tell me how the price of Pleasure goes.

Beau. At the old Rates still; he that gives most is happiest, some few there are for Love!

Will. Ah, one of the last, dear *Beaumond*; and if a Heart or Sword can purchase her, I'll bid as fair as the best. Damn it, I hate a Whore that asks me Money.

Beau. Yet I have known thee venture all thy Stock for a new Woman.

Will. Ay, such a Fool I was in my dull Days of Constancy, but I am now for Change, (and should I pay as often, 'twould undo me)—for Change, my Dear, of Place, Clothes, Wine, and Women. Variety is the Soul of Pleasure, a Good unknown; and we want Faith to find it.

Beau. Thou wouldst renounce that fond Opinion, *Willmore*, didst thou see a Beauty here in Town, whose Charms have Power to fix inconstant Nature or Fortune were she tottering on her Wheel.

Will. Her Name, my Dear, her Name?

Beau. I would not breathe it even in my Complaints, lest amorous Winds should bear it o'er the World, and make Mankind her Slaves;
But that it is a Name too cheaply known, [62]
And she that owns it may be as cheaply purchas'd.

Will. Hah! cheaply purchas'd too! I languish for her.

Beau. Ay, there's the Devil on't, she is—a Whore.

Will. Ah, what a charming Sound that mighty Word bears!

Beau. Damn her, she'll be thine or any body's.

Will. I die for her—

Beau. Then for her Qualities—

Will. No more—ye Gods, I ask no more, Be she but fair and much a Whore—Come let's to her.

Beau. Perhaps tomorrow you may see this Woman.

Will. Death, 'tis an Age.

Feth. Oh, Captain, the strangest News, Captain.

Will. Prithee what?

Feth. Why, Lieutenant *Shift* here tells us of two Monsters arriv'd from *Mexico*, Jews of vast Fortunes, with an old Jew Uncle their Guardian; they are worth a hundred thousand Pounds a piece—Marcy [63] upon's, why, 'tis a Sum able to purchase all *Flanders* again from his most christian Majesty.

Will. Ha, ha, ha, Monsters!

Beau. He tells you Truth, *Willmore*.

Blunt. But hark ye, Lieutenant, are you sure they are not married?

Beau. Who the Devil would venture on such formidable Ladies?

Feth. How, venture on 'em! by the Lord *Harry*, and that would I, tho I'm a Justice of the Peace, and they be Jews, (which to a Christian is a thousand Reasons.)

Blunt. Is the Devil in you to declare our Designs? [*Aside.*]

Feth. Mum, as close as a Jesuit.

Beau. I admire your Courage, Sir, but one of them is so little, and so deform'd, 'tis thought she is not capable of Marriage; and the other is so huge an overgrown Giant, no Man dares venture on her.

Will. Prithee let's go see 'em; what do they pay for going in?

Feth. Pay—I'd have you to know they are Monsters of Quality.

Shift. And not to be seen but by particular Favor of their Guardian, whom I am got acquainted with, from the Friendship I have with the Merchant where they lay. The Giant, Sir, is in love with me, the Dwarf with Ensign *Hunt*, and as we manage Matters we may prove lucky.

Beau. And didst thou see the Show? the Elephant and the Mouse.

Shift. Yes, and pleased them wondrously with News I brought 'em of a famous Mountebank who is coming to *Madrid*, here are his Bills—who amongst other his marvellous Cures, pretends to restore Mistakes in Nature, to new-mould a Face and Body tho never so misshapen, to exact Proportion and Beauty. This News has made me gracious to the Ladies, and I am to bring 'em word of the Arrival of this famous Empiric, and to negotiate the Business of their Reformation.

Will. And do they think to be restor'd to moderate sizes?

Shift. Much pleas'd with the Hope, and are resolv'd to try at any Rate.

Feth. Mum, Lieutenant—not too much of their Transformation; we shall have the Captain put in for a Share, and the Devil would not have him his Rival: *Ned* and I are resolv'd to venture a Cast for 'em as they are—Hah, *Ned.* [Willmore *and* Beaumond *read the Bill.*]

Blunt. Yes, if there were any Hopes of your keeping a Secret.

Feth. Nay, nay, *Ned,* the World knows I am a plaguy Fellow at your Secrets; that, and my Share of the Charge shall be my Part, for *Shift* says the Guardian must be brib'd for Consent: Now the other Moiety of the Money and the Speeches shall be thy part, for thou hast a pretty Knack that way. Now *Shift* shall bring Matters neatly about, and we'll pay him by the Day, or in gross, when we are married—hah, *Shift.*

Shift. Sir, I shall be reasonable.

Will. I am sure *Fetherfool* and *Blunt* have some wise Design upon these two Monsters—it must be so—and this Bill has put an extravagant Thought into my Head—hark ye, *Shift.* [*Whispers to him.*]

Blunt. The Devil's in't if this will not redeem my Reputation with the Captain, and give him to understand that all the Wit does not lie in the Family of the *Willmores,* but that this Noddle of mine can be fruitful too upon Occasion.

Feth. Ay, and Lord, how we'll domineer, *Ned,* hah—over *Willmore* and the rest of the Renegade Officers, when we have married these Lady Monsters, hah, *Ned.*

Blunt.—Then to return back to *Essex* worth a Million.

Feth. And I to *Croyden*—

Blunt.—Lolling in Coach and Six—

Feth.—Be dub'd Right Worshipful—

Blunt. And stand for Knight of the Shire.

Will. Enough—I must have my Share of this Jest, and for divers and sundry Reasons thereunto belonging, must be this very Mountebank expected. [p. 126]

Shift. Faith, Sir, and that were no hard matter, for a day or two the Town will believe it, the same they look for: and the Bank, Operators and Music are all ready.

Will. Well enough, add but a *Harlequin* and *Scaramouch,* and I shall mount in querpo. [p. 126]

Shift. Take no care for that, Sir, your Man, and Ensign *Hunt,* are excellent at those two; I saw 'em act 'em the other day to a Wonder, they'll be glad of the Employment, myself will be an Operator.

Will. No more, get 'em ready, [64] and give it out, the Man of Art's arriv'd: Be diligent and secret, for these two politick Asses must be cozen'd.

Shift. I will about the Business instantly. [*Exit* Shift.]

Beau. This Fellow will do Feats if he keeps his Word.

Will. I'll give you mine he shall—But, dear *Beaumond,* where shall we meet anon?

Beau. I thank ye for that—'Gad, ye shall dine with me.

Feth. A good Motion—

Will. I beg your Pardon now, dear *Beaumond*—I having lately nothing else to do, took a Command of Horse from the General at the last Siege, from which I am just arriv'd, and my Baggage is behind, which I must take order for.

Feth. Pox on't now there's a Dinner lost, 'twas ever an unlucky Rascal.

Beau. To tempt thee more, thou shalt see my Wife that is to be.

Will. Pox on't, I am the lewdest Company in Christendom with your honest Women—but—What, art thou to be noos'd then?

Beau. 'Tis so design'd by my Uncle, if an old Grandee my Rival prevent it not; the Wench is very pretty, young, and rich, and lives in the same House with me, for 'tis my Aunt's Daughter.

Will. Much good may it d'ye, *Harry*, I pity you, but 'tis the common Grievance of you happy Men of Fortune. [*Goes towards the House-door with* Beaumond]

[*Enter* La Nuche, Aurelia, Petronella, Sancho, Women *veil'd a little.*]

Aur. Heavens, Madam, is not that the *English* Captain? [*Looking on* Willmore.]

La Nu. 'Tis, and with him Don *Henrick* the Ambassador's Nephew—how my Heart pants and heaves at sight of him! some Fire of the old Flames remaining, which I must strive to extinguish. For I'll not bate a Ducat of this Price I've set upon myself, for all the Pleasures Youth or Love can bring me—for see *Aurelia*—the sad Memento of a decay'd poor old forsaken Whore in *Petronella*; consider her, and then commend my Prudence.

Will. Hah, Women!—

Feth. Egad, and fine ones too, I'll tell you that.

Will. No matter, Kindness is better Sauce to Woman than Beauty! By this Hand she looks at me—Why dost hold me? [Fetherfool *holds him.*]

Feth. Why, what a Devil, art mad?

Will. Raging, as vigorous Youth kept long from Beauty; wild for the charming Sex, eager for Woman, I long to give a Loose to Love and Pleasure.

Blunt. These are not Women, Sir, for you to ruffle—

Will. Have a care of your Persons of Quality, *Ned.* [*Goes to* La Nuche.]—Those lovely Eyes were never made to throw their Darts in vain.

La Nu. The Conquest would be hardly worth the Pain.

Will. Hah, *La Nuche!* with what a proud Disdain she flung away—stay, I will not part so with you—[*Holds her.*]

[*Enter* Ariadne *and* Lucia *with Footmen.*]

Aria. Who are these before us, *Lucia?*

Luc. I know not, Madam; but if you make not haste home, you'll be troubled with *Carlo* your importunate Lover, who is just behind us.

Aria. Hang me, a lovely Man! what Lady's that? stay.

Pet. What Insolence is this! This Villain will spoil all—

Feth. Why, Captain, are you quite distracted?—dost know where thou art? Prithee be civil—

Will. Go, proud and cruel! [*Turns her from him.*]

[*Enter* Carlo, *and two or three Spanish Servants following:* Petronella *goes to him.*]

Car. Hah, affronted by a drunken Islander, a saucy Tramontane!—Draw—[*To his Servants whilst he takes* La Nuche.] whilst I lead her off—fear not, Lady, you have the Honor of my Sword to guard ye.

Will. Hah, *Carlo*—ye lye—it cannot guard the boasting Fool that wears it—be gone—and look not back upon this Woman. [Snatches her from him] One single Glance destroys thee—

[*They draw and fight; Carlo getting hindmost of his Spaniards, the English beat 'em off: The Ladies run away, all but Ariadne and Lucia.*]

Luc. Heav'ns, Madam, why do ye stay?
Aria. To pray for that dear Stranger—And see, my Prayers are heard, and he's return'd in safety—this Door shall shelter me to o'er-hear the Quarrel. [*Steps aside.*]

[*Enter* Willmore Blunt, Fetherfool *looking big, and putting up his Sword.*]

Feth. The noble Captain be affronted by a starch'd Ruff and Beard, a Coward in querpo, a walking Bunch of Garlick, a pickl'd Pilchard! [65] abuse the noble Captain, and bear it off in State, like a Christmas Sweet-heart; [66] these things must not be whilst *Nicholas Fetherfool* wears a Sword.
Blunt. Pox o' these Women, I thought no good would come on't: besides, where's the Jest in affronting honest Women, if there be such a thing in the Nation?
Feth. Hang't, 'twas the Devil and all—
Will. Ha, ha, ha! Why, good honest homespun Country Gentlemen, who do you think those were?
Feth. Were! why, Ladies of Quality going to their Devotion; who should they be?
Blunt. Why, faith, and so I thought too.
Will. Why, that very one Woman I spoke to is ten Whores in *Surrey*.
Feth. Prithee speak softly, Man: 'Slife, we shall be poniarded for keeping thee company.
Will. Wise Mr. Justice, give me your Warrant, and if I do not prove 'em Whores, whip me.
Feth. Prithee hold thy scandalous blasphemous Tongue, as if I did not know Whores from Persons of Quality.
Will. Will you believe me when you lie with her? for thou'rt a rich Ass, and may'st do it.
Feth. Whores—ha, ha—
Will. 'Tis strange Logic now, because your Band is better that mine, I must not know a Whore better than you.
Blunt. If this be a Whore, as thou say'st, I understand nothing—by this Light such a Wench would pass for a Person of Quality in *London*.
Feth. Few Ladies have I [67] seen at a Sheriff's Feast have better Faces, or worn so good Clothes; and by the Lord *Harry*, if these be of the gentle Craft, I'd not give a Real for an honest Women for my use.
Will. Come follow me into the Church, for thither I am sure they're gone: And I will let you see what a wretched thing you had been had you lived seven Years longer in *Surrey*, stew'd in Ale and Beef-broth.
Feth. O dear *Willmore*, name not those savory things, there's no jesting with my Stomach; it sleeps now, but if it wakes, wo be to your Shares at the Ordinary.
Blunt. I'll say that for *Fetherfool*, if his Heart were but half so good as his Stomach, he were a brave Fellow. [*Aside,* Exeunt.]

Aria. I am resolv'd to follow—and learn, if possible, who 'tis has made this sudden Conquest o'er me. [*All go off.*]

[*Scene draws, and discovers a Church, a great many People at Devotion, soft Music playing. Enter* La Nuche, Aurelia, Petronella *and* Sancho: *To them* Willmore, Fetherfool Blunt; *then* Ariadne, Lucia; Fetherfool *bows to* La Nuche *and* Petronella.]

Feth. Now as I hope to be sav'd, *Blunt*, she's a most melodious Lady. Would I were worthy to purchase a Sin or so with her. Would not such a Beauty reconcile thy Quarrel to the Sex?

Blunt. No, were she an Angel in that Shape.

Feth. Why, what a pox couldst not lie with her if she'd let thee? By the Lord *Harry*, as errant a Dog as I am, I'd fain see any of *Cupid's* Cook-maids put me out of countenance with such a Shoulder of Mutton.

Aria. See how he gazes on her—*Lucia*, go nearer, and o'er-hear 'em. [*Lucia listens.*]

Will. Death, how the charming Hypocrite looks today, with such a soft Devotion in her Eyes, as if even now she were praising Heav'n for all the Advantages it has blest her with.

Blunt. Look how *Willmore* eyes her, the Rogue's smitten heart deep—Whores—

Feth. Only a Trick to keep her to himself—he thought the Name of a *Spanish* Harlot would fright us from attempting—I must divert him—how is't, Captain—Prithee mind this Music—Is it not most Seraphical?

Will. Pox, let the Fiddlers mind and tune their Pipes, I've higher Pleasures now.

Feth. Oh, have ye so; what, with Whores, Captain?—'Tis a most delicious Gentlewoman. [*Aside.*]

Pet. Pray, Madam, mind that Cavalier, who takes such pains to recommend himself to you.

La Nu. Yes, for a fine conceited Fool—

Pet. Catso, a Fool, what else?

La Nu. Right, they are our noblest Chapmen; a Fool, and a rich Fool, and an *English* rich Fool—

Feth. 'Sbud, she eyes me, *Ned*, I'll set myself in order, it may take—hah—[*Sets himself.*]

Pet. Let me alone to manage him, I'll to him—

La Nu. Or to the Devil, so I had one Minute's time to speak to *Willmore*.

Pet. And accosting him thus—tell him—

La Nu. [*In a hasty Tone.*]—I am desperately in love with him, and am Daughter, Wife, or Mistress to some Grandee—bemoan the Condition of Women of Quality in *Spain*, who by too much Constraint are oblig'd to speak first—but were we blest like other Nations where Men and Women meet—[*Speaking so fast, she offering to put in her word, is still prevented by t'other's running on.*]

Pet. What Herds of Cuckolds would *Spain* breed—'Slife, I could find in my Heart to forswear your Service: Have I taught ye your Trade, to become my Instructor, how to cozen a dull phlegmatic greasy-brain'd Englishman?—go and expect your Wishes.

Will. So, she has sent her Matron to our Coxcomb—she saw he was a Cully fit for Game—who would not be a Rascal to be rich, a Dog, an Ass, a beaten, harden'd Coward—by Heaven, I will possess this gay Insensible, to make me hate her—most extremely curse her—See if she be not fallen to Pray'r again, from thence to Flattery, Jilting and Purse-taking, to make the Proverb good—My fair false *Sybil*, what Inspirations are you waiting for from Heaven, new Arts to cheat Mankind!—Tell me, with what Face canst thou be devout, or ask anything from thence, who hast made so leud a use of what it has already lavish'd on thee?

La Nu. Oh my careless Rover! I perceive all your hot Shot [68] is not yet spent in Battle, you have a Volley in reserve for me still—Faith, Officer, the Town has wanted Mirth in your Absence.

Will. And so might all the wiser part for thee, who hast no Mirth, no Gaiety about thee, and when thou wouldst design some Coxcomb's ruin; to all the rest, a Soul thou hast so dull, that neither Love nor Mirth, nor Wit or Wine can wake it to good Nature—thou'rt one who lazily work'st in thy Trade, and sell'st for ready Money so much Kindness; a tame cold Sufferer only, and no more.

La Nu. What, you would have a Mistress like a Squirrel in a Cage, always in Action—one who is as free of her Favors as I am sparing of mine—Well, Captain, I have known the time when *La Nuche* was such a Wit, such a Humor, such a Shape, and such a Voice, (tho to say Truth I sing but scurvily) 'twas Comedy to see and hear me.

Will. Why, yes Faith for once thou wert, and for once mayst be again, till thou know'st thy Man, and knowest him to be poor. At first you lik'd me too, you saw me gay, no marks of Poverty dwelt in my Face or Dress, and then I was the dearest loveliest Man—all this was to my outside; Death, you made love to my Breeches, caress'd my Garniture and Feather, an *English* Fool of Quality you thought me—'Sheart, I have known a Woman dote on Quality, tho he has stunk thro all his Perfumes; one who never went all to Bed to her, but left his Teeth, an Eye, false Back and Breast, sometimes his Palate too upon her Toilet, whilst her fair Arms hug'd the dismember'd Carcase, and swore him all Perfection, because of Quality.

La Nu. But he was rich, good Captain, was he not?

Will. Oh most damnably, and a confounded Blockhead, two certain Remedies against your Pride and Scorn.

La Nu. Have you done, Sir?

Will. With thee and all thy Sex, of which I've try'd an hundred, and found none true or honest.

La Nu. Oh, I doubt not the number: for you are one of those healthy-stomached Lovers, that can digest a Mistress in a Night, and hunger again next Morning: a Pox of your whining consumptive Constitution, who are only constant for want of Appetite: you have a swinging Stomach to Variety, and Want having set an edge upon your Invention, (with which you cut thro all Difficulties) you grow more impudent by Success.

Will. I am not always scorn'd then.

La Nu. I have known you as confidently put your Hands into your Pockets for Money in a Morning, as if the Devil had been your Banker, when you knew you put 'em off at Night as empty as your Gloves.

Will. And it may be found Money there too.

La Nu. Then with this Poverty so proud you are, you will not give the Wall to the Catholic King, unless his Picture hung upon't. No Servants, no Money, no Meat, always on foot, and yet undaunted still.

Will. Allow me that, Child.

La Nu. I wonder what the Devil makes you so termagant on our Sex, 'tis not your high feeding, for your Grandees only dine, and that but when Fortune pleases—For your parts, who are the poor dependent, brown Bread and old *Adam's* Ale [p. 133] is only current amongst ye; yet if little *Eve* walk in the Garden, the starv'd lean Rogues neigh after her, as if they were in Paradise.

Will. Still true to Love you see——

La Nu. I heard an *English* Capuchin swear, that if the King's Followers could be brought to pray as well as fast, there would be more Saints among 'em than the Church has ever canoniz'd.

Will. All this with Pride I own, since 'tis a royal Cause I suffer for; go pursue your Business your own way, ensnare the Fool—I saw the Toils you set, and how that Face was ordered for the Conquest, your Eyes brimful of dying lying Love; and now and then a wishing Glance or Sigh thrown as by chance; which when the happy Coxcomb caught—you feign'd a Blush, as angry and asham'd of the Discovery: and all this Cunning's for a little mercenary Gain—fine Clothes, perhaps some Jewels too, whilst all the Finery cannot hide the Whore!

La Nu. There's your eternal Quarrel to our Sex, 'twere a fine Trade indeed to keep a Shop and give your Ware for Love: would it turn to account think ye, Captain, to trick and dress, to receive [69] all wou'd enter? faith, Captain, try the Trade.

Pet. What in Discourse with this Railer!—come away; Poverty's catching. [*Returns from Discourse with Fetherfool speaks to San.*]

Will. So is the Pox, good Matron, of which you can afford good Penniworths.

La Nu. He charms me even with his angry Looks, and will undo me yet.

Pet. Let's leave this Place, I'll tell you my Success as we go.

[*Exit all, some one way, some another, the Forepart of the Church shuts over, except Willmore Blunt, Aria, and Lucia.*]

Will. She's gone, and all the Plagues of Pride go with her.

Blunt. Heartlikins, follow her—Pox on't, an I'd but as good a Hand at this Game as thou hast, I'll venture upon any Chance—

Will. Damn her, come, let's to Dinner. Where's *Fetherfool?*

Blunt. Follow'd a good Woodman, who gave him the Sign: he'll lodge the Deer e'er night.

Will. Follow'd her—he durst not, the Fool wants Confidence enough to look on her.

Blunt. Oh you know not how a Country Justice may be improved by Travel; the Rogue was hedg'd in at home with the Fear of his Neighbours and the Penal Statutes, now he's broke loose, he runs neighing like a Stone-Horse upon the Common.

Will. However, I'll not believe this—let's follow 'em. [*Exit* Willmore *and* Blunt.]

Aria. He is in love, but with a Courtesan—some Comfort that. We'll after him—'Tis a faint-hearted Lover, Who for the first Discouragement gives over. [*Exit* Ariadne *and* Lucia.]

114

ACT II.

Scene I. *The Street.* [70]

[*Enter* Fetherfool *and* Sancho, *passing over the Stage; after them* Willmore *and* Blunt, *follow'd by* Ariadne *and* Lucia.]

Will. 'Tis so, by Heaven, he's chaffering with her Pimp. I'll spare my Curses on him for having her, he has a Plague beyond 'em.—Harkye, I'll never love, nor lie with Women more, those Slaves to Lust, to Vanity and Interest.

Blunt. Ha, Captain! [Shaking his Head and smiling.]

Will. Come, let's go drink Damnation to 'em all.

Blunt. Not all, good Captain.

Will. All, for I hate 'em all—

Aria. Heavens! if he should indeed! [*Aside.*]

Blunt. But, *Robert*, I have found you most inclined to a Damsel when you had a Bottle in your Head.

Will. Give me thy Hand, *Ned*—Curse me, despise me, point me out for Cowardice if e'er thou see'st me court a Woman more: Nay, when thou knowest I ask any of the Sex a civil Question again—a Plague upon 'em, how they've handled me—come, let's go drink, I say—Confusion to the Race—A Woman!—no, I will be burnt with my own Fire to Cinders e'er any of the Brood shall lay my Flame—

Aria. He cannot be so wicked to keep this Resolution sure—[*She passes by.*] Faith, I must be resolv'd—you've made a pious Resolution, Sir, had you the Grace to keep it— [*Passing on he pauses, and looks on her.*]

Will. Hum—What's that?

Blunt. That—O—nothing—but a Woman—come away.

Will. A Woman! Damn her, what Mischief made her cross my way just on the Point of Reformation!

Blunt. I find the Devil will not lose so hopeful a Sinner. Hold, hold, Captain, have you no Regard to your own Soul? 'dsheartlikins, 'tis a Woman, a very errant Woman.

Aria. Your Friend informs you right, Sir, I am a Woman.

Will. Ay, Child, or I were a lost Man—therefore, dear lovely Creature—

Aria. How can you tell, Sir?

Will. Oh, I have naturally a large Faith, Child, and thou'st a promising Form, a tempting Motion, clean Limbs, well dressed, and a most damnable inviting Air.

Aria. I am not to be sold, nor fond of Praise I merit not.

Will. How, not to be sold too! By this light, Child, thou speakest like a Cherubim, I have not heard so obliging a Sound from the Mouth of Woman-kind this many a Day—I find we must be better acquainted, my Dear.

Aria. Your Reason, good familiar Sir, I see no such Necessity.

Will. Child, you are mistaken, I am in great Necessity; for first I love thee—desperately—have I not damn'd my Soul already for thee, and wouldst thou be so wicked to refuse a little Consolation to my Body? Then secondly, I see thou art frank and good-natur'd, and wilt do Reason *gratis*.

Aria. How prove ye that, good Mr. Philospher?

Will. Thou say'st thou'rt not to be sold, and I'm sure thou'rt to be had—that lovely Body of so divine a Form, those soft smooth Arms and Hands, were made t'embrace as well as be embrac'd; that delicate white rising Bosom to be pressed, and all thy other Charms to be enjoy'd.

Aria. By one that can esteem 'em to their worth, can set a Value and a Rate upon 'em.

Will. Name not those Words, they grate my Ears like Jointure, that dull conjugal Cant that frights the generous Lover. Rate—Death, let the old Dotards talk of Rates, and pay it t'atone for the Defects of Impotence. Let the sly Statesman, who jilts the Commonwealth with his grave Politicks, pay for the Sin, that he may dote in secret; let the brisk Fool inch out his scanted Sense with a large Purse more eloquent than he: But tell not me of Rates, who bring a Heart, Youth, Vigor, and a Tongue to sing the Praise of every single Pleasure thou shalt give me.

Aria. Then if I should be kind, I perceive you would not keep the Secret.

Will. Secrecy is a damn'd ungrateful Sin, Child, known only where Religion and Small-beer are current, despis'd where *Apollo* and the Vine bless the Country: you find none of *Jove's* Mistresses hid in Roots and Plants, but fixed Stars in Heaven for all to gaze and wonder at—and tho I am no God, my Dear, I'll do a Mortal's Part, and generously tell the admiring World what hidden Charms thou hast: Come, lead me to some Place of Happiness—

Blunt. Prithee, honest Damsel, be not so full of Questions; will a Pistole or two do thee any hurt?

Luc. None at all, Sir—

Blunt. Thou speak'st like a hearty Wench—and I believe hast not been one of *Venus'* Hand-maids so long, but thou understand thy Trade—In short, fair Damsel, this honest Fellow here who is so termagant upon thy Lady, is my Friend, my particular Friend, and therefore I would have him handsomely, and well-favor'dly abus'd—you conceive me.

Luc. Truly, Sir, a friendly Request—but in what Nature abus'd?

Blunt. Nature!—why any of your Tricks would serve—but if he could be conveniently strip'd and beaten, or tossed in a Blanket, or any such trivial Business, thou wouldst do me a singular Kindness; as for Robbery he defies the Devil: an empty Pocket is an Antidote against that Ill.

Luc. Your Money, Sir: and if he be not cozen'd, say a *Spanish* Woman has neither Wit nor Invention upon Occasion.

Blunt. Sheartlikins, how I shall love and honor thee for't—here's earnest—[*Talks to her with Joy and Grimace.*]

Aria. But who was that you entertain'd at Church but now?

Will. Faith, one, who for her Beauty merits that glorious Title she wears, it was—a Whore, Child.

Aria. That's but a scurvy Name; yet, if I'm not mistaken in those false Eyes of yours, they look with longing Love upon that—Whore, Child.

Will. Thou are i'th' right, and by this hand, my Soul was full as wishing as my Eyes: but a Pox on't, you Women have all a certain Jargon, or Gibberish, peculiar to your selves; of Value, Rate, Present, Interest, Settlement, Advantage, Price, Maintenance, and the Devil and all of Fopperies, which in plain Terms signify ready Money, by way of Fine before Entrance; so that an honest well-meaning Merchant of Love finds no Credit amongst ye, without his Bill of Lading.

Aria. We are not all so cruel—but the Devil on't is, your good-natur'd Heart is likely accompanied with an ill Face and worse Wit.

Will. Faith, Child, a ready Dish when a Man's Stomach is up, is better than a tedious Feast. I never saw any Man yet cut my piece; some are for Beauty, some are for Wit, and some for the Secret, but I for all, so it be in a kind Girl: and for Wit in Woman, so she say pretty fond things, we understand; tho true or false, no matter.

Aria. Give the Devil his due, you are a very conscientious Lover: I love a Man that scorns to impose dull Truth and Constancy on a Mistress.

Will. Constancy, that current Coin with Fools! No, Child, Heaven keep that Curse from our Doors.

Aria. Hang it, it loses Time and Profit, new Lovers have new Vows and new Presents, whilst the old feed upon a dull repetition of what they did when they were Lovers; 'tis like eating the cold Meat ones self, after having given a Friend a Feast.

Will. Yes, that's the thrifty Food for the Family when the Guests are gone. Faith, Child, thou hast made a neat and a hearty Speech: But prithee, my Dear, for the future, leave out that same Profit and Present, for I have a natural Aversion to hard words; and for matter of quick Dispatch in the Business—give me thy Hand, Child—let us but start fair, and if thou outstripst me, thou'rt a nimble Racer. [*Lucia sees* Shift.]

Luc. Oh, Madam, let's be gone: yonder's Lieutenant Shift, who, if he sees us, will certainly give an Account of it to Mr. Beaumond. Let's get in thro the Garden, I have the Key.

Aria. Here's Company coming, and for several reasons I would not be seen. [*Offers to go.*]

Will. Gad, Child, nor I; Reputation is tender—therefore prithee let's retire. [*Offers to go with her.*]

Aria. You must not stir a step.

Will. Not stir! no Magic Circle can detain me if you go.

Aria. Follow me then at a distance, and observe where I enter; and at night (if your Passion lasts so long) return, and you shall find Admittance into the Garden. [*Speaking hastily.*]

[*He runs out after her.*]
[*Enter* Shift.]

Shift. Well, Sir, the Mountebank's come, and just going to begin in the Piazza; I have order'd Matters, that you shall have a Sight of the Monsters, and leave to court 'em, and when won, to give the Guardian a fourth part of the Portions.

Blunt. Good: But Mum—here's the Captain, who must by no means know our good Fortune, till he see us in State.

[*Enter* Willmore, Shift *goes to him.*]

Shift. All things are ready, Sir, for our Design, the House prepar'd as you directed me, the Guardian wrought upon by the Persuasions of the two Monsters, to take a Lodging there, and try the Bath of Reformation: The Bank's preparing, and the Operators and Music all ready, and the impatient Town flocked together to behold the Man of Wonders, and nothing wanting but your Donship and a proper Speech.

Will. 'Tis well, I'll go fit my self with a Dress, and think of a Speech the while: In the mean time, go you and amuse the gaping Fools that expect my coming. [*Goes out.*]

[*Enter* Fetherfool *singing and dancing*.]

Feth. Have you heard of a *Spanish* Lady,
How she woo'd an *English* Man?
Blunt. Why, how now, Fetherfool?
Feth. Garments gay, and rich as may be,
Decked with Jewels, had she on.
Blunt. Why, how now, Justice, what run mad out of Dog-days?
Feth. Of a comely Countenance and Grace is she,
A sweeter Creature in the World there could not be.
Shift. Why, what the Devil's the matter, Sir?
Blunt. Stark mad, 'dshartlikins.
Feth. *Of a Comely Countenance*—well, Lieutenant, the most heroic and illustrious
Madonna! Thou saw'st her, *Ned*: *And of a comely Count*—The most Magnetic Face—
well—I knew the Charms of these Eyes of mine were not made in vain: I was design'd for
great things, that's certain—*And a sweeter Creature in the World there could not be.*
[*Singing.*]
Blunt. What then the two Lady Monsters are forgotten? the Design upon the Million
of Money, the Coach and Six, and Patent for Right Worshipful, all drown'd in the Joy of
this new Mistress?—But well, Lieutenant, since he is so well provided for, you may put
in with me for a Monster; such a Jest, and such a Sum, is not to be lost.
Shift. Nor shall not, or I have lost my Aim. [*Aside.*]
Feth. [*Putting off his Hat.*] Your Pardons, good Gentlemen; and tho I perceive I shall
have no great need for so trifling a Sum as a hundred thousand Pound, or so, yet a
Bargain's a Bargain, Gentlemen.
Blunt. Nay, 'dsheartlikins, the Lieutenant scorns to do a foul thing, d'ye see, but we
would not have the Monsters slighted.
Feth. Slighted! no, Sir, I scorn your Words, I'd have ye to know, that I have as high a
Respect for Madam Monster, as any Gentleman in Christendom, and so I desire she
should understand.
Blunt. Why, this is that that's handsome.
Shift. Well, the Mountebank's come, Lodgings are taken at his House, and the
Guardian prepar'd to receive you on the aforesaid Terms, and some fifty Pistoles to the
Mountebank to stand your Friend, and the Business is done.
Feth. Which shall be perform'd accordingly, I have it ready about me.
Blunt. And here's mine, put 'em together, and let's be speedy, lest some should bribe
higher, and put in before us. [Fetherfool *takes the Money, and looks pitiful on't.*]
Feth. 'Tis a plaguy round Sum, *Ned*, pray God it turn to Account.
Blunt. Account, 'dsheartlikins, 'tis not in the Power of mortal Man to cozen 'me.
Shift. Oh fie, Sir, cozen you, Sir!—well, you'll stay here and see the Mountebank,
he's coming forth.

[*A Hollowing. Enter from the Front a Bank, a Pageant,* [p. 141] *which they fix on the
Stage at one side, a little Pavilion on't, Music playing, and Operators round
below, or Antiquers.*]
[*Music plays, and an Antique Dance.*]
[*Enter* Willmore *like a Mountebank, with a Dagger in one Hand, and a Viol in the
other,* Harlequin *and* Scaramouche; [71] Carlo *with other* Spaniards *below, and*

Rabble; Ariadne *and* Lucia *above in the Balcony, others on the other side,* Fetherfool *and* Blunt *below.*]

Will. [*bowing*] Behold this little Viol, which contains in its narrow Bounds what the whole Universe cannot purchase, if sold to its true Value; this admirable, this miraculous Elixir, drawn from the Hearts of Mandrakes, Phoenix Livers, and Tongues of Mermaids, [72] and distill'd by contracted Sun-Beams, has besides the unknown Virtue of curing all Distempers both of Mind and Body, that divine one of animating the Heart of Man to that Degree, that however remiss, cold and cowardly by Nature, he shall become vigorous and brave. Oh stupid and insensible Man, when Honor and secure Renown invites you, to treat it with Neglect, even when you need but passive Valour, to become the Heroes of the Age; receive a thousand Wounds, each of which wou'd let out fleeting Life: Here's that can snatch the parting Soul in its full Career, and bring it back to its native Mansion; baffles grim Death, and disappoints even Fate.

Feth. Oh Pox, an a Man [73] were sure of that now—

Will. Behold, here's Demonstration—[*Harlequin stabs himself, and falls* [74] *as dead.*]

Feth. Hold, hold, why, what the Devil is the Fellow mad?

Blunt. Why, do'st think he has hurt himself?

Feth. Hurt himself! why, he's murder'd, Man; 'tis flat *Felo de se*, in any ground in *England*, if I understand Law, and I have been a Justice o'th' Peace.

Will. See, Gentlemen, he's dead—

Feth. Look ye there now, I'll be gone lest I be taken as an Accessory. [*Going out.*]

Will. Coffin him, inter him, yet after four and twenty Hours, as many Drops of this divine Elixir give him new Life again; this will recover whole Fields of slain, and all the Dead shall rise and fight again—'twas this that made the Roman Lemons numerous, and now makes *France* so formidable, and this alone—may be the Occasion of the loss of *Germany.* [*Pours in* Harlequin's *Wound, he rises.*]

Feth. Why this Fellow's the Devil, *Ned*, that's for certain.

Blunt. Oh plague, a damn'd Conjurer, this—

Will. Come, buy this Coward's Comfort, quickly buy; what Fop would be abus'd, mimick'd and scorn'd, for fear of Wounds can be so easily cured? Who is't wou'd bear the Insolence and Pride of domineering great Men, proud Officers or Magistrates? or who wou'd cringe to Statesmen out of Fear? What Cully wou'd be cuckolded? What foolish Heir undone by cheating Gamesters? What Lord wou'd be lampoon'd? What Poet fear the Malice of his satirical Brother, or Atheist fear to fight for fear of Death? Come buy my Coward's Comfort, quickly buy.

Feth. Egad, *Ned*, a very excellent thing this; I'll lay out ten Reels upon this Commodity.

[*They buy, whilst another Part of the Dance is danc'd.*]

Will. Behold this little Paper, which contains a Powder, whose Value surmounts that of Rocks of Diamonds and Hills of Gold; 'twas this made *Venus* a Goddess, and was given her by *Apollo*, from her deriv'd to *Helen*, and in the Sack of *Troy* lost, till recover'd by me out of some Ruins of *Asia*. Come, buy it, Ladies, you that wou'd be fair and wear eternal Youth; and you in whom the amorous Fire remains, when all the Charms are fled: You that dress young and gay, and would be thought so, that patch and paint, to fill up sometimes old Furrows on your Brows, and set yourselves for Conquest, tho in vain; here's that will give you auburn Hair, white Teeth, red Lips, and Dimples on your Cheeks: Come, buy it all you that are past bewitching, and wou'd have handsome, young and active Lovers.

Feth. Another good thing, *Ned.*

Car. I'll lay out a Pistole or two in this, if it have the same Effect on Men.

Will. Come, all you City Wives, that wou'd advance your Husbands to Lord Mayors, come, buy of me new Beauty; this will give it tho now decay'd, as are your Shop Commodities; this will retrieve your Customers, and vend your false and out of fashion'd Wares: cheat, lye, protest and cozen as you please, a handsome Wife makes all a lawful Gain. Come, City Wives, come, buy.

Feth. A most prodigious Fellow!

[*They buy, he sits, the other Part is danc'd.*]

Will. But here, behold the Life and Soul of Man! this is the amorous Powder, which *Venus* made and gave the God of Love, which made him first a Deity; you talk of Arrows, Bow, and killing Darts; Fables, poetical Fictions, and no more: 'tis this alone that wounds and fires the Heart, makes Women kind, and equals Men to Gods; 'tis this that makes your great Lady dote on the ill-favor'd Fop; your great Man be jilted by his little Mistress, the Judge cajol'd by his Seamstress, and your Politician by his Comedian; your young Lady dote on her decrepid Husband, your Chaplain on my Lady's Waiting-Woman, and the young Squire on the Landry-Maid—In fine, Messieurs,

'Tis this that cures the Lover's Pain,
And *Celia* of her cold Disdain.

Feth. A most devilish Fellow this!

Blunt. Hold, shartlikins, *Fetherfool*, let's have a Dose or two of this Powder for quick Dispatch with our Monsters.

Feth. Why Pox, Man, Jugg my Giant would swallow a whole Cart-Load before 'twould operate.

Blunt. No hurt in trying a Paper or two however.

Car. A most admirable Receipt, I shall have need on't.

Will. I need say nothing of my divine Baths of Reformation, nor the wonders of the old Oracle of the Box, which resolves all Questions, my Bills sufficiently declare their Virtue. [*Sits down. They buy.*]

[*Enter* Petronella Elenora *carried in a Chair, dress'd like a Girl of Fifteen.*]

Shift. Room there, Gentlemen, room for a Patient.

Blunt. Pray, Seignior, who may this be thus muzzl'd by old Gaffer Time?

Car. One *Petronella Elenora*, Sir, a famous outworn Courtesan.

Blunt. Elenora! she may be that of *Troy* for her Antiquity, tho fitter for God *Priapus* to ravish than *Paris*.

Shift. Hunt, a word; dost thou see that same formal Politician yonder, on the Jennet, the nobler Animal of the two?

Hunt. What of him?

Shift. 'Tis the same drew on the Captain this Morning, and I must revenge the Affront.

Hunt. Have a care of Revenges in *Spain*, upon Persons of his Quality.

Shift. Nay, I'll only steal his Horse from under him.

Hunt. Steal it! thou may'st take it by force perhaps; but how safely is a Question.

Shift. I'll warrant thee—shoulder you up one side of his great Saddle, I'll do the like on t'other; then heaving him gently up, *Harlequin* shall lead the Horse from between his Worship's Legs: All this in the Crowd will not be perceiv'd, where all Eyes are employ'd on the Mountebank.

Hunt. I apprehend you now—

[*Whilst they are lifting* Petronella *on the Mountebank's Stage,* [75] *they go into the Crowd, shoulder up* Carlo's *Saddle.* Harlequin *leads the Horse forward, whilst* Carlo *is gazing, and turning up his Mustachios; they hold him up a little while, then let him drop: he rises and stares about for his Horse.*]

Car. This is flat Conjuration. [76]

Shift. What's your Worship on foot?

Hunt. I never saw his Worship on foot before.

Car. Sirrah, none of your Jests, this must be by diabolical Art, and shall cost the Seignior dear—Men of my Garb affronted—my Jennet vanished—most miraculous—by St. *Jago* I'll be revenged—hah, what's here [77]—*La Nuche*—[*Surveys her at a distance.*]

[*Enter* La Nuche, Aurelia, Sancho.]

La Nu. We are pursu'd by *Beaumond*, who will certainly hinder our speaking to *Willmore*, should we have the good fortune to see him in this Crowd—and yet there's no avoiding him.

Beau. 'Tis she, how carefully she shuns me!

Aur. I'm satisfied he knows us by the jealous Concern which appears in that prying Countenance of his.

Beau. Stay, Cruel, is it Love or Curiosity, that wings those nimble Feet? [*Holds her.*]

[Lucia *above and* Ariadne.]

Aria. *Beaumond* with a Woman!

Beau. Have you forgot this is the glorious Day that ushers in the Night shall make you mine? the happiest Night that ever favor'd Love!

La Nu. Or if I have, I find you'll take care to remember me.

Beau. Sooner I could forget the Aids of Life, sooner forget how first that Beauty charm'd me.

La Nu. Well, since your Memory's so good, I need not doubt your coming.

Beau. Still cold and unconcern'd! How have I doted, and how sacrific'd, regardless of my Fame, lain idling here, when all the Youth of *Spain* were gaining Honor, valuing one Smile of thine above their Laurels!

La Nu. And in return, I do submit to yield, preferring you above those fighting Fools, who safe in Multitudes reap Honor cheaper.

Beau. Yet there is one—one of those fighting Fools which should'st thou see, I fear I were undone; brave, handsome, gay, and all that Women dote on, unfortunate in every good of Life, but that one Blessing of obtaining Women: Be wise, for if thou seest him thou art lost—Why dost thou blush?

La Nu. Because you doubt my Heart—'tis *Willmore* that he means. [*Aside.*] We've Eyes upon us, Don *Carlo* may grow jealous, and he's a powerful Rival—at night. I shall expect ye.

Beau. Whilst I prepare myself for such a Blessing. [*Exit* Beaumond]

Car. Hah! a Cavalier in conference with *La Nuche!* and entertain'd without my knowledge! I must prevent this Lover, for he's young—and this Night will surprise her. [*Aside.*]

Will. And you would be restor'd? [*To* Petro.]

Pet. Yes, if there be that Divinity in your Baths of Reformation.

Will. There are.

New Flames shall sparkle in those Eyes;
And these grey Hairs flowing and bright shall rise:
These Cheeks fresh Buds of Roses wear,
And all your withered Limbs so smooth and clear,
As shall a general Wonder move,
And wound a thousand Hearts with Love.

Pet. A Blessing on you, Sir, there's fifty Pistoles for you, and as I earn it you shall have more. [*They lift her down.*]

[*Exit* Willmore *bowing.*]

Shift. Messieurs, 'tis late, and the Seignior's Patients stay for him at his Laboratory, tomorrow you shall see the conclusion of this Experiment, and so I humbly take my leave at this time.

[*Enter* Willmore, *below sees* La Nuche, *makes up to her, whilst the last part of the Dance is dancing.*]

La Nu. What makes you follow me, Sir? [*She goes from him, he pursues.*]

Will. Madam, I see something in that lovely Face of yours, which if not timely prevented will be your ruin: I'm now in haste, but I have more to say—[*Goes off.*]

La Nu. Stay, Sir—he's gone—and fill'd me with a curiosity that will not let me rest till it be satisfied: Follow me, *Aurelia*, for I must know my Destiny. [*Goes out.*]

[*The Dance ended, the Bank removes, the People go off.*]

Feth. Come, *Ned*, now for our amorous Visit to the two Lady Monsters.

[*Exit* Fetherfool *and* Blunt.] [78]

122

Scene II. *Changes to a fine Chamber.* [79]

[*Enter* Ariadne *and* Lucia.]

Aria. I'm thoughtful: Prithee, Cousin, sing some foolish Song—

SONG.

Phillis, *whose Heart was unconfin'd*
And free as Flowers on Meads and Plains,
None boasted of her being kind,
'Mongst all the languishing and amorous Swains:
   No Sighs nor Tears the Nymph could move [bis.] [80]
   To pity or return their Love.
Till on a time, the hapless Maid
Retired to shun the heat o'th' Day,
Into a Grove, beneath whose Shade
Strephon, *the careless Shepherd, sleeping lay:*
   But oh such Charms the Youth adorn, [bis.] [80]
   Love is revenged for all her Scorn.
Her Cheeks with Blushes covered were,
And tender Sighs her Bosom warm;
A softness in her Eyes appear,
Unusual Pains she feels from every Charm:
   To Woods and Echoes now she cries, [bis.] [80]
   For Modesty to speak denies.

Aria. Come, help to undress me, for I'll to this Mountebank, to know what success I shall have with my Cavalier. [*Unpins her things before a great Glass that is fasten'd.*]

Luc. You are resolv'd then to give him admittance?

Aria. Where's the danger of a handsome young Fellow?

Luc. But you don't know him, Madam.

Aria. But I desire to do, and time may bring it about without Miracle.

Luc. Your Cousin *Beaumond* will forbid the Banes.

Aria. No, nor old *Carlos* neither, my Mother's precious Choice, who is as solicitous for the old Gentleman, as my Father-in-Law is for his Nephew. Therefore, *Lucia*, like a good and gracious Child, I'll end the Dispute between my Father and Mother, and please myself in the choice of this Stranger, if he be to be had.

Luc. I should as soon be enamor'd on the North Wind, a Tempest, or a Clap of Thunder. Bless me from such a Blast.

Aria. I'd have a Lover rough as Seas in Storms, upon occasion; I hate your dull temperate Lover, 'tis such a husbandly quality, like *Beaumond's* Addresses to me, whom neither Joy nor Anger puts in motion; or if it do, 'tis visibly forc'd—I'm glad I saw him entertain a Woman today, not that I care, but wou'd be fairly rid of him.

Luc. You'll hardly mend yourself in this.

Aria. What, because he held Discourse with a Courtesan?

Luc. Why, is there no danger in her Eyes, do ye think?

Aria. None that I fear, that Stranger's not such a fool to give his Heart to a common Woman; and she that's concern'd where her Lover bestows his Body, were I the Man, I should think she had a mind to't herself.

Luc. And reason, Madam: in a lawful way 'tis your due.

Aria. What all? unconscionable *Lucia!* I am more merciful; but be he what he will, I'll to this cunning Man, to know whether ever any part of him shall be mine.

Luc. Lord, Madam, sure he's a Conjurer.

Aria. Let him be the Devil, I'll try his Skill, and to that end will put on a Suit of my Cousin *Endymion*; [81] there are two or three very pretty ones of his in the Wardrobe, go carry 'em to my Chamber, and we'll fit our selves and away—Go haste whilst I undress. [*Exit* Lucia.]

[Ariadne *undressing before the Glass.*]

[*Enter* Beaumond *tricking himself, and looks on himself.*]

Beau. Now for my charming Beauty, fair *La Nuche*—hah—Ariadne—damn the dull Property, how shall I free myself?

[*She turns, sees him, and walks from the Glass, he takes no notice of her, but tricks himself in the Glass, humming a Song.*]

Aria. Beaumond! What Devil brought him hither to prevent me? I hate the formal matrimonial Fop.

[*He walks about and sings.*]

Sommes [82] *nous pas trop heureux,*
Belle Irise, que nous ensemble.

A Devil on him, he may chance to plague me till night, and hinder my dear Assignation.

[*Sings again.*]

La Nuit et le Sombre voiles
Coverie nos desires ardentes;
Et l'Amour et les Etoiles
Sont nos secrets confidents.

Beau. Pox on't, how dull am I at an excuse? [*Sets his Wig in the Glass, and sings.*]

A Pox of Love and Woman-kind,
And all the Fops adore 'em.

[*Puts on his Hat, cocks it, and goes to her.*]

How is't, Cuz?

Aria. So, here's the saucy freedom of a Husband Lover—a blest Invention this of marrying, whoe'er first found it out.

Beau. Damn this *English* Dog of a Perriwig-maker, what an ungainly Air it gives the Face, and for a Wedding Perriwig too—how dost thou like it, *Ariadne?* [*Uneasy.*]

Aria. As ill as the Man—I perceive you have taken more care for your Perriwig than your Bride.

Beau. And with reason, *Ariadne*, the Bride was never the care of the Lover, but the business of the Parents; 'tis a serious Affair, and ought to be manag'd by the grave and wise: Thy Mother and my Uncle have agreed the Matter, and would it not look very sillily in me now to whine a tedious Tale of Love in your Ear, when the business is at an end? 'tis like saying a Grace when a Man should give Thanks.

Aria. Why did you not begin sooner then?

Beau. Faith, *Ariadne*, because I know nothing of the Design in hand; had I had civil warning, thou shouldst have had as pretty smart Speeches from me, as any Coxcomb Lover of 'em all could have made thee.

Aria. I shall never marry like a *Jew* in my own Tribe; I'll rather be possessed by honest old doting Age, than by saucy conceited Youth, whose Inconstancy never leaves a Woman safe or quiet.

Beau. You know the Proverb of the half Loaf, *Ariadne*; a Husband that will deal thee some Love is better than one who can give thee none: you would have a blessed time on't with old Father *Carlo*.

Aria. No matter, a Woman may with some lawful excuse cuckold him, and 'twould be scarce a Sin.

Beau. Not so much as lying with him, whose reverend Age wou'd make it look like Incest.

Aria. But to marry thee—would be a Tyranny from whence there's no Appeal: A drinking whoring Husband! 'tis the Devil—

Beau. You are deceiv'd, if you think Don *Carlo* more chaste than I; only duller, and more a Miser, one that fears his Flesh more, and loves his Money better.—Then to be condemn'd to lie with him—oh, who would not rejoice to meet a Woollen-Waistcoat, and knit Night-Cap without a Lining, a Shirt so nasty, a cleanly Ghost would not appear in't at the latter Day? then the compound of nasty Smells about him, stinking Breath, Mustaches stuffed with villainous snush, [83] Tobacco, and hollow Teeth: thus prepar'd for Delight, you meet in Bed, where you may lie and sigh whole Nights away, he snores it out till Morning, and then rises to his sordid business.

Aria. All this frights me not: 'tis still much better than a keeping Husband, whom neither Beauty nor Honor in a Wife can oblige.

Beau. Oh, you know not the good-nature of a Man of Wit, at least I shall bear a Conscience, and do thee reason, which Heaven denies to old *Carlo*, were he willing.

Aria. Oh, he talks as high, and thinks as well of himself as any young Coxcomb of ye all.

Beau. He has reason, for if his Faith were no better than his Works, he'd be damn'd.

Aria. Death, who wou'd marry, who wou'd be chaffer'd thus, and sold to Slavery? I'd rather buy a Friend at any Price that I could love and trust.

Beau. Ay, could we but drive on such a Bargain.

Aria. You should not be the Man; You have a Mistress, Sir, that has your Heart, and all your softer Hours: I know't, and if I were so wretched as to marry thee, must see my Fortune lavished out on her; her Coaches, Dress, and Equipage exceed mine by far:

Possess she all the day thy Hours of Mirth, good Humor and Expence, thy Smiles, thy Kisses, and thy Charms of Wit. Oh how you talk and look when in her Presence! but when with me,

>   *A Pox of Love and Woman-kind,* [*Sings.*]
>   *And all the Fops adore 'em.*

How it's, Cuz—then slap, on goes the Beaver, which being cock'd, you bear up briskly, with the second Part to the same Tune—Harkye, Sir, let me advise you to pack up your Trumpery and be gone, your honorable Love, your matrimonial Foppery, with your other Trinkets thereunto belonging; or I shall talk aloud, and let your Uncle hear you.

Beau. Sure she cannot know I love *La Nuche.* [*Aside.*] The Devil take me, spoil'd! What Rascal has inveigled thee? What lying fawning Coward has abus'd thee? When fell you into this Lewdness? Pox, thou art hardly worth the loving now, that canst be such a Fool, to wish me chaste, or love me for that Virtue; or that wouldst have me a ceremonious Whelp, one that makes handsome Legs to Knights without laughing, or with a sneaking modest Squirish Countenance; assure you, I have my Maidenhead. A Curse upon thee, the very thought of Wife has made thee formal.

Aria. I must dissemble, or he'll stay all day to make his peace again—why, have you ne'er—a Mistress then?

Beau. A hundred, by this day, as many as I like, they are my Mirth, the business of my loose and wanton Hours; but thou art my Devotion, the grave, the solemn Pleasure of my Soul—Pox, would I were handsomely rid of thee too. [*Aside.*]—Come, I have business—send me pleas'd away.

Aria. Would to Heaven thou wert gone; [*Aside.*] You're going to some Woman now.

Beau. Oh damn the Sex, I hate 'em all—but thee—farewell, my pretty jealous-sullen-Fool. [*Goes out.*]

Aria. Farewell, believing Coxcomb. [*Enter* Lucia.]

Lucia. Madam, the Clothes are ready in your Chamber.

Aria. Let's haste and put 'em on then. [*Runs out.*]

ACT III.

Scene I. *A House.*

[*Enter* Fetherfool *and* Blunt, *staring about, after them* Shift.]

Shift. Well, Gentlemen, this is the Doctor's House, and your fifty Pistoles has made him entirely yours; the Ladies too are here in safe Custody—Come, draw Lots who shall have the Dwarf, and who the Giant. [*They draw.*]

Feth. I have the Giant.

Blunt. And I the little tiny Gentlewoman.

Shift. Well, you shall first see the Ladies, and then prepare for your Uncle *Moses,* the old *Jew* Guardian, before whom you must be very grave and sententious: You know the old Law was full of Ceremony.

Feth. Well, I long to see the Ladies, and to have the first Onset over.

Shift. I'll cause 'em to walk forth immediately. [*Goes out.*]

Feth. My Heart begins to fail me plaguily—would I could see 'em a little at a Distance before they come slap dash upon a Man. [*Peeping.*]

Hah!—Mercy upon us!—What's yonder!—Ah, *Ned,* my Monster is as big as the Whore of *Babylon*—Oh I'm in a cold Sweat—[Blunt *pulls him to peep, and both do so.*] Oh Lord! she's as tall as the St. *Christopher* in *Notre-dame* at *Paris,* and the little one looks like the Christo upon his Shoulders—I shall ne'er be able to stand the first Brunt.

Blunt. 'Dsheartlikins, whither art going? [*Pulls him back.*]

Feth. Why only—to—say my Prayers a little—I'll be with thee presently. [*Offers to go, he pulls him.*]

Blunt. What a Pox, art thou afraid of a Woman—

Feth. Not of a Woman, *Ned,* but of a She *Gargantua,* [84] I am of a *Hercules* in Petticoats.

Blunt. The less Resemblance the better. 'Shartlikins, I'd rather mine were a *Centaur* than a Woman: No, since my *Naples* Adventure, I am clearly for your Monster.

Feth. Prithee, *Ned,* there's Reason in all things—

Blunt. But villainous Woman—'Dshartlikins, stand your Ground, or I'll nail you to't: Why, what a Pox are you so queasy stomach'd, a Monster won't down with you, with a hundred thousand Pound to boot. [*Pulling him.*]

Feth. Nay, *Ned,* that mollifies something; and I scorn it should be said of *Nich. Fetherfool* that he left his Friend in danger, or did an ill thing: therefore, as thou say'st, *Ned,* tho she were a Centaur, I'll not budge an Inch.

Blunt. Why God a Mercy.

[*Enter the* Giant *and* Dwarf, *with them* Shift *as an* Operator, *and* Harlequin *attending.*] [85]

Feth. Oh—they come—Prithee, *Ned,* advance—[*Puts him forward.*]

Shift. Most beautiful Ladies.

Feth. Why, what a flattering Son of a Whore's this?

Shift. These are the illustrious Persons your Uncle designs your humble Servants, and who have so extraordinary a Passion for your Seignioraships.

Feth. Oh yes, a most damnable one: Wou'd I were cleanlily off the Lay, and had my Money again.

Blunt. Think of a Million, Rogue, and do not hang an Arse thus.

Giant. What, does the Cavalier think I'll devour him? [*To* Shift.]

Feth. Something inclin'd to such a Fear.

Blunt. Go and salute her, or, Adsheartlikins, I'll leave you to her Mercy.

Feth. Oh, dear *Ned,* have pity on me—but as for saluting her, you speak of more than may be done, dear Heart, without a Scaling Ladder. [*Exit* Shift.]

Dwarf. Sure, Seignior *Harlequin,* these Gentlemen are dumb.

Blunt. No, my little diminutive Mistress, my small Epitomy of Woman-kind, we can prattle when our Hands are in, but we are raw and bashful, young Beginners; for this is the first time we ever were in love: we are something awkward, or so, but we shall come on in time, and mend upon Encouragement.

Feth. Pox on him, what a delicate Speech has he made now—'Gad, I'd give a thousand Pounds a Year for *Ned's* concise Wit, but not a Groat for his Judgment in Womankind.

[*Enter* Shift *with a Ladder, sets it against the Giant, and bows to* Fetherfool.]

Shift. Here, Seignior, Don, approach, mount, and salute the Lady.

Feth. Mount! why, 'twould turn my Brains to look down from her Shoulders—But hang't, 'Gad, I will be brave and venture. [*Runs up the Ladder, salutes her, and runs down again.*]

And Egad this was an Adventure and a bold one—but since I am come off with a whole Skin, I am fleshed for the next onset—Madam—has your Greatness any mind to marry? [*Goes to her, speaks, and runs back;* Blunt *claps him on the Back.*]

Giant. What if I have?

Feth. Why then, Madam, without enchanted Sword or Buckler, I'm your Man.

Giant. My Man? my Mouse. I'll marry none whose Person and Courage shall not bear some Proportion to mine.

Feth. Your Mightiness I fear will die a Maid then.

Giant. I doubt you'll scarce secure me from that Fear, who court my Fortune, not my Beauty.

Feth. Hu, how scornful [86] she is, I'll warrant you—why I must confess, your Person is something heroical and masculine, but I protest to your Highness, I love and honor ye.

Dwarf. Prithee, Sister, be not so coy, I like my Lover well enough; and if Seignior Mountebank keep his Word in making us of reasonable Proportions, I think the Gentlemen may serve for Husbands.

Shift. Dissemble, or you betray your Love for us. [*Aside to the Giant.*]

Giant. And if he do keep his Word, I should make a better Choice, not that I would change this noble Frame of mine, cou'd I but meet my Match, and keep up the first Race of Man entire: But since this scanty World affords none such, I to be happy, must be new created, and then shall expect a wiser Lover.

Feth. Why, what a peevish Titt's this; nay, look ye, Madam, as for that matter, your Extraordinariness may do what you please—but 'tis not done like a Monster of Honor, when a Man has set his Heart upon you, to cast him off—Therefore I hope you'll pity a despairing Lover, and cast down an Eye of Consolation upon me; for I vow, most Amazonian Princess, I love ye as if Heaven and Earth wou'd come together.

Dwarf. My Sister will do much, I'm sure, to save the Man that loves her so passionately—she has a Heart.

Feth. And a swinger 'tis—'Sbud—she moves like the Royal Sovereign, [p. 157] and is as long a tacking about. [*Aside.*]

Giant. Then your Religion, Sir.

Feth. Nay, as for that, Madam, we are *English*, a Nation I thank God, that stand as little upon Religion as any Nation under the Sun, unless it be in Contradiction; and at this time have so many amongst us, a Man knows not which to turn his Hand to—neither will I stand with your Hugeness for a small matter of Faith or so—Religion shall shall break no squares.

Dwarf. I hope, Sir, you are of your Friend's Opinion.

Blunt. My little Spark of a Diamond, I am, I was born a *Jew*, with an Aversion to Swines Flesh.

Dwarf. Well, Sir, I shall hasten Seignior Doctor to complete my Beauty, by some small Addition, to appear the more grateful to you.

Blunt. Lady, do not trouble yourself with transitory Parts, 'Dshartlikins thou'rt as handsome as needs be for a Wife.

Dwarf. A little taller, Seignior, wou'd not do amiss, my younger Sister has got so much the Start of me.

Blunt. In troth she has, and now I think on't, a little taller wou'd do well for Propagation; I should be both the Posterity of the antient Family of the *Blunts* of *Essex* should dwindle into Pigmies or Fairies.

Giant. Well, Seigniors, since you come with our Uncle's liking, we give ye leave to hope, hope—and be happy—[Th*ey go out with* Harlequin.] [87]

Feth. Egad, and that's great and gracious—

[Enter Willmore *and an Operator.]*

Will. Well, Gentlemen, and how like you the Ladies?

Blunt. Faith, well enough for the first Course, Sir.

Will. The Uncle, by my endeavor, is entirely yours—but whilst the Baths are preparing, 'twould be well if you would think of what Age, Shape, and Complexion you would have your Ladies form'd in.

Feth. Why, may we chose, Mr. Doctor?

Will. What Beauties you please.

Feth. Then will I have my Giant, *Ned,* just such another Gentlewoman as I saw at Church today—and about some fifteen.

Blunt. Hum, fifteen—I begin to have a plaguy Itch about me too, towards a handsome Damsel of fifteen; but first let's marry, lest they should be boiled away in these Baths of Reformation.

Feth. But, Doctor, can you do all this without the help of the Devil?

Will. Hum, some small Hand he has in the Business? we make an Exchange with him, give him the clippings of the Giant for so much of his Store as will serve to build the Dwarf.

Blunt. Why, then mine will be more than three Parts Devil, Mr. Doctor.

Will. Not so, the Stock is only Devil, the Graft is your own little Wife inoculated.

Blunt. Well, let the Devil and you agree about this matter as soon as you please.

[Enter Shift *as an Operator.]*

Shift. Sir, there is without a Person of an extraordinary Size wou'd speak with you.

Will. Admit him.

[Enter Harlequin, *ushers in* Hunt *as a Giant.]*

Feth. Hah—some o'ergrown Rival, on my Life. [Fetherfool *gets from it.*]

Will. What the Devil have we here? [*Aside.*]

Hunt. Bezolos mano's, Seignior, [p. 159] I understand there is a Lady whose Beauty and Proportion can only merit me: I'll say no more—but shall be grateful to you for your Assistance.

Feth. 'Tis so.

Hunt. The Devil's in't if this does not fright 'em from a farther Courtship. [*Aside.*]

Will. Fear nothing, Seignior—Seignior, you may try your Chance, and visit the Ladies. [*Talks to* Hunt.] [88]

Feth. Why, where the Devil could this Monster conceal himself all this while, that we should neither see nor hear of him?

Blunt. Oh—he lay disguis'd; I have heard of an Army that has done so.

Feth. Pox, no single House cou'd hold him.

Blunt. No—he dispos'd himself in several parcels up and down the Town, here a Leg, and there an Arm; and hearing of this proper Match for him, put himself together to court his fellow Monster.

Feth. Good Lord! I wonder what Religion he's of.

Blunt. Some heathen Papist, by his notable Plots and Contrivances.

Will. 'Tis *Hunt,* that Rogue—[*Aside.*] Sir, I confess there is great Power in Sympathy—Conduct him to the Ladies—[*He tries to go in at the Door.*]—I am sorry you cannot enter at that low Door, Seignior, I'll have it broken down—

Hunt. No, Seignior, I can go in at twice.

Feth. How, at twice! what a Pox can he mean?

Will. Oh, Sir, 'tis a frequent thing by way of Enchantment. [Hunt *being all Doublet, leaps off from another Man who is all Breeches, and goes out; Breeches follows stalking.*]

Feth. Oh Pox, Mr. Doctor, this must be the Devil.

Will. Oh fie, Sir, the Devil! no 'tis all done by an enchanted Girdle—These damn'd Rascals will spoil all by too gross an Imposition on the Fools. [*Aside.*]

Feth. This is the Devil, *Ned,* that's certain—But hark ye, Mr. Doctor, I hope I shall not have my Mistress enchanted from me by this enchanted Rival, hah?

Will. Oh, no, Sir, the Inquisition will never let 'em marry, for fear of a Race of Giants, 'twill be worse than the Invasion of the *Moors,* or the *French*: but go—think of your Mistresses Names and Ages, here's Company, and you would not be seen. [*Exit* Blunt *and* Fetherfool]

[*Enter* La Nuche *and* Aurelia; *Willmore bows to her.*]

La Nu. Sir, the Fame of your excellent Knowledge, and what you said to me this day; has given me a Curiosity to learn my Fate, at least that Fate you threatened.

Will. Madam, from the Oracle in the Box you may be resolved any Question—[*Leads her to the Table, where stands a Box full of Balls; he stares on her.*]—How lovely every absent minute makes her—Madam, be pleas'd to draw from out this Box what Ball you Willmore [*She draws, he takes it, and gazes on her and on it.*] Madam, upon this little Globe is character'd your Fate and Fortune; the History of your Life to come and past—first, Madam—you're—a Whore.

La Nu. A very plain beginning.

Will. My Art speaks simple Truth; the Moon is your Ascendant, that covetous Planet that borrows all her Light, and is in opposition still to *Venus*; and Interest more prevails with you than Love: yet here I find a cross—intruding Line—that does inform me—you have an Itch that way, but Interest still opposes: you are a slavish mercenary Prostitute.

La Nu. Your Art is so, tho call'd divine, and all the Universe is sway'd by Interest: and would you wish this Beauty which adorns me, should be dispos'd about for Charity? Proceed and speak more Reason.

Will. But *Venus* here gets the Ascent again, and spite of—Interest, spite of all Aversion, will make you dote upon a Man—[*Still looking on, and turning the Ball.*] Wild, fickle, restless, faithless as the Winds! [89]—a Man of Arms he is—and by this Line—a Captain—[*Looking on her.*] for *Mars* and *Venus* were in conjunction at his Birth—and Love and War's his business.

La Nu. There thou hast touched my Heart, and spoke so true, that all thou say'st I shall receive as Oracle. Well, grant I love, that shall not make me yield.

Will. I must confess you're ruin'd if you yield, and yet not all your Pride, not all your Vows, your Wit, your Resolution, or your Cunning, can hinder him from conquering absolutely: your Stars are fixed, and Fate irrevocable.

La Nu. No,—I will controul my Stars and Inclinations; and tho I love him more than Power or Interest, I will be Mistress of my fixed Resolves [90]—One Question more— Does this same Captain, this wild happy Man love me?

Will. I do not—find—it here—only a possibility encourag'd by your Love—Oh that you cou'd resist—but you are destin'd his, and to be ruin'd. [*Sighs, and looks on her, she grows in a Rage.*]

La Nu. Why do you tell me this? I am betray'd, and every caution blows my kindling Flame—hold—tell me no more—I might have guess'd my Fate, from my own Soul have guessed it—but yet I will be brave, I will resist in spite of Inclinations, Stars, or Devils.

Will. Strive not, fair Creature, with the Net that holds you, you'll but entangle more. Alas! you must submit and be undone.

La Nu. Damn your false Art—had he but lov'd me too, it had excus'd the Malice of my Stars.

Will. Indeed, his Love is doubtful; for here—I trace him in a new pursuit—which if you can this Night prevent, perhaps you fix him.

La Nu. Hah, pursuing a new Mistress! there thou hast met the little Resolution I had left, and dashed it into nothing—but I have vow'd Allegiance to my Interest—Curse on my Stars, they cou'd not give me Love where that might be advanc'd—I'll hear no more. [*Gives him Money.*]

[*Enter* Shift.]

Shift. Sir, there are several Strangers arriv'd, who talk of the old Oracle. How will you receive 'em?

Will. I've business now, and must be excus'd, a while.—Thus far—I'm well; but I may tell my Tale so often o'er, till, like the Trick of Love, I spoil the pleasure by the repetition.—Now I'll uncase, and see what Effects my Art has wrought on *La Nuche*, for she's the promis'd Good, the Philosophic Treasure that terminates my Toil and Industry. Wait you here. [*Exit* Willmore.]

[*Enter* Ariadne *in Mens Clothes, with* Lucia *so dressed, and other Strangers.*]

Aria. How now, Seignior Operator, where's this renowned Man of Arts and Sciences, this Don of Wonders?—hah! may a Man have a Pistole's Worth or two of his Tricks? will he show, Seignior?

Shift. Whatever you dare see, Sir.

Aria. And I dare see the greatest Bug-bear he can conjure up, my Mistress's Face in a Glass excepted.

Shift. That he can show, Sir, but is now busied in weighty Affairs with a Grandee.

Aria. Pox, must we wait the Leisure of formal Grandees and Statesmen—ha, who's this?—the lovely Conqueress of my Heart, *La Nuche.* [*Goes to her, she is talking with* Aurel.]

La Nu. What foolish thing art thou?

Aria. Nay, do not frown, nor fly; for if you do, I must arrest you, fair one.

La Nu. At whose Suit, pray?

Aria. At Love's—you have stol'n a Heart of mine, and us'd it scurvily.

La Nu. By what marks do you know the Toy, that I may be no longer troubled with it?

Aria. By a fresh Wound, which touched by her that gave it bleeds anew, a Heart all over kind and amorous.

La Nu. When was this pretty Robbery committed?

Ana. Today, most sacrilegiously, at Church, where you debauch'd my Zeal; and when I wou'd have pray'd, your Eyes had put the Change upon my Tongue, and made it utter Railings: Heav'n forgive ye!

La Nu. You are the gayest thing without a Heart, I ever saw.

Aria. I scorn to flinch for a bare Wound or two; nor is he routed that has lost the day, he may again rally, [91] renew the Fight, and vanquish.

La Nu. You have a good opinion of that Beauty, which I find not so forcible, nor that fond Prattle uttered with such Confidence.

Aria. But I have Quality and Fortune too.

La Nu. So had you need. I should have guest the first by your pertness; for your saucy thing of Quality acts the Man as impudently at fourteen, as another at thirty: nor is there any thing so hateful as to hear it talk of Love, Women and Drinking; nay, to see it marry too at that Age, and get itself a Play-fellow in its Son and Heir.

Aria. This Satyr on my Youth shall never put me out of countenance, or make me think you wish me one day older; and egad, I'll warrant them that tries me, [92] shall find me ne'er an hour too young.

La Nu. You mistake my Humor, I hate the Person of a fair conceited Boy.

[*Enter* Willmore *dressed, singing.*]

Will. Vole, vole dans cette Cage,
Petite Oyseau dans cet bocage.
—How now, Fool, where's the Doctor?

Shift. A little busy, Sir.

Will. Call him, I am in haste, and come to cheapen the Price of Monster.

Shift. As how, Sir?

Will. In an honorable way, I will lawfully marry one of 'em, and have pitcht upon the Giant; I'll bid as fair as any Màn.

Shift. No doubt but you will speed, Sir: please you, Sir, to walk in.

Will. I'll follow—*Vole, vole dans cette Cage, &c.*

Luc. Why,'tis the Captain, Madam—[*Aside to* Ariadne]

La Nu. Hah—marry—harkye, Sir,—a word, pray. [*As he is going out she pulls him.*]

Will. Your Servant, Madam, your Servant—*Vole, vole, &c.* [*Puts his Hat off carelessly, and walks by, going out.*]

Luc. And to be marry'd, mark that.

Aria. Then there's one doubt over, I'm glad he is not married.

La Nu. Come back—Death, I shall burst with Anger—this Coldness blows my Flame, which if once visible, makes him a Tyrant—

Will. Fool, what's a Clock, fool? this noise hinders me from hearing it strike. [*Shakes his Pockets, and walks up and down.*]

La Nu. A blessed sound, if no Hue and Cry pursue it.—what—you are resolv'd then upon this notable Exploit?

Will. What Exploit, good Madam?

La Nu. Why, marrying of a Monster, and an ugly Monster.

Will. Yes faith, Child, here stands the bold Knight, that singly, and unarm'd, designs to enter the List with *Thogogandiga* the Giant; a good Sword will defend a worse cause than an ugly Wife. I know no danger worse than fighting for my Living, and I have don't this dozen years for Bread.

La Nu. This is the common trick of all Rogues, when they have done an ill thing to face it out.

Will. An ill thing—your Pardon, Sweet-heart, compare it but to Banishment, a frozen Sentry with brown George [p. 165] and *Spanish* Pay; [p. 165] and if it be not better to be Master of a Monster, than Slave to a damn'd Commonwealth—I submit—and since my Fortune has thrown this good in my way—

La Nu. You'll not be so ungrateful to refuse it; besides then you may hope to sleep again, without dreaming of Famine, or the Sword, two Plagues a Soldier of Fortune is subject to.

Will. Besides Cashiering, a third Plague.

La Nu. Still unconcern'd!—you call me mercenary, but I would starve e'er suffer my self to be possest by a thing of Horror.

Will. You lye, you would by any thing of Horror: yet these things of Horror have Beauties too, Beauties thou canst not boast of, Beauties that will not fade; Diamonds to supply the lustre of their Eyes, and Gold the brightness of their Hair, a well-got Million to atone for Shape, and Orient Pearls, more white, more plump and smooth, than that fair Body Men so languish for, and thou hast set such Price on. [93]

Aria. I like not this so well, 'tis a trick to make her jealous.

Will. Their Hands too have their Beauties, whose very mark finds credit and respect, their Bills are current o'er the Universe; besides these, you shall see waiting at my Door, four Footmen, a Velvet Coach, with Six *Flanders* Beauties more: And are not these most comely Virtues in a Soldier's Wife, in this most wicked peaceable Age?

Luc. He's poor too, there's another comfort. [*Aside.*]

Aria. The most incouraging one I have met with yet.

Will. Pox on't, I grow weary [94] of this virtuous Poverty. There goes a gallant Fellow, says one, but gives him not an Onion; the Women too, faith, 'tis a handsome Gentleman, but the Devil a Kiss he gets *gratis*.

Aria. Oh, how I long to undeceive him of that Error.

La Nu. He speaks not of me; sure he knows me not. [95] [*Aside.*]

Will.—No, Child, Money speaks sense in a Language all Nations understand, 'tis Beauty, Wit, Courage, Honor, and undisputable Reason—see the virtue of a Wager, that new philosophical way lately found out of deciding all hard Questions—*Socrates*, without ready Money to lay down, must yield.

Aria. Well, I must have this gallant Fellow. [*Aside.*]

La Nu. Sure he has forgot this trival thing.

Will.—Even thou—who seest me dying unregarded, wou'd then be fond and kind, and flatter me. [*Soft tone.*]

By Heaven, I'll hate thee then; nay, I will marry to be rich to hate thee: the worst of that, is but to suffer nine Days Wonderment. Is not that better than an Age of Scorn from a proud faithless Beauty? [96]

La Nu. Oh, there's Resentment left—why, yes faith, such a Wedding would give the Town diversion: we should have a lamentable Ditty made on it, entitled, The Captain's Wedding, with the doleful Relation of his being over-laid by an o'er-grown Monster.

Will. I'll warrant ye I escape that as sure as cuckolding; for I would fain see that hardy Wight that dares attempt my Lady Bright, either by Force or Flattery.

La Nu. So, then you intend to bed her?

Will. Yes faith, and beget a Race of Heroes, the Mother's Form with all the Father's Qualities.

La Nu. Faith, such a Brood may prove a pretty Livelihood for a poor decay'd Officer; you may chance to get a Patent to show 'em in *England*, that Novelty.

Will. A provision old *Carlo* cannot make for you against the abandon'd day.

La Nu. He can supply the want of Issue a better way; and tho he be not so fine a fellow as yourself, he's a better Friend, he can keep a Mistress: give me a Man can feed and clothe me, as well as hug and all to bekiss me, [97] and tho his Sword be not so good as yours, his Bond's worth a thousand Captains. This will not do, I'll try what Jealousy will do. [*Aside.*] Your Servant, Captain—your Hand, Sir. [*Takes* Ariadne *by the Hand.*]

Will. Hah, what new Coxcomb's that—hold, Sir—[*Takes her from him.*]

Aria. What would you, Sir, ought with this Lady?

Will. Yes, that which thy Youth will only let thee guess at—this—Child, is Man's Meat; there are other Toys for Children. [*Offers to lead her off.*]

La Nu. Oh insolent! and whither would'st thou lead me?

Will. Only out of harm's way, Child, here are pretty near Conveniences within: the Doctor will be civil—'tis part of his Calling—Your Servant, Sir—[*Going off with her.*]

Aria. I must huff now, tho I may chance to be beaten—come back—or I have something here that will oblige ye to't. [*Laying his hand on his Sword.*] [98]

Will. Yes faith, thou'rt a pretty Youth; but at this time I've more occasion for a thing in Petticoats—go home, and do not walk the Streets so much; that tempting Face of thine will debauch the grave men of business, and make the Magistrats lust after Wickedness.

Aria. You are a scurvy Fellow, Sir. [*Going to draw.*]

Will. Keep in your Sword, for fear it cut your Fingers, Child.

Aria. So 'twill your Throat, Sir—here's Company coming that will part us, and I'll venture to draw. [*Draws, Willmore draws.*]

[*Enter* Beaumond.]

Beau. Hold, hold—hah, *Willmore!* thou Man of constant mischief, what's the matter?

La Nu. Beaumond! undone!

Aria.—Beaumond!—

Will. Why, here's a young Spark will take my Lady Bright from me; the unmanner'd Hot-spur would not have patience till I had finish'd my small Affair with her. [*Puts up his Sword.*]

134

Aria. Death, he'll know me—Sir, you see we are prevented. [*Draws him aside.*]—or—[*Seems to talk to him,* Beaumond *gazes on* La Nuche, *who has pull'd down her Veil.*]

Beau. 'Tis she! Madam, this Veil's too thin to hide the perjur'd Beauty underneath. Oh, have I been searching thee, with all the diligence of impatient Love, and am I thus rewarded, to find thee here encompass'd round with Strangers, fighting, who first should take my right away?—Gods! take your Reason back, take all your Love; for easy Man's unworthy of the Blessings.

Will. Harkye, *Harry*—the—Woman—the almighty Whore—thou told'st me of today.

Beau. Death, do'st thou mock my Grief—unhand me strait, for tho I cannot blame thee, I must hate thee.—[*Goes out.*]

Will. What the Devil ails he? [99]

Aria. You will be sure to come.

Will. At night in the Piazza; I have an Assignation with a Woman, that once dispatch'd, I will not fail ye, Sir.

Luc. And will you leave him with her?

Aria. Oh, yes, he'll be ne'er the worse for my use when he has done with her.

[*Exit* Lucetta *and* Ariadne Willmore *looks with scorn on* La Nuche.]

Will. Now you may go o'ertake him, lie with him—and ruin him: the Fool was made for such a Destiny—if he escapes my Sword. [*He offers to go.*]

La Nu. I must prevent his visit to this Woman—but dare not tell him so. [*Aside.*]—I would not have ye meet this angry Youth.

Will. Oh, you would preserve him for a farther use.

La Nu. Stay—you must not fight—by Heaven, I cannot see—that Bosom—wounded. [*Turns and weeps.*]

Will. Hah! weep'st thou? curse me when I refuse a faith to that obliging Language of thy Eyes—Oh give me one proof more, and after that, thou conquerest all my Soul; Thy Eyes speak Love—come, let us in, my Dear, e'er the bright Fire allays that warms my Heart. [*Goes to lead her out.*]

La Nu. Your Love grows rude, and saucily demands it. [*Flings away.*]

Will. Love knows no Ceremony, no respect when once approached so near the happy minute.

La Nu. What desperate easiness have you seen in me, or what mistaken merit in yourself, should make you so ridiculously vain, to think I'd give myself to such a Wretch, one fal'n even to the last degree of Poverty, whilst all the World is prostrate at my Feet, whence I might chose the Brave, the Great, the Rich? [*He stands spitefully gazing at her.*]—Still as he fires, I find my Pride augment, and when he cools I burn. [*Aside.*]

Will. Death, thou'rt a—vain, conceited, tawdry Jilt, who wou'st [100] draw me in as Rooks their Cullies do, to make me venture all my stock of Love, and then you turn me out despis'd [101] and poor—[*Offers to go.*]

La Nu. You think you're gone now—

Will. Not all thy Arts nor Charms shall hold [102] me longer.

La Nu. I must submit—and can you part thus from me?—[*Pulls him.*]

Will. I can—nay, by Heaven, I will not turn, nor look at thee. No, when I do, or trust that faithless Tongue again—may I be—

La Nu. Oh do not swear—

Will. Ever curst—[*Breaks from her, she holds him.*] [103]

La Nu. You shall not go—Plague of this needless Pride, [*Aside.*]—stay—and I'll follow all the dictates of my Love.

Will. Oh never hope to flatter me to faith again. [*His back to her, she holding him.*]

La Nu. I must, I will; what wou'd you have me do?

Will. [*turning softly to her.*] Never—deceive me more, it may be fatal to wind me up to an impatient height, then dash my eager Hopes. [*Sighing.*] Forgive my roughness—and be kind, *La Nuche,* I know thou wo't—

La Nu. Will you then be ever kind and true?

Will. Ask thy own Charms, and to confirm thee more, yield and disarm me quite.

La Nu. Will you not marry then? for tho you never can be mine that way, I cannot think that you should be another's.

Will. No more delays, by Heaven, 'twas but a trick.

La Nu. And will you never see that Woman neither, whom you're this Night to visit?

Will. Damn all the rest of thy weak Sex, when thou look'st thus, and art so soft and charming. [*Offers to lead her out.*]

La Nu. Sancho—my Coach. [*Turns in scorn.*]

Will. Take heed, what mean ye?

La Nu. Not to be pointed at by all the envying Women of the Town, who'll laugh and cry, Is this the high-priz'd Lady, now fall'n so low, to dote upon a Captain? a poor disbanded Captain? defend me from that Infamy.

Will. Now all the Plagues—but yet I will not curse thee, 'tis lost on thee, for thou art destin'd damn'd. [*Going out.*]

La Nu. Whither so fast?

Will. Why,—I am so indifferent grown, that I can tell thee now—to a Woman, young, fair and honest; she'll be kind and thankful—farewell, Jilt—now should'st thou die for one sight more of me, thou should'st not ha't; nay, should'st thou sacrifice all thou hast couzen'd other Coxcombs of, to buy one single visit, I am so proud, by Heaven, thou shouldst not have it—To grieve thee more, see here, insatiate Woman [*Shows her a Purse or hands full of Gold*] [104] the Charm that makes me lovely in thine Eyes: it had all been thine hadst thou not basely bargain'd with me, now 'tis the Prize of some well-meaning Whore, whose Modesty will trust my Generosity. [*Goes out.*]

La Nu. Now I cou'd rave, t'have lost an opportunity which industry nor chance can give again—when on the yielding point, a cursed fit of Pride comes cross my Soul, and stops the kind Career—I'll follow him, yes I'll follow him, even to the Arms of her to whom he's gone.

Aur. Madam, 'tis dark, and we may meet with Insolence.

La Nu. No matter: *Sancho,* let the Coach go home, and do you follow me—
  Women may boast their Honor and their Pride,
  But Love soon lays those feebler Powr's aside. [*Exeunt.*]

ACT IV.

Scene I. *The Street, or Backside of the Piazza dark.*

[*Enter* Willmore *alone.*]

Will. A Pox upon this Woman that has jilted me, and I for being a fond believing Puppy to be in earnest with so great a Devil. Where be these Coxcombs too? this *Blunt* and *Fetherfool?* when a Man needs 'em not, they are plaguing him with their unseasonable Jests—could I but light on them, I would be very drunk tonight—but first I'll try my Fortune with this Woman—let me see—hereabouts is the Door. [*Gropes about for the Door.*]

[*Enter* Beaumond, *follow'd by* La Nuche, *and* Sancho.]

La Nu. 'Tis he, I know it by his often and uneasy pauses—
Beau. And shall I home and sleep upon my injury, whilst this more happy Rover takes my right away?—no, damn me then for a cold senseless Coward. [*Pauses and pulls out a Key.*]
Will. This Damsel, by the part o'th' Town she lives in, shou'd be of Quality, and therefore can have no dishonest design on me, it must be right down substantial Love, that's certain.
Beau. Yet I'll in and arm myself for the Encounter, for 'twill be rough between us, tho we're Friends. [*Groping about, finds the Door.*]
Will. Oh, 'tis this I'm sure, because the Door is open.
Beau. Hah—who's there?—[Beaumond *advances to unlock the Door, runs against* Willmore *draws.*]
Will. That Voice is of Authority, some Husband, Lover, or a Brother, on my Life—this is a Nation of a word and a blow, therefore I'll betake me to *Toledo*—[*Draws.*]

[Willmore *in drawing hits his Sword against that of* Beaumond, *who turns and fights,* La Nuche *runs into the Garden frighted.*]

Beau. Hah, are you there?
Sancho. I'll draw in defence of the Captain—[Sancho *fights for* Beaumond *and beats out* Willmore.]
Will. Hah, two to one? [*Turns and goes in.*]
Beau. The Garden Door clapped to; sure he's got in; nay, then I have him sure.

[*The Scene changes to a Garden,* La Nuche *in it, to her* Beaumond *who takes hold of her sleeve.*]

La Nu. Heavens, where am I?
Beau. Hah—a Woman! and by these Jewels—should be *Ariadne*. [*feels.*] 'Tis so! [105] Death, are all Women false? [*She struggles to get away, he holds her.*]—Oh, 'tis in vain thou fly'st, thy Infamy will stay behind thee still.

La Nu. Hah, 'tis *Beaumond's* Voice!—Now for an Art to turn the trick upon him; I must not lose his Friendship. [*Aside.*]

[*Enter* Willmore *softly, peeping behind.*]

Will. What a Devil have we here, more Mischief yet;—hah—my Woman with a Man—I shall spoil all—I ever had [106] an excellent knack of doing so.

Beau. Oh Modesty, where art thou? Is this the effect of all your put on Jealousy, that Mask to hide your own new falsehood in? New!—by Heaven, I believe thou'rt old in cunning, that couldst contrive, so near thy Wedding-night, this, to deprive me of the Rites of Love.

La Nu. Hah, what says he? [*Aside.*]

Will. How, a Maid, and young, and to be marry'd too! a rare Wench this to contrive Matters so conveniently: Oh, for some Mischief now to send him neatly off. [*Aside.*]

Beau. Now you are silent; but you could talk today loudly of Virtue, and upbraid my Vice: oh how you hated a young keeping Husband, whom neither Beauty nor Honor in a Wife cou'd oblige to reason—oh, damn your Honor, 'tis that's the sly pretence of all your domineering insolent Wives—Death—what didst thou see in me, should make thee think that I would be a tame contented Cuckold? [*Going, she holds him.*]

La Nu. I must not lose this lavish loving Fool—[*Aside.*]

Will. So, I hope he will be civil and withdraw, and leave me in possession—

Beau. No, tho my Fortune should depend on thee; nay, all my hope [107] of future happiness—by Heaven, I scorn to marry thee, unless thou couldst convince me thou wer't honest—a Whore!—Death, how it cools my Blood—

Will. And fires mine extremely—

La Nu. Nay, then I am provok'd tho I spoil all—[*Aside.*]
And is a Whore a thing so much despis'd?
Turn back, thou false forsworn—turn back, and blush at thy mistaken folly.

[*He stands amaz'd.*]

Beau. La Nuche!

[*Enter* Ariadne *peeping, advancing cautiously undressed,* Lucetta *following.*]

Aria. Oh, he is here—*Lucia*, attend me in the Orange-grove [108]—[*Exit* Lucia.]
Hah, a Woman with him!

Will. Hum—what have we here? another Damsel?—she's gay too, and seems young and handsome—sure one of these will fall to my share; no matter which, so I am sure of one.

La Nu. Who's silent now? are you struck dumb with Guilt? thou shame to noble Love; thou scandal to all brave Debauchery, thou Fop of Fortune; thou slavish Heir to Estate and Wife, born rich and damn'd to Matrimony.

Will. Egad, a noble Wench—I am divided yet.

La Nu. Thou formal Ass disguis'd in generous Lewdness, see—when the Vizor's off, how sneakingly that empty form appears—Nay 'tis thy own—Make much on't, marry with it, and be damn'd. [*Offers to go.*]

Will. I hope she'll beat him for suspecting her. [*He holds her, she turns.*]

Aria. Hah—who the Devil can these be?

La Nu. What silly honest Fool did you mistake me for? what senseless modest thing? Death, am I grown so despicable? have I deserv'd no better from thy Love than to be taken for a virtuous Changeling?

Will. Egad, 'twas an Affront. [*Aside.*]

La Nu. I'm glad I've found thee out to be an errant Coxcomb, one that esteems a Woman for being chaste forsooth! 'Sheart, I shall have thee call me pious shortly, a most—religious Matron!

Will. Egad, she has reason—[*Aside.*]

Beau. Forgive me—for I took ye—for another. [*Sighing.*]

La Nu. Oh did you so? it seems you keep fine Company the while—Death, that I should e'er be seen with such a vile Dissembler, with one so vain, so dull and so impertinent, as can be entertain'd by honest Women!

Will. A Heavenly Soul, and to my Wish, were I but sure of her.

Beau. Oh you do wondrous well t'accuse me first! yes, I am a Coxcomb—a confounded one, to dote upon so false a Prostitute; nay to love seriously, and tell it too: yet such an amorous Coxcomb I was born, to hate the Enjoyment of the loveliest Woman, without I have the Heart: the fond soft Prattle, and the lolling Dalliance, the Frowns, the little Quarrels, and the kind Degrees of making Peace again, are Joys which I prefer to all the sensual, whilst I endeavor to forget the Whore, and pay my Vows to Wit, to Youth and Beauty.

Aria. Now hang me, if it be not *Beaumond.*

Beau. Would any Devil less than common Woman have serv'd me as thou didst? say, was not this my Night? my paid for Night? my own by right of Bargain, and by Love? and hast not thou deceiv'd me for a Stranger?

Will. So—make me thankful, then she will be kind. [*Hugs himself.*]

Beau.—Was this done [109] like a Whore of Honor think ye? and would not such an Injury make me forswear all Joys of Womankind, and marry in mere spite?

La Nu. Why where had been the Crime had I been kind?

Beau. Thou dost confess it then.

La Nu. Why not?

Beau. Those Bills of Love the oftner paid and drawn, make Women better Merchants than Lovers.

La Nu. And 'tis the better Trade.

Will. Oh Pox, there she dashed all again. I find they calm upon't, and will agree, therefore I'll bear up to this small Frigate and lay her aboard. [*Goes to* Ariadne.]

La Nu. However I'm glad the Vizor's off; you might have fool'd me on, and sworn I was the only Conqueror of your Heart, had not Good-nature made me follow you, to undeceive your false Suspicions of me: How have you sworn never to marry? how rail'd at Wives, and satir'd Fools oblig'd to Wedlock? And now at last, to thy eternal Shame, thou hast betray'd thy self to be a most pernicious honorable Lover, a perjur'd—honest— nay, a very Husband. [*Turns away, he holds her.*]

Aria. Hah, sure 'tis the Captain.

Will. Prithee, Child, let's leave 'em to themselves, they'll agree matters I'll warrant them when they are alone; and let us try how Love and Good-nature will provide for us.

Aria. Sure he cannot know me?—Us!—pray who are you, and who am I?

Will. Why look ye, Child, I am a very honest civil Fellow, for my part, and thou'rt a Woman for thine; and I desire to know no more at present.

Aria. 'Tis he, and knows not me to be the same he appointed today—Sir, pursue that Path on your right Hand, that Grove of Orange-Trees, and I'll follow you immediately.

Will. Kind and civil—prithee make haste, dear Child. [*Exit* Willmore.]

Beau. And did you come to call me back again? [*Lovingly.*]

La Nu. No matter, you are to be marry'd, Sir—

Beau. No more, 'tis true, to please my Uncle, I have talk'd of some such thing; but I'll pursue it no farther, so thou wilt yet be mine, and mine entirely—I hate this *Ariadne*—for a Wife—by Heaven I do.

Aria. A very plain Confession. [*Claps him on the back.*]

Beau. Ariadne!

La Nu. I'm glad of this, now I shall be rid of him. [*Aside.*]—How is't, Sir? I see you struggle hard 'twixt Love and Honor, and I'll resign my Place—[*Offers to go, Ariadne pulls her back.*]

Aria. Hold, if she take him not away, I shall disappoint my Man—faith, I'll not be out-done in Generosity. [*Gives him to* La Nuche.] Here—Love deserves him best—and I resign him—Pox on't I'm honest, tho that's no fault of mine; 'twas Fortune who has made a worse Exchange, and you and I should suit most damnably together. [*To* Beaumond]

Beau. I am sure there's something in the Wind, she being in the Garden, and the Door left open. [*Aside.*]—Yes, I believe you are willing enough to part with me, when you expect another you like better.

Aria. I'm glad I was before-hand with you then.

Beau. Very good, and the Door was left open to give admittance to a Lover.

Aria. 'Tis visible it was to let one in to you, false as you are.

La Nu. Faith, Madam, you mistake my Constitution, my Beauty and my Business is only to be belov'd not to love; I leave that Slavery for you Women of Quality, who must invite, or die without the Blessing; for likely the Fool you make choice of wants Wit or Confidence to ask first; you are fain to whistle before the Dogs will fetch and carry, and then too they approach by stealth: and having done the Drudgery, the submissive Curs are turn'd out for fear of dirtying your Apartment, or that the Mungrils should scandalize ye; whilst all my Lovers of the noble kind throng to adore and fill my Presence daily, gay as if each were triumphing for Victory.

Aria. Ay this is something; what a poor sneaking thing an honest Woman is!

La Nu. And if we chance to love still, there's a difference, your Hours of Love are like the Deeds of Darkness, and mine like cheerful Birds in open Day.

Aria. You may, you have no Honor to lose.

La Nu. Or if I had, why should I double the Sin by Hypocrisy? [Lucia *squeaks within, crying, help, help.*]

Aria. Heavens, that's *Lucia's* Voice.

Beau. Hah, more caterwauling?

[*Enter* Lucia *in haste.*]

Luc. Oh, Madam, we're undone; and, Sir, for Heaven's sake do you retire.

Beau. What's the matter?

Luc. Oh you have brought the most villainous mad Friend with you—he found me sitting on a Bank—and did so ruffle me.

Aria. Death, she takes *Beaumond* for the Stranger, and will ruin me.

140

Luc. Nay, made love so loud, that my Lord your Father-in-law, who was in his Cabinet, heard us from the Orange-Grove, and has sent to search the Garden—and should he find a Stranger with you—do but you retire, Sir, and all's well yet. [*To* Beaumond.]

Aria. The Devil's in her Tongue. [*Aside.*]

Luc. For if Mr. *Beaumond* be in the House, we shall have the Devil to do with his Jealousy.

Aria. So, there 'tis out.

Beau. She takes me for another—I am jilted everywhere—what Friend?—I brought none with me.—Madam, do you retire—[*To* La Nuche.]

La Nu. Glad of my Freedom too—[*Goes out.*]

[A clashing of Swords within. Enter *Willmore* fighting, pressed back by three or four Men, and *Abevile, Ariadne* and *Lucetta* run out.]

Beau. Hah, set on by odds; hold, tho thou be'st my Rival, I will free thee, on condition thou wilt meet me tomorrow morning in the Piazza [110] by day break. [*Puts himself between their Swords, and speaks to* Willmore *Aside.*]

Will. By Heaven I'll do it.

Beau. Retire in safety then, you have your pass.

Abev. Fall on, fall on, the number is increas'd. [Fall on Beaumond

Beau. Rascals, do you not know me? [Falls in with 'em and beats them back, and goes out [111] with them.

Will. Nay, and you be so well acquainted, I'll leave you—unfortunate still I am; my own well meaning, but ill Management, is my eternal Foe: Plague on 'em, they have wounded me—yet not one drop of Blood's departed from me that warm'd my Heart for Woman, and I'm not willing to quit this Fairy-ground till some kind Devil have been civil to me.

[*Enter* Ariadne *and* Lucia.]

Aria. I say, 'tis he: thou'st made so many dull Mistakes tonight, thou darest not trust thy Senses when they're true—How do you, Sir?

Will. That Voice has Comfort in't, for 'tis a Woman's: hah, more Interruption?

Aria. A little this way, Sir. [*Exit Aria, and* Willmore *into the Garden.*]

[*Enter* Beaumond, Abevile *in a submissive Posture.*]

Beau. No more excuses—By all these Circumstances, I know this *Ariadne* is a Gipsy. What difference then between a money-taking Mistress and her that gives her Love? only perhaps this sins the closer by't, and talks of Honor more: What Fool wou'd be a Slave to empty Name, or value Woman for dissembling well? I'll to *La Nuche*—the honester o'th' two—*Abevile*—get me my Music ready, and attend me at *La Nuche's.* [*Exit severally.*]

Luc. He's gone, and to his Mistress too.

[*Enter* Ariadne *pursu'd by* Willmore.]

Will. My little *Daphne*, 'tis in vain to fly, unless like her, you cou'd be chang'd into a Tree: *Apollo's* self pursu'd not with more eager Fire than I. [*Holds her.*]

Aria. Will you not grant a Parley e'er I yield?

Will. I'm better at a Storm.

Aria. Besides, you're wounded too.

Will. Oh leave those Wounds of Honor to my Surgeon, thy Business is to cure those of Love. Your true bred Soldier ever fights with the more heat for a Wound or two.

Aria. Hardly in Venus' Wars.

Will. Herself ne'er thought so when she snatched her Joys between the rough Encounters of the God of War. Come, let's pursue the Business we came for: See the kind Night invites, and all the ruffling Winds are hushed and still, only the Zephirs spread their tender Wings, courting in gentle Murmurs the gay Boughs; 'twas in a Night like this, Diana taught the Mysteries of Love to the fair Boy Endymion. I am plaguy full of History and Simile tonight.

Aria. You see how well he far'd for being modest.

Will. He might be modest, but 'twas not over-civil to put her Goddessship to asking first; thou seest I'm better bred—Come let's haste to silent Grots that attend us, dark Groves where none can see, and murmuring Fountains.

Aria. Stay, let me consider first, you are a Stranger, inconstant too as Island Winds, and every day are fighting for your Mistresses, of which you've had at least four since I saw you first, which is not a whole day.

Will. I grant ye, before I was a Lover I ran at random, but I'll take up now, be a patient Man, and keep to one Woman a Month.

Aria. A Month!

Will. And a fair Reason, Child; time was, I wou'd have worn one Shirt, or one pair of Shoos so long as have let the Sun set twice upon the same Sin: but see the Power of Love; thou hast bewitched me, that's certain.

Aria. Have a care of giving me the ascendant over ye, for fear I make ye marry me.

Will. Hold, I bar that cast, Child; no, I'm none of those Spirits that can be conjur'd into a Wedding-ring, and dance in the dull matrimonial Circle all my Days.

Aria. But what think you of a hundred thousand Crowns, and a Beauty of sixteen?

Will. As of most admirable Blessings: but harkye, Child, I am plaguily afraid thou'rt some scurvy honest thing of Quality by these odd Questions of thine, and hast some wicked Design upon my Body.

Aria. What, to have and to hold I'll warrant.—No Faith, Sir, Maids of my Quality expect better Jointures than a Buff-coat, Scarf and Feather: such Portions as mine are better Ornaments in a Family than a Captain and his Commission.

Will. Why well said, now thou hast explain'd thy self like a Woman of Honor— Come, come, let's away.

Aria. Explain myself! How mean ye?

Will.—Thou say'st I am not fit to marry thee—and I believe this Assignation was not made to tell me so, nor yet to hear me whistle to the Birds. [112]

Aria. Faith no, I saw you, lik'd ye, and had a mind to ye.

Will. Ay, Child—

Aria. In short, I took ye for a Man of Honor.

Will. Nay, if I tell the Devil take me.

Aria. I am a Virgin in Distress.

Will. Poor Heart.

Aria. To be marry'd within a Day or two to one I like not.

Will. Hum—and therefore wouldst dispose of a small Virgin Treasure (too good for silly Husbands) in a Friend's Hands: faith, Child—I was ever a good religious charitable Christian, and shall acquit myself as honestly and piously in this Affair as becomes a Gentleman.

[*Enter* Abevile *with Music.*]

Abev. Come away, are ye all arm'd for the Business?

Aria. Hah, arm'd! we are surpriz'd again.

Will. Fear not. [*Draws.*]

Aria. Oh God, Sir, haste a way, you are already wounded: but I conjure you, as a Man of Honor, be here at the Garden Gate tonight again, and bring a Friend, in case of Danger, with you; and if possible I'll put myself into your Hands, for this Night's Work has ruin'd me—[*Speaking quick, and pushing him forwards runs off.*]

Abev. My Master sure not gone yet—[*Peeping advancing.*]

Will. Rascals, tho you are odds, you'll find hot Work in vanquishing. [*Falls on 'em.*]

Abev. Hold, Sir, I am your Page. Do you not know me? and these the Music you commanded—shall I carry 'em where you order'd, Sir?

Will. They take me for some other, this was lucky. [*Aside.*] O, aye—'tis well—I'll follow—but whither?—Plague of my dull Mistakes, the Woman's gone—yet stay—[*Calls 'em.*]

For now I think on't, this Mistake may help me to another—stay—I must dispose of this mad Fire about me, which all these Disappointments cannot lay—Oh for some young kind Sinner in the nick—How I cou'd souse upon her like a Bird of Prey, and worry her with Kindness. [*Aside.*]—Go on, I follow. [*Exeunt.*]

[*Scene changes to* La Nuche's *House.*]
[*Enter* Petronella *and* Aurelia *with Light.*]

Aur. Well, the Stranger [113] is in Bed, and most impatiently expects our Patrona, who is not yet returned.

Pet. Curse of this Love! I know she's in pursuit of this Rover, this *English* Piece of Impudence; Pox on 'em, I know nothing good in the whole Race of 'em, but giving all to their Shirts when they're drunk. What shall we do, *Aurelia?* This Stranger must not be put off, nor *Carlo* neither, who has fin'd [p. 182] again as if for a new Maidenhead.

Aur. You are so covetous, you might have put 'em off, but now 'tis too late.

Pet. Put off! Are these Fools to be put off think ye? a fine Fop *Englishman*, and an old doting Grandee?—No, I cou'd put the old trick on 'em still, had she been here but to have entertain'd 'em: but hark, one knocks, 'tis *Carlo* on my Life—

[*Enter* Carlo, *gives* Petronella *Gold.*]

Car. Let this plead for me.

Pet. Sweet Don, you are the most eloquent Person.

Car. I would regale tonight—I know it is not mine, but I've sent five hundred Crowns to purchase it, because I saw another bargaining for't; and Persons of my Quality must not be refus'd: you apprehend me.

Pet. Most rightly—that was the Reason then she came [114] so out of Humor home—and is gone to Bed in such a sullen Fit.

Car. To Bed, and all alone! I would surprise her there. Oh how it pleases me to think of stealing into her Arms like a fine Dream, Wench, hah.

Aur. 'Twill be a pleasant one, no doubt.

Pet. He lays the way out how he'll be cozen'd. [*Aside.*]—The Seigniora perhaps may be angry, [115] Sir, but I'll venture that to accommodate you; and that you may surprise her the more readily, be pleased to stay in my Chamber, till you think she may be asleep.

Car. Thou art a perfect Mistress of thy Trade.

Pet. So, now will I to the Seigniora's Bed myself, dressed and perfum'd, and finish two good Works at once; earn five hundred Crowns, and keep up the Honor of the House. [*Aside.*]—Softly, sweet Don. [*Lights him out.*]

Aur. And I will do two more good things, and disappoint your Expectations; jilt the young *English* Fool, and have old *Carlo* well bang'd, if t'other have any Courage.

[*Enter* La Nuche *in Rage, and* Sancho.]

La Nu. *Aurelia*, help, help me to be reveng'd upon this wretched unconsidering Heart.

Aur. Heavens, have you made the Rover happy, Madam?

La Nu. Oh wou'd I had! or that or any Sin wou'd change this Rage into some easier Passion: Sickness and Poverty, Disgrace and Pity, all met in one, were kinder than this Love, this raging Fire of a proud amorous Heart.

[*Enter* Petronella.]

Pet. Heavens, what's the matter?

Aur. Here's *Petronella*, dissemble but your Rage a little.

La Nu. Damn all dissembling [116] now, it is too late—
The Tyrant Love reigns absolute within,
And I am lost, *Aurelia*.

Pet. How, Love! forbid it Heaven! will Love maintain ye?

La Nu. Curse on your Maxims, will they ease my Heart? Can your wise Counsel fetch me back my Rover?

Pet. Hah, your Rover, a Pox upon him.

La Nu. He's gone—gone to the Arms of some gay generous Maid, who nobly follows Love's diviner Dictates, [117] whilst I 'gainst Nature studying thy dull Precepts, and to be base and infamously rich, have barter'd all the Joys of human Life—Oh give me Love: I will be poor and love.

Pet. She's lost—but hear me—

La Nu. I won't, from Childhood thou hast trained me up in Cunning, read Lectures to me of the use of Man, but kept me from the knowledge of the Right; taught me to jilt, to flatter and deceive: and hard it was to learn th' ungrateful Lessons. But oh how soon plain Nature taught me Love, and show'd me all the cheat of thy false Tenets [118]—No—give me Love with any other Curse.

Pet. But who will give you that when you are poor? when you are wretchedly despis'd and poor?

La Nu. Hah!

Pet. Do you not daily see fine Clothes, rich Furniture, Jewels and Plate are more inviting than Beauty unadorn'd? be old, diseas'd, deform'd, be anything, so you be rich and splendidly attended, you'll find yourself lov'd and ador'd by all—But I'm an old fool still—Well, *Petronella*, had'st thou been half as industrious in thy Youth as in thy Age—thou hadst not come to this. [*Weeps.*]

La Nu. She's in the right.

Pet. What can this mad poor Captain do for you, love you whilst you can buy him Breeches, and then leave you? A Woman has a sweet time on't with any Soldier-Lover of 'em all, with their Iron Minds, and Buff Hearts; feather'd Inamorato's have nothing that belongs to Love but his Wings, the Devil clip 'em for *Petronella.*

La Nu. True—he can ne'er be constant. [*Pausing.*]

Pet. Heaven forbid he should! No, if you are so unhappy as that you must have him, give him a Night or two and pay him for't, and send him to feed again: But for your Heart, 'Sdeath, I would as soon part with my Beauty, or Youth, and as necessary a Tool 'tis for your Trade—A Courtesan and love! but all my Counsel's thrown away upon ye. [*Weeps.*]

La Nu. No more, I will be rul'd—I will be wise, be rich; and since I must yield somewhere, and some time, *Beaumond* shall be the Man, and this the Night; he's handsome, young, and lavishly profuse: This Night he comes, and I'll submit to Interest. Let the gilded Apartment be made ready, and strew it o'er with Flowers, adorn my Bed of State; let all be fine; perfume my Chamber like the Phœnix's Nest, I'll be luxurious in my Pride tonight, and make the amorous prodigal Youth my Slave.

Pet. Nobly resolv'd! and for these other two who wait your coming, let me alone to manage. [*Goes out.*]

[*Scene changes to a Chamber, discovers* Fetherfool *in Bed.*]

Feth. This Gentlewoman is plaguy long in coming:—some Nicety now, some perfum'd Smock, or Point Night-Clothes to make her more lovely in my Eyes: Well, these Women are right City Cooks, they stay so long to garnish the Dish, till the Meat be cold—but hark, the Door opens.

[*Enter* Carlo *softly, half undressed.*]

Car. This Wench stays long, and Love's impatient; this is the Chamber of *La Nuche*, I take it: If she be awake, I'll let her know who I am; if not, I'll steal a Joy before she thinks of it.

Feth. Sure 'tis she, pretty modest Rogue, she comes i'th' dark to hide her Blushes—hum, I'm plaguy eloquent o'th' sudden—who's there? [*Whispering.*]

Car. 'Tis I, my Love.

Feth. Hah, sweet Soul, make haste.—There 'twas again.

Car. So kind, sure she takes me for some other, or has some inkling of my Design—[*To himself.*] Where are you, Sweetest?

Feth. Here, my Love, give me your Hand—[*Puts out his Hand;* Carlo *kneels and kisses it.*

Car. Here let me worship the fair Shrine before I dare approach so fair a Saint. [*Kisses the Hand.*]

Feth. Hah, what a Pox have we here?—wou'd I were well out o' t'other side—perhaps—'tis her Husband, and then I'm a dead Man, if I'm discover'd. [*Removes to t'other side,* Carlo *holds his Hand.*]

Car. Nay, do not fly—I know you took me for some happier Person. [*Fetherfool struggles,* Carlo *rises and takes him in his Arms, and kisses him.*]

Feth. What, will you ravish me? [*In a shrill Voice.*]

Car. Hah, that Voice is not *La Nuche's*—Lights there, Lights.

Feth. Nay, I can hold a bearded *Venus*, Sir, as well as any Man. [Holds *Carlo.*]

Car. What art thou, Rogue, Villain, Slave? [They fall to Cuffs, and fight till they are bloody, fall from the Bed and fight on the Floor.]

[*Enter* Petronella, Sancho, *and* Aurelia.]

Pet. Heaven, what noise is this?—we are undone, part 'em, *Sancho*. [*They part 'em.*]

Feth. Give me my Sword; nay, give me but a Knife, that I may cut yon Fellow's Throat—

Car. Sirrah, I'm a Grandee, and a *Spaniard*, and will be reveng'd.

Feth. And I'm an *English-man*, and a Justice, and will have Law, Sir.

Pet. Say 'tis her Husband, or anything to get him hence. [*Aside to* Sancho, *who whispers him.*]

These *English*, Sir, are Devils, and on my Life 'tis unknown to the Seigniora that he's i'th' House. [*To* Carlo *aside.*]

Car. Come, I'm abus'd, but I must put it up for fear of my Honor; a Statesman's Reputation is a tender thing: Convey me out the back way. I'll be reveng'd. [*Goes out.*]

Feth. [*Aurelia whispers to him aside.*] How, her Husband! Prithee convey me out; my Clothes, my Clothes, quickly—

Aur. Out, Sir! he has lock'd the Door, and designs to have ye murder'd.

Feth. Oh, gentle Soul—take pity on me—where, oh what shall I do?—my Clothes, my Sword and Money.

Aur. Quickly, *Sancho*, tie a Sheet to the Window, and let him slide down by that—Be speedy, and we'll throw your Clothes out after ye. Here, follow me to the Window.

Feth. Oh, any whither, any whither. [119] That I could not be warn'd from whoring in a strange Country, by my Friend *Ned Blunt's* Example—if I can but keep it secret now, I care not. [*Exeunt.*]

[*Scene, the Street, a Sheet ty'd to the Balcony, and* Fetherfool *sitting cross to slide down.*]

Feth. So—now your Neck, or your Throat, chose ye either, wise Mr. *Nicholas Fetherfool*—But stay, I hear Company. Now dare not I budge an Inch.

[*Enter* Beaumond *alone.*]

Beau. Where can this Rascal, my Page, be all this while? I waited in the Piazza so long, that I believed he had [120] mistook my Order, and gone directly to *La Nuche's* House—but here's no sign of him—

Feth. Hah—I hear no noise, I'll venture down. [*Goes halfway down and stops.*]

146

[*Enter* Abevile, Harlequin, *Music and* Willmore.]

Will. Whither will this Boy conduct me?—but since to a Woman, no matter whither 'tis. [121]

Feth. Hah, more Company; now dare not I stir up nor down, they may be Bravoes to cut my Throat.

Beau. Oh sure these are they—

Will. Come, my Heart, lose no time, but tune your Pipes. [Harlequin *plays on his Guitar, and sings.*]

Beau. How, sure this is some Rival. [*Goes near and listens.*]

Will. Harkye, Child, hast thou ne'er an amorous Ditty, short and sweet, hah—

Abev. Shall I not sing that you gave me, Sir?

Will. I shall spoil all with hard Questions—Ay, Child—that that. [Abevile *sings,* [122] Beaumond *listens, and seems angry the while.*]

SONG.

A Pox upon this needless Scorn!
Silvia, *for shame the Cheat give o'er;*
The end to which the fair are born,
Is not to keep their Charms in store,
But lavishly dispose in haste,
Of Joys—which none but Youth improve;
Joys which decay when Beauty's past:
And who when Beauty's past will love?
When Age those Glories shall deface,
Revenging all your cold Disdain,
And Silvia *shall neglected pass,*
By every once admiring Swain;
And we can only Pity pay,
When you in vain too late shall burn:
If Love increase, and Youth delay,
Ah, Silvia, *who will make return?*
Then haste, my Silvia, *to the Grove,*
Where all the Sweets of May *conspire,*
To teach us every Art of Love,
And raise our Charms of Pleasure higher;
Where, whilst embracing we should lie
Loosely in Shades, on Banks of Flowers:
The duller World whilst we defy,
Years will be Minutes, Ages Hours.

Beau. 'Sdeath, that's my Page's Voice: Who the Devil is't that ploughs with my Heifer!

Aur. Don Henrick, Don Henrick—[*The Door opens,* Beaumond *goes up to't;* Willmore *puts him by, and offers to go in, he pulls him back.*]

Will. How now, what intruding Slave art thou?]

Beau. What Thief art thou that basely, and by dark, rob'st me of all my Rights? [*Strikes him, they fight, and Blows light on* Fetherfool *who hangs down.*]

[Sancho *throws* Fetherfool's *Clothes out,* Harlequin *takes 'em up in confusion; they fight out Beaumond, all go off, but* Willmore *gets into the House:* Harlequin *and* Fetherfool *remain.* Fetherfool *gets down, runs against* Harlequin *in the dark, both seem frighted.*]

Harl. Que questo.
Feth. Ay, *un pouer dead Home,* murder'd, kill'd.
Harl. [*In Italian.*] You are the first dead Man I ever saw walk.
Feth. Hah, Seignior *Harlequin!*
Harl. Seignior *Nicholas!*
Feth. A Pox *Nicholas* ye, I have been mall'd and beaten within doors, and hang'd and bastinado'd without doors, lost my Clothes, my Money, and all my Moveables; but this is nothing to the Secret taking Air. Ah, dear *Seignior,* convey me to the Mountebanks, there I may have Recruit and Cure under one.

ACT V.

Scene I. *A Chamber.*

[La Nuche *on a Couch in an Undress,* Willmore *at her Feet, on his Knees, all unbraced: his Hat, Sword, &c. on the Table, at which she is dressing her Head.*]

Will. Oh Gods! no more!
I see a yielding in thy charming Eyes;
The Blushes on thy Face, thy trembling Arms,
Thy panting Breast, and short-breath'd Sighs confess,
Thou wo't be mine, in spite of all thy Art.
La Nu. What need you urge my Tongue then to repeat
What from my Eyes you can so well interpret?

[*Bowing down her Head to him and sighing.*]

—Or if it must—dispose me as you please—
Will. Heaven, I thank thee! [*Rises with Joy.*]
Who wou'd not plough an Age in Winter Seas,
Or wade full seven long Years in ruder Camps,
To find out this Rest [123] at last?—[*Leans on, and kisses her Bosom.*]
Upon thy tender Bosom to repose;
To gaze upon thy Eyes, and taste thy Balmy Kisses, [*Kisses her.*]
—Sweeter than everlasting Groves of Spices,
When the soft Winds display the opening Buds:
—Come, haste, my Soul, to Bed—
La Nu. You can be soft I find, when you wou'd conquer absolutely.
Will. Not infant Angels, not young sighing *Cupids*
Can be more; this ravishing Joy that thou hast promis'd me,

Has form'd my Soul to such a Calm of Love,
It melts e'en at my Eyes.

    La Nu. What have I done? that Promise will undo me.
—This Chamber was prepar'd, and I was dressed,
To give Admittance to another Lover.

    Will. But Love and Fortune both were on my side—Come, come to Bed—consider
nought but Love—[*They going out, one knocks.*]

    La Nu. Hark!

    Beau. [*without.*] By Heav'n I will have entrance.

    La Nu. 'Tis he whom I expect; [124] as thou lov'st Life
And me, retire a little into this Closet.

    Will. Hah, retire!

    La Nu. He's the most fiercely jealous of his Sex,
And Disappointment will enrage him more.

    Will. Death: let him rage whoe'er he be; dost think
I'll hide me from him, and leave thee to his Love?
Shall I, pent up, thro the thin Wainscot hear
Your Sighs, your amorous Words, and sound of Kisses?
No, if thou canst cozen me, do't, but discreetly,
And I shall think thee true:
I have thee now, and when I tamely part
With thee, may Cowards huff and bully me. [*Knocks again.*]

    La Nu. And must I be undone because I love ye?
This is the Mine from whence I fetched my Gold. [125]

    Will. Damn the base Trash: I'll have thee poor, and mine;
'Tis nobler far, to starve with him thou lov'st
Than gay without, and pining all within.

      [*Knocking, breaking the Door,* Willmore *snatches up his Sword.*]

    La Nu. Heavens, here will be murder done—he must not see him. [*As Beaumond
breaks open the Door, she runs away with the Candle, they are by dark,* [126] Beaumond
enters with his Sword drawn.*]

    Will. What art thou?

    Beau. A Man. [*They fight.*]

      [*Enter* Petronella *with Light,* La Nuche *following,* Beaumond *runs to her.*]

Oh thou false Woman, falser than thy Smiles,
Which serve but to delude good-natur'd Man,
And when thou hast him fast, betray'st his Heart!

    Will. Beaumond!

    Beau. Willmore! Is it with thee I must tug for Empire? For I lay claim to all this
World of Beauty. [*Takes* La Nuche, *looking with scorn on* Willmore.]

    La Nu. Heavens, how got this Ruffian in?

    Will. Hold, hold, dear *Harry*, lay no Hands on her till thou can'st make thy Claim
good.

    Beau. She's mine, by Bargain mine, and that's sufficient.

Will. In Law perhaps, it may for ought I know, but 'tis not so in Love: but thou'rt my Friend, and I'll therefore give thee fair Play—if thou canst win her take her: But a Sword and a Mistress are not to be lost, if a Man can keep 'em.

Beau. I cannot blame thee, thou but acts thy self—
But thou fair Hypocrite, to whom I gave my Heart,
And this exception made of all Mankind,
Why would'st thou, as in Malice to my Love,
Give it the only Wound that cou'd destroy it?

Will. Nay, if thou didst forbid her loving me, I have her sure.

Beau. I yield him many Charms; he's nobly born,
Has Wit, Youth, Courage, all that takes the Heart,
And only wants what pleases Women's Vanity,
Estate, the only good that I can boast:
And that I sacrifice to buy thy Smiles.

La Nu. See, Sir—here's a much fairer Chapman—you may be gone—[*To* Willmore.]

Will. Faith, and so there is, Child, for me, I carry all about me, and that by Heaven is thine: I'll settle all upon thee, but my Sword, and that will buy us Bread. I've two led Horses too, one thou shalt manage, and follow me thro Dangers.

La Nu. A very hopeful comfortable Life;
No, I was made for better Exercises.

Will. Why, everything in its turn, Child, yet a Man's but a Man.

Beau. No more, but if thou valuest her,
Leave her to Ease and Plenty.

Will. Leave her to Love, my Dear; one hour of right-down Love,
Is worth an Age of living dully on:
What is't to be adorn'd [127] and shine with Gold,
Dressed like a God, but never know the Pleasure?
—No, no, I have much finer things in store for thee. [*Hugs her.*]

La Nu. What shall I do?
Here's powerful Interest prostrate at my Feet, [*Pointing to* Beaumond]
Glory, and all than Vanity can boast;
—But there—Love unadorn'd, no covering but his Wings, [*To* Willmore.]
No Wealth, but a full Quiver to do mischiefs,
Laughs at those meaner Trifles—

Beau. Mute as thou art, are not these Minutes mine?
But thou—ah false—hast dealt 'em out already,
With all thy Charms of Love, to this unknown—
Silence and guilty Blushes say thou hast:
He all disorder'd too, loose and undressed,
With Love and Pleasure dancing in his Eyes,
Tell me too plainly how thou hast deceiv'd me.

La Nu. Or if I have not, 'tis a Trick soon done,
And this ungrateful Jealousy wou'd put it in my Head. [*Angrily.*]

Beau. Wou'd! by Heaven, thou hast [128]—he is not to be fool'd,
Or sooth'd into belief of distant Joys,
As easy as I have been: I've lost so kind
An Opportunity, where Night and Silence both
Conspire with Love, had made him rage like Waves

Blown up by Storms:—no more—I know he has
—Oh what, *La Nuche!* robb'd me of all that I
Have languish'd for—

La Nu. If it were so, you should not dare believe it—[*Angrily turns away, he kneels and holds her.*]

Beau. Forgive me; oh so very well I love,
Did I not know that thou hadst been a Whore,
I'd give thee the last proof of Love—and marry thee.

Will. The last indeed [129]—for there's an end of Loving;
Do, marry him, and be curst by all his Family:
Marry him, and ruin him, that he may curse thee too.—But hark ye, Friend, this is not fair; 'tis drawing Sharps on a Man that's only arm'd with the defensive Cudgel, I'm for no such dead doing Arguments; if thou art for me, Child, it must be without the folly, for better for worse; there's a kind of Nonsense in that Vow Fools only swallow.

La Nu. But when I've worn out all my Youth and Beauty, and suffer'd every ill of Poverty, I shall be compell'd to begin the World again without a Stock to set up with. No faith, I'm for a substantial Merchant in Love, who can repay the loss of Time and Beauty; with whom to make one thriving Voyage sets me up forever, and I need never put to Sea again. [Comes to *Beaumond*]

Beau. Nor be expos'd to Storms of Poverty, the *Indies* shall come to thee—See here—this is the Merchandize my Love affords. [*Gives her a Pearl, and Pendants of Diamond.*]

La Nu. Look ye, Sir, will not these Pearls do better round my Neck, than those kind Arms of yours? these Pendants in my Ears, than all the Tales of Love you can whisper there?

Will. So—I am deceiv'd—deal on for Trash—and barter all thy Joys of Life for Baubles—this Night presents me one Adventure more—I'll try thee once again, inconstant Fortune; and if thou fail'st me then—I will forswear thee [*Aside.*] Death, hadst thou lov'd my Friend for his own Value, I had esteem'd thee; but when his Youth and Beauty [130] cou'd not plead, to be the mercenary Conquest of his Presents, was poor, below thy Wit: I cou'd have conquer'd so, but I scorn thee at that rate—my Purse shall never be my Pimp—Farewell, *Harry.*

Beau. Thou'st sham'd me out of Folly—stay—

Will. Faith—I have an Assignation with a Woman—a Woman Friend! young as the infant-day, and sweet as Roses e'er the Morning Sun have kiss'd their Dew away. She will not ask me Money neither.

La Nu. Hah! stay—[*Holds him, and looks on him.*]

Beau. She loves him, and her Eyes betray her Heart.

Will. I am not for your turn, Child—Death, I shall lose my Mistress fooling here—I must be gone. [*She holds him, he shakes his Head and sings.*]

> No, no, I will not hire your Bed,
> Nor Tenant to your Favors be;
> I will not farm your White and Red,
> You shall not let your Love to me:
> I court a Mistress—not a Landlady. [bis.] [131]

Beau. He's in the right; and shall I waste my Youth and powerful Fortune on one who all this while has jilted me, seeing I was a lavish loving Fool?—No—this Soul and Body shall not be divided—[*Gives her to* Willmore.]

Will. I am so much thy Friend, another time I might be drawn to take a bad Bargain off thy Hands—but I have other Business at present: wo't do a kind thing, *Harry,*—lend me thy Aid to carry off my Woman tonight? 'tis hard by in the Piazza, perhaps we may find Resistance.

Beau. Myself and Sword are yours. I have a Chair waits below too, may do you Service.

Will. I thank ye—Madam—your Servant.

La Nu. Left by both! [132]

Beau. You see our Affairs are pressing. [*Bows, and smiles carelessly. Exit* Willmore *singing, and* Beaumond] [133]

La Nu. Gone! where's all your Power, ye poor deluded Eyes? Curse on your feeble Fires, that cannot warm a Heart which every common Beauty kindles. Oh—he is gone forever.

[*Enter* Petronella.]

Pet. Yes, he is gone, to your eternal Ruin: not all the Race of Men cou'd have produc'd so bountiful and credulous a Fool.

La Nu. No, never; fetch him back, my *Petronella*: Bring me my wild Inconstant, or I die—[*Puts her out.*]

Pet. The Devil fetch him back for *Petronella*, is't he you mean? you've had too much of him; a Curse upon him, he'as ruin'd you.

La Nu. He has, he shall, he must complete my ruin.

Pet. She raves, the Rogue has given her a *Spanish* Philtre.

La Nu. My Coach, my Veil—or let 'em all alone; undressed thus loosely to the Winds commit me to darkness, and no Guide but pitying *Cupid.* [*Going out,* Petronella *holds her.*]

Pet. What, are you mad?

La Nu. As Winds let loose, or Storms when they rage high. [*Goes out.*]

Pet. She's lost, and I'll shift for myself, seize all her Money and Jewels, of which I have the Keys; and if Seignior Mountebank keeps his Word, be transform'd to Youth and Beauty again, and undo this *La Nuche* at her own Trade—[*Goes in.*]

Scene II. *The Street.*

[*Enter* Willmore, Beaumond, *Chair following.*]

Will. Set down the Chair; you're now within call, I'll to the Garden-Door, and see if any Lady Bright appear—Dear *Beaumond,* stay here a minute, and if I find occasion, I'll give you the Word.

Beau. 'Tis hard by my Lodgings; if you want Conveniences, I have the Key of the Back-way through the Garden, whither you may carry your Mistress. *Willmore* I thank thee—let me first secure my Woman. [*Goes out.*]

Beau. I thought I'd lov'd this false, this jilting Fair, even above my Friendship; but I find I can forgive this Rogue, tho I am sure he has rob'd me of my Joys.

[*Enter* Ariadne *with a Casket of Jewels.*]

Aria. Not yet! a Devil on him, he's Dear-hearting it with some other kind Damsel—Faith, 'tis most wickedly done of me to venture my Body with a mad unknown Fellow. Thus a little more Delay will put me into a serious Consideration, and I shall e'en go home again, sleep and be sober. [*She walks about.*]

Beau. Hah, a Woman! Perhaps the same he looks for—I'll counterfeit his Voice and try my Chance—Fortune may set us even.

Aria. Hah, is not that a Man? Yes—and a Chair waiting. [*She peeps.*]

Beau. Who's there?

Aria. A Maid.

Beau. A Miracle—Oh art thou come, Child?

Aria. 'Tis he, you are a civil Captain, are you not, to make a longing Maid expect thus? What Woman has detain'd you?

Beau. Faith, my Dear, tho Flesh and Blood be frail, yet the dear Hopes of thee has made me hold out with a Herculean Courage—Stay, where shall I carry her? not to my own Apartment; *Ariadne* may surprise me: I'll to the Mountebank here i'th' Piazza, he has a Cure for all things, even for longing Love, and for a Pistole or two will do Reason.—Hah, Company: Here, step into this Chair. [*She goes in, they go off just as* Willmore *enters.*]

Will. Hum, a Woman of Quality and jilt me—Egad, that's strange now—Well, who shall a Man trust in this wicked World?

[*Enter* La Nuche *as before.*]

La Nu. This should be he, he saunters about like an expecting Lover. [Willmore *peeping and approaching.*]

Will. By this Light a Woman, if she be the right—but right or wrong so she be Feminine: harkye, Child, I fancy thee some kind thing that belongs to me.

La Nu. Who are you? [*In a low tone.*]

Will. A wandering Lover that has lost his Heart, and I have shrewd Guess 'tis in thy dear Bosom, Child.

La Nu. Oh you're a pretty Lover, a Woman's like to have a sweet time on't, if you're always so tedious.

Will. By yon bright Star-light, Child, I walk'd here in short turns like a Sentinel, all this live-long Evening, and was just going (Gad forgive me) to kill myself.

La Nu. I rather think some Beauty has detain'd you: Have you not seen *La Nuche?*

Will. La Nuche!—Why, she's a Whore—I hope you take me for a civiller Person, than to throw myself away on Whores—No, Child, I lie with none but honest Women I: but no disputing now, come—to my Lodging, my dear—here's a Chair waits hard by. [*Exeunt.*]

Scene III. *Willmore's Lodging.*

[*Enter* Harlequin *with* Fetherfool's *Clothes on his Shoulder, leading him halting by one Hand,* Blunt *(drunk) by the other in the dark;* [134] Fetherfool *bloody, his Coat put over his Shoulders.*]

Feth. Peano, Peano, Seignior, gently, good *Edward*—for I'll not halt before a Cripple; I have lost a great part of my agil Faculties.

Blunt. Ah, see the Inconstancy of fickle Fortune, *Nicholas*—A Man today, and beaten tomorrow: but take comfort, there's many a proper fellow has been robb'd and beaten on this Highway of whoring.

Feth. Ay, *Ned*, thou speak'st by woful Experience—but that I should miscarry after thy wholesome Documents—but we are all mortal, as thou say'st, *Ned*—Would I had never crossed the Ferry from *Croydon*; a few such Nights as these wou'd learn a Man Experience enough to be a Wizard, if he have but the ill luck to escape hanging.

Blunt. 'Dsheartlikins, I wonder in what Country our kinder Stars rule: In *England* plunder'd, sequester'd, imprison'd and banish'd; in *France*, starv'd, walking like the Sign of the naked Boy, with *Plymouth* Cloaks [p. 198] in our Hands; in *Italy* and *Spain* robb'd, beaten, and thrown out at Windows.

Feth. Well, how happy am I, in having so true a Friend to condole me in Affliction— [*Weeps.*] I am oblig'd to Seignior *Harlequin* too, for bringing me hither to the Mountebank's, where I shall not only conceal this Catastrophe from those fortunate Rogues our Comrades, but procure a little Album Græcum [p. 199] for my Backside. Come, Seignior, my Clothes—but, Seignior—*un Portavera Poco* [135] *palanca.* [*Dresses himself.*]

Harl. Seignior.

Feth. Entende vos Signoria Englesa?

Harl. Em Poco, em Poco, Seignior.

Feth. Per quelq arts, did your Seigniorship escape Cudgeling?

Harl. La art de transformatio.

Feth. Transformatio—Why, wert thou not born a Man?

Harl. No, Seignior, *un vieule Femme.*

Feth. How, born an old Woman?

Blunt. Good Lord! born an old Woman! And so by transformation became invulnerable.

Feth. Ay—in—invulnerable—what would I give to be invulnerable? and egad, I am almost weary of being a Man, and subject to beating: wou'd I were a Woman, a Man has but an ill time on't: if he has a mind to a Wench, the making Love is so plaguy tedious— then paying is to my Soul insupportable. But to be a Woman, to be courted with Presents, and have both the Pleasure and the Profit—to be without a Beard, and sing a fine Treble—and squeak if the Men but kiss me—'twere fine—and what's better, I am sure never to be beaten again.

Blunt. Pox on't, do not use an old Friend so scurvily; consider the Misery thou'lt endure to have the Heart and Mind of a jilting Whore possess thee: What a Fit of the Devil must he suffer who acts her Part from fourteen to fourscore! No, 'tis resolv'd thou remain *Nicholas Fetherfool* still, shalt marry the Monster, and laugh at Fortune.

Feth. 'Tis true, should I turn Whore to the Disgrace of my Family—what would the World say? who wou'd have thought it, cries one? I cou'd never have believ'd it, cries another. No, as thou say'st, I'll remain as I am—marry and live honestly.

Blunt. Well resolv'd, I'll leave you, for I was just going to serenade my Fairy Queen, when I met thee at the Door—some Deeds of Gallantry must be perform'd, Seignior, *Bonus Nochus.* [Exit *Blunt.*]

[*Enter* Shift *with Light.*]

Feth. Hah, a Light, undone!

Harl. Patientia, Patientia, Seignior.

Shift. Where the Devil can this Rogue *Hunt* be? Just now all things are ready for marrying these two Monsters; they wait, the House is hushed, and in the lucky Minute to have him out of the way: sure the Devil owes me a spite. [Runs against *Harlequin*, puts out his Candle.]

Harl. Qui est là? [136]

Shift. 'Tis *Harlequin*: Pox on't, is't you?

Harl. Peace, here's *Fetherfool*, I'll secure him, whilst you go about your Affair. [*Exit* Shift.]

Feth. Oh, I hear a Noise, dear *Harlequin* secure me; if I am discover'd [137] I am undone—hold, hold—here's a Door—[*They both go in.*]

[*Scene changes to a Chamber, discovers the* She-Giant *asleep in a great Chair.*]
[*Enter* Fetherfool *and* Harlequin.]

Feth. [138] Hah—my Lady Monster! have I to avoid *Scylla* run upon *Carybdis?*—hah, she sleeps; now wou'd some magnanimous Lover make good Use of this Opportunity, take Fortune by the Fore-lock, put her to't, and make sure Work—but Egad, he must have a better Heart, or a better Mistress than I.

Harl. Try your Strength, I'll be civil and leave you. [*In* Italian *he still speaks.*]

Feth. Excuse me, Seignior, I should crackle like a wicker Bottle in her Arms—no, Seignior, there's no venturing without a Grate between us: the Devil wou'd not give her due Benevolence—No, when I'm marry'd, I'll e'en show her a fair pair of Heels, her Portion will pay Postage—But what if the Giant should carry her? that's to be fear'd, then I have cock'd and dressed, and fed, and ventur'd all this while for nothing.

Harl. Faith, Seignior, if I were you, I wou'd make sure of something, see how rich she is in Gems.

Feth. Right, as thou say'st, I ought to make sure of something, and she is rich in Gems: How amiable looks that Neck with that delicious row of Pearls about it.

Harl. She sleeps.

Feth. Ay, she sleeps as 'twere her last. What if I made bold to unrig her? So if I miss the Lady, I have at least my Charges paid: what vigorous Lover can resist her Charms?—[*Looks on her.*]

But shou'd she wake and miss it, and find it about me, I shou'd be hang'd—[*Turns away.*]—So then, I lose my Lady too—but Flesh and Blood cannot resist—What if I left the Town? then I lose my Lady still; and who wou'd lose a Hog for the rest of the Proverb?—And yet a Bird in Hand, Friend *Nicholas*—Yet sweet Meat may have sour Sauce—And yet refuse when Fortune offers—Yet Honesty's a Jewel—But a Pox upon Pride, when Folks go naked—

Harl. Well said. [*Encouraging him by Signs.*]

Feth. Ay—I'll do't—but what Remedy now against Discovery and Restitution?

Harl. Oh, Sir, take no care, you shall—swallow 'em.

Feth. How, swallow 'em! I shall ne'er be able to do't.

Harl. I'll show you, Seignior, 'tis easy.

Feth. 'Gad that may be, 'twere excellent if I cou'd do't; but first—by your leave. [*Unties the Necklace, breaks the String, and* Harlequin *swallows one to show him.*]

Harl. Look ye, that's all—

Feth. Hold, hold, Seignior, an you be so nimble, I shall pay dear for my Learning—let me see—Friend *Nicholas*, thou hast swallow'd many a Pill for the Disease of the Body, let's see what thou canst perform for that of the Purse. [*Swallows 'em.*]—so—a comfortable business this—three or four thousand pound in Cordial-Pearl: 'Sbud, *Mark Anthony* was never so treated by his *Egyptian* Crocodile—hah, what noise is that?

Harl. Operator, Operator, Seignior.

Feth. How, an Operator! why, what the Devil makes he here? some Plot upon my Lady's Chastity; were I given to be jealous now, Danger wou'd ensue—Oh, he's entering, I would not be seen for all the World. Oh, some place of Refuge—[*Looking about.*]

Harl. I know of none.

Feth. Hah, what's this—a Clock Case?

Harl. Good, good—look you, Sir, do you do thus, and 'tis impossible to discover ye.

[*Goes into the Case, and shows him how to stand; then* Fetherfool *goes in, pulls off his Periwig, his Head out, turning for the Minutes o'th' top: his Hand out, and his Fingers pointing to a Figure.*]

[*Enter* Shift *and* Hunt.]

Feth. Oh Heaven, he's here.

Shift. See where she sleeps; get you about your business, see your own little Marmoset and the Priest be ready, that we may marry and consummate before Day; and in the Morning our Friends shall see us abed together, give us the good morrow, and the Work's done. [*Exit* Hunt.]

Feth. Oh Traitor to my Bed, what a Hellish Plot's here discover'd! [Shift *wakes the* Giant.]

Giant. Oh, are you come, my Sweetest?

Feth. Hah, the Mistress of my Bosom false too! ah, who wou'd trust faithless Beauty—oh that I durst speak.

Shift. Come let's away, your Uncle and the rest of the House are fast asleep, let's away e'er the two Fools, Blunt and Fetherfool, arrive.

Giant. Hang 'em, Pigeon-hearted Slaves—

Shift. A Clock—let's see what hour 'tis—[*Lifts up the Light to see,* Fetherfool *blows it out.*]—How! betray'd—I'll kill the Villain. [*Draws.*]

Feth. Say you so, then 'tis time for me to uncase.

Shift. Have you your Lovers hid? [*Gets out, all groping in the dark,* Fetherfool *gets the* Giant *by the Hand.*]

Giant. Softly, or we're undone; give me your Hand, and be undeceiv'd.

Feth. 'Tis she, now shall I be reveng'd. [*Leads her out.*]

Shift. What, gone! Death, has this Monster got the Arts of Woman? [Harlequin *meets him in the dark, and plays tricks with him.*]

[*Exit all.*] [139]
[*Enter* Willmore *and* La Nuche *by dark.*]

Will. Now we are safe and free, let's in, my Soul, and gratefully first sacrifice to Love, then to the Gods of Mirth and Wine, my Dear. [*Exit passing over the Stage.*]

[*Enter* Blunt *with* Petronella, *embracing her, his Sword in his Hand, and a Box of* *Jewels.*]

Pet. I was damnably afraid I was pursu'd. [*Aside.*]

Blunt. Something in the Fray I've got, pray Heaven it prove a Prize, after my cursed ill luck of losing my Lady Dwarf: Why do you tremble, fair one?—you're in the Hands of an honest Gentleman, Adshartlikins.

Pet. Alas, Sir, just as I approach! Seignior Doctor's Door, to have myself surrounded with naked Weapons, then to drop with the fear my Casket of Jewels, which had not you by chance stumbled on and taken up, I had lost a hundred thousand Crowns with it.

Blunt. Ha um—a hundred thousand Crowns—a pretty trifling Sum—I'll many her out of hand. [*Aside.*] [140]

Pet. This is an *Englishman*, of a dull honest Nation, and might be manag'd to advantage, were but I transform'd now. [*Aside.*] I hope you are a Man of Honor; Sir, I am a Virgin, fled from the rage of an incens'd Brother; cou'd you but secure me with my Treasure, I wou'd be devoted yours.

Blunt. Secure thee! by this Light, sweet Soul, I'll marry thee;—*Belvile's* Lady ran just so away with him—this must be a Prize—[*Aside.*] But hark—prithee, my Dear, step in a little, I'll keep my good Fortune to myself.

Pet. See what trust I repose in your Hands, those Jewels, Sir.

Blunt. So—there can be no jilting here, I am secur'd from being cozen'd however. [*Exit* Petronella.]

[*Enter* Fetherfool.]

Feth. A Pox on all Fools, I say, and a double Pox on all fighting Fools; just when I had miraculously got my Monster by a mistake in the dark, convey'd her out, and within a moment of marrying her, to have my Friend set upon me, and occasion my losing her, was a Catastrophe which none but thy termagant Courage (which never did any Man good) cou'd have procur'd.

Blunt. 'Dshartlikins, I cou'd kill myself.

Feth. To fight away a couple of such hopeful Monsters, and two Millions—'owns, was ever Valour so improvident?

Blunt. Your fighting made me mistake: for who the Pox wou'd have look'd for *Nicholas Fetherfool* in the person of a Hero?

Feth. Fight, 'Sbud, a Million of Money wou'd have provok'd a Bully; besides, I took you for the damn'd Rogue my Rival.

Blunt. Just as I had finish'd my Serenade, and had put up my Pipes to be gone, out stalk'd me your two-handed Lady, with a Man at her Girdle like a bunch of Keys, whom I taking for nothing less than someone who had some foul design upon the Gentlewoman, like a true Knight-Errant, did my best to rescue her.

Feth. Yes, yes, I feel you did, a Pox of your heavy hand.

Blunt. So whilst we two were lovingly cuffing each other, comes the Rival, I suppose, and carries off the Prize.

Feth. Who must be Seignior *Lucifer* himself, he cou'd never have vanish'd with that Celerity else with such a Carriage—But come, all we have to do is to raise the Mountebank and the Guardian, pursue the Rogues, have 'em hang'd by Law, for a Rape, and Theft, and then we stand fair again.

Blunt. Faith, you may, if you please, but Fortune has provided otherwise for me. [*Aside.*]

[*Exit* Blunt *and* Fetherfool.]
[Enter *Beaumond* and *Ariadne.*]

Beau. Sure none lives here, or Thieves are broken in, the Doors are all left open.

Aria. Pray Heaven this Stranger prove but honest now. [*Aside.*]

Beau. Now, my dear Creature, everything conspires to make us happy, let us not defer it.

Aria. Hold, dear Captain, I yield but on Conditions, which are these—I give you up a Maid of Youth and Beauty, ten thousand Pound in ready Jewels here—three times the value in Estate to come, of which here be the Writings, you delivering me a handsome proper fellow, Heart-whole and sound, that's all—your Name I ask not till the Priest declare it, who is to seal the Bargain. I cannot deceive, for I let you know I am Daughter-in-law to the *English* Ambassador.

Beau. Ariadne!—How vain is all [141] Man's Industry and Care
To make himself accomplish'd;
When the gay fluttering Fool, or the half-witted rough unmanner'd Brute,
Who in plain terms comes right down to the business,
Out-rivals him in all his Love and Fortunes. [*Aside.*]

Aria. Methinks you cool upon't, Captain.

Beau. Yes, *Ariadne.*

Aria. Beaumond!

Beau. Oh what a World of Time have I misspent for want of being a Blockhead—
'Sdeath and Hell,
Wou'd I had been some brawny ruffling Fool,
Some forward impudent unthinking Sloven,
A Woman's Tool; for all besides unmanageable.
Come, swear that all this while you thought 'twas I.
The Devil has taught ye Tricks to bring your Falsehood off.

Aria. Know 'twas you! no, Faith, I took you for as errant a right-down Captain as ever Woman wished for; and 'twas uncivil egad, to undeceive me, I tell you that now.

[*Enter* Willmore *and* La Nuche *by dark.*]

Will. Thou art all Charms, a Heaven of Sweets all over, plump smooth round Limbs, small rising Breasts, a Bosom soft and panting—I long to wound each Sense. Lights there—who waits?—there yet remains a Pleasure unpossest, the sight of that dear Face—Lights there—where are my Vermin? [Exit *Willmore.*]

Aria. My Captain with a Woman—and is it so—

[*Enter* Willmore *with Lights, sees* Ariadne, *and goes to her.*]

Will. By Heaven, a glorious Beauty! now a Blessing on thee for showing me so dear a Face—Come, Child, let's retire and begin where we left off.

La Nu. A Woman!

Aria. Where we left off! pray, where was that, good Captain?

Will. Within upon the Bed, Child—come—I'll show thee.

Beau. Hold, Sir.

Will. Beaumond! come fit to celebrate my Happiness; ah such a Woman-friend!

Beau. Do ye know her?

Will. All o'er, to be the softest sweetest Creature—

Beau. I mean, do ye know who she is?

Will. Nor care; 'tis the last Question I ever ask a fine Woman.

Beau. And you are sure you are thus well acquainted.

Will. I cannot boast of much acquaintance—but I have plucked a Rose from her Bosom—or so—and given it her again—we've past the hour of the Berjere together, that's all—

Beau. And do you know—this Lady is my—Wife? [*Draw.*]

Will. Hah! hum, hum, hum, hum—[*Turns and sings, sees* La Nuche, *and returns quick with an uneasy Grimace.*]

Beau. Did you not hear me? Draw.

Will. Draw, Sir—what on my Friend?

Beau. On your Cuckold, Sir, for so you've doubly made me: Draw, or I'll kill thee—[*Passes at him, he fences with his Hat,* La Nuche *holds* Beaumond]

Will. Hold, prithee hold.

La Nu. Put up your Sword, this Lady's innocent, at least in what concerns this Evening's business; I own—with Pride I own I am the Woman that pleas'd so well tonight.

Will. La Nuche! kind Soul to bring me off with so handsome a lye: How lucky 'twas she happen'd to be here!

Beau. False as thou art, why shou'd I credit thee?

La Nu. By Heaven, 'tis true, I will not lose the glory on't.

Will. Oh the dear perjur'd Creature, how I love thee for this dear lying Virtue—Harkye, Child, hast thou nothing to say for thy self, to help us out withal?—[*To* Ariadne *aside.*]

Aria. I! I renounce ye—false Man.

Beau. Yes, yes, I know she's innocent of this, for which I owe no thanks to either of you, but to myself who mistook her in the dark.

La Nu. And you it seems mistook me for this Lady; I favor'd your Design to gain your Heart, for I was told, that if this Night I lost you, I shou'd never regain you: now I am yours, and o'er the habitable World will follow you, and live and starve by turns, as Fortune pleases.

Will. Nay, by this Light, Child, I knew when once thou'dst try'd me, thou'dst ne'er part with me—give me thy Hand, no Poverty shall part us. [*Kisses her.*]—so—now here's a Bargain made without the formal Foppery of Marriage.

La Nu. Nay, faith Captain, she that will not take thy word as soon as the Parson's of the Parish, deserves not the Blessing.

Will. Thou art reform'd, and I adore the Change.

[*Enter the* Guardian, Blunt, *and* Fetherfool.]

Guar. My Nieces stol'n, and by a couple of the Seignior's Men! the Seignior fled too! undone, undone!

Will. Hah, now's my Cue, I must finish this Jest. [*Goes out.*]

[*Enter* Shift *and* Giant, Hunt *and* Dwarf.]

Guar. Oh impudence, my Nieces, and the Villains with 'em! I charge ye, Gentlemen, to lay hold on 'em.

Dwarf. For what, good Uncle, for being so courageous to marry us?

Guar. How, married to Rogues, Rascals, *John Potages!* [142]

Blunt. Who the Devil wou'd have look'd for jilting in such Hobgoblins?

Feth. And hast thou deceiv'd me, thou foul filthy Synagogue? [143]

[*Enter* Willmore *like a Mountebank as before.*]

Blunt. The Mountebank! oh thou cheating Quack, thou sophisticated adulterated Villain.

Feth. Thou cozening, lying, Fortune-telling, Fee taking Rascal.

Blunt. Thou juggling, conjuring, canting Rogue!

Will. What's the matter, Gentlemen?

Blunt. Hast thou the Impudence to ask, who took my Money to marry me to this ill-favor'd Baboon?

Feth. And me to this foul filthy o'ergrown Chronicle?

Blunt. And hast suffered Rogues, thy Servants, to marry 'em: Sirrah, I will beat thee past Cure of all thy hard-nam'd Drugs, thy *Guzman Medicines.* [p. 209]

Feth. Nay, I'll peach him in the Inquisition for a Wizard, and have him hang'd for a Witch.

Shift. Sir, we are Gentlemen, and you shall have the thirds of their Portion, what wou'd you more? [*Aside to the* Guardian.] Look ye, Sir. [*Pulls off their Disguise.*]

Blunt. Hunt!

Feth. Shift! We are betray'd: all will out to the Captain.

Will. He shall know no more of it than he does already for me, Gentlemen. [*Pulls off his Disguise.*]

Blunt. Willmore!

Feth. Ay, ay, 'tis he.

Blunt. Draw, Sir—you know me—

Will.—For one that 'tis impossible to cozen. [*All laugh.*]

Beau. Have a care, Sir, we are all for the Captain.

Feth. As for that, Sir, we fear ye not, d'ye see, [144] were you *Hercules* and all his Myrmidons. [145] [*Draws, but gets behind.*]

Will. Fools, put up your Swords, Fools, and do not publish the Jest; your Money you shall have again, on condition you never pretend to be wiser than your other Men, [146] but modestly believe you may be cozen'd as well as your Neighbours. [*The* Guardian *talking with* Hunt *and* Shift *and* Giant *this while.*]

Feth. La you, *Ned,* why shou'd Friends fall out?

Blunt. Cozen'd! it may be not, Sir; for look ye, Sir, the *Essex* Fool, the cozen'd dull Rogue can show Moveables or so—nay, they are right too—[*Shows his Jewels.*] This is no *Naples* Adventure, Gentlemen, no Copper Chains; [p. 209] all substantial Diamonds, Pearls and Rubies—[Willmore *takes the Casket, and looks in it.*]

La Nu. Hah, do not I know that Casket, and those Jewels!

Feth. How the Pox came this Rogue by these?

Will. Hum, *Edward*, I confess you have redeem'd your Reputation, and shall hereafter pass for a Wit—by what good fortune came you by this Treasure?—what Lady—

Blunt. Lady, Sir! alas no, I'm a Fool, a Country Fop, an Ass, I; but that you may perceive your selves mistaken, Gentlemen, this is but an earnest of what's to come, a small token of remembrance, or so—and yet I have no Charms, I; the fine Captain has all the Wit and Beauty—but thou'rt my Friend, and I'll impart. [Brings out *Petronella* veil'd.]

[*Enter* Aurelia *and* Sancho.]

Aur. Hither we trac'd her, and see she's yonder.

Sancho. Sir, in the King's Name lay hold of this old Cheat, she has this Night robb'd our *Patrona* of a hundred thousand Crowns in Money and Jewels.

Blunt. Hah! [*Gets from her.*] [147]

La Nu. You are mistaken, Friend *Sancho*, she only seiz'd 'em for my use, and has deliver'd 'em in trust to my Friend the Captain.

Pet. Hah, *La Nuche!*

Blunt. How! cozen'd again!

Will. Look ye, Sir, she's so beautiful, you need no Portion, that alone's sufficient for Wit.

Feth. Much good may do you with your rich Lady, *Edward.*

Blunt. Death, this Fool laugh at me too—well, I am an errant right-down Loggerhead, a dull conceited cozen'd silly Fool; and he that ever takes me for any other, 'Dshartlikins, I'll beat him. I forgive you all, and will henceforth be good-natur'd; wo't borrow any Money? Pox on't, I'll lend as far as e'er 'twill go, for I am now reclaim'd.

Guar. Here is a Necklace of Pearl lost, which, Sir, I lay to your Charge. [*To* Fetherfool.]

Feth. Hum, I was bewitched I did not rub off with it when it was mine—who, I? if e'er I saw a Necklace of Pearl, I wish 'twere in my Belly.

Blunt. How a Necklace! unconscionable Rogue, not to let me share: well, there is no Friendship in the World; I hope they'll hang him.

Shift. He'll ne'er confess without the Rack—come, we'll toss him in a Blanket.

Feth. Hah, toss me in a Blanket, that will turn my Stomach most villainously, and I shall disembogue [p. 211] and discover all.

Shift. Come, come, the Blanket. [*They lay hold on him.*] [148]

Feth. Hold, hold, I do confess, I do confess—

Shift. Restore, and have your Pardon.

Feth. That is not in Nature at present, for Gentlemen, I have eat 'em.

Shift. 'Sdeath, I'll dissect ye. [*Goes to draw.*]

Will. Let me redeem him; here Boy, take him to my Chamber, and let the Doctor glister him soundly, and I'll warrant you your Pearl again.

Feth. If this be the end of travelling, I'll e'en to old *England* again, take the Covenant, get a Sequestrator's Place, grow rich, and defy all Cavaliering.

Beau. 'Tis Morning, let's home, *Ariadne*, and try, if possible, to love so well to be content to marry; if we find that amendment in our Hearts, to say we dare believe and trust each other, then let it be a Match.

Aria. With all my Heart.

Will. You have a hankering after Marriage still, but I am for Love and Gallantry.

So tho by several ways we gain our End,
Love still, like Death, does to one Center tend.

EPILOGUE
Spoken by Mrs. *BARRY*.

POETS are Kings of Wit, and you appear
A Parliament, by Play-Bill, summon'd here; [p. 212]
When e'er in want, to you for aid they fly,
And a new Play's the Speech that begs supply:
But now—
The scanted Tribute is so slowly paid,
Our Poets must find out another Trade;
They've tried all ways th' insatiate Clan to please,
Have parted with their old Prerogatives,
Their Birth-right Satiring, and their just pretence
Of judging even their own Wit and Sense;
And write against their Consciences, to show
How dull they can be to comply with you.
They've flatter'd all the Mutineers i'th' Nation,
Grosser than e'er was done in Dedication;
Pleas'd your sick Palates with Fantastic Wit,
Such as was ne'er a treat before to th' Pit;
Giants, fat Cardinals, Pope Joans *and Fryers,*
To entertain Right Worshipfuls and Squires:
Who laugh and cry Ads Nigs, 'tis woundy good,
When the fuger's all the Jest that's understood.
And yet you'll come but once, unless by stealth,
Except the Author be for Commonwealth;
Then half Crown more you nobly throw away, [149]
And tho my Lady seldom see a Play,
She, with her eldest Daughter, shall be boxed that day.
Then Prologue comes, Ads-lightikins, cries Sir John,
You shall hear notable Conceits anon:
How neatly, Sir, he'll bob the Court and French *King,*
And tickle away—you know who—for Wenching.
All this won't do, [150] *they e'en may spare their Speeches,*
For all their greasing [p. 213] *will not buy 'em Britches;*
To get a penny new found ways must take,
As forming Popes, and Squibs and Crackers make.
In Coffee-Houses some their talent vent,
Rail for the Cause against the Government,
And make a pretty thriving living on't,
For who would let a useful Member want.
Things being brought to this distressed Estate,
'Twere fit you took the matter in Debate.
There was a time, when Loyally by you,
True Wit and Sense received Allegiance due,

Our King of Poets had his Tribute pay'd,
His Peers secured beneath his Laurel's shade.
What Crimes have they committed, they must be
Driven to the last and worst Extremity?
Oh, let it not be said of English *Men,*
Who have to Wit so just and noble been,
They should their Loyal Principles recant,
And let the glorious Monarch of it want.

THE DUTCH LOVER.

ARGUMENT.

Roderigo—the natural son of the great Count d' Olivarez, minister to Philip IV of Spain—was, upon his father's disgrace, given over when very young to the care of a certain Don Ambrosio, and by him brought up as his own child. Ambrosio has one son, Marcel, and two daughters, Hippolita and Cleonte. Marcel, whilst in Flanders, promised Hippolita to his friend Alonzo. This Alonzo is the son of a lady Octavia and Don Manuel. But Manuel's rival in Octavia's love, Alonzo, stole their boy when an infant and brought him up to arms, giving him his own name. Pedro, an old servant, who is cognizant of this, is sworn to secrecy. Alonzo arrives in Madrid purposing to wed Hippolita as he desires to ally himself with so ancient and powerful a family as Ambrosio's. Hippolita, however, having been betrayed by a German named Antonio, has fled, and now resides in a house of pleasure in the town, having assumed the habit of a Venetian courtesan. Alonzo meeting Euphemia, sister to his friend Lovis, becomes enamored of her, and the lady grants him a rendezvous at a house where they will be uninterrupted—it happens this house is the bagnio where Hippolita is secreted. Marcel, on his way to visit Clarinda, whom he loves, recognizes Alonzo and follows him to his rendezvous, Olinda, Euphemia's maid, mistakenly introduces Marcel to her mistress. Euphemia is veiled and Marcel, who has heard that his sister is living in that house, in his turn mistakes the lady for Hippolita, more especially as he meets Antonio there. The two men fight, but Alonzo entering interferes. Antonio escapes, bearing away Hippolita. Euphemia, whom Marcel in a passion of revenge would kill, is soon discovered not to be Hippolita, and the angry brother duly retires from the scene. Alonzo, however, leaving the house is accosted for Marcel by Dormida, Clarinda's maid, who gives him the key to their house. Alonzo enters followed by Marcel who is close on his heels. They jostle and fight in the darkness of the hall within, and Alonzo departs leaving Marcel wounded. Dormida fearing trouble drags Clarinda forth and meeting Alonzo in the street they throw themselves on his honorable protection. A complete stranger, in his dilemma he escorts them to the mansion of Ambrosio, and they chance on Cleonte's chamber. She has just had a visit from Silvio (under which name Roderigo passes), who is burning with passion for her but shrinks from his supposed sister. Cleonte offers the two ladies a refuge and Alonzo retires. With the aid of his friend Lovis he assumes the habit of Haunce van Ezel, a Dutch boor who is contracted to Euphemia, and, as Haunce, courts Lovis' sister with the full approbation of their father Don Carlo. When Haunce himself appears he is greeted with some familiarity as having been at the house before. The Dutch Lover, who has newly arrived, chances on a strife between Antonio and Hippolita and interfering disarms Antonio, wounding him in the face. Cleonte meantime has introduced her guest Clarinda to Silvio, and Marcel seeing them together concludes that his own brother is the man who fought him on the previous night and indeed his favored rival. At once he challenges him and they arrange to have a duel in a grove near the town. Here, however, comes Hippolita disguised in man's attire, awaiting Antonio to whom she has sent a billet signed 'Alonzo'. She retires, whilst Silvio appears, and when he is engaged with Marcel, Alonzo rushes in and parts them. Alonzo avows that it was he who caused the confusion with Clarinda, and arranges to meet Marcel later in another spot. Antonio next arrives and Hippolita, calling herself Alonzo, draws, but Alonzo himself insists on taking up the quarrel. At the clash of steel

Marcel returns and all four fight, Marcel with Hippolita, whom he wounds, Alonzo with Antonio, whom he disarms—Hippolita reveals herself, Alonzo claims her, but Antonio declaring that he is bound to her by sacred vows rescues her from Marcel's vengeance and obtains his forgiveness. All return to Ambrosio's house where they find Cleonte and Clarinda. Explanations ensue, and Marcel is at Clarinda's feet. Pedro, however, who attends Alonzo, recognizes his old fellow-servant, Dormida, duenna to Clarinda, and learning Don Manuel is dead, reveals that Alonzo is Clarinda's brother, also handing over papers left by Don Alonzo the foster-father, which bestow 12,000 crowns a year on his adopted son, Alonzo portions Clarinda and gives her to Marcel. Francisca, woman to Cleonte, informs Silvio that Cleonte will yield to him—Silvio, suddenly revolted, declares he will present himself, but secretly resolves to poinard his sister. Marcel who has overheard the conference, beside himself with rage, dashes on Silvio with dagger drawn and when checked by Ambrosio and the rest who rush in at Francisca's cries makes known the cause of his wrath. Francisca confesses that Cleonte had sent no such message, but herself purposed to take her mistress' place that night and receive Silvio. Ambrosio then reveals the secret of Silvio's birth and gives Cleonte to him, in his joy even taking Hippolita to his arms since Antonio has married her. Alonzo, meanwhile, disguised as Haunce has been united to Euphemia. He is discovered by the arrival on the scene of the real Haunce accompanied by Gload, a foolish tutor. Carlo is soon reconciled to the new bridegroom, whilst Haunce and Gload joining in a masquerade find themselves unexpectedly wedded to Olinda and Dorice, two women attendant on the lady Euphemia.

SOURCE.

Mrs. Behn founded the plot of *The Dutch Lover* upon the stories of Eufemie and Theodore, Don Jame and Frederic, in a pseudo-Spanish novel entitled '*The History of Don Fenise*, a new Romance written in Spanish by Francisco de Las Coveras, And now Englished by a Person of Honor, London, Printed for Humphrey Moseley,' 8vo, 1651. There is of course no such Spanish author as 'the ingenious Don Francisco de las Coveras'. The chief merit of the book is purely bibliographical: it is a very rare volume and difficult to meet with. The Bodleian indeed contains a copy, but it is not to be found in the British Museum library. The somewhat morbid theme of overwhelming passion barred by consanguinity eventually discovered to be false, which is here exemplified in the love of Silvio for Cleonte, occurs more than once in the later Jacobean and Carolan drama. In Beaumont and Fletcher's tragicomedy *A King and no King* (1611: 4to, 1619), we have Arbaces enamored of Panthea, his reputed sister; similar motives are to be found in Arthur Wilson's *The Swizzer* (1631); but in Middleton's *Women beware Women* (circa 1612: 4to, 1657), no contrivance can legitimize the incestuous loves of Hippolito and Isabella, and death is the only solution. In Massinger's *The Unnatural Combat* (1621: 4to, 1639), the demoniac Malefort pursues his daughter Theocrine with the same baleful fires as Francesco Cenci looked on Beatrice, but the height of horror, harrowing the soul with pity and anguish, culminates in Ford's terrible scenes '*Tis Pity She's a Whore* (4to, 1633), so tenderly tragic, so exquisitely beautiful for all their moral perversity, that they remain unequalled outside Shakespeare.

In the Restoration Theatre the theme of consanguinity was originally dealt with no less than three times by Dryden: comically, in *The Spanish Friar* (1681), when Lorenzo—after all the love-brokerage of pursy Father Dominic—discovers Elvira to be his sister: tragically, in *Don Sebastian* (1690), when Sebastian and Almeyda are separated by the disclosures of old Alvarez: sentimentally and romantically, in *Love Triumphant* (1693-4), when Alphonso wins Victoria whom he has long loved, even whilst she was supposed to be his sister. Otway it will be remembered turns the pathetic catastrophe of *The Orphan* (1680), upon a deceit which produces similar though unhappy circumstances. In 1679, *Oedipus*, a joint production of Dryden and Lee, was brought out with great success at the Duke's Theatre, Dorset Gardens.

Unhallowed and incestuous passions again form the plot of *The Fatal Discovery; or, Love in Ruins* (4to, 1698), produced at Drury Lane, a play seemingly derived from *Bandello, Part II*, Novel 35, which coincides with the thirtieth tale of the *Heptameron*. In various forms, however, this legend is to be found in the literature of all countries, and a cognate tradition is even attached to certain districts. *Innocence Distress'd; or, The Royal Penitents*, a tragedy by Robert Gould (ob. 1709), never performed but published by subscription (8vo, 1737), for the benefit of his daughter Hannah, is based on the same story. Gould's work is weak and insipid.

Later in the eighteenth century we have Horace Walpole's *The Mysterious Mother* (8vo, 1768), an unacted drama of extraordinary power and undissipated gloom on the same terrible theme; whilst Shelley's *The Cenci*, published in 1819, which the poet most emphatically intended for the boards, remains a masterpiece of supreme genius.

Wagner in *Die Walküre* shows the irresistible passion of Siegmund and Sieglinde, brother and sister, from whose union sprang the mighty hero Siegfried; and in *Gengangere* (Ghosts), 1881, Ibsen threw, by the sickly craving of the fibreless Oswald Alving for Regina, a lurid light across that awesome tragedy of shadows, Nemesis, and blank despair.

THEATRICAL HISTORY.

The Dutch Lover was produced at the Duke's Theatre, Dorset Garden, in February, 1673, but owing to the manifold disadvantages under which it was put on the stage it did not meet with that success it certainly deserved. It was indeed, to quote the preface, 'hugely injured in the acting.' The performers were anything but word perfect and hopelessly forgot or confused their business, which, more especially in a play of such a type as this romantic comedy so full of busy and complicated detail demanding close and continuous attention, was enough to mystify the audience completely and foredoom the piece to failure. The worst sinner was Haunce himself, who hardly spoke one of his lines but gagged from start to finish. Not unnaturally, Mrs. Behn resented this and avows that she would have trounced him roundly in print except 'de mortuis...' Although the original cast is not given, this detail enables us to fix the representative of Haunce as Angel, a leading comedian, who died in the spring of 1673, his name last appearing as de Boastado in Ravenscroft's *Careless Lovers*.

In addition to these serious detriments the costumes were very poor, especially the disguise of Alonzo as the Hollander, and Haunce's own 'fantastical travelling habit,' dresses on the aptness of which the probability of the intrigue can be made so largely to depend.

Yet another mishap occurred. The epilogue, which had been promised by a friend, did not come to hand, and accordingly the present epilogue was hastily composed. Though containing nothing notably witty or pointed it does not fall below the generality of these productions. Of the prologue we have no means of judging as it was unfortunately lost before it could find its way into print.

Had *The Dutch Lover* received fair treatment from the actors it should surely have commanded no small success in its day. Technically it is well contrived, and exhibits the skill and clever stage-craft of its authoress in a high degree, qualities which have often given a long lease of life to plays of infinitely less merit.

AN EPISTLE TO THE READER. [p. 221]

Good, Sweet, Honey, Sugar-Candied Reader,

Which I think is more than anyone has called you yet, I must have a word or two with you before you do advance into the Treatise; but 'tis not to beg your pardon for diverting you from your affairs, by such an idle Pamphlet as this is, for I presume you have not much to do and therefore are to be obliged to me for keeping you from worse employment, and if you have a better you may get you gone about your business: but if you will misspend your Time, pray lay the fault upon yourself; for I have dealt pretty fairly in the matter, told you in the Title Page what you are to expect within. Indeed, had I hung a sign of the Immortality of the Soul, of the Mystery of Godliness, or of Ecclesiastical Policie, and then had treated you with Indiscerpibility and Essential Spissitude (words, which though I am no competent Judge of, for want of Languages, yet I fancy strongly ought to mean just nothing) with a company of Apocryphal midnight Tales cull'd out of the choicest Insignificant Authors; If I had only proved in Folio that Apollonius was a naughty knave, or had presented you with two or three of the worst principles transcrib'd out of the peremptory and ill-natur'd (though prettily ingenious) Doctor of Malmesbury [p. 221] undigested and ill-manag'd by a silly, saucy, ignorant, impertinent, ill educated Chaplain I were then indeed sufficiently in fault; but having inscrib'd Comedy on the beginning of my Book, you may guess pretty near what penny-worths you are like to have, and ware your money and your time accordingly. I would not yet be understood to lessen the dignity of Plays, for surely they deserve a place among the middle if not the better sort of Books; for I have heard the most of that which bears the name of Learning, and which has abused such quantities of Ink and Paper, and continually employs so many ignorant, unhappy souls for ten, twelve, twenty years in the University (who yet poor wretches think they are doing something all the while) as Logic etc. and several other things (that shall be nameless lest I misspell them) are much more absolutely nothing than the errantest Play that e'er was writ. Take notice, Reader, I do not assert this purely upon my own knowledge, but I think I have known it very fully prov'd, both sides being fairly heard, and even some ingenious opposers of it most abominably baffl'd in the Argument: Some of which I have got so perfectly by rote, that if this were a proper place for it, I am apt to think myself could almost make it clear; and as I would not undervalue Poetry, so neither am I altogether of their judgement who believe no wisdom in the world beyond it. I have often heard indeed (and read) how much the World was anciently oblig'd to it for most of that which they call'd Science, which my want of letters makes me less assured of than others happily may be: but I have heard some wise men say that no considerable part of useful knowledge was this way communicated, and on the other way, that it hath serv'd to propagate so many idle superstitions, as all the benefits it hath or can be guilty of, can never make sufficient amends for; which unaided by the unlucky charms of Poetry, could never have possessed a thinking Creature such as man. However true this is, I am myself well able to affirm that none of all our English

Poets, and least the Dramatique (so I think you call them) can be justly charg'd with too great reformation of men's minds or manners, and for that I may appeal to general experiment, if those who are the most assiduous Disciples of the Stage, do not make the fondest and the lewdest Crew about this Town; for if you should unhappily converse them through the year, you will not find one Dram of sense amongst a Club of them, unless you will allow for such a little Link-Boy's Ribaldry thick larded with unseasonable oaths & impudent defiance of God, and all things serious; and that at such a senseless damn'd unthinking rate, as, if 'twere well distributed, would spoil near half the Apothecaries trade, and save the sober people of the Town the charge of Vomits; And it was smartly said (how prudently I cannot tell) by a late learned Doctor, who, though himself no great asserter of a Deity, (as you'll believe by that which follows) yet was observed to be continually persuading of this sort of men (if I for once may call them so) of the necessity and truth of our Religion; and being ask'd how he came to bestir himself so much this way, made answer that it was because their ignorance and indiscreet debauch made them a scandal to the profession of Atheism. And for their wisdom and design I never knew it reach beyond the invention of some notable expedient, for the speedier ridding them of their Estate, (a devilish clog to Wit and Parts), than other grouling Mortals know, or battering half-a-dozen fair new Windows in a Morning after their debauch, whilst the dull unjantee [p. 222] Rascal they belong to is fast asleep. But I'll proceed no farther in their character, because that miracle of Wit (in spite of Academic frippery) the mighty Echard [p. 222] hath already done it to my satisfaction; and whoever undertakes a Supplement to anything he hath discoursed, had better for their reputation be doing nothing.

Besides this Theme is worn too thread-bare by the whiffling would-be Wits of the Town, and of both the stone-blind-eyes of the Kingdom. And therefore to return to that which I before was speaking of, I will have leave to say that in my judgement the increasing number of our latter Plays have not done much more towards the amending of men's Morals, or their Wit, than hath the frequent Preaching, which this last age hath been pester'd with, (indeed without all Controversy they have done less harm) nor can I once imagine what temptation anyone can have to expect it from them; for sure I am no Play was ever writ with that design. If you consider Tragedy, you'll find their best of Characters unlikely patterns for a wise man to pursue: For he that is the Knight of the Play, no sublunary feats must serve his Dulcinea; for if he can't bestrid the Moon, he'll ne'er make good his business to the end, and if he chance to be offended, he must without considering right or wrong confound all things he meets, and put you half-a-score likely tall fellows into each pocket; and truly if he come not something near this Pitch I think the Tragedy's not worth a farthing; for Plays were certainly intended for the exercising of men's passions not their understandings, and he is infinitely far from wise that will bestow one moment's meditation on such things: And as for Comedy, the finest folks you meet with there are still unfitter for your imitation, for though within a leaf or two of the Prologue, you are told that they are people of Wit, good Humor, good Manners, and all that: yet if the Authors did not kindly add their proper names, you'd never know them by their Characters; for whatsoe'er's the matter, it hath happen'd so spitefully in several Plays, which have been pretty well received of late, that even those persons that were meant to be the ingenious Censors of the Play, have either prov'd the most debauch'd, or most unwitty people in the Company: nor is this error very lamentable, since as I take it Comedy was never meant, either for a converting or a conforming Ordinance: In short, I think a Play the best divertisement that wise men have: but I do also think them nothing so who do discourse as formally about the rules of it, as if 'twere the grand affair of human life. This being my opinion of Plays, I studied only to make this as entertaining as I could, which whether I have been successful in, my gentle Reader, you may for your shilling judge. To tell you my thoughts of it, were to little purpose, for were they very ill, you may be sure I would not have expos'd it; nor did I so till I had first consulted most of those who have a reputation for judgement of this kind; who were at least so civil (if not kind) to it as did encourage me to venture it upon the Stage, and in the Press: Nor did I take their single word for it, but us'd their reasons as a confirmation of my own.

Indeed that day 'twas Acted first, there comes me into the Pit, a long, lither, phlegmatic, white, ill-favor'd, wretched Fop, an Officer in Masquerade newly transported with a Scarf & Feather out of France, a sorry Animal that has nought else to shield it from the uttermost contempt of all mankind, but that respect which we afford to Rats and Toads, which though we do not well allow to live, yet when considered as a part of God's Creation, we make honorable mention of them. A thing, Reader—but no more of such a Smelt: This thing, I tell ye, opening that which serves it for a mouth, out issued such a noise as this to those that sate about it, that they were to expect a woful Play, God damn him, for it was a woman's. Now how this came about I am not sure, but I suppose he brought it piping hot from some who had with him the reputation of a villainous Wit: for Creatures of his size of sense talk without all imagination, such scraps as they pick up from other folks. I would not for a world be taken arguing with such a property as this; but if I thought there were a man of any tolerable parts, who could upon mature deliberation distinguish well his right hand from his left, and justly state the difference between the number of sixteen and two, yet had this prejudice upon him; I would take a little pains to make him know how much he errs. For waving the examination why women having equal education with men, were not as capable of knowledge, of whatsoever sort as well as they: I'll only say as I have touch'd before, that Plays have no great room for that which is men's great advantage over women, that is Learning; We all well know that the immortal Shakespeare's Plays (who was not guilty of much more of this than often falls to women's share) have better pleas'd the World than Johnson's works, though by the way 'tis said that Benjamin was no such Rabbi neither, for I am inform'd that his Learning was but Grammar high; (sufficient indeed to rob poor Sallust of his best orations) and it hath been observ'd that they are apt to admire him most confoundedly, who have just such a scantling of it as he had; and I have seen a man the most severe of Johnson's Sect, sit with his Hat remov'd less than a hair's breadth from one sullen posture for almost three hours at *The Alchemist*; who at that excellent Play of *Harry the Fourth* (which yet I hope is far enough from Farce) hath very hardly kept his Doublet whole; but affectation hath always had a greater share both in the action and discourse of men than truth and judgement have; and for our Modern ones, except our most unimitable Laureat, I dare to say I know of none that write at such a formidable rate, but that a woman may well hope to reach their greatest heights. Then for their musty rules of Unity, and God knows what besides, if they meant anything, they are enough intelligible and as practible by a woman; but really methinks they that disturb their heads with any other rule of Plays besides the making them pleasant, and avoiding of scurrility, might much better be employed in studying how to improve men's too imperfect knowledge of that ancient English Game which hight long Laurence: [p. 224] And if Comedy should be the picture of ridiculous mankind I wonder anyone should think it such a sturdy task, whilst we are furnish'd with such precious Originals as him I lately told you of; if at least that Character do not dwindle into Farce, and so become too mean an entertainment for those persons who are us'd to think. Reader, I have a complaint or two to make to you and I have done; Know then that this Play was hugely injur'd in the Acting, for 'twas done so imperfectly as never any was before, which did more harm to this than it could have done to any of another sort; the Plot being busy (though I think not intricate) and so requiring a continual attention, which being interrupted by the intolerable negligence of some that acted in it, must needs much spoil the beauty on't. My Dutch Lover spoke but little of what I intended for him, but supplied it with a great deal of idle stuff, which I was wholly unacquainted with until I had heard it first from him; so that Jack-pudding ever us'd to do: which though I knew before, I gave him yet the Part, because I knew him so acceptable to most o'th' lighter Periwigs about the Town, and he indeed did vex me so, I could almost be angry: Yet, but Reader, you remember, I suppose, a fusty piece of Latin that has past from hand to hand this thousand years they say (and how much longer I can't tell) in favor of the dead. I intended him a habit much more notably ridiculous, which if ever it be important was so here, for many of the Scenes in the three last Acts depended upon the mistakes of the Colonel for Haunce, which the ill-favor'd likeness of their Habits is suppos'd to cause. Lastly my Epilogue was promis'd me by a Person who had surely made it good, if any, but he failing of his word, deput'd one, who has made it as you see, and to make out your pennyworth you have it here. The Prologue is by misfortune lost. Now, Reader, I have eas'd my mind of all I had to say, and so sans farther compliment, Adieu.

DRAMATIS PERSONÆ.

MEN.

Ambrosio, A Nobleman of *Spain*.
Marcel, His Son.
Silvio, Supposed Bastard Son to *Ambrosio*.
Antonio, A *German* that has debauch'd *Hippolyta*.
Alonzo, A *Flanders* Colonel contracted to *Hippolyta* and newly arriv'd at Madrid.
Lovis, His Friend.
Carlo, Father to *Lovis* and *Euphemia*.
Haunce van Ezel, A Dutch Fop contracted to *Euphemia*, newly arriv'd at *Madrid*.
Gload, His Cash-keeper.
Pedro, An old Servant to *Alonzo*.
Boy, Page to *Marcel*. [151]
Servant to *Carlo*. [151]
A Friar. [151]

WOMEN.

Euphemia, In love with *Alonzo*.
Hippolyta, In love with *Antonio*, Daughter to *Ambrosio*.
Cleonte, In love with *Silvio*, Daughter to *Ambrosio*.
Clarinda, Sister unknown to *Alonzo*, in love with *Marcel*.
Dormida, Her Governess.
Francisca, Woman to *Cleonte*.
Olinda, Maid to *Euphemia*.
Dorice, Maid to *Euphemia*.

Swains, Four Shepherds, Four Nymphs, Dutch Men and Dutch Women. [151]

The Scene, *Madrid*.

THE *DUTCH* LOVER.

ACT I.

Scene I. *A Street.* [152]

[*Enter* Alonzo *and* Lovis *in travelling Habits, attended by* Pedro *and* Gload.]

Lo. Dear *Alonzo!* I shall love a Church the better this Month for giving me a sight of thee, whom I so little expected in this part of the World, and less in so sanctifi'd a Place. What Affair could be powerful enough to draw thee from the kind obliging Ladies of *Brabant?*
Alon. First the sudden Orders of my Prince *Don John*, and next a fair Lady.

Lo. A Lady! Can any of this Country relish with a Man that has been us'd to the Freedom of those of *Bruxels*, from whence I suppose you are now arriv'd?

Alon. This morning I landed, from such a Storm, as set us all to making Vows of Conversion, (upon good Conditions) and that indeed brought me to Church.

Lo. In that very Storm I landed too, but with less Sense of Danger than you, being diverted with a pleasant Fellow that came along with me, and who is design'd to marry a Sister of mine against my Will—And now I think of him, *Gload*, where hast thou left this Master of thine?

Glo. At the Inn, Sir, in as lamentable a Pickle, as if he were still in the Storm; recruiting his emptied Stomach with Brandy, and railing against all Women-kind for your Sister's sake, who has made him undertake this Voyage.

Lo. Well, I'll come to him, go home before. [*Exit* Gload.]

Alon. Prithee what thing is this?

Lo. Why, 'tis the Cashier to this Squire I spoke of, a Man of Business, and as wise as his Master, but the graver Coxcomb of the two. But this Lady, *Alonzo*, who is this Lady thou speak'st of? shall not I know her? We were wont to divide the Spoils of Beauty, as well as those of War between us.

Alon. O but this is no such Prize, thou wouldst hardly share this with the Danger, there's Matrimony in the Case.

Lo. Nay, then keep her to thy self, only let me know who 'tis that can debauch thee to that scandalous way of Life; is she fair? will she recompense the Folly?

Alon. Faith, I know not, I never saw her yet, but 'tis the Sister of *Marcel*, whom we both knew last Summer in *Flanders*, and where he and I contracted such a Friendship, that without other Consideration he promis'd me *Hippolyta*, for that's his Sister's Name.

Lo. But wo't thou really marry her?

Alon. I consider my Advantage in being allied to so considerable a Man as *Ambrosio*, her Father; I being now so unhappy as not to know my Birth or Parents.

Lo. I have often heard of some such thing, but durst not ask the Truth of it.

Alon. 'Tis so, all that I know of myself is, that a *Spanish* Soldier, who brought me up in the Army, dying, confessed I was not his Son, (which till then I believ'd) and at the Age of twelve left me to shift for myself: the Fortune he enrich'd me with, was his Horse and Arms, with a few Documents how to use them, as I had seen him do with good success: This Servant, [*Points to* Pedro] and a Crucifix of Value. And from one Degree to another, I arriv'd to what you knew me, Colonel of the Prince's Regiment, and the Glory of his Favor.

Lo. Honor is the Child of Virtue, and finds an Owner everywhere.

Alon. Oh, Sir, you are a Courtier, and have much the odds of a Soldier in Parleys of this nature: but hither I am come—

Lo. To be undone—Faith, thou look'st ill upon't.

Alon. I confess I am not altogether so brisk as I should have been upon another Occasion; you know, *Lovis*, I have been us'd to Christian [153] Liberty, and hate this formal Courtship. Pox on't, wou'd 'twere over.

Lo. Where all Parties are agreed, there's little need of that; and the Ladies of *Spain*, whatever Gravity they assume, are as ready as any you ever met withal.

Alon. But there's a damn'd Custom that does not at all agree with Men so frank and gay as thou and I; there's a deal of Danger in the Achievement, which some say heightens the Pleasure, but I am of another Opinion.

Pedro. Sir, there is a Female in a Veil has follow'd us ever since we came from Church.

Alon. Some amorous Adventure: See [*Enter* Olinda.] she advances: Prithee retire, there may be danger in it. [*Puts* Lovis *back.*]

Lo. Oh then, I must by no means leave you. [Lovis *advances.*]

Olin. Which of these two shall I chose? [*She looks on both.*]

Sir, you appear a Stranger. [*To* Lovis.]

Alon. We are both so, Lady.

Olin. I shall spoil all, and bring [*She looks again on both.*] the wrong. Sir, you should be a Cavalier, that—

Alon. Would gladly obey your Orders.

Lo. Nay, I find 'tis all one to you which you chose, so you have one of us: but would not both do better?

Olin. No, Sir, my Commission's but to one.

Alon. Fix and proceed then, let me be the Man.

Olin. What shall I do? they are both well: [*Aside.*]

but I'll e'en chose, as 'twere, for myself; and hang me if I know which that shall be, [*looks on both.*] Sir, there is a Lady of Quality and Beauty, who guessing you to be Men of Honor, has sent me to one of you.

Alon. Me, I am sure.

Lo. Me, me, he's engag'd already.

Alon. That's foul Play, *Lovis.*

Alon. Well, I must have but one, and therefore I'll wink and chose.

Lo. I'll not trust blind Fortune.

Alon. Prithee, *Lovis*, let thee and I agree upon the matter, and I find the Lady will be reasonable; cross or pile who shall go.

Lo. Go, Sir, whither?

Alon. To the Lady that—

Lo. Sent for neither of us that I can hear of yet.

Alon. You will not hear me out, but I'll end the Difference by choosing you, Sir; and if you'll follow me [*To* Alonzo.] at a Distance, I will conduct you where this Lady is.

Alon. Fair Guide, march on, I'll follow thee. [*Offers to go.*]

Lo. You are not mad, Sir, 'tis some abuse, and dangerous. [*Pulls him back.*]

Alon. Be not envious of my Happiness: Forbear a Wench, for fear of Danger!

Lo. Have a care, 'tis some Plot. [*Holds him.*] Where did this Lady see us? we are both Strangers in the City.

Alon. No matter where.

Olin. At Church, Sir, just now.

Alon. Ay, ay, at Church, at Church, enough.

Lo. What's her Name?

Alon. Away, thou art fuller of Questions than a Fortune-teller: Come, let's be gone.

Lo. Sure you do not mean to keep your Word, Sir?

Alon. Not keep my Word, *Lovis?* What wicked Life hast thou known me lead, should make thee suspect I should not? When I have made an Interest in her, and find her worth communicating, I will be just upon Honor—Go, go.

Lo. Well, go your ways; if Marriage do not tame you, you are past all Hopes: but pray, Sir, let me see you at my Lodgings, the *Golden Fleece* here at the Gate.

Alon. I'll attend thee here, and tell thee my Adventure: Farewell. [*Exit* Lovis.] *Pedro,* go you and inquire for the House of Don *Ambrosio,* and tell him I will wait on him in the Evening, by that time I shall get myself in Order.

[*Exit* Alonzo *and* Olinda; Pedro *the other way*.]

Scene II. Ambrosio's *House.*

[*Enter* Silvio, *melancholy*.]

Silv. I must remove *Marcel,* for his nice Honor [154]
Will ne'er permit that I should court my Sister;
My Passion will admit of no Restraint,
'Tis grown so violent; and fair *Cleonte's* Charms
Each Day increase to such a killing Number,
That I must speak or die.

[*Enter* Francisca.]

Franc. What, still with folded Arms and down-cast looks?
Silv. Oh *Francisca!*
My Brother's Presence now afflicts me more
Than all my Fears of Cruelty from *Cleonte;*
She is the best, the sweetest, kindest Sister—
Franc. Ay, Sir, but she will never make the kindest Mistress.
Silv. At least she should permit me to adore her,
Were but *Marcel* away.
Hast thou no Stratagem to get him absent?
For I can think of nothing but my Sister. [*Sighs.*]
Franc. I know of one, nor other Remedy for you than loving less.
Silv. Oh, 'tis impossible:
Thou know'st I've tried all ways, made my Addresses
To all the fairest Virgins in *Madrid;*
Nay, and at last fell to the worst Debauchery,
That of frequenting every common House:
But Souls that feed so high on Love as mine,
Must nauseate coarser Diet.
No, I must still love on, [155] and tell her so,
Or I must live no longer.
Franc. That methinks you might do even in the Presence of *Marcel.* A Brother is allow'd to love a Sister.
Silv. But I shall do't in such a way, *Francisca,*
Be so transported, and so passionate,
I shall betray what he will ne'er endure.
And since our other Sister, loose *Hippolyta,* was lost,
He does so guard and watch the fair *Cleonte*—
Franc. Why, quarrel with him, Sir: you know you are so much dearer to my Lord your Father than he is, that should he perceive a Difference between ye, he would soon

dismiss him the House; and 'twere but Reason, Sir, for I am sure Don *Marcel* loves you not.

 Silv. That I excuse, since he the lawful Heir to all my Father's Fortunes, sees it every Day ready to be sacrific'd to me, who can pretend no Title to't, but the unaccountable Love my Father bears me.

 Franc. Can you dissemble, Sir?

 Silv. The worst of any Man, but would endeavor it, If it could any ways advance my Love.

 Franc. Which I must find some way to ruin. [*Aside.*]
Then court his Mistress.

 Silv. The rich *Flavia?*

 Franc. That would not incense him, for her he is to marry; But 'tis the fair *Clarinda* has his Heart.

 Silv. To act a feigned Love, and hide a real one,
Is what I have already try'd in vain.
Even fair *Clarinda* I have courted too,
In hope that way to banish from my Soul
The hopeless Flame *Cleonte* kindled there;
But 'twas a Shame to see how ill I did dissemble.

 Franc. Stay, Sir, here comes *Marcel.* I'll leave you.

[Exit Francisca.]
[Enter Marcel, with a Letter open in his Hand, which he kisses.]

 Mar. Kind Messenger of Love! Thus, thus a thousand times
I bid thee welcome from my fair *Clarinda.*
Thus joyful Bridegrooms, after long Despairs, [156]
Possess the yielding Treasure in their Arms:
Only thus much the happier Lover I,
Who gather all the Sweets of this fair Maid
Without the ceremonious Tie of Marriage;
That tie that does but nauseate the Delight,
Be far from happy Lovers; we'll embrace
And unconfin'd and free as whispering Air,
That mingles wantonly with spreading Flowers.

 Silv. What's all this?

 Mar. Silvio, the Victory's won.
The Heart that nicely stood it out so long,
Now yields upon Conditions.

 Silv. What Victory? or what Heart?

 Mar. I am all Rapture, cannot speak it out;
My Senses have carous'd too much of Joy; [157]
And like young Drunkards, proud of their new try'd Strength,
Have made my Pleasure less by the excess.

 Silv. This is wondrous.
Impart some of your over-charge to me,
The Burden lightened will be more supportable.

 Mar. Read here, and change thy Wonder, [158] when thou knowest

How happy Man can be. [*Gives him a Letter.*]

[*Silvio* reads.]

Marcel,
Dormida *will have me tell you what Effects your Vows have made, and how easily they
have drawn from me a Consent to see you, as you desir'd, this Night in my Chamber: you
have sworn to marry me, and Love will have me credit you, and then methinks I ought not
to deny you anything, nor question your Virtue.* Dormida *will wait to throw you down the
Key, when all are in Bed, that will conduct you to*

Your Clarinda.

    Silv. Damn her for a Dissembler!
Is this the chaste, the excellent *Clarinda*,
Who whilst I courted, was as cold and nice,
As a young Nun the day she is invested?
    Mar. How now, Brother! what, displeased with it? [*Takes the Letter.*]
    Silv. A little, Sir, to see another's Happiness,
Whilst I, where e'er I pay my Vows and Sighs,
Get nothing but Disdain; and yet this Shape
And Face I never thought unhandsome.
    Mar. These be the least approaches to a Heart;
'Tis not dull looking well will do the feat,
There is a Knack in Love, a critical Minute:
And Women must be watched as Witches are, [p. 234]
E'er they confess, and then they yield apace.

[*Enter a* Boy.]

    Boy. Sir, there's without a Servant of Don *Alonzo's,* who says his Master will be here
tonight. [Marcel *is surprised.*] [159]
    Mar. Alonzo! now I begin to wake
From Love, like one from some delightful Dream,
To reassume my wonted Cares and Shame.
—I will not speak with him. [*Exit* Boy.]
Oh *Hippolyta!* thou poor lost thing, *Hippolyta!*
How art thou fallen from Honor, and from Virtue,
And liv'st in Whoredom with an impious Villain,
Who in revenge to me has thus betray'd thee.
Keep thy self closer than thou'st done thy Sin;
For if I find thee out, by all that's good,
Thou hadst more Mercy on thy slaughter'd Honor,
Than I will have for thee.
And thou, *Antonio,* that hast betray'd her, [160]
Who till profan'd by thee, was chaste as Shrines,
And pure as are the Vows are offer'd there,
That Rape which thou'st committed on her Innocence,
I will revenge as shall become her Brother. [*Offers to go out in rage.*]
    Silv. Stay, *Marcel,*

I can inform you where these Lovers are.

    Mar. Oh tell me quickly then,
That I may take them in their foul Embraces,
And send their Souls to Hellena

    Silv. Last Night I made a youthful Sally to
One of those Houses where Love and Pleasure
Are sold at dearest Rates.

    Mar. A Bordello; forwards pray.

    Silv. Yes, at the Corner of St. *Jerom's*; where after seeing many Faces which pleas'd me not, I would have took my leave; but the Matron of the House, a kind obliging Lady, [161] seeing me so nice, and of Quality, (tho disguis'd) told me she had a Beauty, such an one as had Count *d' Olivarez* [p. 235] in his height of Power seen, he would have purchas'd at any rate. I grew impatient to see this fine thing, and promis'd largely: then leading me into a Room as gay, and as perfum'd as an Altar upon a Holy-day, I saw seated upon a Couch of State—

    Mar. Hippolyta!

    Silv. Hippolyta our Sister, dressed like a *Venice* Courtesan, [p. 235]
With all the Charms of a loose Wanton,
Singing and playing to her ravished Lover,
Who I perceiv'd assisted to expose her.

    Mar. Well, Sir, what follow'd?

    Silv. Surpriz'd at sight of this, I did withdraw,
And left them laughing at my little Confidence.

    Mar. How! left them? and left them living too?

    Silv. If a young Wench will be gadding,
Who can help it?

    Mar. 'Sdeath you should, were you that half her Brother, Which my Father too dotingly believes you. [*Enrag'd.*]

    Silv. How! do you question his Belief, *Marcel?*

    Mar. I ne'er consider'd it; be gone and leave me.

    Silv. Am I a Dog [162] that thus you bid me vanish?
What mean you by this Language? [*Comes up to him.*]
And how dare you upbraid me with my Birth,
Which know, *Marcel*, is more illustrious far
Than thine, being got when Love was in his reign,
With all his Youth and Heat about him?
I, like the Birds [163] of bravest kind, was hatched
In the hot Sun-shine of Delight; whilst
Thou, *Marcel*, wer't poorly brooded
In the cold Nest of Wedlock.

    Mar. Thy Mother was some base notorious Strumpet,
And by her Witchcraft reduc'd my Father's Soul,
And in return she paid him with a Bastard,
Which was thou.

    Silv. Marcel, thou ly'st. [*Strikes him.*]

    Mar. Tho 'twere no point of Valour, but of Rashness
To fight thee, yet I'll do't.

    Silv. By Heaven, I will not put this Injury up.

[They fight, Silvio *is wounded.]*

[Fight again. Enter Ambrosio, *and* Cleonte *between;* Silvio *falls into the Arms of* Cleonte.]

Amb. Hold! I command you hold;
Ah, Traitor to my Blood, what hast thou done?

[To Marcel, *who kneels and lays his Sword at his Feet.]*

Silv. In fair *Cleonte's* Arms!
O I could kiss the Hand that gives me Death,
So I might thus expire.
Mar. Pray hear me, Sir, before you do condemn me.
Amb. I will hear nothing but thy Death pronounc'd,
Since thou hast wounded him, if it be mortal.
Have I not charg'd thee on thy Life, *Marcel,*
Thou shouldst not hold Discourse with him of any kind?
Mar. I did foresee my Fate, but could not shun it.

[Takes his Sword and goes out.]

Amb. What ho! *Biscay,* a Surgeon; [164] on your Lives a Surgeon; where be the Rascals? *[Goes out.]*
Silv. I would not have a Surgeon search my Wound
With rude and heavy Hands:
Yours, fair *Cleonte,* can apply the Balsam
Far more successfully,
For they are soft and white as Down of Swans, [165]
And every Touch is sovereign.
Cleo. But I shall die with looking on your Wounds.
Silv. And I shall die unless you cure them, Sister.
Cleo. With the expence of mine to save your Life,
Is both my Wish and Duty.
Silv. I thank you, pretty Innocence. *[Leads him in.]*

Scene III. *A Grove.*

[Discovers Euphemia *veil'd, walking alone.]*

Euph. Olinda stays long; I hope she has overtook the Cavalier. Lord, how I am concern'd; if this should be Love now, I were in fine condition, at least if he be married, or a Lover: Oh that I fear: hang me, if it has not disorder'd me all over. But see, where she comes with him too.

[Enter Olinda *and* Alonzo.]

Olin. Here he is, Madam, I hope 'tis the right Man.

Alon. Madam, you see what haste I make to obey your kind Commands.

Euph. 'Twas as kindly done, Sir; but I fear when you know to what end 'tis, you'll repent your Haste.

Alon. 'Tis very likely; but if I do, you are not the first of your Sex that has put me to Repentance: But lift up your Veil, and if your Face be good—[*Offers to lift up her Veil.*]

Euph. Stay, you're too hasty.

Alon. Nay, let's have fair Play on both sides, I'll hide nothing from you. [*Offers again.*]

Euph. I have a Question or two to ask you first.

Alon. I can promise nothing till I see my Reward. I am a base Barterer, here's one for t'other; you saw your Man and lik'd him, [166] and if I like you when I see you—[*Offers again.*]

Euph. But if you do not, must all my liking be castaway?

Alon. As for that, trust to my good Nature; a frank Wench has hitherto taken me as much as Beauty. And one Proof you have already given of that, in this kind Invitation: come, come, do not lose my little new-gotten good Opinion of thee, by being coy and peevish. [*Offers again.*]

Euph. You're strangely impatient, Sir.

Alon. O you should like me the better for that, 'tis a sign of Youth and Fire.

Euph. But, Sir, before I let you see my Face—

Alon. I hope I must not promise you to like it.

Euph. No, that were too unreasonable, but I must know whether you are a Lover.

Alon. What an idle Question's that to a brisk young Fellow? A Lover! yes, and that as often as I see a new Face.

Euph. That I'll allow.

Alon. That's kindly said; and now do I find I shall be in love with thine as soon as I see't, for I am half so with thy Humor already.

Euph. Are you not married, Sir?

Alon. Married!

Euph. Now I dread his Answer. [*Aside.*] Yes, married.

Alon. Why, I hope you make no Scruple of Conscience, to be kind to a married Man.

Euph. Now do I find, you hope I am a Courtesan that come to bargain for a Night or two; but if I possess you, it must be forever.

Alon. For ever let it be then. Come, let's begin on any Terms.

Euph. I cannot blame you, Sir, for this mistake, since what I've rashly done, has given you cause to think I am not virtuous.

Alon. Faith, Madam, Man is a strange ungovern'd thing; yet I in the whole course of my Life have taken the best care I could, to make as few Mistakes as possible: and treating all Women-kind alike, we seldom err; for where we find one as you profess to be, we happily light on a hundred of the sociable and reasonable sort.

Euph. But sure you are so much a Gentleman, that you may be convinc'd?

Alon. Faith, if I be mistaken, I cannot devise what other use you can make of me.

Euph. In short this; I must leave you instantly; and will only tell you I am the sole Daughter of a rich Parent, young, and as I am told not unhandsome; I am contracted to a Man I never saw, nor I am sure shall not like when I do see, he having more Vice and Folly than his Fortune will excuse, tho a great one; and I had rather die than marry him.

Alon. I understand you, and you would have me dispatch this Man.

Euph. I am not yet so wicked. The Church is the only place I am allowed to go to, and till now could never see the Man that was perfectly agreeable to me: Thus veil'd, I'll venture to tell you so.

Alon. What the Devil will this come to? her Mien and Shape are strangely graceful, and her Discourse is free and natural. What a damn'd Defeat is this, that she should be honest now! [*Aside.*]

Euph. Well, Sir, what Answer? I see he is uneasy. [*Aside.*]

Alon. Why, as I was saying, Madam, I am a Stranger.

Euph. I like you the better for that.

Alon. But, Madam, I am a Man unknown, unown'd in the World; and much unworthy the Honor you do me—Would I were well rid of her, and yet I find a damnable Inclination to stay too. [*Aside.*]

Will nothing but Matrimony serve your turn, Madam? Pray use a young Lover as kindly as you can.

Euph. Nothing but that will do, and that must be done.

Alon. Must! 'slife this is the first [167] of her Sex that ever was before-hand with me, and yet that I should be forc'd to deny her too. [*Aside.*]

Euph. I fear his Answer, *Olinda.* [*Aside.*]

Olin. At least 'tis but making a Discovery of your Beauty, and then you have him sure.

Alon. Madam, 'tis a matter of Moment, and requires Deliberation; besides I have made a kind of Promise—

Euph. Never to marry?

Alon. No, faith, 'tis not so well: But since now I find we are both in haste, I am to be marry'd.

Euph. This I am sure is an Excuse; but I'll fit him for't. [*Aside.*]
To be marry'd said you?
That Word has kill'd me, Oh I feel it drill
Through the deep Wound his Eyes have lately made:
'Twas much unkind to make me hope so long.

[*She leans on* Olinda, *as if she swooned, who pulls off her Veil: he stands gazing at a Distance.*]

Olin. Sure she does but counterfeit, and now I'll play my Part. Madam, Madam!

Alon. What wondrous thing is that! I should not look upon't, it changes Nature in me.

Olin. Have you no pity, Sir? Come nearer pray.

Alon. Sure there's Witchcraft in that Face, it never could have seiz'd me thus else, I have lov'd a thousand times, yet never felt such joyful Pains before.

Olin. She does it rarely. What mean you, Sir?

Alon. I never was a Captive to this Hour.
If in her Death such certain Wounds she give,
What Mischiefs she would do, if she should live!
Yet she must live, and live that I may prove
Whether this strange Disorder here be Love. [*To his heart.*] [168]
Divine, divinest Maid. [*Kneels.*]

Olin. Come nearer, Sir, you'll do a Lady no good at that Distance. Speak to her, Sir.
[*He rises and comes to her, gazing still.*]

Alon. I know not what to say,
I am unus'd to this soft kind of Language:
But if there be a Charm in Words, and such
As may conjure her to return again;
Prithee instruct [169] me in them, I'll say anything,
Do anything, and suffer all the Wounds
Her Eyes can give.
   Euph. Sure he is real. [*Aside.*]
Alas! I am discover'd; how came my Veil off? [*She pretends to recover, and wonder that her Veil is off.*]
   Alon. That you have let me see that lovely Face,
May move your Pity, not your Anger, Madam;
Pity the Wounds 't has made, pity the Slave,
Who till this Moment boasted of his Freedom.
   Euph. May I believe all this? for that we easily do in things we wish.
   Alon. Command me [170] things impossible to all
Sense but a Lover's, I will do't: to show
The Truth of this, I could even give you
The last Proof of it, and take you at your Word,
To marry you.
   Euph. O wondrous Reformation! marry me! [*Laughs.*]
   Alon. How, do you mock my Grief?
   Euph. What a strange dissembling thing is Man! To put me off too, you were to be married.
   Alon. Hah, I had forgotten *Hippolyta.* [*He starts.*]
   Euph. See, *Olinda,* the Miracle increases, he can be serious too. How do you, Sir?
   Alon. 'Tis you have robb'd me of my native Humor,
I ne'er could think till now.
   Euph. And to what purpose was it now?
   Alon. Why, Love and Honor were at odds within me,
And I was making Peace between them.
   Euph. How fell that out, Sir?
   Alon. About a Pair of Beauties; Women,
That set the whole World at odds.
She that is Honor's Choice I never saw,
And love has taught me new Obedience here.
   Euph. What means he? I fear he is in earnest. [*Aside.*]
   Olin. 'Tis nothing but his Aversion to Marriage, which most young Men dread now a-days.
   Euph. I must have this Stranger, or I must die; for whatever Face I put upon't, I am far gone in Love, but I must hide it. [*Aside.*] Well, since I have mist my Aim, you shall never boast my Death; [171] I'll cast myself away upon the next handsome young Fellow I meet, tho I die for't; and so farewell to you, loving Sir. [*Offers to go.*]
   Alon. Stay, do not marry, as you esteem the Life of him that shall possess you.
   Euph. Sure you will not kill him.
   Alon. By Heaven, I Willmore
   Euph. O I'll trust you, Sir: Farewell, farewell.
   Alon. You shall not go in triumph thus,

Unless you take me with you.

Euph. Well, since you are so resolv'd (and so in love) I'll give you leave to see me once more at a House at the Corner of St. *Jerom's*, where this Maid shall give you Entrance.

Alon. Why, that's generously said.

Euph. As soon 'tis dark you may venture.

Alon. Till then will be an Age, farewell, fair Saint,
To thee and all my quiet till we meet. [*Exeunt.*]

ACT II.

Scene I. *The Street.*

[*Enter* Marcel *in a Cloak alone.*]

Mar. The Night comes on, and offers me two Pleasures,
The least of which would make another blest,
Love and Revenge: but I, whilst I dispute
Which Happiness to chose, neglect them both.
The greatest Bliss that Mankind can possess,
Persuades me this way, to my fair *Clarinda:*
But tyrannic Honor
Presents the Credit of my House before me,
And bids me first redeem its fading Glory,
By sacrificing that false Woman's Heart
That has undone its Fame. [172]
But stay, Oh Conscience, when I look within,
And lay my Anger by, I find that Sin
Which I would punish in *Antonio's* Soul,
Lie nourish'd up in mine without Controul.
To fair *Clarinda* such a Siege I lay,
As did that Traitor to *Hippolyta*;
Only *Hippolyta* a Brother has,
Clarinda, none to punish her Disgrace:
And 'tis more Glory the defenc'd to win,
Than 'tis to take unguarded Virtue in.
I either must my shameful Love resign,
Or my more brave and just Revenge decline.

[*Enter* Alonzo *dressed, with* Lovis. Marcel *stays.*]

Alon. But to be thus in love, is't not a Wonder, *Lovis?*

Lo. No, Sir, it had been much a greater, if you had stay'd a Night in Town without being so; and I shall see this Wonder as often as you see a new Face of a pretty Woman.

Alon. I do not say that I shall lose all Passion for the fair Sex hereafter; but on my Conscience, this amiable Stranger has given me a deeper Wound than ever I received from any before.

Lo. Well, you remember the Bargain.

Alon. What Bargain?

Lo. To communicate; you understand.

Alon. There's the Devil on't, she is not such a Prize: Oh, were she not honest, Friend! [*Hugs him.*]

Lo. Is it so to do? What, you pretend to be a Lover, and she honest, now only to deprive me of my Part: remember this, *Alonzo.*

Mar. Did not I hear *Alonzo* nam'd? [*Aside.*]

Alon. By all that's good I am in earnest, Friend;
Nay thy own Eyes shall convince thee
Of the Power of hers.
Her Veil fell off, and she appear'd to me,
Like unexpected Day, from out a Cloud;
The lost benighted Traveller
Sees not th' Approach of the next Morning's Sun [173]
With more transported Joy,
Than I this ravishing and unknown Beauty.

Lo. Hey day! What Stuff's here? Nay, now I see thou art quite gone indeed.

Alon. I fear it. Oh, had she not been honest!
What Joy, what Heaven of Joys she would distribute!
With such a Face, and Shape, a Wit, and Mein—
But as she is, I know not what to do.

Lo. You cannot marry her.

Alon. I would not willingly, tho I think I'm free: For *Pedro* went to *Marcel* to tell him I was arriv'd, and would wait on him; but was treated more like a Spy, than a Messenger of Love: They sent no Answer back, which I tell you, *Lovis,* angers me: 'twas not the Entertainment I expected from my brave Friend *Marcel.* But now I am for the fair Stranger who by this expects me.

Mar. 'Tis *Alonzo.* O how he animates my Rage, and turns me over to Revenge, upon *Hippolyta* and her false Lover! [*Aside.*]

Lo. Who's this that walks before us? [*They go out.*] [174]

Alon. No matter who.

Mar. I am follow'd. [*They enter again.*]

Lo. See, he stops. [Marcel *looks back.*]

Alon. Let him do what he please, we will out-go him. [*They go out.*]

Lo. This Man whoe'er he be still follows us.

Alon. I care not, nothing shall hinder my Design, I'll go tho I make my passage thro his Heart. [*They enter at another Door,* [p. 245] *he follows.*]

Lo. See, he advances, pray stand by a little. [*They stand by.*]

Mar. Sure there's some Trick in this, but I'll not fear it. This is the Street, and hereabout's the House. [*Looks about.*] This must be it, if I can get admittance now [*Knocks.*]

[*Enter* Olinda *with a Light.*]

Olin. O, Sir, are you come? my Lady grew impatient. [*They go in.*]

Mar. She takes me for some other: This is happy. [*Aside.*]

Alon. Gods! is not that the Maid that first conducted me to the fair thing that rob' me of my Heart?

Lo. I think it is.

Alon. She gives admittance to another Man.
All Women-kind are false, I'll in and tell her so. [*Offers to go.*]

Lo. You are too rash, 'tis dangerous.

Alon. I do despise thy Counsel, let me go.

Lo. If you are resolv'd, I'll run the Hazard with you. [*They both go in.*]

Scene II. *The Scene changes to a Chamber.*

[*Enter from one side* Olinda, *lighting in* Marcel *muffled as before in his Cloke, from the other* Antonio *leading in* Euphemia *veil'd.*]

Mar. By Heaven's, 'tis she: Vile Strumpet! [Throws off his Cloke, and snatches her from him.]

Euph. Alas, this is not he whom I expected.

Ant. Marcel! I had rather have encounter'd my evil Angel than thee. [*Draws.*]

Mar. I do believe thee, base ungenerous Coward. [*Draws.*]

[*They fight,* Marcel *disarms* Antonio, *by wounding his Hand. Enter* Alonzo, *goes betwixt them, and with his Sword drawn opposes* Marcel, *who is going to kill* Antonio; *Lovis follows him.*]

Alon. Take Courage, Sir. [*To* Antonio, *who goes out mad.*]

Mar. Prevented! whoe'er thou be'st.
It was unjustly done,
To save his Life who merits Death,
By a more shameful way.
But thank the Gods she still remains to meet
That Punishment that's due to her foul Lust.

[*Offers to run at her,* Alonzo *goes between.*]

Alon. 'Tis this way you must make your Passage then.

Mar. What art thou, that thus a second time
Dar'st interpose between Revenge and me?

Alon. 'Tis *Marcel!* What can this mean? [*Aside.*]
Dost not thou know me, Friend? look on me well.

Mar. Alonzo here! Ah I shall die with Shame. [*Aside.*]
As thou art my Friend, remove from that bad Woman,
Whose Sins deserve no sanctuary.

Euph. What can he mean? I dare not show my Face. [*Aside.*]

Alon. I do believe this Woman is a false one,
But still she is a Woman, and a fair one:
I would not suffer thee to injure her,
Tho I believe she has undone thy quiet,
As she has lately mine.

Mar. Why, dost thou know it then?
Stand by, I shall forget thou art my Friend else,

And thro thy Heart reach hers.

    Alon. Nothing but Love could animate him thus,
He is my Rival. [*Aside.*]
    Marcel, I will not quit one inch of Ground;
Do what thou dar'st, for know I do adore her,
And thus am bound by Love to her Defence.

[Offers to fight Marcel, who retires in wonder.]

    Euph. Hold, noble Stranger, hold.
    Mar. Have you such Pity on your Lover there? [*Offers to kill her,* Alonzo *stays him.*]
    Euph. Help, help. [*Her Veil falls off.*]

[Enter Hippolyta dressed like a Courtesan: Sees Marcel.]

    Hip. Oh Gods, my Brother! in pity, Sir, defend me From the just Rage of that incensed Man. [*Runs behind* Lovis, *whilst* Marcel *stands gazing on both with wonder.*]
    Lo. I know not the meaning of all this, but
However I'll help the Lady in Distress.
Madam, you're safe, whilst I am your Protector. [*Leads her out.*]
    Mar. I've lost the Power of striking where I ought,
Since my misguided Hand so lately err'd.
Oh Rage, dull senseless Rage, how blind and rude
It makes us.
Pardon, fair Creature, my unruly Passion,
And only blame that Veil which hid that Face,
Whose Innocence and Beauty had disarm'd it:
I took you for the most perfidious Woman,
The falsest loosest thing.
    Alon. How! are you a Stranger to her?
    Mar. Yes I am. Have you forgiven me, Madam?
    Euph. Sir, I have. [Marcel *bows and offers to go out.*]
    Alon. Stay, Friend, and let me know your Quarrel.
    Mar. Not for the World, *Alonzo.*
    Alon. This is unfriendly, Sir.
    Mar. Thou dost delay me from the noblest Deed,
On which the Honor of my House depends,
A Deed which thou wilt curse thy self for hindering
Farewell. [*Goes out.*]
    Alon. What can the meaning of this be?
    Euph. Oh do not ask, but let us quickly leave this dangerous Place.
    Alon. Does it not belong to you?
    Euph. No, but you would like me the better if it did: for, Sir, it is a—
    Alon. Upon my Life, a Bawdy-house.
    Euph. So they call it.
    Alon. You do amaze me.
    Euph. Truth is, not daring to trust my Friends or Relations with a Secret that so nearly concern'd me as the meeting you, and hearing of a new come Courtesan living in

this House, I sent her word I would make her a Visit, knowing she would gladly receive it from a Maid of my Quality: When I came, I told her my Business, and very frankly she offer'd me her House and Service—Perhaps you'll like me the worse for this bold Venture, but when you consider my promis'd Husband is every day expected, you will think it but just to secure myself any way.

Alon. You could not give me a greater Proof than this of what you say you bless me with, your Love.

Euph. I will not question but you are in earnest; at least if any doubt remain, these will resolve it. [*Gives him Letters.*]

Alon. What are these, Madam?

Euph. Letters, Sir, intercepted from the Father of my design'd Husband out of *Flanders* to mine.

Alon. What use can I make of them?

Euph. Only this: Put yourself into an Equipage very ridiculous, and pretend you are my foolish Lover arriv'd from *Flanders*, call yourself *Haunce van Ezel*, and give my Father these, as for the rest I'll trust your Wit.

Alon. What shall I say or do now? [*Aside.*]

Euph. Come, come, [175] no study, Sir; this must be done,
And quickly too, or you will lose me.

Alon. Two great Evils! if I had but the Grace to chose the least now, that is, lose her. [*Aside.*]

Euph. I'll give you but tonight to consider it.

Alon. Short warning this: but I am damnably in love, and cannot withstand Temptation. [*Kisses her Hand.*]

Euph. I had forgot to tell you my Name's *Euphemia*, my Father's you'll find on the Letters, and pray show your Love in your haste. Farewell.

Alon. Stay, fair *Euphemia*, and let me pay my Thanks, and tell you that I must obey you.

Euph. I give a Credit where I give a Heart.
Go inquire my Birth and Fortune: as for you,
I am content with what I see about you.

Alon. That's bravely said, nor will I ask one Question about you, not only to return the Bounty, but to avoid all things that look like the Approaches to a married Life. If Fortune will put us together, let her e'en provide for us.

Euph. I must be gone: Farewell, and pray make haste. [*Looks kindly on him.*]

Alon. There's no resisting those Looks, *Euphemia*: One more to fortify me well; for I shall have need of every Aid in this Case. [*Look at one another and go.*] [176]

Scene III. *A Street.*

[*Enter* Antonio *in haste with* Hippolyta; *weeping as passing over the Stage.*]

Ant. Come, let us haste, I fear we are pursu'd.

Hip. Ah, whither shall we fly?

Ant. We are near the Gate, and must secure ourselves with the Darkness of the Night in *St. Peter's* Grove, we dare not venture into any House. [*Exeunt.*]

[*Enter* Clarinda *and* Dormida *above in the Balcony.*]

Clar. Can'st thou not see him yet?

Dorm. Good lack a-day, what an impatient thing is a young Girl in love!

Clar. Nay, good *Dormida*, let not want of Sleep make thee testy.

Dorm. In good time—are you my Governess, or I yours, that you are giving me Instructions? Go get you in, or I shall lay down my Office.

Clar. Nay, wait a little longer, I'm sure he will come.

Dorm. You sure! you have wondrous Skill indeed in the Humors of Men: how came you to be so well acquainted with them? you scarce ever saw any but Don *Marcel*, and him too but thro a Grate or Window, or at Church; and yet you are sure. I am a little the elder of the two, and have manag'd as many Intrigues of this kind as any Woman, and never found a constant just Man, as they say, of a thousand; and yet you are sure.

Clar. Why, is it possible *Marcel* should be false?

Dorm. Marcel! No, no, Sweet-heart, he is that Man of a thousand.

Clar. But if he should, you have undone me, by telling me so many pretty things of him.

Dorm. Still you question my Ability, which by no means I can endure; get you in I say.

Clar. Do not speak so loud, you will wake my Mother.

Dorm. At your Instructions again; do you question my Conduct and Management of this Affair? Go watch for him yourself: I'll have no more to do with you back nor edge. [*Offers to go.*]

Clar. Will you be so barbarous to leave me to myself, after having made it your Business this three Months to solicit a Heart which was but too ready to yield before; after having sworn to me how honorable all his Intents were; nay, made me write to him to come tonight? And now when I have done this, and am all trembling with fear and shame (and yet an infinite Desire to see him too) [*Sighs*] thou wilt abandon me: go, when such as you oblige, 'tis but to be insolent with the more freedom.

Dorm. What, you are angry I'll warrant. [*Smiles.*]

Clar. I will punish myself to pay thee back, and will not see *Marcel*.

Dorm. What a pettish Fool is a Maid in love at fifteen! how unmanageable! But I'll forgive all—go get you in, I'll watch for your Lover; I would not have you disoblige a Man of his Pretensions and Quality for all the World. [Clarinda *goes in.*]

[*Enter* Alonzo *below.*]

Alon. Now do I want *Lovis* extremely, to consult with him about this Business: For am afraid the Devil, or Love, or both are so great with me, that I must marry this fai Enchantress, which is very unlucky; [177] but, since *Ambrosio* and *Marcel* refuse to see me, I hold my self no longer engag'd in Honor to *Hippolyta*.

Dorm. [*above.*] Whist, whist, Sir, Sir.

Alon. Who's there?

Dorm. 'Tis I, your Servant, Sir; oh you are a fine Spark, are you not, to make so fair a Creature wait so long for you? there, there's the Key, open the Door softly and come in [*Throws him down a Key in a Handkerchief.*]

Alon. What's this? But I'll ask no Questions, so fair a Creature, said she? Now i 'twere to save my Life cannot I forbear, I must go in: Shou'd *Euphemia* know this, sh would call it Levity and Inconstancy; but I plead Necessity, and will be judg'd by th amorous Men, and not the jealous Women: For certain this Lady, whoe'er she be, designs me a more speedy Favor than I can hope from *Euphemia*, and on easier Terms too. This is the Door that must conduct to the languishing *Venus*. [Opens the Door and goes in, leaving it unshut.

[*Enter* Marcel *with his Sword drawn.*]

Mar. Thus far I have pursu'd the Fugitives,
Who by the help of hasty Fear and Night,
Are got beyond my Power; unlucky Accident!
Had I but kill'd *Antonio*, or *Hippolyta*,
Either had made my Shame supportable.
But tho I have mist the Pleasure of Revenge,
I will not that of Love.
One Look from fair *Clarinda* will appease
The Madness which this Disappointment rais'd.

[*Walks looking towards the Window.*]

None appears yet: *Dormida* was to throw me down the Key. The Door is open, left so to give me entrance. [*Goes to the Door.*]

Scene IV. *Changes to a dark Hall.*

[*Discovers* Alonzo *groping about in the Hall.*]

Alon. Now am I in a worse Condition than before, can neither advance nor retreat: I do not like this groping alone in the Dark thus. Whereabouts am I? I dare not call: were this fair thing she spoke of but now half so impatient as I, she would bring a Light, and conduct me.

[*Enter* Marcel.]

Mar. 'Tis wondrous dark.
Alon. Hah, a Man's Voice that way; that's not so well: it may be some Lover, Husband, or Brother; none of which are to be trusted in this Case, therefore I'll stand upon my Guard. [*Draws:* Marcel *coming towards him jostles him.*] [178]
Mar. Who's there?
Alon. A Man.
Mar. A Man! none such inhabit here. [*Draws.*]
Thy Business?
Alon. This shall answer you, since there's no other way.

[*They fight,* Alonzo *wounds* Marcel, *who fights him to the Door;* Alonzo *goes out,*
Marcel *gropes to follow.*]

188

Mar. This is not just, ye Gods, to punish me, and let the Traitor 'scape unknown too: Methought 'twas *Silvio's* Voice, or else a sudden thought of Jealousy come into my Head would make me think so.

[*Enter* Clarinda *and* Dormida *with Light.*]

Clar. I tell you I did hear the noise of fighting.
Dorm. Why, between whom should it be? I'll be sworn *Marcel* came in alone.
Clar. Marcel! and wounded too! oh I'm lost. [*Sees him, weeps.*]
Mar. Keep your false Tears to bathe your Lover's Wounds. For I perhaps have given him some [179]—Thou old Assistant to her Lust, whose greatest Sin is wishing, tell me who 'twas thou didst procure for her. [*In rage to* Dormida.]
Dorm. Alas! I cannot imagine who it should be, unless Don *Silvio*, who has sometimes made Addresses to her: But oh the House is up, Madam, we are undone; let's fly for Heavens sake.
Clar. Oh *Marcel*, can you believe—[*A Noise.*]
Dorm. Come, come, I'll not be undone for your Fiddle-faddles; I'll lay it all on you, if I be taken. [*Pulls out* Clarinda.]
Mar. Sot that I was, I could not guess at this today, by his Anger at the Letter I foolishly show'd him; he is my Rival, and 'tis with him she's fled; and I'll endeavor to pursue them. [*Offers to go.*] But oh my Strength complies with their Design, [*Leaning on his Sword.*] and shamefully retires to give them leave to play their amorous Game out. [*Goes faintly out.*]

Scene V. *Changes to the Street. Discovers* Alonzo *alone.*

Alon. This Act of mine was rash and ill-natur'd,
And I cannot leave the Street with a good Conscience,
Till I know what mischief I have done.

[*Enter* Dormida *and* Clarinda.]

Hah, Ladies from the same House! these are Birds that I have frighted from their Nests I am sure: I'll proffer my Service to them.
Dorm. Why do not you make more haste?
Clar. How can she go, whose Life is left behind?
Besides, I know not whither we should go.
Ye Powers that guard the Innocent, protect us.
Alon. These must be some whom I have injur'd.
Ladies—you seem as in distress.
Dorm. Oh, Sir, as you are a Gentleman, assist a pair of Virgins.
Alon. What's this, a mumping Matron? I hope the other's young, or I have offer'd my Service to little purpose.
Clar. Sir, if you will have the Charity to assist us,
Do it speedily, we shall be very grateful to you.
Alon. Madam, I will, but know not where to carry ye; my Lodging is in an Inn, and is neither safe nor honorable: but Fortune dares no less than protect the Fair, and I'll venture my Life in your Protection and Service. [*Exeunt.*]

[*Enter* Marcel *faintly.*]

Mar. Stay, Traitor, stay—oh they are out of sight,
But may my Curse o'ertake them in their flight. [*Exit.*]

Scene VI. *Chamber of* Cleonte.

[*She is discover'd in her Night-Gown, at a Table, as undressing,* Francisca *by her.*]

Cleo. Francisca, thou art dull tonight. [*Sighs.*]
Franc. You will not give me leave to talk.
Cleo. Not thy way indeed, hast thou no Stories but of Love, and of my Brother *Silvio?*
Franc. None that you wish to hear: But I'll do what you please, so you will not oblige me to sigh for you.
Cleo. Then prithee sing to me.
Franc. What Song, a merry, or a sad?
Cleo. Please thy own Humor, for then thou'lt sing best.
Franc. Well, Madam, I'll obey you, and please myself.

SINGS.

Amyntas *led me to a Grove,*
Where all the Trees did shade us;
The Sun itself, tho it had strove,
Yet could not have betrayed us.
The place secure from human Eyes,
No other fear allows,
But when the Winds that gently rise
Do kiss the yielding Boughs.

Down there we sat upon the Moss,
And did begin to play
A thousand wanton Tricks, to pass
The Heat of all the Day.
A many Kisses he did give,
And I return'd the same:
Which made me willing to receive
That which I dare not name.

His charming Eyes no aid requir'd,
   To tell their amorous Tale;
On her that was already fir'd,
   'Twas easy to prevail.
He did but kiss, and clasp me round,
   Whilst they his thoughts expressed,
And laid me gently on the Ground;
   Oh!—who can guess the rest?

[*After the Song, enter* Silvio *all undressed, gazing wildly on* Cleonte; *his Arm ty'd up.*]

   Cleo. My Brother *Silvio,* at this late hour, and in my Lodgings too! How do you, Sir?
are you not well?
   Silv. Oh, why did Nature give me being?
Or why create me Brother to *Cleonte?* [*Aside.*]
Or give her Charms, and me the sense to adore 'em?
   Cleo. Dear Brother—[*Goes to him.*]
   Silv. Ah, *Cleonte*—[*Takes her by the Hand and gazes.*]
   Cleo. What would you, Sir?
   Silv. I am not—well—
   Cleo. Sleep, Sir, will give you ease.
   Silv. I cannot sleep, my Wounds do rage and burn so, as they put me past all power
of rest.
   Cleo. We'll call your Surgeon, Sir.
   Silv. He can contribute nothing to my Cure,
But I must owe it all to thee, *Cleonte.*
   Cleo. Instruct me in the way, give me your Arm,
And I will bathe it in a thousand Tears, [*Goes to untie his Arm.*]
And breathe so many Sighs into your Wound—
   Silv. Let that slight hurt alone, and search this—here. [*To his Heart.*]
   Cleo. How! are you wounded there,
And would not let us know it all this while?
   Silv. I durst not tell you, but design'd to suffer,
Rather than trouble you with my Complaints:
But now my Pain is greater than my Courage.
   Franc. Oh, he will tell her, that he loves her sure. [*Aside.*]
   Cleo. Sit down and let me see't. [*He sits down, she puts her Hand into his Bosom.*]
   Franc. Oh foolish Innocence—[*Aside.*]
   Cleo. You have deceiv'd me, Brother, here's no Wound.
   Silv. Oh take away your Hand—
It does increase my Pain, and wounds me deeper.
   Cleo. No, surely, Sir, my Hand is very gentle.
   Silv. Therefore it hurts me, Sister; the very thoughts
Of Touches by so soft and fair a Hand,
Playing about my Heart, are not to be endur'd with Life. [*Rises in passion.*]
   Cleo. Alas, what means my Brother?
   Silv. Can you not guess, fair Sister? have my Eyes

So ill expressed my Soul? or has your Innocence
Not suffer'd you to understand my Sighs?
Have then a thousand Tales, which I have told you,
Of Broken Hearts, and Lovers Languishments,
Not serv'd to tell you, that I did adore you?
    Cleo. Oh let me still remain in Innocence,
Rather than sin so much to understand you.
    Franc. I can endure no more—[*Goes out.*]
    Silv. Can you believe it Sin to love a Brother? it is not so in Nature.
    Cleo. Not as a Brother, Sir; but otherwise,
It is, by all the Laws of Men and Heaven.
    Silv. Sister, so 'tis that we should do no Murder,
And yet you daily kill, and I, among the number
Of your Victims, [180] must charge you with the sin
Of killing me, a Lover, and a Brother.
    Cleo. What wou'd you have me do?
    Silv. Why—I would have thee—do—I know not what—
Still to be with me—yet that will not satisfy;
To let me look—upon thee—still that's not enough.
I dare not say to kiss thee, and embrace thee;
That were to make me wish—I dare not tell thee what—
    Cleo. I must not hear this Language from a Brother. [*She offers to go.*]
    Silv. What a vile thing's a Brother? Stay, take this Dagger, and add one Wound more

[*He kneels and offers her a Dagger,* [181] *and holds her by the Coat.*]

To those your Eyes have given, and after that
You'll find no trouble from my Sighs and Tears.

[*Enter* Francisca.]

    Franc. By this she understands him, curse on her Innocence, 'Tis fuel to his flame—
[*Aside.*] Madam, there is below a Lady, who desires to speak with the Mistress of the House.
    Cleo. At this hour a Lady! who can it be?
    Franc. I know not, but she seems of Quality.
    Cleo. Is she alone?
    Franc. Attended by a Gentleman and an old Woman.
    Cleo. Perhaps some one that needs a kind Assistance; my Father is in Bed, and I'll venture to know their Business; bring her up.
    Franc. 'Twere good you should retire, Sir. [*To* Silvio, *and Exit.*]
    Silv. I will, but have a care of me, *Cleonte,*
I fear I shall grow mad, and so undo thee:
Love me—but do not let me know't too much. [*Goes out.*]

[*Enter* Francisca *with Lights; follow'd by* Alonzo, Clarinda, *and* Dormida: Alonzo *gazes on* Cleonte *a while.*]

Cleo. Is't me you would command?

Clar. I know not what to say, I am so disorder'd. [*Aside.*]

Alon. What Troops of Beauties she has! sufficient to take whole Cities in—Madam, I beg—[*Takes* Clarinda *by the Hand, and approaches* Cleonte.]

Cleo. What, Sir?

Alon. That you would receive into Protection—

Cleo. What pray, Sir?

Alon. Would you would give me leave to say, a Heart
That your fair Eyes have lately made unfit
For its old Quarters.

Cleo. I rather think you mean this Lady, Sir. [Alonzo *looks with wonder on* Clarinda.]

Alon. She's heavenly fair too, and has surpriz'd my Heart,
Just as 'twas going to the other's Bosom,
And rob'd her at least of one half of it. [*Aside.*]

Clar. Madam, I am a Virgin in distress,
And by misfortune forc'd to seek a Sanctuary,
And humbly beg it here.

Cleo. Intreaties were not made for that fair Mouth;
Command and be obey'd.
But, Sir, to whom do you belong?

Alon. I belong to a very fair Person,
But do not know her Name.

Cleo. But what are you, pray, Sir?

Alon. Madam, a Wanderer; a poor lost thing,
That none will own or pity.

Cleo. That's sad indeed; but whoe'er you are, since you belong to this fair Maid you'll find a Welcome everywhere.

Alon. And if I do not, I am cashier'd. [*Aside.*]
Madam, if telling you I am her Brother,
Can make me more acceptable,
I shall be yet more proud of the Alliance.

Cleo. What must I call your Sister, Sir, when I would pay my Duty?

Alon. There I am routed again with another hard Question. [*Aside.*]

Clar. Madam, my Name's *Clarinda.*

Alon. Madam, I'll take my leave, and wish the Heart I leave with you tonight, may persuade you to suffer my Visits tomorrow, till when I shall do nothing but languish.

Cleo. I know not what loss you have suffer'd tonight; but since your fair Sister' Presence with us allows it, you need not doubt a welcome.

Alon. I humbly thank you, Madam. [*Kisses her Hand, and looks amorously o* Clarinda.]

Franc. Madam, pray retire, for Don *Marcel* is come into the House all bloody enrag'd against somebody.

Clar. I'm troubled at his Hurt, but cannot fear his Rage. Good night, Sir. [*They g out.*]

Alon. They are gone; now had I as much mind to have kissed the other's Hand, bu that 'twas not a Ceremony due to a Sister—What the Devil came into my Head, to say sh was so? nothing but the natural itch of talking and lying: they are very fair; but what that to me? *Euphemia* surpasses both: But a Pox of her terms [182] of Marriage, I'll set that to her Beauty, and then these get the Day, as far as natural Necessity goes: But I'll home and sleep upon't, and yield to what's most powerful in the Morning.

Tonight these Strangers do my Heart possess,
But which the greatest share, I cannot guess:
My Fate in Love resembles that in War,
When the rich Spoil falls to the common share. [*Goes out.*]

Scene VII. *The Street.*

[*Enter* Alonzo, *as out of the House, gazing upon it.*]

Alon. Sure I shall know this House again tomorrow. [*To him* Lovis.]

Lo. I wonder what should be become of *Alonzo*, I do do not like these Night-works of his—Who's there?

Alon. Lovis!

Lo. Alonzo?

Alon. The same, where hast thou been?

Lo. In search of you this two Hours.

Alon. O, I have been taken up with new Adventures, since I saw thee; but prithee what became of thine? for methought it was a likely Woman.

Lo. Faith, Sir, I thought I had got a Prize; but a Pox on't, when I came into the Street, e'er she had recover'd Breath to tell me who she was, the Cavalier you rescu'd from *Marcel*, laid claim to her; thank'd me for her Preservation, and vanished. I hope you had better luck with your Female, whose Face I had not the good fortune to see.

Alon. Not so good as I could have wished, for she stands still on her honorable terms.

Lo. Of Matrimony, ha, ha, a very Jilt, I'll warrant her; Come, come, you shall see her no more.

Alon. Faith, I fear I must.

Lo. To what purpose?

Alon. To persuade her to Reason.

Lo. That you'll soon do, when she finds you will not bite at t'other Bait.

Alon. The worst is, if I see her again, it must be at her Father's House; and so transform'd from Man to Beast—I must appear like a ridiculous Lover she expects out of *Flanders.*

Lo. A very Cheat, a trick to draw thee in: be wise in time.

Alon. No, on my Conscience she's in earnest, she told me her Name, and his I am to represent.

Lo. What is't, I pray?

Alon. Haunce van Ezel. [183]

Lo. Hah! her Name too, I beseech you? [*Impatiently.*]

Alon. Euphemia: And such a Creature 'tis—

Lo. 'Sdeath, my Sister all this while: This has call'd up all that's Spaniard in me, and makes me raging mad. [*Aside.*] But do you love her, Sir?

Alon. Most desperately, beyond all Sense or Reason.

Lo. And could you be content to marry her?

Alon. Anything but that—But thou know'st my engagement elsewhere; and I have hopes that yet she'll be wise, and yield on more pleasant terms.

194

Lo. I could be angry now; but 'twere unreasonable to blame him for this. [*Aside.*] Sir, I believe by your Treatment from *Ambrosio* and *Marcel*, you may come off there easily.

Alon. That will not satisfy my Honor, tho 'twill my Love; that I have not *Hippolyta*, I will owe to my own Inconstancy, not theirs: besides, this may be a Cheat, as you say.

Lo. But does *Euphemia* love you?

Alon. Faith, I think she has too much Wit to dissemble, and too much Beauty to need that Art.

Lo. Then you must marry her.

Alon. Not if I can avoid it.

Lo. I know this Lady, Sir, and know her to be worth your Love: I have it in my Power too, to serve you, if you proceed suddenly, which you must do, or lose her; for this *Flandrian* Boor your Rival is already arriv'd, and designs tomorrow to make his first Address to *Euphemia*.

Alon. Oh, he must not, shall not see her.

Lo. How will you hinder him?

Alon. With this. [*To his Sword.*] Where is this Rival? tell me: Conduct me to him strait; I find my Love above the common rate, and cannot brook this Rival.

Lo. So, this blows the flame—His Life will be no hindrance to you in this Affair, if you design to love on.

Alon. Do'st know him?

Lo. Yes, he is a pleasant Original for you to be copy'd by: It is the same Fop, I told you was to marry my Sister, and who came along with me to *Madrid.*

Alon. How! *Euphemia* thy Sister?

Lo. Yes, indeed is she, and whom my Father designs to cast away upon this half Man, half Fool; but I find she has Wit to make a better Choice: she yet knows nothing of my Arrival, and till you resolve what to do, shall not; and my *Dutchman* does nothing without me.

Alon. If thou hast the management of him, he's likely to thrive.

Lo. But not in his Amour, if you please: In short, Sir, if you do really love my Sister, I am content to be so ungracious a Child to contribute to the cheating my Father of this same hopeful Son he expects, and put you upon him; but what you do, must be speedily then.

Alon. I am oblig'd to thee for this frank Offer, and will be instructed by thee.

Lo. If you're resolv'd, I'll warrant you Success.

Alon. I think I am resolv'd in spite of all my Inclinations to Libertinism.

Lo. Well, Sir, I'll get you such a Suit then, as that our Hero makes his first approach in, as ridiculously gay as his Humor, which you must assume too.

Alon. Content.

Lo. Tonight I must pay my Duty to my Father, and will prepare your way, and acquaint my Sister with it; 'tis but a Frolic if we succeed not.

Alon. God-a-mercy, Lad, let's about it then e'er we sleep, lest I change my Resolution before Morning. [*Exeunt.*]

ACT III.

Scene I. *House of* Carlo.

[*Enter* Alonzo *dressed ridiculously, meeting* Lovis, *they laugh at each other.*]

Lo. Very *Haunce* all over, the Taylor has play'd his part, play but yours as well, and I'll warrant you the Wench.

Alon. But prithee, why need I act the Fool thus, since *Haunce* was never seen here?

Lo. To make good the Character I always gave of him to my Father; but here he comes, pray be very rude, and very impertinent.

Alon. Lord, Lord, how shall I look thus damnably set out, and thus in love!

[*Enter* Don Carlo.]

Lo. This, Sir, is Monsieur *Haunce*, your Son that must be.

Alon. Beso los manos, signor: [p. 263] Is your Name Don *Carlo?* and are you the Gravity of this House? and the Father of Donna *Euphemia?* and are you—

Car. Sir, I guess by all these your Demands at once, your Name to be *Myn heer Haunce van Ezel.*

Alon. Your Judgment's good; but to my Questions.

Car. In truth I have forgot them, there were so many.

Alon. Are you he who is to be my Father?

Car. 'Tis so negotiated—and if all Circumstances concur—For, Sir, you must conceive, the Consequence of so grand a Conjunction—

Alon. Less of your Compliments, Sir, and more of your Daughter, I beseech you. 'Sheart, what a formal Coxcomb 'tis. [*Aside.*]

Lo. Prithee give him way. [*Aside.*]

Alon. By this Light I'll lose thy Sister first; Why, who can endure the grave approaches to the Matter? 'Dslife, I would have it as I would my Fate, sudden and unexpected.

Car. Pray, how long have you been landed?

Alon. So, now shall I be plagu'd with nothing but wise Questions, to which I am able to make no Answer. [*Aside.*] Sir, it is your Daughter that I desire to see impatiently.

Car. Have you no Letters from my very good Friend your Father?

Alon. What if I have not? cannot I be admitted to your Daughter without a Pass?

Car. O lack, Sir—

Alon. But to let you see I come with full Power (tho I am old enough to recommend myself) here is my Commission for what I do. [*Gives him Letters.*]

Car. I remember amongst his other Faults, my Son writ me word he had Courage: If so, I shall consider what to do. [*Reads.*] Sir, I find by these your Father's Letters, you are not yet arriv'd.

Alon. I know that, Sir, but I was told I should express my Love in my haste; therefore outsailing the Pacquet, I was the welcome Messenger myself; and since I am so forward, I beseech you, Sir—[Carlo *coming to embrace him.*]

Now dare not I proceed, he has so credulous a consenting Face. [*Aside.*]

196

Car. Spare your Words, I understand their meaning; a prudent Man speaks least, as the *Spaniard* has it: and since you are so forward, as you were saying, I shall not be backward; but as your Father adviseth here, hasten the uniting of our Families, with all celerity; for delay in these Affairs is but to prolong time, as the wise Man says.

Alon. You are much in the right, Sir. But my Wife, I desire to be better acquainted with her.

Car. She shall be forth-coming, Sir. Had you a good Passage? for the Seas and Winds regard no Man's necessity.

Alon. No, no, a very ill one; your Daughter, Sir.

Car. Pray, how long were you at Sea?

Alon. Euphemia, Sir, *Euphemia*, your Daughter. This Don's fuller of Questions than of Proverbs, and that's a Wonder. [*Aside.*]

Car. They say *Flanders* is a very fine Country, I never saw it; but—

Alon. Nor 'tis no matter, Sir, if you never do, so I saw your Daughter. He'll catechize me home to my *Dutch* Parents by and by, of which I can give him no more account than—[*Aside.*]

Car. Are they as dissatisfied with their new Governor, as they were with *Don John*? [p. 265] for they love change.

Alon. A Pox of their Government, I tell you I love your Daughter.

Car. I fear 'tis so, he's valiant; and what a dangerous Quality is that in *Spain!* 'tis well he's rich. [*Aside.*]

Lo. Pray, Sir, keep him not long in Discourse, the Sea has made him unfit for—

Alon. Anything but seeing my Mistress.

Lo. I'll have mercy upon thee, and fetch her to thee. [*Exit* Lovis.]

Car. Sir, you must know, that we suffer not our Women in Spain to converse so frequently with your Sex, and that thro a cautious—well consider'd prudent—Consideration.

Alon. But, Sir, do you consider what an impatient thing a young Lover is? Or is it so long since you were one yourself, you have forgot it? 'Tis well he wanted Words. [*Enter* Euphemia *and* Lovis.] But yonder's *Euphemia*, whose Beauty is sufficient to excuse every Defect in the whole Family, tho each were a mortal sin; and now 'tis impossible to guard myself longer from those fair Eyes. [*Aside.*]

Car. I must not urge him to speak much before *Euphemia*, lest she discover he wants Wit by his much Tongue: [*Aside.*] There's my Daughter, Sir, go and salute her.

Alon. Oh, I thank you for that, Sir. [*He stands ridiculously looking on her.*]

Car. You must be bold, Sir.

Alon. Well, Sir, since you command me—[*Goes rudely to kiss her.*]

Car. I did not mean kissing by saluting.

Alon. I cry you Mercy, [184] Sir, so I understood you.

Car. Fie upon't, that he should be no more a Master of Civility.

Lo. I fear, Sir, my Sister will never like this Humor in her Lover; he wants common Conversation.

Car. Conversation—ye foolish Boy, he has Money, and needs none of your Conversation. And yet if I thought he were valiant—

[*This while* Alonzo *and* Euphemia *make signs of Love with their Eyes.*]

Lo. I hope, Sir, he does not boast [185] of more of that than he really has.

Car. That Fault I myself have been guilty of, and can excuse; but the thing itself I shall never endure: you know I was forc'd to send you abroad, because I thought you addicted to that. I shall never sleep in quiet—Valiant! that's such a thing, to be Rich, or Wise and Valiant. [*Goes to* Euphemia.]

Lo. Colonel, pray to the business, for I fear you will betray yourself.

Car. But look upon his Wealth, *Euphemia*, and you will find those Advantages there which are wanting in his Person; but I think the Man's well.

Euph. I must not seem to yield too soon. [*Aside.*] Sir, there be many Spaniards born that are as rich as he, and have Wit too.

Car. She was ever very averse to this Marriage. [*Aside.*] This Man is half a *Spaniard*, his Mother was one, and my first Mistress, and she I can tell you, was a great Fortune—

Euph. I, Sir, but he is such a Fool—

Car. You are a worse, to find fault with that in a Husband.

Alon. Stand aside, Sir, are you to court your Daughter or I?

Car. I was inclining her—

Alon. You inclining her! an old Man wants Rhetoric; set me to her. [*Goes to* Euphemia.]

Car. This capricious Humor was tolerable in him, Whilst I believ'd it the Effects of Folly, but now 'tis that of Valour: Oh, I tremble at the Sight of him. [*Retires.*]

Euph. Now, I see you are a Cavalier of your Word.

Alon. Faith, *Euphemia*, you might have believ'd, and taken me upon better Terms, if you had so pleas'd: To marry you is but an ill-favor'd Proof to give you of my Passion.

Euph. Do you repent it?

Alon. Would to God 'twere come but to that, I was just upon the Point of it when you enter'd. But I know not what the Devil there is in that Face of yours, but it has debauch'd every sober Thought about me: Faith, do not let us marry yet.

Euph. If we had not proceeded too far to retreat, I should be content.

Alon. What shall I come to? all on the sudden to leave delicious whoring, drinking and fighting, and be condemn'd to a dull honest Wife. Well, if it be my ill Fortune, may this Curse light on thee that has brought me to't: may I love thee even after we are married to that troublesome Degree, that I may grow most damnable jealous of thee, and keep thee from the Sight of all Mankind, but thy own natural Husband, that so thou may'st be depriv'd of the greatest Pleasure of this Life, the Blessing of Change.

Euph. I am sorry to find so much ill Nature in you; would you have the Conscience to tie me to harder Conditions than I would you?

Alon. Nay, I do not think I shall be so wickedly loving; but I am resolv'd to marry thee and try.

Euph. My Father, Sir, on with your Disguise. [*To them* Carlo.]

Car. Well, Sir, how do you like my Daughter?

Alon. So, so, she'll serve for a Wife.

Car. But do you find her [186] willing to be so?

Alon. 'Tis not a half-penny matter for that, as long as my Father and you are agreed upon the matter,

Car. Well, *Euphemia*, setting all foolish Modesty aside, how do you like this Man?

Euph. As one, whom in Obedience to you, I am content to cast myself away upon.

Car. How seems his Humor to you?

Euph. Indifferent, Sir, he is not very courtly, something rough and hasty.

Car. I fear she has found his ill Quality of Valour too; and since 'tis certain 'tis so, [187] why should it be said that I ruin'd a Child to satisfy my Appetite of Riches? [*Aside.*] Come, Daughter, can you love him, or can you not? For I'll make but short Work on't; you are my Daughter, and have a Fortune great enough to enrich any Man; and I'm resolv'd to put no Force upon your Inclinations.

Euph. How's this! nay, then 'tis time I left dissembling. [*Aside.*] Sir, this Bounty in you has strangely overcome me, and makes me asham'd to have withstood your Will so long.

Car. Do not dissemble with me, I say do not; for I am resolv'd you shall be happy.

Euph. Sir, my Obedience shall—

Car. No more of your Obedience; I say again, do not dissemble, for I'm not pleas'd with your Obedience.

Euph. This Alteration is very strange and sudden; pray Heaven he have not found the Cheat. [*Aside.*] Love, Sir, they say will come after Marriage; pray let me try it.

Car. Few have found it so; nor shall you experience it at so dear a Rate as your Ruin.

Euph. But, Sir, methinks I am grown to love him more since he spoke to me, than before.

Car. The Effects of your Obedience again.

Euph. This is a strange Alteration, Sir; not all my Tears and Prayers before I saw him, could prevail with you. I beseech you, Sir, believe me.

Car. Nor should now, had I not another Reason for't.

Euph. Oh, I fear—But, Sir—

Car. Go to, I'll be better satisfy'd e'er I proceed farther—both of your Inclinations, and his Courage. [*Aside.*]

Euph. Do you consider his Wealth, Sir?

Car. That shall not now befriend him.

Alon. Sir, I bar whispering; 'tis not in my Bargain, nor civil: I'll have fair Play for my Money.

Car. I am only knowing my Daughter's Pleasure; she is a little peevish, as Virgins use in such Cases; but wou'd that were all, and I'd endeavor to reconcile her.

Alon. I thank you, Sir; in the mean time I'll take a Walk for an Hour or two, to get me a better Stomach both to my Dinner and Mistress.

Car. Do so, Sir. Come, *Euphemia,* I will give you a Proof of my Indulgence, thou shalt marry no valiant Fools! valiant, quoth ye. Come, come—had he been peaceable and rich—Come, come—[*Exit with* Euphemia.]

Lo. Well, now I'll go look after my *Dutchman,* lest he surprise us [188] here, which must not be; where shall I find you?

Alon. I'll wait upon my Prince, and then on you here.

Lo. Do so, and carry on this Humor. Adieu.

Scene II. *A flat Grove.*

[*Enter* Haunce *in a fantastical travelling Habit, with a Bottle of Brandy in his Hand as sick:* Gload *marches after.*]

Hau. Ah, ah, a pox of all Sea-Voyages. [189] [*Drinks.*] Here, *Gload,* take thee t'other Sope, and then let's home. [Gload *drinks.*] Ah, ah, a pox of all Sea-Voyages.

Glo. Sir, if I may advise, take t'other turn in the Grove, for I find by my Nose you want more airing.

Hau. How, Sirrah! by your Nose? have a care, you know 'tis ill jesting with me when I'm angry.

Glo. Which is as often as you are drunk; I find it has the same Effects on me too: but truly, Sir, I meant no other than that you smell a little of the Vessel, a certain sour remains of a Storm about you.

Hau. Ah, ah, do not name a Storm to me, unless thou wilt have the Effects on't in thy Face. [*Drinks.*]

Glo. Sha, sha, bear up, Sir, bear up.

Hau. Salerimente, a Sea-phrase too! Why, ye Rascal, I tell you I can endure nothing that puts me in mind of that Element. [*Drinks.*]

Glo. The Sight of *Donna Euphemia* will—[Gload *drinks between whiles too.*]

Hau. Hold, hold, let me consider whether I can endure to hear her nam'd or not; for I think I am so thoroughly mortify'd, I shall hardly relish Woman-kind again this—two Hours. [*Drinks.*]

Glo. You a Man of Courage, and talk thus!

Hau. Courage! Why, what dost thou call Courage?—*Hector* himself would not have chang'd his ten Years Siege for our ten Days Storm at Sea—a Storm—a hundred thousand fighting Men are nothing to't; Cities sacked by Fire nothing: 'tis a resistless Coward that attacks a Man at disadvantage; an unaccountable Magic, that first conjures down a Man's Courage, and then plays the Devil over him. And in fine, it is a Storm—

Glo. Good lack that it should be all these terrible things, and yet that we should outbrave it.

Hau. No god-a-mercy to our Courages [190] tho, I tell you that now, *Gload*; but like an angry Wench, when it had huffed and bluster'd itself weary, it lay still again. [*Drinks.*]

Glo. Hold, hold, Sir, you know we are to make Visits to Ladies, Sir; and this replenishing of our Spirits, as you call it, Sir, may put us out of Case.

Hau. Thou art a Fool, I never made love so well as when I was drunk; it improves my Parts, and makes me witty; that is, it makes me say anything that comes next, which passes now-a-days for Wit: and when I am very drunk, I'll home and dress me, and the Devil's in't if she resist me so qualify'd and so dress'd.

Glo. Truly, Sir, those are things that do not properly belong to you.

Hau. Your Reason, your Reason; we shall have thee witty too in thy Drink, hah! [*Laughs.*]

Glo. Why, I say, Sir, none but a Cavalier ought to be soundly drunk, or wear a Sword and Feather; and a Cloke and Band were fitter for a Merchant.

Hau. Salerimente, I'll beat any *Don* in *Spain* that does but think he has more right to any sort of Debauchery, or Gallantry than I, I tell you that now, *Gload*.

Glo. Do you remember, Sir, how you were wont to go at home? when instead of a Periwig, you wore a slink, greasy Hair of your own, thro which a pair of large thin Souses [p. 271] appear'd, to support a formal Hat, on end thus—[*Imitates him.*]

Hau. Ha, ha, ha, the Rogue improves upon't. [*Gives him Brandy.*]

Glo. A Collar instead of a Cravat twelve inches high; with a blue, stiff, starched, lawn Band, set in print like your Whiskers; a Doublet with small Skirts hooked to a pair of wide-kneed Breeches, which dangled halfway over a Leg, [191] all to be dash'd and dirty'd as high as the gartering.

Hau. Ha, ha, ha, very well, proceed. [*Drinks.*]

Glo. Your Hands, defil'd with counting of damn'd dirty Money, never made other use of Gloves, than continually to draw them thro—thus—till they were dwindled into the scantling of a Cats-gut.

Hau. Ha, ha, ha, a pleasant Rascal. [*Drinks.*]

Glo. A Cloke, half a yard shorter than the Breeches, not thorough lin'd, but fac'd as far as 'twas turn'd back, with a pair of frugal Butter-hams, [p. 271] which was always manag'd—thus—

Hau. Well, Sir, have you done, that I may show you this Merchant revers'd?

Glo. Presently, Sir; only a little touch at your Debauchery, which unless it be in damn'd Brandy, you dare not go to the Expence of. Perhaps at a Wedding, or some Treat where your Purse is not concern'd, you would most insatiably tipple; otherwise your two Stivers-Club is the highest you dare go, where you will be condemn'd for a Prodigal, (even by your own Conscience) if you add two more extraordinary to the Sum, and at home sit in the Chimney-Corner, cursing the Face of Duke *de Alva* upon the Jugs, for laying an Imposition on Beer: And now, Sir, I have done.

Hau. And dost thou not know, when one of those thou hast described, goes but half a League out of Town, that he is so transform'd from the Merchant to the Gallant in all Points, that his own Parents, nay the Devil himself cannot know him? Not a young English Squire newly come to an Estate, above the management of his Wit, has better Horses, gayer Clothes, swears, drinks, and does everything with a better grace than he; damns the stingy Cabal of the two Stiver-Club, and puts the young King of *Spain* and his Mistress together in a Rummer [192] of a Pottle; [p. 272] and in pure Gallantry breaks the Glasses over his Head, scorning to drink twice in the same: and a thousand things full as heroic and brave I cou'd tell you of this same Holy-day Squire. But come, t'other turn, and t'other sope, and then for *Donna Euphemia.* For I find I begin to be reconcil'd to the Sex.

Glo. But, Sir, if I might advise, let's e'en sleep first.

Hau. Away, you Fool, I hate the sober Spanish way of making Love, that's unattended with Wine and Music; give me a Wench that will out-drink the Dutch, out-dance the French, and out—out—kiss the English.

Glo. Sir, that's not the Fashion [193] in *Spain.*

Hau. Hang the Fashion; I'll manage her [194] that must be my Wife, as I please, or I'll beat her into Fashion.

Glo. What, beat a Woman, Sir?

Hau. Sha, all's one for that; if I am provok'd, Anger will have its Effects on whomsoe'er it light; so said *Van Trump,* when he took his Mistress a Cuff o'th' Ear for finding fault with an ill-fashion'd Leg he made her: I lik'd his Humor well, therefore come thy ways. [*Exeunt.*]

Scene III. *Draws off. A Grove.* [195]

[*Discovers* Antonio *sleeping on the Ground;* Hippolyta *sitting by, who sings.*]

> *Ah false* Amyntas, *can that Hour*
>   *So soon forgotten be,*
> *When first I yielded up my Power*
>   *To be betray'd by thee?*
> *God knows with how much Innocence*
>   *I did my Heart resign*
> *Unto thy faithless Eloquence,*
>   *And gave thee what was mine.*
>
> *I had not one Reserve in store,*
>   *But at thy Feet I laid*
> *Those Arms which conquer'd heretofore,*
>   *Tho now thy Trophies made.*
> *Thy Eyes in silence told their Tale*
>   *Of Love in such a way,*
> *That 'twas as easy to prevail,*
>   *As after to betray.*

[*She comes forth, weeps.*]

Hip. My Grief's too great to be diverted this way. [*Pointing to* Antonio.]
Why should this Villain sleep, this treacherous Man—
Who has forever robb'd me of my rest?
Had I but kept my Innocence entire,
I had out-brav'd my Fate, and broke my Chains,
Which now I bear like a poor guilty Slave,
Who sadly crys, If I were free from these,
I am not from my Crimes; so still lives on,
And drags his loathed Fetters after him.
Why should I fear to die, or murder him?
It is but adding one Sin more to th' number.
This—would soon do't—but where's the Hand to guide it? [*Draws a Dagger, sighs.*]
For 'tis an act too horrid for a Woman. [*Turns away.*]
But yet thus sleeping I might take that Soul, [*Turns to him.*]
Which waking all the Charms of Art and Nature
Had not the Power t'effect.
Oh were I brave, I could remember that,
And this way be the Mistress of his Heart.
But mine forbids it should be that way won;
No, I must still love on, in spite of me,
And wake him quickly, lest one Moment's thought
Upon my Shame should urge me to undo him.
Antonio, *Antonio.*

202

[He wakes, rises, and looks amazedly to see the Dagger in her Hand.]

Ant. Vile Woman, why that Dagger in that Hand?
Hip. To've kill'd thee with,
But that my Love o'ercame my juster Passion,
And put it in thy Power to save thy self;
Thank that, and not my Reason for thy Life.
Ant. She's doubly arm'd, with that and Injury,
And I am wounded and defenceless. *[Aside.]*
Hippolyta, why all this Rage to me? *[Kindly smiles.]*
Hip. Antonio, thou art perjur'd, false and base. *[In great Rage.]*
Ant. What said my fairest Mistress? *[Goes to her looking softly.]*
Hip. I said that thou wert perjur'd, false and base. *[Less in Rage.]*
Ant. My dear *Hippolyta*, speak it again,
I do not understand thee, *[Takes her by the Hand.]*
Hip. I said that thou wert perjur'd, my *Antonio*. *[Sighs.]*
Ant. Thou wert to blame, but 'twas thy Jealousy.
Which being a Fault of Love I will excuse.
Give me that Mark of Anger, prithee do,
It misbecomes thy Hand.
Hip. I've nothing left but this I can command,
And do not ravish this too.
Ant. It is unkind thus to suspect my Love;
Will you make no Allowance for my Humor?
I am by Nature rough, and cannot please,
With Eyes and Words all soft as others can,
But I can love as truly my blunt way.
Hip. You were so soft when first you conquer'd me. *[Sighs.]*
That but the Thoughts of that dear Face and Eyes,
So manag'd, and so set for Conquest out,
Would make me kind even to another Man;
Could I but thus embrace and hide my Eyes,
And call him my *Antonio*.

[She leans on his Bosom, he the while gets her Dagger.]

Ant. Stand off, false Woman, I despise thy Love,
Of which to every Man I know thou deal'st
An equal share.
Hip. I do not wonder that I am deceiv'd,
But that I should believe thee, after all thy Treachery.
But prithee tell me why thou treat'st me thus?
Why didst thou with the sacred Vows of Marriage,
After a long and tedious Courtship to me,
Ravish me from my Parents and my Husband?
For so the brave *Alonzo* was by promise.
Ant. Why, I will tell thee; 'twas not love to thee,

But hatred to thy Brother Don *Marcel*,
Who made Addresses to the fair *Clarinda*,
And by his Quality destroy'd my Hopes.
    Hip. And durst you not revenge yourself on him?
    Ant. His Life alone could not appease my Anger;
And after studying what I had to do—
    Hip. The Devil taught thee this.
    Ant. Yes, and you I chose,
Because you were contracted to *Alonzo*,
That the disgrace might be more eminent.
    Hip. I do believe thee, for when I reflect
On all thy Usage since thou hast betray'd me,
I find thou hast not paid me back one Sigh,
Or Smile for all that I have given thee.
    Ant. Hear me out.
    Hip. Most calmly.
    Ant. From Town to Town you know I did remove you,
Under pretence to shun your Brother's Anger:
But 'twas indeed to spread your Fame abroad.
But being not satisfy'd till in *Madrid*,
Here in your native Town, I had proclaim'd you;
The House from whence your Brother's Fury chas'd us,
Was a Bordello, where 'twas given out
Thou wert a *Venice* Courtesan to hire,
Whilst you believ'd it was your nuptial Palace. [*Laughs.*]
    Hip. Dost think I did not understand the Plot?
Yes, and was mad till some young Lovers came.
But you had set a Price too high upon me,
No brisk young Man durst venture,
I had expos'd myself at cheaper Rates.
    Ant. Your Price, I pray, young Sinner? [*Pulls off his Hat in scorn.*]
    Hip. Thy Life; he that durst say *Antonio* lives no more,
Should have possessed me *gratis*.
    Ant. I would have taken care none should have don't;
To show, and offer you to Sale, was equally as shameful.
    Hip. Well, what hast thou more to do? this is no
Place to inhabit in, nor shall thou force me further;
And back into the Town thou dar'st not go.
    Ant. Perhaps I had been kinder to you,
Had you continu'd still to give me that—
Might have begot a Passion in me.
    Hip. I have too much Repentance for that Sin,
To increase it, at the Price of being belov'd by thee.
    Ant. Consider what you do, this Place is silent,
And far from anything that may assist you.
Come lead me to the Covert of this Grove. [*Takes her rudely.*]

[*Enter* Haunce *and* Gload *drunk;* Haunce *seeing them, offers to go out again.*]

Glo. Hold, hold, Sir, why do you run away?

Hau. Thou Fool, dost not see the Reason?

Glo. I see a Man and a Lady, Sir.

Hau. Why, you Coxcomb, they are Lovers; Or some that are going to do the deed of Love.

Ant. How! Men here? Your Business.

Hau. Prithee, Friend, do not trouble yourself with ours, but follow your own; my Man is a little saucy in his Drink indeed, but I am sober enough to understand how things go.

Ant. Leave us then.

Hau. Leave us then—good Words, good Words, Friend; for look ye, I am in a notable Humor at present, and will be intreated.

Glo. Yes, Sir, we will be intreated.

Ant. Pray leave us then.

Hau. That's something—but hark ye, Friend, say a Man had a mind to put in for a share with you.

Ant. Rude Slaves, leave us.

Hau. Ha, Slaves!

Glo. Slaves said you, Sir? hah—

Hip. Oh, as you're a Gentleman, assist me. [*To* Haunce.]

Hau. Assist thee? this Fellow looks as he would not have his Abilities call'd in question; otherwise I am amorous enough to do thee a kindness. [*Offers still to go, she holds him.*]

Hip. Sir, you mistake me; this is a Ravisher—

Hau. A Ravisher! ha, ha, ha, dost like him the worse for that? No, no, I beg your Pardon, Madam.

Hip. Have you no Manhood, Sir?

Glo. She is in earnest; now if I durst stay, how I would domineer over my Master; never try'd perhaps, I may be valiant thus inspir'd. Lady, I am your Champion, who dares ravish you, or me either?

Ant. Rascal, unhand her. [*He comes up to them,* Gload *puts the Lady before him.*]

Hau. How now, *Gload* engag'd! nay, I scorn to be out-done by my Man. Sirrah march off with the Baggage, whilst I secure the Enemy.

Ant. Rash Man, what mean you?

Hau. I say, standoff, and let him go quietly away with the Wench, or look you—

Ant. Unmanner'd Fool, I will chastise thy Boldness. [*Goes up to him with his Dagger.*]

Hau. How, how, hast thou no other Weapon?

Ant. No, if I had, thou durst not have encounter'd me.

Hau. I scorn thy Words, and therefore there lies my Sword; and since you dare me at my own Weapon, I tell you I am good at Snick-a-Sne [p. 278] as the best *Don* of you all—[*Draws a great Dutch Knife.*]

Ant. Can I endure this Affront?

Glo. The best way to make a Coward fight, is to leave him in Danger—Come Lady—[*Goes out.*]

Ant. Thou base unmanner'd Fool, how darest thou [196] offer at a Gentleman, with so despis'd a thing as that?

Hau. Despis'd a thing? talk not so contemptibly of this Weapon, I say, do not, but come on if you dare.

Ant. I can endure no longer—[*Flies at him,* Haunce *cuts his Face, and takes away, after a-while, his Dagger.*] Injustice! can such a Dog, and such a Weapon vanquish me?

Hau. Beg your Life; for I scorn to stain my Victory in Blood—that I learnt out of *Pharamond.* [p. 278] [*Aside.*]

Ant. He does not merit Life, that could not defend [197] it against so poor and base a thing as thou: Had but *Marcel* left me my Sword—

Hau. O then I perceive you are us'd to be vanquish'd, and therefore I scorn to kill thee; live, live.

Ant. How the Rascal triumphs over me!

Hau. And now, like a generous Enemy, I will conduct thee to my Tent, and have thy Wounds dressed—That too I had out of *Pharamond.* [*Aside.*]

Ant. What if I take the offer of this Sot? so I may see *Hippolyta again.* But I forget—[*Aside.*]

Hau. Will you accept my Offer?

Ant. For some Reasons I dare not venture into the Town.

Hau. My Lodging is at St. Peter's Gate, hard by; and on the Parole of a Man of Prowess you shall be safe and free—*Pharamond* again. [*Aside.*]

Ant. I'll trust him, for worse I cannot be. [*Aside.*] Lead on, I'll follow, Sir—

Hau. Not so, for tho the Captive ought to follow the Victor, yet I'll not trust my Enemy at my backside. Politicks too.—[*Aside.*]

Ant. You must command—[*Go out.*]

Scene IV. *The Garden.*

[*Enter* Silvio *and* Francisca.]

Silv. Well, dear *Francisca,* will *Cleonte* come, And all alone into the Garden?

Franc. My Lord, she will; I have at last prevail'd, to what intent she knows not; this is an Hour wherein you'll scarce be interrupted: The amorous Entertainment you have prepar'd for her, will advance your Design; such Objects heighten the Desire. Is all ready on your part?

Silv. It is, and I am prepared for all the Resistance she can make, and am resolv'd to satisfy my insupportable Flame, since there's no other hope left me.

Franc. She's coming, Sir, retire. [*Exit* Silvio *into the Garden.*] Oh, how he kills me! Well, at least this pleasure I have whilst I am dying, that when he possesses the fair *Cleonte,* he forever ruins his Interest in her Heart, and must find nothing but her mortal Hate and Scorn.

[*Enter* Cleonte.]

Cleo. Francisca, why art thou so earnest for my coming into the Garden so early?

Franc. Because, Madam, here without Interruption you may learn what the Lady *Clarinda* has to tell you.

Cleo. Is that all? go wait upon her hither then.

Franc. Yes, when your more pleasant Affair is dispatch'd, I will—[*Aside.*]

206

[Exit Francisca.]

Cleo. Can this be Love I feel?
This strange unusual something in my Soul,
That pleads so movingly for *Silvio* there;
And makes me wish him not allied to me?

[A noise of rural Music is heard within the Trees, as Pipes, Flutes, and Voices.]

Hah! what pleasant Noise is this? sure 'tis i' the Air—Bless me, what strange things be these!

[Enter Swains playing upon Pipes, after them four Shepherds with Garlands and Flowers, and four Nymphs dancing an amorous Dance to that Music; wherein the Shepherds make Love to the Nymphs, and put the Garlands on their Heads, and go out; the Nymphs come and lay them at Cleonte's *Feet, and sing.]*

1 Nymph. Here at your Feet, we tribute pay,
Of all the Glories of the May.
2 Nymph. Such Trophies can be only due
To Victors so divine as you,
Both. Come, follow, follow, where Love leads the way,
To Pleasures that admit of no Delay.
1 Nymph. Come follow to the amorous Shade,
Covered with Roses, and with Jessamine.
2 Nymph. Where the Love-sick Boy is laid,
Panting for Love's charming Queen.
Both. Come follow, follow, where we lead the way,
To Pleasures that admit of no delay. [Lead her out.]

[The Scene changes to a fine Arbor, they leave her and vanish.]

Cleo. I am all Wonder.

[Enter Silvio *in rapture, not yet seeing* Cleonte.]*

Silv. I'm all on Fire, till I enjoy my Sister;
Not all the Laws of Birth and Nature
Can hinder me from loving—Nor is't just:
Why should the charm of fair *Cleonte's* Eyes,
Me less than Aliens to her Blood surprise?
And why (since I love Beauty everywhere,
And that *Cleonte* has the greatest share)
Should not I be allowed to worship her?
The empty Words of Nature and of Blood,
Are such as Lovers never understood.
Prudence in love 'twere Nonsense to approve,

And he loves most that gives a Loose to Love.

    Cleo. Silvio here!

    Silv. Hah—yonder she's! [*Sees her.*]

And now my Passion knows no Bounds, nor Laws.

    Cleonte, come, come satisfy my Flame.

[*Runs to her, and takes her passionately by the hand.*]

These private Shades are ours, no jealous Eye

Can interrupt our Heaven of Joy.

    Cleo. What mean you? do you know I am your Sister?

    Silv. Oh that accursed Name!—why should it check me? [*He pauses.*]

Wouldst thou had rather been some mis-begotten Monster,

That might have startled Nature at thy Birth:

Or if the Powers above would have thee fair,

Why wert thou born my Sister?

Oh, if thou shouldst preserve thy Soul, and mine,

Fly from this Place and me; make haste away,

A strange wild Monster is broke in upon thee;

A thing that was a Man, but now as mad

As raging Love can make him.

Fly me, or thou art lost forever.

    Cleo. Remember, *Silvio*, that you are my Brother,

And can you hurt your Sister? [*Weeps.*]

    Silv. Shouldst thou repeat those Ties a thousand times,

'Twill not redeem thee from the Fate that threatens thee.

Be gone, whilst so much Virtue does remain about me,

To wish thee out of Danger.

    Cleo. Sure, *Silvio*, this is but to try my Virtue. [*Weeps still.*]

    Silv. No, look on my Eyes, *Cleonte*, and thou shalt see them flame with a strange wicked Fire.

[*Looks wildly on her.*]

Yet do not look, thy Eyes increase it.

—Alas! [*Turns away, and hides his Eyes.*]

And I shall still forget I am thy Brother:

Go, go, whilst I have power to take my Eyes away,

For if they turn again, it will be fatal.

    Cleo. Pray hear me, Sir.

    Silv. Oh, do not speak; thy Voice has Charms

As tempting as thy Face; but whilst thou art silent and unseen,

Perhaps my Madness may be moderate;

For as it is, the best Effects of it

Will prompt me on to kill thee.

    Cleo. To kill me!

    Silv. Yes; for shouldst thou live, adorn'd with so much Beauty,

So much my Passion is above my Reason,

In some such fit as does possess me now
I should commit a Rape, a Rape upon thee:
Therefore be gone, and do not tempt Despair,
That merciless rude thing, but save thy Honor,
And thy Life.

 Cleo. I will obey you, Sir. [*Goes into the Garden.*]

 Silv. She's gone—and now [*Walks, and talks in stopping.*] my hot Fit abates—she is my Sister—that is, my Father's Daughter—but—what if his Wife deceiv'd him—or perhaps—(which is the likelier thing) my Mother play'd the false one—for 'twas her Trade to do so—and I'm not Son to *Ambrosio*—Oh, that she were in being to confess this Truth, for sure 'tis Truth; then I might love, and might enjoy *Cleonte*—enjoy *Cleonte!* [*In transport.*] Oh that Thought! what Fire it kindles in my Veins, and now my cold Fit's gone—[*Offers to go, but starts and returns.*]

—No, let me pause a while—
For in this Ague of my Love and Fear,
Both the Extremes are mortal—[*Goes into the Garden.*]

[*Enter* Ambrosio *and* Marcel.]

 Amb. I'm reconcil'd to you, since your Brother *Silvio* would have it so.

 Mar. My Blood flows to my Face, to hear him named.

 Amb. Let there be no more Differences between you: But *Silvio* has of late been discontented, keeps home, and shuns the Conversation which Youth delights in; goes not to Court as he was wont. Prithee, *Marcel*, learn thou the cause of it.

 Mar. I do believe I shall, my Lord—too soon. [*Aside.*]

 Amb. I'm now going to my *Villa*, and shall not return till Night; by the way I mean to visit your Wife, that was design'd to be, the rich *Flavia*, and see if I can again reconcile her to you; for your Neglect has been great, and her Anger is just.

 Mar. I rather wish it should continue, Sir, for I have yet no Inclinations to marry.

 Amb. No more, I'll have it so, if I can.

 Mar. I'm silent, Sir. [*Exit* Ambrosio *and* Marcel.]

[*Enter as from out of the Garden,* Cleonte, Clarinda, Francisca, Dormida, *from amongst the Trees, sadly;* Silvio *who starts at sight of them.*]

 Cleo. I am satisfied you knew not of my Brother's [198] being in the Garden. [*To* Francisca.] [198]

 Silv. Clarinda with my Sister! and in our House! she's very fair—and yet how dull and blasted all her Beauties seems, when they approach the fair *Cleonte's*—I cannot shun a tedious Compliment; to see the fair *Clarinda* [*Goes to* Clarinda.] [199] here, is a Happiness beyond my Hope; I'm glad to see her kind to the Sister, who always treated the Brother with so much Scorn and Rigour.

 Clar. Silvio! sure I'm betray'd. [*Aside.*] [*He talks to her.*]

[*Enter* Marcel, *and is amaz'd.*]

Mar. Hah! *Silvio* with *Clarinda* in our House! Oh, daring Villain! to make this place a Sanctuary To all thy Lusts and Treachery! Now I'm convinc'd, 'twas he that wounded me, And he that fled last Night with that false Woman. [Cleonte *goes to* Marcel.]

Silv. You need not fear me now, fair Maid, I'm disarm'd of all my dangerous Love.

Mar. It was by his contrivance that she came, [*To* Cleonte.] do not excuse him, but send her quickly from you, lest you become as infamous as she.—

Cleo. Oh, how I hate her now; I know my Brother *Silvio* loves her.

Mar. How every Gesture shows his Passion, whilst she seems pleas'd to hear him. I can endure no more—

Cleo. What will you do? [She goes to them.]

Mar. Nothing, dear Sister,
But if I can be wise and angry too:
For 'tis not safe t'attack him in the Garden.
How now, *Silvio*—under the Name of Brother,
I see you dare too much. [*Snatches away his Sister and* Clarinda.]

Silv. What mean you by this rude Address, *Marcel*?

Mar. I'll tell ye, Sir, anon. Go get you in. [To the Women, who go in.]

Silv. Well, Sir, your Business now?

Mar. It is not safe to tell you here, tho I have hardly Patience to stay till thou meet me in St. *Peter's* Grove.

Silv. I will not fail you, Sir, an Hour hence. [*Goes in after them.*]

Mar. I dare not in this Rage return to upbraid *Clarinda*, lest I do things that misbecome a Man. [*Goes out.*] [200]

ACT IV.

Scene I. Carlo's *House.*

[*After a Noise of Music without, enter Haunce dressed as* Alonzo *was, follow'd by Gload, in Masquerade.*]

Hau. Hold, hold, I do not like the Salutations I receive from all I meet in this House.

Glo. Why, Sir, methinks they are very familiar Scabs all.

Hau. *Salerimente*, they all salute me as they were my old Acquaintance. Your servant, *Myn heer Haunce*, cries one; your servant, Monsieur *Haunce*, cries another.

[*Enter* Servant.]

Serv. Your servant, Sir, you come indeed like a Bridegroom all beset with Dance and Fiddle.

Hau. Bridegroom! ha, ha, ha, dost hear, *Gload*? 'tis true faith. But how the Devil came he to know it, man, hah?

Serv. My Master, Sir, was just asking for you, he longs to speak with you.

Hau. Ha, ha, with me, Sir? why, ha, ha, who the pox am I?

Serv. You, Sir, why, who should you be?

Hau. Who should I be? why, who should I be?

Serv. *Myn heer Haunce van Ezel*, Sir.

Hau. Ha, ha, ha, well guest, i'faith now.

Glo. Why how should they guess otherwise, coming so attended with Music, as prepar'd for a Wedding?

Hau. Ha, ha, ha, say'st thou so? faith, 'tis a good Device to save the Charges of the first Compliments, hah: but hark ye, hark ye, Friend, are you sure this is the House of Don *Carlo?*

Serv. Why, Sir, have you forgot it?

Hau. Forgot it! ha, ha, ha, dost hear, *Gload?* forgot it! why how the Devil should I remember it?

Glo. Sir, I believe this is some new-fashion'd Civility in Spain, to know every Man before he sees him.

Hau. No, no, you fool, they never change their Fashion in Spain, Man.

Glo. I mean their manner of Address, Sir.

Hau. It may be so, I'll see farther. Friend, is Don *Carlo* within?

Serv. He has not been out since, Sir.

Hau. Since, ha, ha, ha, since when? hah.

Serv. Since you saw him, Sir.

Hau. Salerimente, will you make me mad? why you damnable Rascal, when did I see him? hah.

Serv. Here comes my Master himself, Sir, [*Enter* Carlo.] let him inform you, if you grow so hot upon the Question.

Car. How now, Son, what, angry? You have e'en tir'd yourself with walking, and are out of Humor.

Hau. Look there again—the old Man's mad too; why how the pox should he know I have been walking? Indeed, Sir, I have, as you say, been walking [*Playing with his Hat.*]—and am—as you say, out of Humor—But under favor, Sir, who are you? Sure 'tis the old Conjurer, and those were his little Imps I met. [*Surlily to him.*] [201]

Car. Sure, Son, you should be a Wit, by the shortness of your Memory.

Hau. By the Goodness of yours, you should be none, ha, ha, ha. Did I not meet with him there, *Gload,* hah? But pray refresh my Memory, and let me know you; I come to seek a Father amongst you here, one Don *Carlo.*

Car. Am I not the Man, Sir?

Hau. How the Devil should I know that now, unless by instinct?

Glo. The old Man is mad, and must be humor'd.

Hau. Cry you Mercy, Sir, I vow I had quite forgot you. Sir, I hope Donna *Euphemia*—

Car. Oh, Sir, she's in a much better Humor than when you saw her last, complied with our Desires more than I cou'd hope or wish.

Hau. Why look you here again—I ask'd after her Health, not her Humor.

Car. I know not what Arts you made use of, but she's strangely taken with your Conversation and Person.

Glo. Truly, Sir, you are mightily beholden to her, that she should have all this good Will to your Person and Conversation before she sees you.

Hau. Ay, so I am; therefore, Sir, I desire to see your Daughter, for I shall hardly be so generous as she has been, and be quits with her before I see her.

Car. Why, Sir, I hop'd you lik'd her when you saw her last.

Hau. Stark mad—I saw her last! why, what the Devil do you mean? I never saw her in all my Life, man. Stark mad, as I am true Dutch—[*Aside.*]

Car. A Lover always thinks the time tedious: But here's my Daughter.

[Enter Euphemia *and* Olinda.]

Hau. Ay, one of these must be she: but 'tis a Wonder I should not know which she is by instinct. [*Aside.*] [202]

[Stands looking very simply [203] *on both.]*

Euph. This is not *Alonzo*—has he betray'd me? [*Aside.*]

Car. Go, Sir, she expects you.

Hau. Your pardon, Sir; let her come to me, if she will, I'm sure she knows me better than I do her.

Glo. How should she know you, Sir?

Hau. How? by instinct, you Fool, as all the rest of the House does: don't you, fair Mistress?

Euph. I know you—

Hau. Yes, you know me; you need not be so coy mun, the old Man has told me all.

Euph. What has he told you?—I am ruin'd. [*Aside.*]

Hau. Faith, much more than I believ'd, for he was very full of his new-fashion'd Spanish Civility, [204] as they call it; But ha, ha, I hope, fair Mistress, you do not take after him?

Euph. What if I do, Sir?

Hau. Why then I had as lieve marry a Steeple with a perpetual Ring of Bells.

Glo. Let me advise you, Sir; methinks you might make a handsomer Speech for the first, to so pretty a Lady—Fakes, and were I to do't—

Hau. I had a rare Speech for her thou knowest, and an Entertainment besides, that was, tho I say it, unordinary: But a pox of this new way of Civility, as thou call'st it, it has put me quite beside my part.

Glo. Tho you are out of your complimenting Part, I am not out of my dancing one, and therefore that part of your Entertainment I'll undertake for. 'Slife, Sir, would you disappoint all our Ship's Company?—

Hau. That's according as I find this proud Tit in Humor.

Car. And why so coy? pray why all this Dissimulation? Come, come, I have told him your Mind, and do intend to make you both happy immediately.

Euph. How, Sir, immediately!

Car. Yes, indeed; nay, if you have deceiv'd me, and dissembled with me, when I was so kind, I'll show you Trick for Trick i'faith—[*Goes to* Haunce.]

Euph. What shall we do, *Olinda?*

Olin. Why marry Don *Alonzo*, Madam.

Euph. Do not rally, this is no time for Mirth.

Olin. Fie upon't, Madam, that you should have so little Courage; your Father takes this Fellow to be *Alonzo.*

Car. What Counsel are you giving there, hah?

Olin. Only taking leave of our old Acquaintance, since you talk of marrying us so soon.

Car. What Acquaintance, pray?

Olin. Our Maiden-heads, Sir.

Hau. Ha, ha, ha, a pleasant Wench, faith now; I believe you would be content to part with yours with less warning.

Olin. On easy Terms perhaps, but this marrying I do not like; 'tis like going a long Voyage to Sea, where after a while even the Calms are distasteful, and the Storms dangerous: one seldom sees a new Object, 'tis still a deal of Sea, Sea; Husband, Husband, every day,—till one's quite cloy'd with it.

Car. A mad Girl this, Son.

Hau. Ay, Sir, but I wish she had left out the simile, it made my Stomach wamble. [205]

Glo. Pray, Sir, let you the Maid alone as an Utensil belonging to my Place and Office, and meddle you with the Mistress.

Hau. Faith now, thou hast the better Bargain of the two; my Mistress looks so scurvily and civil, that I don't know what to say to her—Lady—hang't, that look has put me quite out again.

Car. To her, Son, to her—

Hau. Hark ye, Lady—Well, what next now? Oh pox, quite out, quite out; tell me whether the old Man ly'd or no, when he told me you lov'd me.

Euph. I love you!

Hau. Look you there now, how she looks again.

Car. She's only bashful, Sir, before me; therefore if you please to take a small Collation, that has waited within for you this three Hours—

Hau. That's strange now, that anything should wait for me, who was no more expected here than *Bethlehem-Gaber* [206]: [p. 289] Faith now, Lady, this Father of yours is very simple.

Euph. To take you for his Son.

Hau. I meant to have surpriz'd you I vow, before you had dreamt of me; and when I came, you all knew me as well as if you had cast a Figure for me.

Car. Well, Son, you'll follow.

Euph. You will not leave me alone, Sir, with a Man?

Hau. Go your ways, go your ways—I shall know more of your Secrets before [Gload *makes Grimaces to Olinda of Love.*] night yet, you little pouting Hypocrite you.

Euph. You know my Secrets! why, who are you?

Hau. Ha, ha, ha, that's a very good one faith now: who am I, quoth thou? why there's not a Child thus high in all your Father's House would have ask'd me so simple a Question.

Olin. Madam, I find by this Man, this is your expected Lover, whom you must flatter, or you are undone, 'tis *Haunce van Ezel.* [*To* Euphemia.]

Euph. The Fop himself.

Hau. Oh, do you know me now?

Euph. 'Tis impossible.

Hau. This is an extreme the other way now. [*Aside.*]

Impossible, ha, ha, ha! No, no, poor thing, do not doubt thy Happiness: for look ye to confirm you, here are my Bills of Exchange with my own natural Name to them, if you can read written Hand—[*Shows her Papers.*]

Glo. Not love you! I'll swear you lye now, you little Jade, I am now in Masquerade and you cannot judge of me; but I am Book-keeper and Cashier to my Master, and my Love will turn to account, I'll warrant you.

Olin. There may be use made of him. [*Aside.*]

I shall think of it. But pray why are you thus accouter'd?

Glo. Fakes, to entertain [207] your Lady, we have brought the whole Ship's Company too in Masquerade.

Olin. That indeed will be very proper at this time of the Day, and the first Visit too.

Glo. Shaw, that's nothing, you little think what Blades we are mun—Sir, I'll call in the Fiddles and the Company.

Hau. Well remember'd, faith, now I had e'en forgot it.

Euph. What's the meaning of this? [*Fiddles strike up.*]

Hau. To show you the difference between the damnable dull Gravity of the *Spanish*, and brisk Gaiety of the *Dutch*. Come, come, begin all.

[*Enter* Dutchmen *and Women dancing.*]

Nay, I'll show you what I can do too, come, *Gload.* [*They two dance.*] [208] There's for you now, and yet you have not seen half my good Qualities; I can sing the newest Ballad that has been made, so I can. [*Sings a* Dutch *Song.*]

Euph. Be these your Friends, Sir? they look as if you had ransack'd a Hoy [p. 291] for them.

Hau. How! look on them well, they are all States or States-fellows, I tell you that now, and they can bear witness who I am too.

Euph. Now I'm convinced, and am sorry I doubted my Happiness so long: I had such a Character of you.

Hau. Of me! oh Lord, I vow now—as they say—I don't know—ha, ha—

Euph. I heard you were the most incorrigible Fool, the most intolerable Fop.

Hau. Ha, ha, ha, do you hear, *Gload*—who, I a Fop? I vow they were mistaken in me, for I am counted as pretty a Merchant as any walks the Change; can write a very plain Hand, and cast Account as well—my man *Gload*—can't I, Sirrah?

Glo. Yes indeed, forsooth, can he.

Hau. Egad, a Fool, a Fop, quoth ye—[*Walks angry.*]

Olin. By all means flatter him, Madam.

Euph. I'm satisfy'd, Sir.

Hau. I care not whether you are or no, for I shall have you whether you will or no, mun.

Euph. 'Tis very likely; but there is a certain troublesome Fellow in love with me, that has made me vow whenever I marry to ask him leave.

Hau. How, ask his leave? I scorn to ask any Body's leave, I tell you that, tho 'twere my Mistress—

Euph. I cannot marry you then.

Hau. How, not marry me? look here now: [*Ready to cry.*]

Gload, can't you marry, and let no living Soul know it?

Euph. Oh no, Sir, I love your Life better, which would be endanger'd.

Hau. Why, what a cursed Custom you have in *Spain*, a Man can neither marry, nor console his Neighbour's Wife without having his Throat cut. Why, what if he will not give you leave?

Euph. Why, then you must fight him.

Hau. How! fight him, I fight him!

Glo. Why, yes, Sir, you know you can fight, you try'd but this very Morning—

Hau. Softly, you damn'd Rogue, not a Word of my Prowess aloud. *Salerimente,* I shall be put to fight when I am sober, shall I, for your damn'd prating, ye Rascal?

Euph. I am glad you have that good Quality.

[Olinda *speaking to* Gload, *pushes him to speak.*]

Glo. Ay, Madam—my Master—has many more:
But if you please to tell him his Rival's Name—

Hau. I'll have your Ears for this, Sirrah, the next time I'm soundly drunk, and you know that won't be long. [*Aside.*] Lord, Madam, my Man knows not what he says. Ye Rascal, say I have no Courage—or I will drink myself to the Miracle of Valour, and exercise it all on thee.

Glo. I know what I do, Sir, you had Courage this Morning, is the Fit over?

Hau. Have I not slept since, you Rogue, have I not?

Glo. I have a trick to save your Honor, Sir, and therefore I will stand in't you have Courage.

Hau. A Pox of your Trick, the Rogue knows I dare not chastise him now, for fear they should think I have Valour.

Glo. Madam, my Master's modest, but tell him who 'tis he must fight with—

Hau. Oh, for a Tun of Rhenish—that I might abundantly beat thee—

Euph. Your Rival's Name's *Alonzo,* Sir.

Hau. Oh the Devil, a thundering Name too; but will this same—*Alonzo* make no allowance for necessity?—I vow 'tis pure necessity in me to marry you: the old Men being agreed upon the Matter, I am but an Instrument—alas, not I, [*Crys.*] A very Tool, as they say, so I am.

Glo. Lord, Sir, why do you cry? I meant no harm.

Hau. No harm, you Rascal—to say I am valiant.

Glo. Why, yes, Sir, and if you would say so too, at worst 'twas but getting Don *Lovis* to have fought for you; you know that's a small courtesy to a Friend.

Hau. Faith, now thou art in the right; he'll do his Business for him, I'll warrant him. [*Wipes his Eyes.*]
Nay then, Madam, I have Courage, and will to this Don—this *Alonzo* you speak of; and if he do not resign you, and consign you too, I'll make him; yes, make him, do ye see—If *Lovis* should refuse me now—[*Aside.*]

Glo. Shaw, Sir, he makes nothing to kill a Man, ten or twenty.

Euph. Well, since you are so resolv'd, my Brother will tell you where to find this *Alonzo*; and tell him, I must marry you today, for I am resolv'd not to lie alone tonight.

Hau. What would not a Man do for so kind a Mistress?

Euph. Well, get you about it strait then, lest my Father's coming prevent it. [*Exeunt* Euphemia *and* Olinda.]

Hau. I am gone—but if *Lovis* should fail—

Glo. He would beat you, if he thought you doubted him.

Hau. I'll keep my Fears then to myself. [*Go out.*]

Scene II. *The Street.*

[*Enter* Hippolyta *dressed like a Man, with a Paper.*]

Hip. Thus I dare look abroad again:
Methinks I am not what I was,
My Soul too is all Man;
Where dwells no Tenderness, no womanish Passions.
I cannot sigh, nor weep, nor think of Love,
But as a foolish Dream that's gone and past.
Revenge has took possession of my Soul,
And drove those Shadows thence; and shows me now
Love, in so poor, so despicable a Shape,
So quite devested of his Artful Beauty,
That I'm asham'd I ever was his Votary.
Well, here's my Challenge to *Antonio*;
But how to get it to him is the Question.
Base as he is, he'll not refuse to come,
And since he never saw the wrong'd *Alonzo*,
Sure I may pass for him. Who's here?—

[*Enter* Haunce *and* Gload. *She stands aside.*]

Hau. Gload, if it were possible I could be sober, and valiant at once, I should now be provok'd to exercise it: for I cannot find *Lovis*, and then how I shall come off, the Lord knows. And then again, for letting the Lady go, whom I rescu'd in the Grove this Morning.

Glo. Should I disobey a Lady, Sir? for she commanded me to let her go so soon as she came into the Gate. And, Sir, look, here comes Don *Lovis*.

[*Enter* Lovis *and* Alonzo.]

Hau. Oh, Brother *Lovis*, where the Devil have you been all this Day? I stay'd for you to go with me to your Sister's, as long as Flesh and Blood could forbear.

Lo. Why, have you been there without me?

Hau. Yes, marry have I, Sir.

Alon. I am undone then—[*Aside.*]

Hau. I needed no Recommendation mun, for when I came they were all as well acquainted with me—I never saw them before; but by the way, they are all no wiser than they should be, except your Sister, who is the pretty'st loving, sweet Rogue—

Alon. How's this?

Lo. But have you seen my Sister?

Hau. Seen her! yes, and will marry her too mun before Night, an she were a thousand Sisters—but harkye, *Lovis*, the business is this—you must know that before I marry her, I am to seek out a certain Fellow, they call—they call *Alonzo*, ay, ay, *Alonzo*—a Pox on him, a troublesome Rascal they say he is; and his leave, it seems, must be asked to marry your Sister.

Lo. Well, Sir, and what if he will not give you leave?

Hau. Why then, you must know I am to get him very well favor'dly beaten.

Alon. Sure this is the Coxcomb himself.

Hau. Now for your Sister's sake, who loves me, poor thing, I will not run the danger of beating him myself, but must desire that small courtesy of thee.

Lo. How! I beat him?

Hau. You beat him, yes, you; what a Pox do you scruple such a kindness to a Friend? I know you make no more of killing a Man next your Heart in a Morning, than I do of eating a pickled Herring.

Lo. But she desir'd you to do't.

Hau. That's all one so it be done, mun; besides, why should I run myself into a Premunire, when I need not? Your Father is bound by Agreement to mine, to deliver me the Wares (that is, his Daughter) safe and sound; and I have no more to do, but to protest against him in case of Non-performance. 'Twill be a dear Commodity to me at this rate. [*Cries.*]

Lo. Well, Sir, I'll see what may be done.

Hau. Spoke like a Friend now: Well, you must about it instantly, for I must be married today.

Alon. Must you so, Sir?—

Hau. Yes marry must I, Sir—Who the Devil's this now? [*To* Lovis.]

Alon. That same *Alonzo* whom you inquire for.

Hau. Are you so, Sir?—Why, what then, Sir,—*Lovis, Lovis.* [*Runs behind* Lovis.] [209]

Alon. What then, Sir? then I tell you, I will not be beaten.

Hau. Look ye here now—*Lovis.*

Lo. Ha, ha, ha, canst thou be angry with him? [*To* Alonzo.]

Hau. I, can you be angry with me?

Alon. I know not why an Ass should have more privilege than any other rude Beast.

Lo. Ha, ha, ha, this Humor's so pleasant in thee, I wish thou wouldst pursue it a little—*Haunce*, bear up to him, he's but a mere Huff, ha, ha, ha. [*Claps him on the Back, he goes fearfully forward.*]

Glo. I, Sir, as long as Don *Lovis* is here, you may say what you Willmore

Hau. May I so?—and why, Sir?—am I, Sir—an Ass, Sir? [*Runs behind* Lovis.]

Alon. 'Sdeath, you Rascal, do you question me?

Hau. Oh, hold, Sir, hold, not I, God forbid I should question it, *Lovis*—is it, indeed, *Alonzo*, hah?

Lo. Yes indeed is it.

Hau. And wilt thou not do so much as to beat him for me a little?

Lo. Not I, I dare not, he's a terrible Man.

Hau. Why look you here now, you damn'd Rogue, [*To* Gload.] Have not you serv'd me finely, hah?

Glo. Why, Sir, 'tis but crying Peccavi.

Hau. Peccavi, and be hang'd to you—Lord, Sir, [*To* Alonzo.] why are you so angry? I came but to ask you a civil Question, from my Wife that must be.

Alon. You must ask me leave, first.

Hau. Yes, yes, Sir, so she said mun; for she must marry me tonight.

Alon. Yes, you shall have it with this—too. [*Draws.*]

Hau. Why look you [Haunce *runs away,* Lovis *stays him.*] here now, here's damn'd doings. For my part, I declare it here upon [210] my Death-bed, I am forc'd to what I do, and you kill me against my Willmore

Alon. Do'st think we are not discover'd in our Design? I'd kill the Dog if I thought we were.

Lo. I believe not; and perceive by my Sister's Message, that we are to come to her, and prevent this Fellow's marrying her.

Alon. Well, Sir, I'll spare your Life, and give your Mistress leave to marry tonight.

Hau. How, Sir, tonight?—But is he in earnest, *Lovis?*

Lo. In very good earnest.

Hau. Tan, ta, ra, ra, ra—hay, Boys, what a Night we'll have on't, *Gload,* for Fiddles and Dancing.

Alon. Tell your Mistress I will dispatch a little Affair, and wait on her.

Glo. And pray, Sir, may I have leave to marry the Maid too?

Alon. We'll consider on't.

Hau. I am not such a Fool to venture tho, till I know the Coast is clear, for his very Looks are terrible; but go you, *Gload,* and tell her what he says. [*Alonzo* talks to *Lovis.*]

[Enter *Hippolyta* from aside.]

Hip. These be the Men that rescu'd me this morning,
And are not to be employ'd in my Affair.
But yonder Stranger has a noble Look,
And from him I'll intreat this Favor—Sir—[*To* Alonzo.]

Alon. With me, Sir?

Hip. Yes, please you to walk a little this way, Sir. [*Takes him aside.*]

Hau. Well, make you sure of Fiddles, for look ye, we'll appear tonight like ourselves.

Glo. It shall be done, Sir.

Hip. I am a Stranger and a Gentleman,
And have an humble Suit to you.

Alon. You may command me anything.

Hip. Sir, there is a Gentleman, if I may call him so, that dares do ill; has put a base Affront upon a Lady—a Lady whom all brave Men are bound to vindicate: I've writ him here a Challenge, and only beg you'll give it him; I will attend you in St. *Peter's* Grove, where I desire the perfidious *Antonio* (for that's his Name, to whom this is directed) to meet me.

Alon. I'm pleas'd to see this Gallantry in a Man so young, and will serve you in this, or whatever else you shall command. But where is this *Antonio?*

Hip. That I'll inquire of these. Sir, pray can you give any account of the Cavalier [*To* Haunce, *who starts as afraid.*] [211] you fought with this Morning in St. *Peter's* Grove, that had a Lady with him?

Hau. So, now perhaps I shall be hang'd for that. [*Aside.*]
I fight, Sir! I never fought in my Life, nor saw no Man, not I.

Glo. 'Sha, you may confess it, Sir; there's no Law against killing in *Spain.*

Hip. How, have you murder'd him? [*Takes hold of him.*]

Hau. This Rogue has a mind to have me dispatch'd. [*Aside.*] Hold, Sir, the Man's as well and alive as you are, and is now at my Lodgings: look ye, here's the Dagger I disarm'd him of—but that I do not love to boast. [*Shows it.*]

Hip. It is the same.

Alon. Sir, I shall not fail to wait on you with the Answer I receive.

Hip. I humbly thank you, Sir.

Alon. So prithee, dear *Lovis*, go make my excuse to your Sister for a moment, and let her get all things ready against I come; let the Priest too wait, for I see my Destiny, which I can no longer prevent, draws on apace. [*Exit* Lovis.] Come, Sir, you must conduct me to *Antonio*.

[*Exeunt* Alonzo, Haunce, *and* Gload.]

Hip. So now the Work's half done, that will redeem
All the lost Credit of our Family.
To kill, or to be kill'd, I care not which, [*Weeps.*]
So one or both expire; be strong, my Soul,
And let no feeble Woman dwell about thee.
Hence Fears and Pity, such poor things as these
Cannot the Storms of my Revenge appease:
Those Showers must from his treacherous Heart proceed,
If I can live and see *Antonio* bleed. [*Sighs, and Exit.*]

Scene III. *A deep Grove.*

[*Enter* Marcel *alone.*]

Mar. The hour is almost come which I appointed,
And yet no *Silvio* appears, the time seems long to me;
But he that's circled in his Mistress' Arms,
Forgets the hasty hours,
And passes them as unregarded by,
As Men do Beggars who demand a Charity.

[*Enter* Hippolyta.]

Young Man, hast thou encounter'd none within this Grove?

Hip. Not any, Sir,—*Marcel!* my injur'd Brother!

Mar. Why dost thou turn away, and hide thy Face?

Hip. 'Tis not my Face I hide, but Sorrow there. [*Weeps.*]

Mar. Trust me, thou weepest; would I could do so too,
That I might be less angry;
And Silence best expresses Grief:
But thine's a saucy Sorrow dares approach
A Face so fair and young.

Hip. If the Ingrate for whom I grieve had thought so, I might have spar'd my Tears. Farewell, Sir.

Mar. Stay, hast thou been a Lover?

Hip. A very, very passionate one.

Mar. And wert thou not belov'd?

Hip. At first, to draw me in, the cunning Artist Made me believe I was.

Mar. Oh! I could kiss thee now, for the alliance
Between thy Grief and mine.
Hadst thou a loose and wanton Sister too,
Then thou wert perfect wretched, as I am. [Weeps.]
But prithee leave me, now I think of it:
For shouldst thou stay, thou'dst rob me of my Anger;
For since a Youth like thee can be unhappy,
With such a Shape, and so divine a Face,
Methinks I should not quarrel with my Star,
But bow to all my faithless Mistress' Scorns.

[Hollowing within.] So ho, ho, so ho, ho—

Mar. So ho, so ho, ho, ho—'Tis my false Rival.
Now leave me, Sir, to reassume my Anger.
    Hip. I will obey—farewell—
My own Despair makes me neglect his Life. [Goes out.]

[Enter *Silvio*.]

    Mar. 'Tis *Silvio*.
    Silv. You see I have obey'd you, Sir.
    Mar. Come, Sir, your Sword.
    Silv. You are my Brother, and 'twere an impious Action,
To fight you unprovok'd: give me a cause,
Nay, and a just one too, or I shall find it hard
—To wound *Cleonte's* Brother. [Aside sighing.]
    Mar. Thou cam'st prepar'd to talk, and not to fight.
I cannot blame thee for't, for were I *Silvio*,
Thus I would do to save a Life belov'd: [Offers to fight, *Silvio* steps back.]
But 'twill not serve you now.
    Silv. Your Reason, Sir, and I'm ready, if it be just.
    Mar. Oh do not urge me to repeat my Wrongs,
For if thou dost, I hardly shall have Man enough remain
To fight thee fairly. [*Offers still.*]
    Silv. Surely he knows my Passion for *Cleonte*—[*Aside.*]
I urge the Reason still.
    Mar. Hast thou forgot thy last Night's Treachery?
How like a Thief thou stol'st into her Lodgings?
    Silv. 'Tis so—'tis true, *Marcel*, I rudely did intrude—
    Mar. Oh, quickly haste—this looks like Women's jangling. [*Offers to fight again.*]
    Silv. Oh, is it bravely done, [212] *Marcel*, to punish
A Passion which you ought to pity rather?
'Tis what I cannot reconcile nor justify:
And so distracted it has made me too—
I will not fight in so unjust a Cause.
Kill me, and I'll embrace you whilst I die;
A thousand Wounds imprinted on this Body, [213]

Will bring less Pain than that her Eyes have caus'd.
Here strike—Pity my Pain and ease me.

[*Opens his Arms, and throws away his Sword.*]

  Mar. I find thou hast a Charm about thy Tongue,
And thou implor'st thy Death in such a way,
I cannot hurt thee; and it gives me hopes
Thou art not yet so bless'd to be belov'd,
For then thou wouldst not be thus desperate.
  Silv. Oh yes, I am belov'd.
  Mar. Oh do not say thou art,
Nor take me from a Calmness, that may spare thee.
  Silv. Not say I am belov'd! thou canst not hire me
With Life or fuller Joy, to say I am not.
If there be Truth and Love in Innocence, she loves me.
  Mar. Yet, yet, ye Gods, I can endure—say, but thou art not,
For I would yet preserve thee.
  Silv. Oh, canst thou wish that I should fall so low,
To save my Life with Lies; the poorest Sin of all the number?
  Mar. Then once again thou hast debauch'd my Pity. [*Takes to his Sword.*] [214]
  Silv. Her Passion I will justify, but not my own;
Her's is as pure as Prayers of Penitence;
But mine—I cannot give a Name to.

[*They fight: Enter* Alonzo, *and parts them.*]

  Alon. How now, what's here to do! *Marcel?*
  Mar. Alonzo! the only Man I wish to shun.
  Silv. I'm glad, who e'er thou be'st thou hast prevented us.
  Alon. Thou hast more Wit than he, then I find: Your Quarrel, Sir, may a Man have leave to enquire into't?
  Mar. This is that *Silvio*, that noble Youth my Brother, whom thou hast often heard me name.
  Alon. An excellent Character for an Enemy, Noble, and Brother: For shame put up your Swords, and I'll be Judge between ye.
  Mar. The Case is soon decided; I will not tell you with how tedious a Courtship I won the Heart, as I thought, of a young Beauty of this Town—and yesterday receiv'd a Billet from her, to wait on her at night, to receive the recompence of all my Pains and Sufferings—In this extasy of Joy I show'd him the Paper; and he getting thither before me, rob'd me of my Prize.
  Silv. I am so pleas'd at this mistake of thine, I can forgive it freely.
  Mar. Not content with this, most treacherously, hid in the shades of Night, he met me in the Hall of this false Woman, and stabb'd me, which did secure his flight with her; and wouldst thou have me put this Injury up?
  Alon. Faith, you must, and your Sword too,
Unless you mean to keep it drawn on me.
'Twas I that wounded you i' th' dark; and it was I

That rob'd you of *Clarinda*.

Mar. Thou?

Alon. I, am I so unlikely a Man to do such a feat?

Mar. How dare you, Sir, do this?

Alon. I dare do anything, but break my Word, as thou hast basely done with me—But I am now in haste, and should be glad to know where to meet you anon.

Mar. I'll wait on you at the farther side of this Grove by the River.

Alon. I will not fail you—[*Exit* Alonzo.]

Mar. Come, Sir, till I can better prove you are my Rival, I will believe you are my Friend and Brother.

Silv. When thou shalt know my miserable Story,
Thou wilt believe and pity me. [*Go out.*]

[*Enter again* Hippolyta *from out of the Wood.*]

Hip. I wonder this Cavalier stays so long,
Pray Heaven he meet *Antonio*.

[*Enter* Alonzo.]

Your Servant, Sir.

Alon. The Cavalier to whom you sent me, Sir, Will wait upon you here.

Hip. I humbly thank you, Sir, and should be glad to know how I might pay my Gratitude.

Alon. My Duty ends not here; I have a Sword to serve you.

Hip. You shame me with this Generosity; but, Sir, I hope my own will be sufficient in so good a Cause.

Alon. Tho you are young, I question not your Bravery; But I must beg to stay and see fair play, And offer you my Service when you've done.

Hip. The Enemy appears, Sir,—and since you are so good, I beg you would retire behind those Trees; for if he see us both, since he is single, he will suspect some treachery.

Alon. You've reason, Sir, and I'll obey you. [*Goes aside.*]

[*Enter* Antonio *reading a Paper.*]

SIR,

I do desire you to meet me in St. Peter's *Grove, with your Sword in your Hand, about an Hour hence; you will guess my Business, when you know my name to be*
                                                                    Alonzo.

Alon. How's that? [*Aside.*]

Ant. I wish't had been another Enemy,
Since from the Justice of his Cause I fear
An ill success; would I had seen *Hippolyta*,
That e'er I dy'd I might have had her pardon.
This Conscience—'tis ominous,
But ne'er appears in any horrid shape,
Till it approaches Death—

[Goes forward, sees Hippolyta, who jostles him in passing by; he stops and looks.]

Hip. You seem, Sir, to be he whom I expect.
Ant. I'm call'd *Antonio*, Sir—
Hip. And I *Alonzo*; the rest we need not ask,
For thou art well acquainted with my Injuries,
And I with thy Perfidiousness. *[Draws.]*
Ant. I know of none you have receiv'd from me,
If on *Hippolyta's* account you fight:
She lov'd me, and believ'd; and what dull Lover
Would have refus'd a Maid so easily gain'd?
Hip. Ah, Traitor, by how base a way
Thou wouldst evade thy Fate?
Didst thou not know she was my Wife by promise?
Did not *Marcel, Ambrosio*, all consent
To make her mine as soon as I arriv'd?
Alon. Who the Devil's that young Bully that takes my Name, and my Concerns upon
him? *[Aside.]*
Hip. But why should I expect a Truth from thee,
Who after so much time, so many Vows,
So many Tears, Despairs and Sighs, at last
Didst gain a Credit with this easy Fool,
Then left her to her shames, and her despairs?—Come, Sir—
Or I shall talk my self to calmness—*[Aside.]*
Ant. I'm ready, Sir, to justify the Deed.

[They offer to fight, Alonzo *steps forth.]*

Alon. Hold! hold! fair Thief that rob'st me of my Name,
And wouldst my Honor too; *[Puts her by.]*
If thou hast wrong'd the fair *Hippolyta*, *[To* Antonio.]
No Man but I has right to do her justice.
Or you are both my Rivals—tell me which,
Which of you is it I must kill—or both?
I am *Alonzo*, who dares love *Hippolyta?*
Hip. Let not your friendship, Sir, proceed so far,
To take my Name, to take my Quarrel on you.
Alon. In this Dispute none's more concern'd than I,
And I will keep my ground in such a cause,
Tho all the Rivals that her Beauty makes me,
Were arm'd to take my Life away.
Ant. Come, Sir, I care not which of you's *Alonzo*. *[They go to fight, she holds*
Alonzo.]
Hip. This Gallantry's too much, brave Stranger.
Antonio, hurt him not; I am the wrong'd *Alonzo*,
And this a perfect Stranger to the business,
Who seeing me appear less Man than he,

And unacquainted with my Deeds abroad,
In Bounty takes my Name and Quarrel on him.
    Alon. Take heed, young Man, and keep thy Virtue in,
Lest thus misguided it become a Crime.
But thou, he says, hast wrong'd *Hippolyta,* [To *Antonio.*]
And I am he must punish it.
    Hip. Sure it is he indeed—
For such a Miracle my Brother render'd him, [*Aside.*]
Hold, hold, thou Wonder of thy Sex—[*They fight.*]
    Alon. Stand by, I shall be angry with thee else,
And that will be unsafe—

[*As* Alonzo *fights with one Hand, he keeps her off with t'other; she presses still forward on* Antonio *with her Sword, endeavoring to keep back* Alonzo.]

[*Enter to them* Marcel.]

    Mar. Sure I heard the Noise of Swords this way! [*Draws.*]
Hah, two against one! Courage, Sir. [*To* Antonio.]

[*They fight all four,* Marcel *with* Hippolyta *whom he wounds, and* Alonzo *with* Antonio, *who is disarmed.*]

    Hip. Good Heaven, how just thou art!
    Mar. What, dost thou faint already?—Hah, the pretty talking Youth I saw but now!

[*Runs to her, and holds her up.*]

Alas, how dost thou?
    Hip. Well, since thy Hand has wounded me—
    Ant. My Life is yours, nor would I ask the Gift,
But to repair my Injuries to *Hippolyta.*
    Alon. I give it thee—[*Gives him his Sword.*]
    Mar. How, *Antonio!*—
What unkind Hand has rob'd me of the justice
Of killing thee?
    Alon. His that was once thy Friend, *Marcel.*
    Mar. Oh! dost thou know my Shame? [*Turns away.*]
    Alon. I know thou art false to Friendship,
And therefore do demand mine back again, thou'st us'd it scurvily.
    Mar. Thou knowst too much to think I've injur'd thee.
    Alon. Not injur'd me! Who was it promis'd me *Hippolyta?*
Who his Alliance, and his Friendship too?
And who has broke them all, but thou perfidious?
Come, 'tis *Hippolyta* that I demand.
    Mar. By this he should not know my Sister's Shame. [*Aside.*]
Oh, Sir, you must not have *Hippolyta.*
    Alon. How! not have *Hippolyta!*

Tho every Step were guarded by a Brother,
Tho she were circled roundabout with Rivals,
Ye should not all have Power to keep her from me.
Not have *Hippolyta!*—
'Sdeath, Sir, because I do not know my Birth,
And cannot boast a little empty Title,
I must not have *Hippolyta.*—
Now I will have her; and when you know I can,
You shall petition me to marry her.
And yet I will not do't. Come, Sir—[*Offers to fight.*]

    Hip. Hold, hold, brave Man, or turn your Sword on me.
I am the unhappy Cause of all your Rage:
'Tis I, generous *Alonzo*, that can tell you
What he's asham'd to own,
And thou wilt blush to hear.

    Mar. Hippolyta! thou wretched wicked Woman:
Thus I reward thy Sins—[*Offers to kill her,* Antonio *steps between.*]

    Ant. Hold, Sir, and touch her not without my leave,
She is my Wife; by sacred Vows my Wife.

    Alon. I understand no riddling; but whoever thou be'st.
Man or Woman, thou'rt worth our Care—
She faints—come, let us bear her hence. [*She faints,* Antonio *kneels to her.*]

    Ant. Oh stay, *Hippolyta*, and take me with thee,
For I've no use of Life when thou art gone. [*Weeps.*]
Here, kill me, brave *Marcel*—and yet you need not;
My own Remorse, and Grief will be sufficient.

    Mar. I credit thee, and leave thee to their Mercy.

    Hip. That Goodness, Sir, has call'd me back to Life,
To pay my humble Thanks; could you have Mercy too,
To pardon me—you might redeem my Soul.

    Mar. Some Pity I have yet, that may preserve thee too,
Provided this Repentance be not feign'd.

    Ant. My Life, Sir, is Security for both.

    Mar. Doubt not, I'll take the Forfeit, Sir—Come, *Hippolyta.*
Thy Father's House shall once again receive thee.

    Ant. Lean on my Arm, my dearest.

    Mar. Sir, by the way, I'll let you know her Story,
And then perhaps you will not blame my Friendship.

    Alon. And in return, I'll give you back *Clarinda*—
And beg your Pardon for the Wound I gave you. [*Exeunt, leading* Hippolyta.]

ACT V.

Scene I. *A Garden.*

[*Enter* Cleonte, Clarinda *weeping, and* Dormida *and* Francisca.]

Cleo. Fear not, I'll use my Interest both with your
Mother and my Father, to set your Heart at rest,
Whose Pain I feel by something in my own.

Clar. The Gods reward your Bounty, fair *Cleonte.*

Dorm. I, I, Madam, I beseech you make our Peace with my good Lady her Mother,
whatsoever becomes of the rest, for she'll e'en die with Grief—[*Weeps.*]
She had but two fair Pledges of her Nuptial Bed.
And both by cruel Fate are ravished from her.
Manuel a Child was lost,
And this; not holy Relics were more strictly guarded,
Till false *Marcel* betray'd me to debauch her. [*Weeps aloud.*]

Cleo. Alas, had you a Brother once? [*To* Clarinda.]

Clar. Madam, I might have had: but he was lost e'er I was born.

Cleo. Ah! would my *Silvio* had been so. [*Aside.*]
By what strange Accident, *Clarinda?*

Dorm. Madam, I can inform you best. [*Puts herself between.*]

Cleo. Do then, *Dormida.*

Dorm. Madam, you must know, my Lady *Octavia*, for that's her name, was in her
Youth the very Flower of Beauty and Virtue: Oh such a Face and Shape! had you but
seen her—And tho I say it, Madam, I thought myself too somebody then.

Clar. Thou art tedious: Madam, 'tis true my Mother had the Reputation of both those
Attractions, which gain'd her many Lovers: amongst the rest, Don *Manuel*, and Don
Alonzo, were most worthy her Esteem.

Dorm. Ay, Madam, Don *Alonzo*, there was a Man for you, so obliging and so
bountiful—Well, I'll give you Argument of both to me: for you must know I was a
Beauty then, and worth obliging. [*Puts herself between.*] And he was the Man my Lady
lov'd, tho Don *Manuel* were the richer: but to my own Story—

Cleo. Forward, *Clarinda.*

Clar. But as it most times happens,
We marry where our Parents like, not we;
My Mother was dispos'd of to Don *Manuel.*

Dorm. Ay, Madam; but had you seen Don *Alonzo's* Rage, and how my Lady took
this Disappointment—But I who was very young, and very pretty, as I told you before—

Clar. Forbear, Madam; 'tis true,
Alonzo was so far transported,
That oft he did attempt to kill my Father;
But bravely tho, and still he was prevented:
But when at the Intreaties of my Mother,
The King confin'd my Father,
Alonzo then study'd a new Revenge;
And thinking that my Father's Life depended

Upon a Son he had, scarce a Year old,
He did design to steal him; and one Evening,
When with the Nurse and Maid he took the Air,
This desperate Lover seiz'd the smiling Prize,
Which never since was heard of.
 Cleo. I guess the Grief the Parents must sustain.
 Dorm. It almost caus'd their Deaths; nor did kind Heaven
Supply them with another till long after,
Unhappy this was born:
Which just her Father liv'd to see, and dy'd. [*Weeps.*]
Then she was Daughter, Son and Husband too,
To her afflicted Mother: But as I told you, Madam, I was then in my Prime—
 Clar. Now, Madam, judge what her Despair must be,
Who is depriv'd of all her Joys in me. [*Weeps.*]
 Cleo. Francisca, see who it is that knocks so hastily. [*One knocks.*]
 Franc. Oh, Madam, 'tis Don *Marcel* leading a wounded Man.
 Cleo. Oh my Fears, [215] 'tis *Silvio!*
 Franc. 'Tis not Don *Silvio.*

[*Enter* Marcel, *leading* Hippolyta *wounded, followed by* Alonzo *and* Pedro.]

 Cleo. Alas, what Youth is this you lead all bleeding?
 Mar. One that deserves your Care; where's my Father?
 Cleo. Not yet return'd.
 Mar. 'Tis well; and you, Sir, I must confine till I know how to satisfy my Honor, and that of my wrong'd Sister. [*To* Antonio.]
 Ant. The holy Man will soon decide our Difference:
Pray send for one, and reconcile us all.
 Hip. I fear, *Antonio,* still thou dost dissemble.
 Ant. So let me find Forgiveness when I die,
If any fear of Death have wrought this change,
But a pure Sense of all my Wrongs to thee,
Knowing thy constant Love, and Virtue to me.
 Mar. I will secure your fear—*Francisca,* send for Father *Joseph* to me, and conduct these Gentlemen to the Lodgings next the Garden.

[*Exeunt* Francisca, Antonio *and* Hippolyta.]

 Alon. Prithee, *Marcel,* are thee and I awake, or do we dream? thou, that thou art in thy Father's House; and I, that I see those two fair Women there? Pray, lovely Fugitive, how came you hither? [*To* Clarinda.]
 Mar. I thought thou wert mistaken;
'Twas *Silvio* brought her hither, that false Man.
But how came you to know her?
 Alon. Know her! 'slife, I question my Sense.
Pray, Lady, are you Flesh and Blood? [*To* Cleonte.]
 Cleo. Yes surely, Sir; for 'twere pity you should have bestow'd your Heart on a Shadow, and I well remember you gave it one of us last Night.

Alon. A Dream, a Dream! but are you indeed the same fair Person, and is this the same House too?

Cleo. I am afraid your Heart's not worth the keeping, since you took no better notice where you dispos'd of it.

Alon. Faith, Madam, your wrong a poor Lover, who has languish'd in search of it all this live-long day.

Cleo. Brother, I beseech you, receive the innocent *Clarinda*, who, I fear, will have the greatest Cause of Complaint against you. [*To* Marcel. *Gives him to* Clarinda.]

Alon. But pray, fair one, let you and I talk a little about that same Heart you put me in mind of just now. [*To* Cleonte, *with whom he seems to talk.*]

Pedro. Surely that's my old Mistress, *Dormida*; twenty years has not made so great an Alteration in that ill-favor'd Face of hers, but I can find a Lover there.

[*Goes to her, they seem to talk earnestly, and sometimes pleasantly, pointing to* Clarinda.]

Mar. Enough, *Clarinda*: I'm too well convinc'd,
Would thou hadst still remain'd a Criminal.
Now how can I reward thy Faith and Love?

Clar. I know, *Marcel*, it is not in thy Power,
Thy faithless Story I'm acquainted with.

Mar. Do not reproach me with my Shame, *Clarinda*.
'Tis true, to gain thee to consent to my Desires,
I made an honorable Pretence of loving.
Pardon a Lover all the ways he takes
To gain a Mistress so belov'd and fair.
But I have since repented of that Sin,
And came last Night for thy Forgiveness too.

Pedro. This is News indeed; 'tis fit I keep this Secret no longer from my Master. Don *Manuel* being dead, my Vow's expir'd. [*Aside.*]

[Pedro *goes to* Alonzo.]

Clar. And do you mean no more to love me then?

Mar. In spite of me, above my Sense or Being.

Clar. And yet you'll marry *Flavia*.

Mar. Against my Will I must, or lose a Father.

Clar. Then I must die, *Marcel*.

Mar. Do not unman my Soul, it is too weak To bear the Weight of fair *Clarinda's* Tears. [*Weeps.*] [216]

Alon. Why was this Secret kept from me so long?

Pedro. I was oblig'd by Vow, Sir, to Don *Alonzo*, my dead Master, not to restore you till Don *Manuel's* Death; believing it a Happiness too great for his Rival, for so he was upon your Mother's score.

Alon. Have I a Mother living?

Pedro. Here in Madrid, Sir, and that fair Maid's your Sister. [*Pointing to* Clarinda.]

Alon. I scarce can credit thee, but that I know thee honest.

Pedro. To confirm that belief, Sir, here are the Writings of twelve thousand Crowns a Year, left you by your Foster-Father the brave *Alonzo*, whose Name he gave you too. [*Gives him Papers, he reads.*]

Alon. I am convinc'd—How now, *Marcel*, what all in Tears? why, who the Devil would love in earnest?

Come, come, make me Judge between you.

Mar. You'll soon decide it then, my Heart's *Clarinda's*; But my forc'd Vows are given to another.

Alon. Vows! dost think the Gods regard the Vows of Lovers? they are things made in necessity, and ought not to be kept, nor punish'd when broken; if they were—Heaven have mercy on me poor Sinner.

[*Enter* Ambrosio.]

Mar. My Father return'd! [*Bows, and goes to him, and then leads* Alonzo *to him.*]
Sir, this is the gallant Man that was design'd to be your Son-in-Law.

Amb. And that you were not so, Sir, was my misfortune only.

Alon. I am glad to find it no slight to my Person,
Or unknown Quality that depriv'd me of that Honor.

Mar. To convince you of that, *Alonzo*, I know my Father will bestow this other Sister on you; more fair and young, and equally as rich. [*Ambrosio* calls *Marcel* aside.]

Alon. How, his Sister! Fool that I was, I could not guess at this; and now have I been lying and swearing all this while how much I lov'd her. Well, take one time with another, a Man falls into more Danger by this amorous Humor, than he gets good turns by it.

Mar. Pardon me, Sir, I knew not you had design'd her elsewhere—Dear *Alonzo*, my Father—

Alon. Ay, Sir, I am much oblig'd to him. Oh Pox, would I were well with *Euphemia*.

Mar. I protest I could wish—

Alon. Ay, so could I, Sir, that you had made a better Judgment of my Humor: All must out, I have no other way to avoid this Compliment else. Why look ye, *Marcel*—Your Sister is—Pox, I am ill at Dissimulation, and therefore in plain Terms, I am to be married this very Evening to another.

Mar. This was happy, and has sav'd me an Excuse. [*Aside.*]
But are you in earnest, How is it possible, being so lately come into *Madrid*?

Alon. Destiny, Destiny, *Marcel*, which there was no avoiding, tho I mist of *Hippolyta*.

Mar. Who is it, prithee?

Alon. A Woman I hope, of which indeed I would have been better assur'd; but she was wilful. She's call'd *Euphemia*.

Mar. Our next Neighbour, the Daughter of old *Carlo*.

Alon. The same.

Mar. Thou art happy to make so good a Progress in so short a time, but I am—

Alon. Not so miserable as you believe. Come, come, you shall marry *Clarinda*.

Mar. 'Tis impossible.

Alon. Where's the hindrance?

Mar. Her want of Fortune; that's enough, Friend.

Alon. Stand by and expect the best—[*Goes to* Ambrosio.] Sir, I have an humble Suit to you.

Amb. I shall be infinitely pleas'd you could ask me anything in my Power; but, Sir, this Daughter I had dispos'd of, before I knew you would have mist of *Hippolyta.*

Alon. Luckier than I expected. [*Aside.*] Sir, that was an Honor I could not merit, and am contented with my Fate: But my Request is, that you would receive into your Family a Sister of mine, whom I would bestow on Don *Marcel.*

Mar. Hah, what mean you, Sir? a Sister of yours?

Alon. Yes, she will not be unwelcome—This is she.

Amb. This is the Daughter to *Octavia*—Her Mother was a Lady whom once I did adore, and 'twas her fault she was not more happy with me, than with Don *Manuel.* Nor have I so wholly forgot that Flame, but I might be inclin'd to your Proposal: But, Sir, she wants a Fortune.

Alon. That I'll supply.

Mar. You supply, Sir? On what kind Score, I pray?

Alon. That which you'll suffer without being jealous, When you shall know she is indeed my Sister.

Clar. How! this brave Man my Brother?

Alon. So they tell me, and that my Name is *Manuel.* Had you not such a Brother?

Dorm. Oh ye Gods, is this the little *Manuel?*

Pedro. Yes, *Dormida*, and for a farther Proof see this. [*Opens his Master's Bosom and shows a Crucifix.*]

Dorm. This I remember well, it is Don *Manuel*:
Pray let me look upon you: Just like my Lord—Now
may the Soul of Don *Alonzo* rest in Peace,
For making so hopeful a Man of you.

Alon. Amen. But, Sir, if you approve of my Sister,
I'll make her as worthy of *Marcel*, as *Flavia.*

Amb. I've lost the Hopes of her—She's not to be reconcil'd. [*Aside.*]
Clarinda needs no more than to belong to you,
To make her valuable—and I consent with Joy. [*Gives her to Marcel.*]

Mar. And I with Joys unutterable take her.

Alon. Pedro, there rests no more than that you wait on my Mother, and let her know all that has happen'd to myself and Sister, and that I'll pay my Duty to her e'er I sleep.

Dorm. The very Joy to find her Son again, will get my Pardon too: and then perhaps *Pedro* and I may renew our old Amours.

Alon. Sir, I have another Request to make.

Amb. You must command, Sir.

Alon. That is, that you will permit this fair Company to honor me this Evening at my Father-in-law's, Don *Carlo.*

Amb. How, has Don *Carlo* married the Lady Octavia?

Alon. No, Sir, but a worse matter than that, I am to marry his Daughter.

Amb. Oh, Sir, *Euphemia* has too much Beauty and Virtue to make you doubt your Happiness.

Alon. Well, Sir, I must venture that. But your Company I'll expect, the Ladies may clap on their Vizards, and make a Masquerading Night on't: tho such Freedoms are not very usual in *Spain*, we that have seen the World, may absolve one another.

Amb. My Garden joins to that of Don *Carlo*, and that way we will wait on you, as soon as I have dispatched a small Affair.

Alon. Your humble servant, Sir. [*Goes out; Ambrosio the other way.*]

Mar. Sister, go you and prepare my Father to receive *Hippolyta*, whilst I go see them married.

[*Exeunt* Cleonte *and* Clarinda.]

[Marcel *passing over the Garden, sees* Silvio *enter in Passion, followed by* Francisca.]

Silv. Do not, *Francisca*—do not blow my Flame,
The Cure thou bring'st is much the greater Hellena [*Offers to go, but stops.*]
    Mar. Hah, *Silvio!* unseen I'll hear the Business. [*Goes aside.*]
    Silv. I would fain shun thee, but this impious Weight
Of Love upon my Soul hinders my flight:
I'm fixed—like conscious Guilt it keeps me here,
And I am now insensible of Fear.
Speak on, thou Messenger of sacred Love—speak on.
    Franc. The fair *Cleonte*, Sir, whose Soul's inflam'd
No less than yours; tho with a virgin Modesty
She would conceal it, pitying now your Pain,
Has thro my Intercession—
    Silv. Oh quickly speak! What Happiness design'd me?
    Franc. To admit you, Sir, this Night into her Chamber.
    Mar. Death to my Soul! What's this? [*Aside.*]
    Silv. Her Chamber? is that all? will that allay this Fever
In my Blood?—No, no, *Francisca*,
'Tis grown too high for amorous Parleys only;
Her Arms, her charming Bosom, and her Bed,
Must now receive me; or I die, *Francisca*.
    Franc. I mean no other, Sir; why, can you think
A Maid in love as much as you can be,
Assisted with the silence of the Night,
(Which veils her Blushes too) can say—I dare not?
Or if she do, she'll speak it faintly o'er,
And even whilst she so denies will yield.
Go, go prepare yourself for this Encounter,
And do not dally as you did today,
And fright your Pleasure with the Name of Sister—
    Mar. Oh cursed Witch! [*Aside.*]
    Franc. What say you, Sir?
    Silv. That Name has check'd my Joy—
And makes it strangely silent and imperfect. [*Walks away.*]
    Franc. Why do you go, before you answer me? [*Follows him into the Garden.*]
    Mar. I'll follow him, and kill them. [*Comes out with a Dagger.*]
Oh, who would be allied unto a Woman,
Nature's loose Handy-Work? the slight Employs
Of all her wanton Hours?—Oh, I could rave now—
Abandon Sense and Nature.
Hence, all considerate Thoughts, and in their Room,
Supply my Soul with Vengeance, that may prove

Too great to be allay'd by Nature, or by Love. [*Goes into the Garden after them.*]

[*Enter again* Silvio *melancholy, followed by* Francisca.]

Franc. But will you lose this Opportunity,
Her Lodgings too being so near your own?
Silv. Hell take her for her Wickedness.
Oh that ten thousand Mountains stood between us,
And Seas as vast and raging as her Lust,
That we might never meet—Oh perfect Woman!
I find there is no Safety in thy Sex;
No trusting to thy Innocence:
That being counterfeit, thy Beauty's gone,
Dropt like a Rose o'er-blown;
And left thee nothing but a wither'd Root,
That never more can bloom.
Franc. Alas, I fear I have done ill in this. [*Aside.*]
Silv. I now should hate her: but there yet remains
Something within, so strangely kind to her,
That I'm resolv'd to give her one proof more,
Of what I have vow'd her often; yes, I'll kill her—
Franc. How, kill her, Sir? Gods, what have I done! [*Aside.*]
Silv. Yes, can I let her live, and say I lov'd her?
No, she shall tempt no more vain yielding Men.
Franc. Consider, Sir, it is to save your Life she does it.
Silv. My Life!
'Twere better she and I were buried
Quick in one Grave, than she should fall to this,
She has out-sinn'd even me in this Consent.

[*Enter* Marcel *from amongst the Trees softly with his Dagger behind* Silvio.]

Mar. Oh, here they are—
Franc. My Lord, defend yourself, your are undone else.
Silv. Hah, *Marcel!* [*Draws.*]
Franc. Help, help.
Mar. Hell take thy Throat.

[*Enter* Ambrosio, Clarinda, Cleonte, *and the rest of the House.*]

Amb. Hold, Villain, hold.
How dar'st thou thus rebel—ungrateful Wretch?
Mar. This cause, Sir, is so just, that when you hear it,
You'll curse me, that I let him live thus long:
He loves my Sister, Sir; and that leud Woman
Repays his lustful Flame, and does this Evening
Invite him to her Bed—Oh, let me kill him. [*Offers to go to him.*]
Amb. That he should love *Cleonte* I'll allow,

232

And her returns too, whilst they are innocent.

Mar. But, Sir, he does not love her as a Sister.

Amb. If that be all his Crime, I still forgive him.

Silv. Yes, Sir, 'tis true, I do adore my Sister,
But am so far from that foul thing he nam'd,
That could I think I had a secret Thought
That tended that way, I would search it—thus—[*Goes to stab himself.*]

Cleo. What mean you by this Desperation?

Silv. Oh, take away this Woman from my sight. [*Pointing to* Cleonte.]
For she will finish what this has ill begun. [*Holds his Dagger up.*]

Franc. Thus low, Sir, for you Mercy I must kneel; [*Kneels.*]
Which yet I must despair of, when you know
How very very wicked [217] I have been. [*Weeps.*]
Cleonte, Sir, is chaste as Angels are.

Silv. My Sister innocent! how soon I do believe thee!

Franc. Yes, Sir, nor knows of that vile Message which I brought you.

Silv. What Devil set thee on to tempt me then?

Franc. The worst of Devils, hopeless, raging Love;
And you, my Lord, were the unhappy Object.

Mar. Oh sinful Woman, what was thy Design?

Cleo. What means all this? [*Aside.*]

Franc. At least to have enjoy'd him once; which done,
Thinking that it had been the fair *Cleonte*,
It would have made him hate her.

Silv. Should all thy other Sins be unrepented,
The Piety of this Confession saves thee.
Pardon, *Cleonte*, my rude Thoughts of thee, [*Kneels, she takes him up.*]
I had design'd to have kill'd thee—
Had not this Knowledge of thy Innocence
Arriv'd before I'd seen thee next.
And, Sir, your Pardon too I humbly beg, [*To* Ambrosio.]
With license to depart; I cannot live
Where I must only see my beauteous Sister;
That Torment is too great to be supported,
That still must last, and never hope a Cure.

Amb. Since you are so resolv'd, I will unfold
A Secret to you, that perhaps may please you.

Silv. Low at your Feet I do implore it, Sir. [*Kneels.*]

Amb. Your Quality forbids this Ceremony. [*Takes him up.*]

Silv. How, Sir!

Amb. Your Father was the mighty Favorite, the Count *d'Olivarez*; [218] your Mother, *Spain's* celebrated Beauty, *Donna Margarita Spiniola*, by whom your Father had two natural Sons, *Don Lovis de Harro*, and yourself *Don Roderigo*. The Story of his Disgrace, you know, with all the World; 'twas then he being banished from the Court, he left you to my Care then very young. I receiv'd you as my own, and as more than such educated you, and as your Father oblig'd me to do, brought you always up about their Majesties; for he hoped, if you had Beauty and Merits, you might inherit part of that Glory he lost.

Mar. This is wondrous.

Amb. This Truth you had not known so soon, had you not made as great an Interest at Court as any Man so young ever did, and if I had not acquitted myself in all Points as became the Friend of so great and brave a Man, as Count *d'Olivarez*: the Fortune he left you was two Millions of Crowns.

Silv. Let me embrace your feet for this blest News. Is not the fair *Cleonte* then my Sister?

Amb. No, Sir, but one whom long since I design'd your Wife, if you are pleas'd [219] to think her worthy of it. [*Offers her.*]

Silv. Without her, Sir, I do despise my Being;
And do receive her as a Blessing sent
From Heaven to make my whole Life happy.

Amb. What say you, *Cleonte?*

Cleo. Sir, I must own a Joy greater than is fit for a Virgin to express.

Mar. Generous Don *Roderigo*, receive me as your Friend, and pardon all the Fault you found in me as a Brother. [*Embraces him.*]

Silv. Be ever dear unto my Soul, *Marcel.*

Mar. Now is the time to present *Hippolyta* and *Antonio* to my Father, whilst his Humor is so good. And you, dear Brother, I must beg to join with us in so just a Cause.

Silv. You need not doubt my Power, and less my Willmore

Mar. Do you prepare him then, whilst I bring them in: for by this I know my Confessor has made them one. [*Exit* Marcel.]

Silv. Sir, I've a Suit to you.

Amb. You cannot ask what I can deny.

Silv. Hippolyta, Sir, is married to *Antonio*, And humbly begs your Pardon for her past fault.

Amb. Antonio and *Hippolyta!* oh, name them not.

[*Enter* Antonio *and* Hippolyta, *a* Fryar, *and* Marcel.]

Mar. Pray, Sir, forgive them, your Honor being safe,
Since Don *Antonio* has by marrying her,
Repair'd the Injury he did us all,
Without which I had kill'd him.

Amb. Thou art by Nature more severe than I,
And if thou think'st our Honor satisfy'd,
I will endeavor to forget their Faults.

Ant. We humbly thank you, Sir, and beg your Blessing,
At least bestow it on *Hippolyta*;
For she was ever chaste, and innocent,
And acted only what became her Duty;
Since by a sacred Vow she was my Wife.

Amb. How cam'st thou then to treat her so inhumanly?

Ant. In pure revenge to Don *Marcel* her Brother,
Who forc'd my Nature to a stubbornness,
Which whilst I did put on, I blush to own;
And still between Thoughts so unjust, and Action,
Her Virtue would rise up and check my Soul,
Which still secur'd her Fame.

Hip. And I have seen in midst of all thy Anger,
Thou'st turn'd away, and chang'd thy Words to Sighs;
Dropt now and then a Tear, as if asham'd,
Not of thy Injuries, but my little Merit.

Amb. How weak and easy Nature makes me—Rise,
I must forgive you both.
Come, Sir, I know you long to be secur'd
Of what you say you love so much, *Cleonte*.

Franc. But, Madam, have you fully pardon'd me?

Silv. We will all join in your behalf, *Francisco*.

Cleo. I can forgive you, when you can repent. [*Exeunt.*]

Scene II. Carlo's *House*. [220]

[*Enter* Olinda *and* Dorice.]

Olin. But is the Bride-Chamber dressed up, and the Bed made as it ought to be?

Dorm. As for [221] the making, 'tis as it use to be, only the Velvet Furniture.

Olin. As it use to be? Oh ignorance! I see these young Wenches are not arriv'd yet to bare Imagination: Well, I must order it myself, I see that.

Dorm. Why, *Olinda*, I hope they will not go just to Bed upon their marrying, without some signs of a Wedding, as Fiddles, and Dancing, and so forth.

Olin. Good Lord, what Joys you have found out for the first Night of a young Bride and Bridegroom. Fiddles and Dancing, ha, ha, ha! they'll be much merrier by themselves, than Fiddles and Dancing can make them, you Fool.

[*Enter* Haunce *and* Gload.]

Bless me! what is't I see! [*Stares on* Haunce.]

Hau. Why! what the Devil means she? look about me, *Gload*, and see what I have that's so terrible.

Olin. Oh, I have no Power to stir, it is a Sprite.

Hau. What does she mean now, *Gload?*

Glo. She desires to be satisfy'd whether we be Flesh and Blood, Sir, I believe.

Hau. Do'st see nothing that's Devil-wise about me?

Glo. No, indeed, Sir, not I.

Hau. Why then the Wench is tippled, that's all, a small Fault.

Olin. O, in the name of Goodness, Sir, what are you?

Glo. Ay, Ay, Sir, 'tis that she desires to know.

Olin. Who are you, Sir?

Hau. Why who should I be, but he that's to be your Master anon?

Glo. Yes, who should he be but *Myn heer Haunce van Ezel?*

Olin. What, did you come in at the Door?

Hau. Yes, marry did I; what, do you think I creep in like a Lapland Witch [p. 323] through the Key-holes?

Dorm. Nay, nay, this cannot be the Bridegroom.

Olin. No, for 'tis but a moment since we left him, you know, in my Lady's Chamber.

Hau. Very drunk, by this good Light.

Dorm. And therefore it cannot be *Myn heer Haunce.*

Hau. What a Devil [222] will you persuade me out of my Christian Name?

Olin. The Priest has yet scarce done his Office, who is marrying him above to my Lady.

Hau. Salerimente, here's brave doing, to marry me, and never give me notice; or thou art damnable drunk, or very mad.

Glo. Yes, and I am married to you too, am I not? [*To* Olinda.]

Olin. You? we know neither of you.

Hau. Ha, ha, ha, here's a turn for you.

[*Enter* Carlo.]

Car. Why, *Olinda, Dorice, Olinda,* where be these mad Girls? 'tis almost Night, and nothing in Order. Why, what now? Who's here?

Hau. So the old Man's possessed too—Why, what a Devil ails you, Sir? [*Goes roughly to him.*]

Car. From whence come you, Sir? and what are you?

Hau. Gload, let's be gone, for we shall be transmigrated into some strange Shapes anon, for all the House is enchanted. Who am I, quoth ye? before I came you all knew me; and now you are very well acquainted with me, you have forgot me.

Car. If you be my Son *Haunce,* how came you here?

Hau. If I be your Son *Haunce,* where should I be else?

Car. Above with your Wife, not below amongst the Maids.

Hau. What Wife? what Wife? Ha, ha, ha, do not provoke me, lest I take you a slap in the Face, I tell you that now.

Car. Oh, I find by his Humor this is he, and I am finely cheated and abus'd. I'll up and know the Truth. [*Goes out.*] [223]

Hau. And so will I. [*Follows.*]

Glo. Why, but Mistress *Olinda,* you have not, indeed, forgot me, have you?

Olin. For my Lover I have, but perhaps I may call you to mind, as my Servant hereafter.

Glo. Since you are so proud and so fickle, you shall stand hereafter as a Cipher with me; and I'll begin upon a new Account with this pretty Maid: what say you forsooth?

Dorm. I am willing enough to get a Husband as young as I am.

Glo. Why, that's well said, give your Hand upon the Bargain—God-ha'-Mercy, [224] with all my Heart, i'faith. [Go in.] [225]

[*Scene draws off, discovers a Chamber. Enter* Alonzo, Euphemia, *and* Lovis; *to them* Carlo, Haunce, *and the rest.*]

Car. Oh, I am cheated, undone, abus'd.

Lo. How, Sir, and where?

[Haunce *sees* Alonzo *dressed like him, goes gazing about him, and on himself, calling* Gload *to do the same.*]

Car. Nay, I know not how, or where; but so I am: and when I find it, I'll turn you all out of Doors. Who are you, Sir? quickly tell me.

236

Alon. If you be in such haste, take the shortest Account, I am your Son.

Car. I mean, Sir, what's your Name, and which of you is *Haunce van Ezel?*

Hau. Ay, which of us is *Haunce van Ezel?* tell us that, Sir; we shall handle ye i'faith now—

Alon. He, Sir, can best inform you. [*Pointing to* Haunce.]

Hau. Who, I! I know no more than the great Turk, not I, which of us is me; my Hat, my Feather, my Suit, and my Garniture all over, faith now; and I believe this is me, for I'll trust my Eyes before any other Sense about me. What say'st thou now, *Gload?* guess which of us is thy own natural Master now if thou canst.

Glo. Which, Sir?—why—let me see—let me see, [*Turns them both about.*] fakes, I cannot tell, Sir.

Car. Come, come, the Cheat is plain, and I'll not be fobb'd off, therefore tell me who you are, Sir. [*To* Alonzo.]

Alon. One that was very unwilling to have put this Trick upon you, if I could have persuaded *Euphemia* to have been kind on any other Terms, but nothing would down with her but Matrimony.

Car. How long have you known her?

Alon. Faith, Sir, too long by at least an Hour.

Car. I say again, what are you, Sir?

Alon. A Man I am, and they call me *Alonzo.*

Car. How! I hope not the great fighting Colonel whom my Son serv'd as a Volunteer in *Flanders.*

Alon. Even he, Sir.

Car. Worse and worse, I shall grow mad, to think that in spite of all my Care, *Euphemia* should marry with so notorious a Man of War.

Hau. How! is this *Alonzo,* and am I cozen'd? pray tell me truly, are you not me indeed?

Alon. All over, Sir, only the inside a little less Fool.

Hau. So here's fine juggling—are not you a rare Lady, hah? [*To* Euphemia; *cries.*]

Euph. I assure you, Sir, if this Man had not past for you, I had never had him.

Hau. Had him! Oh, you are a flattering thing, I durst ha' sworn you could no more ha' been without me, than a Barber's Shop without a Fiddle, so I did: Oh, what a damnable Voyage have I back again without a Wife too—[*Crys again.*]

Lo. If that be all, we'll get you one before you go; that shall be my care.

Hau. A Pox of your care: well, I will get myself most soundly drunk tonight, to be reveng'd of these two damnable Dons. Come, *Gload,* let us about something in order to't. [*Exit with* Gload.]

Euph. Pray, Sir, be persuaded, he's worth your owning.

Car. Tell not me of owning; what Fortune has he?

Lo. His Horse and Arms, the Favor of his Prince, and his Pay.

Car. His Horse and Arms I wholly dislike, as Implements of War; and that same Princely Favor, as you call it, will buy no Lands; and his Pay he shall have when he can get it.

Lo. But, Sir, his coming to *Madrid* was to take possession of a Place the Prince has promis'd him.

Car. Has promis'd him? what! I shall marry my Daughter to the Promises of e'er a Prince in *Christendom,* shall I? No, no; Promises, quoth ye?

Alon. Well, Sir, will this satisfy you? [*Gives him a Parchment.*]

Euph. If it should not, let us consider what next to do.

Alon. No consideration, *Euphemia*; not so much as that we are married, lest it lessen our Joys.

Car. Twelve thousand Crowns a Year!—Sir, I cry you mercy, and wish you joy with my Daughter.

Lo. So his Courage will down with him now.

Alon. To satisfy you farther, Sir, read this. [*Gives him another Paper.*] And now, *Euphemia*, prepare yourself to receive some gallant Friends of mine, whom you must be acquainted with, and who design to make a merry Night on't.

Euph. A whole Night, *Alonzo?*

Alon. By no means, *Euphemia*, for the first too, which if the thoughts of its being part of my Duty do not hinder, will be a pleasant enough to me.

Car. So considerable an Office at Court too!—Let me embrace you, Sir; and tell you how happy I am in so brave Son-in-law.

Alon. With that assurance, Sir, I'll take a more than ordinary freedom with you, and teach *Euphemia* a franker way of living, than what a native *Spaniard* would have allow'd her.

Car. She shall be what sort of Wife you'll have her.

[*Enter Servant, after a noise of Music.*]

Alon. What Music's that?

Serv. It waits upon some Ladies and Gentlemen who ask for you, Sir.

Alon. Wait them in, they are those Friends of mine I told you of. [*He goes and brings them in.*]

[*Enter* Marcel *and* Clarinda, Silvio *and* Cleonte, Antonio *and* Hippolyta, Dormida *and* Francisca; *all salute* Euphemia.]
[*Enter* Haunce *and* Gload *in Masquerade to the Company,* Olinda *and* Dorice *masked.*]

Hau. Well, the Devil's in't if we shall not appear ridiculous enough, hah, *Gload?*

Glo. Ay, Sir, the more ridiculous the better.

Hau. I was always of that mind.—Ha, ha, Boys, who be all these Dons and Donnas?—Harkye, *Lovis*, I hope the Wife you promis'd me is amongst these fair Ladies, for so I guess they are both, fair and Ladies.

Lo. You guess right, Sir.

Alon. Now, Ladies and Gentlemen, command your Music, and do what likes you best.

Lo. Here's the Lady I recommend to you, take her, Sir, be thankful. [*Gives him* Olinda.]

Olin. This is the Fool that I am to manage.

Dorm. And this is my Lot. [*Takes* Gload.]

[*Music plays, they all dance.*]

Lo. There is within a young Father ready to join your Hands: take this opportunity, and make sure of a Wife.

Hau. I warrant you, Sir.

238

[Exeunt Haunce, Olinda, Gload, *and* Dorice.]
[Enter Pedro.]

Pedro. Your Mother, Sir, whom I found more dead than living, for the loss of your Sister, was very near dying outright with Joy, to hear of your Arrival, and most impatiently expects you.

Dorm. And are we all forgiven, *Pedro?*

Pedro. Yes, you and I are like to be Fellow-Servants together again, *Dormida.*

Dorm. And Fellow-Lovers too I hope, *Pedro.*

Pedro. The Devil's in't if Age have not allay'd Flames of all sorts in thee; but if you contribute to my allowance—

Dorm. Thou know'st I could never keep anything from thee, *Pedro.*

Alon. Come, Ladies, there is a small Banquet attends you in the next Room.

Silv. We'll wait on you, Sir.

[Enter Haunce, Gload, Olinda, *and* Dorice.]

Hau. Hold, hold, and give me Joy too, for I am married, if she has not mistaken her Man again, and I my Woman.

Olin. No, you are the Man I look for, and I no Cheat, having all about me that you look for too, but Money. *[Discovers herself.]*

Alon. How, *Olinda!*

Olin. Yes, indeed, Sir, I serv'd my Lady first, and then thought it no Offence to take the Reward due to that Service.

Hau. Here's a *Spanish* Trick for you now, to marry a Wife, before one sees her.

Euph. What, *Dorice* married too?

Dorm. After your Example, Madam.

Glo. Yes, indeed, forsooth, and I have made bold too after the Example of my Master.

Hau. Now do they all expect I should be dissatisfied; but, Gentlemen, in sign and token that I am not, I'll have one more merry Frisk before we part, 'tis a witty Wench; faith and troth, after a Month 'tis all one who's who; therefore come on, *Gload.* *[They dance together.]*

Alon. Monsieur *Haunce*, I see you are a Man of Gallantry. Come let us in, I know every Man here desires to make this Night his own, and sacrifice it to Pleasure.

The Ladies too in Blushes do confess.
Equal Desires; which yet they'll not confess.
Theirs, tho less fierce, more constant will abide;
But ours less current grow the more they're try'd.

EPILOGUE

HISS 'em, and cry 'em down, 'tis all in vain,
Incorrigible Scriblers can't abstain:
But impudently i'th' old Sin engage;
Tho doom'd before, nay banish'd from the Stage.
Whilst sad Experience our Eyes convinces,
That damn'd their Plays which hang'd the German *Princess;* [p. 329]
And we with Ornament set off a Play,
Like her dressed fine for Execution-day.
And faith, I think, with as small hopes to live;
Unless kind Gallants the same Grace you'd give
Our Comedy as Her; beg a Reprieve.
Well, what the other mist, let our Scribe get,
A Pardon, for she swears she's the less Cheat.
She never gull'd you Gallants of the Town
Of Sum above four Shillings, or half a Crown. [p. 329]
Nor does she, as some late great Authors do,
Bubble the Audience, and the Players too.
Her humble Muse soars not in the High-rode
Of Wit transverst, or Bawdy A-la-mode;
Yet hopes her plain and easy Style is such,
As your high Censures will disdain to touch.
Let her low Sense creep safe from your Bravadoes,
Whilst Rotas [p. 330] *and Cabals aim at Granadoes.*

THE ROUNDHEADS; OR,
THE GOOD OLD CAUSE.

ARGUMENT.

The historical state of affairs 1659-60 was briefly as follows:—the Protectorate of Richard Cromwell expired 22 April, 1659. Hereupon Fleetwood and some other officers recalled the Long Parliament (Rump), which was constituted the ruling power of England, a select council of state having the executive. Lambert, however, with other dissentients was expelled from Parliament, 12 October, 1659. He and his troops marched to Newcastle; but the soldiers deserted him for General Fairfax, who had declared for a free Parliament, and were garrisoned at York. Here Monk, entering England 2 January, 1660, joined them with his forces. Lambert, deprived of his followers, was obliged to return to London. His prompt arrest by order of Parliament followed, and he, Sir Harry Vane and other members of the Committee of Safety were placed in strict confinement. On 5 March Lambert was imprisoned in the Tower, whence he escaped on 10 April, only to be recaptured a fortnight later. There are vivid pictures in Aubrey, Pepys, and other writers, of the wild enthusiasm at the fall of the Rump Parliament, with bonfires blazing, all the church bells ringing, and the populace of London carousing and pledging King Charles on their knees in the street. 'They made little gibbets and roasted rumps of mutton. Nay, I saw some very good rumps of beef,' writes Aubrey, and Pepys is even more vivid in his tale than the good antiquary.

King Charles landed at Dover, 26 May, amid universal rejoicings.

Mrs. Behn has (quite legitimately) made considerable departures from strict historical fact and the sequence of events for her dramatic purposes.

Lambert and Fleetwood are scheming for the supreme power, and both intrigue with Lord Wariston, the chairman of the Committee of Safety, for his good word and influence. Lambert meantime fools Fleetwood by flattery and a feigned indifference. Lady Lambert, who is eagerly expecting her husband to be proclaimed King, and is assuming the state and title of royalty to the anger of Cromwell's widow, falls in love with a cavalier, Loveless. Her friend, Lady Desbro', a thorough loyalist at heart, though wedded to an old parliamentarian, has long been enamored of Freeman, the cavalier's companion. Lambert surprises Loveless and Freeman with his wife and Lady Desbro', but Lady Lambert pretending they have come to petition her, abruptly dismisses them both and so assuages all suspicion. At a meeting of the Committee the two gallants are sent to prison for a loyal outburst on the part of Loveless. Ananias Goggle, a lay elder, who having offered liberties to Lady Desbro' is in her power, is by her obliged to obtain her lover's release, and she at once holds an interview with him. They are interrupted by Desbro' himself, but Freeman is concealed and makes an undiscovered exit behind the shelter of Goggle's flowing cloak.

Loveless is brought to Lady Lambert at night. She endeavours to dazzle him by showing the regalia richly set out and adorned with lights. He puts by, however, crown and sceptre and rebukes her overweening ambition. Suddenly the Committee, who have been drinking deep, burst in upon them dancing a riotous dance. Loveless is hurriedly concealed under the coverlet of a couch, and Lady Lambert sits thereon seemingly at her devotions. Her husband takes his place by her side, but rolls off as the gallant slips to the ground. The lights fall down and are extinguished, the men fly howling and bawling 'A

Plot! A Plot!' in drunken terror. Lambert is cajoled and hectored into believing himself mistaken owing to his potations. The ladies hold a council to correct and enquire into women's wrongs, but on a sudden, news is brought that Lambert's followers have turned against him and that he is imprisoned in the Tower. The city rises against the Parliament and the Rump is dissolved. Loveless and Freeman rescue Lady Lambert and Lady Desbro', whose old husband has fallen down dead with fright. The parliamentarians endeavor to escape, but Wariston, Goggle, and Hewson—a leading member of the Committee—are detected and maltreated by the mob. As they are hauled away to prison the people give themselves up to general merry-making and joy.

SOURCE.

The purely political part of *The Roundheads; or, The Good Old Cause* was founded by Mrs. Behn on John Tatham's *The Rump*; or, *The Mirror of the Late Times* (4to, 1660, 4to, 1661, and again 1879 in his collected works,) which was produced on the eve of the Restoration, in February, 1660, at the Private House, i.e. small theatre, in Dorset Court. The company which played here had been brought together by William Beeston, but singularly little is known of its brief career and only one name has been recorded, that of George Jolly, the leading actor. Tatham was the author of the Lord Mayor's pageants 1657-64. His plays, four in number, together with a rare entertainment, *London's Glory* (1660), have been well edited by Maidment and Logan.

The Rump met with great success. It is certainly a brisk and lively piece, and coming at the juncture it did must have been extraordinarily effective. As a topical key-play reflecting the moment it is indeed admirable, and the crescendo of overwhelming satire, all the keener for the poet's deep earnestness, culminating in the living actors, yesterday's lords and law-givers, running to and fro the London streets, one bawling 'Ink or pens, ink or pens!', another 'Boots or shoes, boots or shoes to mend!', a third 'Fine Seville oranges, fine lemons!', whilst Mrs. Cromwell exchanges Billingsgate with a crowd of jeering boys, must have caused the house absolutely to rock with merriment.

With all its point and cleverness *The Rump*, however, from a technical point of view, is ill-digested and rough. The scenes were evidently thrown off hastily, and sadly lack refining and revision. Mrs. Behn has made the happiest use of rather unpromising material. The intrigues between Loveless and Lady Lambert, who in Tatham is very woodeny and awkward, between Freeman and Lady Desbro', which give *The Roundheads* unity and dramatic point, are entirely her own invention. In the original *Rump* neither cavaliers nor Lady Desbro' appear. Ananias Goggle also, the canting lay elder of Clements, with his subtle casuistry that jibs at 'the person not the office,' a dexterous character sketch, alive and acute, we owe to Mrs. Behn.

Amongst the many plays, far too numerous even to catalogue, that scarify the puritans and their zealot tribe, *The Cheats* (1662), by Wilson, and Sir Robert Howard's *The Committee* (1662), which long kept the stage, and, in a modified form, *The Honest Thieves*, was seen as late as the second half of the nineteenth century, are pre-eminently the best. Both possess considerable merit and are worthy of the highest comic traditions of the theatre.

As might have been expected, the dissolution of the Rump Parliament let loose a flood of political literature, squibs, satires and lampoons. Such works as *The famous Tragedy of the Life and Death of Mrs. Rump ... as it was presented on a burning stage at Westminster, the 29th of May, 1660* (4to, 1660), are of course valueless save from a purely historical interest. A large number of songs and ballads were brought together and published in two parts, 1662, reprint 1874. This collection (*The Rump*), sometimes witty, sometimes angry, sometimes obscene, is weighty evidence of the loathing inspired by the republicans and their misrule, but it is of so personal and topical a nature that the allusions would hardly be understood by anyone who had not made a very close and extended study of those critical months.

THEATRICAL HISTORY.

The Roundheads; or, The Good Old Cause was produced at the Duke's Theatre in 1682. They were unsettled and hazardous times. The country was convulsed by the judicial murders and horrors which followed in the train of the pseudo-Popish Plot engineered by the abominable Gates and his accomplices. King and Parliament were at hopeless variance. The air was charged with strife, internecine hatreds and unrest. In such an atmosphere and in such circumstances politics could not but make themselves keenly felt upon the stage. The actors were indeed 'abstracts and brief chronicles of the time', and the theatre became a very Armageddon for the poets. As *A Lenten Prologue refus'd by the Players* (1682) puts it:—

'Plots and Parties give new matter birth
And State distractions serve you here for mirth!
. . . .
The Stage, like old Rump Pulpits, is become
The scene of News, a furious Party's drum.'

Produced on 4 December, 1682, Dryden and Lee's excellent Tragedy, *The Duke of Guise*, which the Whigs vainly tried to suppress, created a furore. Crowne's *City Politics* (1683) is a crushing satire, caricaturing Oates, Stephen College, old Sergeant Maynard and their faction with rare skill. Southerne's *Loyal Brother* (1682), eulogizes the Duke of York; the scope of D'Urfey's *Sir Barnaby Whigg* (1681), can be told by its title, indeed the prologue says of the author:—

'That he shall know both parties now he glories,
By hisses th' Whigs, and by their claps the Tories.'

His *Royalist* (1682) follows in the same track.

Even those plays which were entirely non-political are inevitably prefaced with a mordant prologue or wound up by an epilogue that has party venom and mustard in its tail.

It would be surprising if so popular a writer as Mrs. Behn had not put a political play on the stage at such a juncture, and we find her well to the fore with *The Roundheads*, which she followed up in the same year with *The City Heiress*, another openly topical comedy.

The cast of *The Roundheads* is not given in any printed copy, and we have no exact means of apportioning the characters, which must have entailed the whole comic strength of the house. It is known that Betterton largely refrained from appearing in political comedies, and no doubt Smith took the part of Loveless, whilst Freeman would have fallen to Joseph Williams. Nokes was certainly Lambert; and Leigh, Wariston. Mrs. Leigh probably played Lady Cromwell or Gilliflower; Mrs. Barry, Lady Lambert; and Mrs. Currer, Lady Desbro'. The piece seems to have been very successful, and to have kept the stage at intervals for some twenty years.

To the Right Noble [226]
HENRY FITZ-ROY, [p. 337]

Duke of *Grafton*, Earl of *Sutton*, Viscount of *Ipswich*, Baron of *Sudbury*, Knight of the most Noble Order of the Garter, and Colonel of his Majesties Regiment of Foot-Guards, &c.

May it please Your Grace,

    Dedications which were Originally design'd, as a Tribute to the Reverence and just esteem we ought to pay the *Great* and *Good* ; are now so corrupted with Flattery, that they rarely either find a Reception in the World, or merit that Patronage they wou'd implore. But I without fear Approach the great Object, being above that mean and mercenary Art; nor can I draw the Lovely Picture half so charming and so manly as it is; and that Author may more properly boast of a Lucky Hitt, whose choice and Fortune is so good, than if he had pleas'd all the different ill Judging world besides in the business of the *Play*; for none that way, can ever hope to please all; in an Age when Faction rages, and different Parties disagree in all things—But coming the first day to a new Play with a Loyal Title, and then even the sober and tender conscienc'd, throng as to a forbidden Conventicle, fearing the Cub of their old Bear of Reformation should be expos'd, to be the scorn of the wicked, and dreading (tho' but the faint shadow of their own deformity) their *Rebellion, Murders, Massacres* and *Villainies*, from forty upwards, should be represented for the better undeceiving and informing of the World, flock in a full Assembly with a pious design to Hiss and Rail it as much out of countenance as they would *Monarchy, Religion, Laws*, and *Honesty*; throwing the *Act of Oblivion* in our Teeths, as if that (whose mercy cannot make them forget their old Rebellion) cou'd hinder honest Truths from breaking out upon 'em in Edifying Plays, where the Loyal hands ever out-do their venom'd Hiss; a good and happy Omen, if Poets may be allow'd for Prophets as of old they were: and 'tis as easily seen at a new Play how the Royal Interest thrives, as at a City Election, how the *Good Old Couse* [227] is carried on; as a Noble Peer lately said, *Tho' the Tories have got the better of us at the Play, we carried it in the City by many Voices, God be praised!*

    This Play, call'd *The Roundheads*, which I humbly lay at your Graces feet, Pardon the Title, and Heaven defend you from the bloody Race, was carried in the House *nemine contra dicente*, by the Royal Party, and under your Grace's Illustrious Patronage is safe from any new Seditious affronts abroad; Your Grace alone, whom Heaven and Nature has form'd the most adorable Person in the whole Creation, with all the advantages of a glorious Birth, has a double right and power to defend all that approach you for sanctuary; your very Beauty is a Guard to all you deign to make safe: for You were born for Conquest every way; even what *Phanatick*, what peevish *Politician*, testy with *Age, Diseases*, miscarried *Plots*, disappointed *Revolutions*, envious of *Power*, of *Princes*, and of *Monarchy*, and mad with *Zeal* for *Change* and *Reformation*, could yet be so far lost to sense of Pleasure, as not to turn a Rebel to Revenge the *Good old Cause*, and the patronage to *Plebean* sedition with only looking on you, 'twou'd force his meager face to blushing smiles, and make him swear he had mistook the side, curse his own Party, and if possible, be reconciled to Honesty again: such power have charms like Yours to calm the soul, and will in spite of You plead for me to the disaffected, even when they are at Wars with your Birth and Power. But this *Play*, for which I humbly beg your Grace's Protection, needs it in a more peculiar manner, it having drawn down Legions upon its head, for its Loyalty—*what, to Name us* cries one, *'tis most abominable, unheard of daring* cries another—*she deserves to be swing'd* cries a third; as if twere all a Libel, a Scandal impossible to be prov'd, or that their Rogueries were of so old a Date their Reign were past Remembrance or History; when they take such zealous care to renew it daily to our memories: And I am satisfied, that they that will justify the best of these Traitors, deserves the fate of the worst, and most manifestly declare to the World by it, they wou'd be at the *Old Game* their fore-Fathers play'd with so good success: yet if there be any honest loyal man allied to any here nam'd, I heartily beg his pardon for any offensive Truth I have spoken, and 'tis a wonderful thing that amongst so Numerous a Flock they will not allow of one mangy Sheep; not one Rogue in the whole Generation of the Association.

Ignoramus the 1st *and the* 2d. [228]

But as they are I leave 'em to your Grace to Judge of 'em; to whom I humbly present this small Mirror, of the late wretched Times: wherein your Grace may see something of the Miseries three the Most Glorious Kingdoms of the Universe were reduc'd to; where your Royal Ancestors victoriously Reign'd for so many hundred years: How they were Governed, Parcell'd out, and deplorably enslav'd, and to what Low, Prostituted Lewdness they fell at last: where the Nobility and Gentry were the most contemn'd and despis'd part of them, and such Mean (and till then obscure) Villains Rul'd, and Tyrannized, that no *Age*, nor *Time*, or scarce a Parish Book makes mentions or cou'd show there was any such Name or Family. Yet these were those that impudently Tug'd for Empire, and Prophan'd that illustrious Throne and Court, so due then, and possessed now (through the infinite Mercies of God to this bleeding Nation) by the best of Monarchs; a Monarch, who had the divine goodness to Pardon even his worst of Enemies what was past; Nay, out of his Vast and God-like Clemency, did more than Heaven itself can do, put it out of his Power by *an Act of Oblivion*, to punish the unparalell'd Injuries done His Sacred Person, and the rest of the Royal Family: How great his Patience has been since, I leave to all the World to judge: but Heaven be prais'd, he has not yet forgot the Sufferings and Murders of the Glorious Martyr of ever Blessed memory, Your Graces Sacred Grandfather, and by what Arts and Ways that Devilish Plot was laid! and will like a skilful Pilate, by the wreck of one Rich Vessel, learn how to shun the danger of this present Threatening and save the rest from sinking; The Clouds already begin to disappear, and the face of things to change, thanks to Heaven, his Majesties infinite Wisdom, and the Over-Zeal of the (falsely called) *True Protestant Party*; Now we may pray for the King and his Royal Brother, defend his Cause, and assert his Right, without the fear of a taste of the Old Sequestration call'd a *Fine*; Guard the Illustrious Pair, good Heaven, from Hellish Plots, and all the Devilish Machinations of Factious Cruelties: and you, great Sir, (whose Merits have so Justly deserv'd that glorious Command so lately trusted to your Care, which Heaven increase, and make your glad Regiment Armies for our safety. May you become the great Example of Loyalty and Obedience, and stand a firm and unmoveable Pillar to *Monarchy*, a Noble Bullwark to *Majesty*; defend the Sacred Cause, employ all that Youth, Courage, and Noble Conduct which God and Nature purposely has endued you with, to serve the Royal Interest: You, Sir, who are obliged by a double Duty to Love, Honor, and Obey his Majesty, both as a Father and a King! O undissolvable Knot! O Sacred Union! what Duty, what Love, what Adoration can express or repay the Debt we owe the first, or the Allegiance due to the last, but where both meet in one, to make the Tie Eternal; Oh what Counsel, what Love of Power, what fancied Dreams of Empire, what fickle Popularity can inspire the heart of Man, or any Noble mind, with Sacrilegious thoughts against it, can harbour or conceive a stubborn disobedience: Oh what Son can desert the Cause of an Indulgent Parent, what Subject, of such a Prince, without renouncing the Glory of his Birth, his Loyalty, and good Nature.

Ah Royal lovely Youth! beware of false Ambition; wisely believe your Elevated Glory, (at least) more happy then a Kings, you share their Joys, their pleasures and magnificence, without the toils and business of a *Monarch*, their careful days and restless thoughtful nights; know, you art blest with all that Heaven can give, or you can wish; your Mind and Person such, so excellent, that Love knows no fault it would wish to mend, nor Envy to increase! blest with a Princess of such undisputable charming Beauty, as if Heaven, designing to take a peculiar care in all that concerns your Happiness, had form'd her on purpose, to complete it.

Hail happy glorious Pair! the perfect joy and pleasure of all that look on ye, for whom all Tongues and Hearts have Prayers and Blessings; May you out-live Sedition, and see your Princely Race as Numerous as Beautiful, and those all great and Loyal Supporters of a long Race of *Monarchs* of this Sacred Line, This shall be the perpetual wish, this the Eternal Prayer of

SIR,
Your Graces most Humble,
and most Obedient Servant,
A. BEHN.

THE ROUND-HEADS;
or, the Good Old Cause.

PROLOGUE,

Spoken by the Ghost of *Hewson* ascending from Hell dress'd as a Cobbler.

I am the Ghost of him who was a true Son
Of the late Good Old Cause, *ycleped* Hewson, [229]
Rous'd by strange Scandal from th' eternal Flame
With noise of Plots, [p. 341] *of wondrous Birth and Name,*
Whilst the sly Jesuit robs us of our Fame.
Can all their Conclave, tho with Hell th' agree,
Act Mischief equal to Presbytery? [p. 341]
Look back on our Success in Forty One, [p. 341]
Were ever braver Villainies carried on,
Or new ones now more hopefully begun?
And shall our Unsuccess our Merit lose,
And make us quit the Glory of our Cause?
No, hire new Villains, Rogues without Remorse,
And let no Law nor Conscience stop your Course;
Let Politicians order the Confusion,
And let the Saints pay pious Contribution.
Pay those that rail, and those that can delude
With scribbling Nonsense the loose Multitude.
Pay well your Witnesses, they may not run
To the right Side, and tell who set 'em on.

Pay 'em so well, that they may ne'er recant,
And so turn honest merely out of want.
Pay Juries, that no formal Laws may harm us,
Let Treason be secur'd by Ignoramus. [p. 341]
Pay Bully Whig, who loyal Writers bang,
And honest Tories in Effigy hang:
Pay those that burn the Pope to please the Fools,
And daily pay Right Honorable Tools;
Pay all the Pulpit Knaves that Treason brew,
And let the zealous Sisters pay 'em too;
Justices, bound by Oath and Obligation,
Pay them the utmost Price of their Damnation,
Not to disturb our useful Congregation.
Nor let the Learned Rabble be forgot,
Those pious Hands that crown our hopeful Plot.
No, modern Statesmen cry, 'tis Lunacy
To barter Treason with such Rogues as we.
But subtiler Oliver *did not disdain*
His mightier Politicks with ours to join.
I for all Uses in a State was able,
Cou'd Mutiny, cou'd fight, hold forth, and cobble.
Your lazy Statesman may sometimes direct,
But your small busy Knaves the Treason act.

DRAMATIS PERSONÆ.

MEN.

Lord *Fleetwood*, [p. 343] Competitor for the Crown
Lord *Lambert*, [p. 343] Competitors for the Crown, but *Lambert* is General of the Army.
Lord *Wariston*, [p. 343] Chairman of the Committee of Safety.
Hewson, [p. 343] Chairman of the Committee of Safety.
Desbro, [p. 343] Commanders, and Committee-men.
Duckingfield, [p. 343] Commanders, and Committee-men.
Corbet, [p. 343] Commanders, and Committee-men.
Lord *Whitlock*. [p. 343]
Ananias Goggle, Lay Elder of *Clement's* Parish. [p. 343]
A Rabble of the Sanctify'd Mobile. [230]
Corporal *Right*, an *Oliverian* Commander, but honest, and a Cavalier in his Heart.
Loveless, a Royalist, a Man of Honor, in love with Lady *Lambert*.
Freeman, his Friend, of the same Character, in love with Lady *Desbro*.
Captain of the Prentices. [230]
Two Pages to Lady *Lambert*.
Tom, Page to Lady *Desbro*. [230]
Page to Lady *Fleetwood*.
A Felt-maker.
A Joyner.
Doorkeeper.

Two Clerks.
Three Soldiers.

WOMEN.

Lady *Lambert*, [p. 343] in love with *Loveless*.
Lady *Desbro*, [p. 343] in love with *Freeman*.
Lady *Fleetwood*. [p. 343]
Lady *Cromwell*. [p. 343]
Gilliflower, Lady *Lambert's* Old Woman.
Several Ladies, for Redress of Grievances.
Women Servants to Lady *Lambert*.

Petitioners, Servants, Guards, [230] Footmen, Fiddlers,
and a Band of Loyal City Apprentices.

ACT I.

Scene I. *The Street*.

[*Enter three* Soldiers, *and Corporal* Right.]

Cor. Ah, Rogue, the World runs finely round, the business is done.
1 Sold. Done! the Town's our own, my fine Rascal.
2 Sold. We'll have Harlots by the Belly, Sirrah.
1 Sold. Those are Commodities I confess I wou'd fain be trucking for—but no words of that, Boy.
Cor. Stand, who goes there?

[*To them a* Joyner *and a* Felt-maker.]

1 Sold. Who are you for?—hah!
Joy. Are for, Friend? we are for Gad and the Lord *Fleetwood*. [p. 344]
1 Sold. *Fleetwood*! knock 'em down, *Fleetwood*, that sniveling Thief?
Felt. Why, Friends, who are ye for?
Cor. For! who shou'd we be for, but *Lambert*, Noble *Lambert*? Is this a time o'th' day to declare for *Fleetwood*, with a Pox? indeed, i'th' Morning 'twas a Question had like to have been decided with push a Pike. [231]
2 Sold. Dry blows wou'd ne'er ha' don't, some must have sweat Blood for't; but—'tis now decided.
Joy. Decided!
2 Sold. Yes, decided, Sir, without your Rule for't.
Joy. Decided! by whom, Sir? by us the Free-born Subjects of *England*, by the Honorable Committee of Safety, or the Right Reverend City? without which, Sir, I humbly conceive, your Declaration for *Lambert* is illegal, and against the Property of the People.
2 Sold. Plain *Lambert*; here's a saucy Dog of a Joyner; Sirrah, get ye home, and mind your Trade, and save the Hangman a labor.

Joy. Look ye, Friend, I fear no Hang-man in *Christendom*; for Conscience and Public Good, for Liberty and Property, I dare as far as any Man.

2 Sold. Liberty and Property, with a Pox, in the Mouth of a Joyner: you are a pretty Fellow to settle the Nation—what says my Neighbour Felt-maker?

Felt. Why, verily, I have a high respect for my honorable Lord *Fleetwood*, he is my intimate Friend; and till I find his Party the weaker, I hope my Zeal will be strengthened for him.

2 Sold. Zeal for *Fleetwood!* Zeal for a Halter, and that's your due: Why, what has he ever done for you? Can he lead you out to Battle? Can he silence the very Cannon with his Eloquence alone?—Can he talk—or fight—or—

Felt. But verily he can pay those that can, and that's as good—and he can pray—

2 Sold. Let him pray, and we'll fight, and see whose business is done first; we are for the General who carries Charms in every Syllable; can act both the Soldier and the Courtier, at once expose his Breast to Dangers for our sakes—and tell the rest of the pretended Slaves a fair Tale, but hang 'em sooner than trust 'em.

1 Sold. Ay, ay, a *Lambert*, a *Lambert*, he has Courage, *Fleetwood's* an Ass to him.

Felt. Hum—here's Reason, Neighbour. [*To the Joyner.*]

Joy. That's all one, we do not act by Reason.

Cor. *Fleetwood's* a Coward.

2 Sold. A Blockhead.

1 Sold. A sniveling Fool; a General in the Hangings, no better.

Joy. What think you then of *Vane*? [p. 345]

2 Sold. As of a Fool, that has dreamt of a new Religion, and is only fit to reign in the Fifth Monarchy [p. 345] he preaches so much up? but no King in this Age.

Felt. What of *Haslerig*? [p. 346]

2 Sold. A Hangman for *Haslerig*. I cry, No, no, One and all, a *Lambert*, a *Lambert*; he is our General, our Protector, our Keiser, our—even what he pleases himself.

1 Sold. Well, if he pleases himself, he pleases me.

2 Sold. He's our Rising Sun, and we'll adore him, for the Speaker's Glory's set.

Cor. At nought, Boys; how the Rogue look'd when his Coach was stop'd!

Joy. Under favor, what said the Speaker?

2 Sold. What said he? prithee, what cou'd he say that we wou'd admit for Reason? Reason and our Bus'ness are two things: Our Will was Reason and Law too, and the Word of Command lodg'd in our Hilts: *Cobbet* and *Duckenfield* show'd 'em Cockpit-Law.

Cor. He understood not Soldier's Dialect; the Language of the Sword puzzled his Understanding; the Keenness of which was too sharp for his Wit, and over-rul'd his Robes—therefore he very mannerly kiss'd his Hand, and wheel'd about—

2 Sold. To the place from whence he came.

Cor. And e'er long to the place of Execution.

1 Sold. No, damn him, he'll have his Clergy.

Joy. Why, is he such an Infidel to love the Clergy?

Cor. For his Ends; but come let's go drink the General's Health, *Lambert*; not *Fleetwood*, that Son of a Custard, always quaking.

2 Sold. Ay, ay, *Lambert* I say—besides, he's a Gentleman.

Felt. Come, come, Brother Soldier, let me tell you, I fear you have a *Stewart* in your Belly.

250

Cor. I am sure you have a Rogue in your Heart, Sirrah, which a Man may perceive thro that sanctified Dog's Face of yours; and so get ye gone, ye Rascals, and delude the Rabble with your canting Politicks. [*Every one beats 'em.*]

Felt. Nay, an you be in Wrath, I'll leave you.

Joy. No matter, Sir, I'll make you know I'm a Freeborn Subject, there's Law for the Righteous, Sir, there's Law. [*Go out.*] [232]

Cor. There's Halters, ye Rogues—

2 Sold. Come, Lads, let's to the Tavern, and drink Success to Change; I doubt not but to see 'em chop about, till it come to our great Hero again—Come to the Tavern.

[*Going out, are met by* Loveless *and* Freeman, *who enter, and stay the* Corporal.]

Cor. I'll follow ye, Comrade, presently.

[*Exit the rest of the Soldiers.*] [233]

—Save ye, noble Colonel.

Free. How is't, Corporal?

Cor. A brave World, Sir, full of Religion, Knavery, and Change: we shall shortly see better Days.

Free. I doubt it, Corporal.

Cor. I'll warrant you, Sir,—but have you had never a Billet, no Present, nor Love—remembrance today, from my good Lady *Desbro?*

Free. None, and wonder at it. Hast thou not seen her Page today?

Cor. Faith, Sir, I was employ'd in Affairs of State, by our Protector that shall be, and could not Callis

Free. Protector that shall be! who's that, *Lambert*, or *Fleetwood*, or both?

Cor. I care not which, so it be a Change; but I mean the General:—but, Sir, my Lady *Desbro* is now at Morning-Lecture here hard by, with the Lady *Lambert*.

Lo. Seeking the Lord for some great Mischief or other.

Free. We have been there, but could get no opportunity of speaking to her—*Loveless*, know this Fellow—he's honest and true to the Hero, tho a Red-Coat. I trust him with my Love, and have done with my Life.

Lo. Love! Thou canst never make me believe thou art earnestly in love with any of that damn'd Reformation.

Free. Thou art a Fool; where I find Youth and Beauty, I adore, let the Saint be true or false.

Lo. 'Tis a Scandal to one of us to converse with 'em; they are all sanctify'd Jilts; and there can neither be Credit nor Pleasure in keeping 'em company; and 'twere enough to get the Scandal of an Adherer to their devilish Politicks, to be seen with 'em.

Free. What, their Wives?

Lo. Yes, their Wives. What seest thou in 'em but Hypocrisy? Make love to 'em, they answer in Scripture.

Free. Ay, and lie with you in Scripture too. Of all Whores, give me your zealous Whore; I never heard a Woman talk much of Heaven, but she was much for the Creature too. What do'st think I had thee to the Meeting for?

Lo. To hear a Rascal hold forth for Bodkins and Thimbles, Contribution, my beloved! to carry on the good Cause, that is, Roguery, Rebellion, and Treason, profaning the sacred Majesty of Heaven, and our glorious Sovereign.

Free. But—were there not pretty Women there?

Lo. Damn 'em for sighing, groaning Hypocrites.

Free. But there was one, whom that handsome Face and Shape of yours, gave more occasion for sighing, than any Mortification caus'd by the Cant of the Lay-Elder in the half Hogs-Head: Did'st thou not mind her?

Lo. Not I, damn it, I was all Rage; and hadst not thou restrain'd me, I had certainly pull'd that Rogue of a Holder forth by the Ears from his sanctify'd Tub. 'Sdeath, he hum'd and haw'd all my Patience away, nosed and snivel'd me to Madness. Heaven! That thou shouldst suffer such Vermin to infect the Earth, such Wolves amongst thy Flocks, such Thieves and Robbers of all Laws of God and Man, in thy Holy Temples. I rave to think to what thou'rt fall'n, poor *England!*

Free. But the she Saint—

Lo. No more; were she as fair as Fancy could imagine, to see her there wou'd make me loath the Form; she that can listen to the dull Nonsense, the bantering of such a Rogue, such an illiterate Rascal, must be a Fool, past sense of loving, *Freeman.*

Free. Thou art mistaken.—But, didst thou mind her next the Pulpit?

Lo. A Plague upon the whole Congregation: I minded nothing but how to fight the Lord's Battle with that damn'd sham Parson, whom I had a mind to beat.

Free. My Lady *Desbro* is not of that Persuasion, but an errant Heroic [p. 349] in her Heart, and feigns it only to have the better occasion to serve the Royal Party. I knew her, and lov'd her before she married.

Lo. She may chance then to be sav'd.

Free. Come, I'll have thee bear up briskly to some one of 'em, it may redeem thy Sequestration; which, now thou see'st no hopes of compounding, puts thee out of Patience.

Lo. Let 'em take it, and the Devil do 'em Good with it; I scorn it should be said I have a Foot of Land in this ungrateful and accursed Island; I'd rather beg where Laws are obey'd, and Justice perform'd, than be powerful where Rogues and base-born Rascals rule the roast.

Free. But suppose now, dear *Loveless,* that one of the Wives of these Pageant Lords should fall in love with thee, and get thy Estate again, or pay the double for't?

Lo. I wou'd refuse it.

Free. And this for a little dissembl'd Love, a little Drudgery—

Lo. Not a Night, by Heaven—not an Hour—no, not a single Kiss. I'd rather make love to an *Incubus.*

Free. But suppose 'twere the new Protectress herself, the fine Lady *Lambert?*

Lo. The greatest Devil of all; damn her, do'st think I'll cuckold the Ghost of old *Oliver?* [p. 349]

Free. The better; There's some Revenge in't; do'st know her?

Lo. Never saw her, nor care to do.

Cor. Colonel, do you command me anything?

Free. Yes, I'll send thee with a Note—Let's step into a Shop and write it; *Loveless,* stay a moment, and I'll be with thee. [*Exit* Freeman *and* Corporal.]

[*Enter* L. Lambert, L. Desbro, Gilliflower, Pages *with great Bibles, and Footmen. Loveless walks sullenly, not seeing 'em.*]

[L. Lambert's *Train carried.*]

L. Lam. O, I'm impatient to know his Name; ah, *Desbro*, he betray'd all my Devotion; and when I would have pray'd, Heav'n knows it was to him, and for him only.

L. Des. What manner of Man was it?

L. Lam. I want Words to describe him; not tall, nor short; well made, and such a Face—

> Love, Wit and Beauty [234] revel'd in his Eyes;
> From whence he shot a thousand winged Darts
> That pierc'd quite through my Soul.

L. Des. Seem'd he a Gentleman?

L. Lam. A God! altho his outside [235] were but mean;
But he shone thro like Lightning from a Cloud,
And shot more piercing Rays.

L. Des. Staid he long?

L. Lam. No, methought he grew [236] displeas'd with our Devotion,
And seem'd to contradict the Parson with his angry Eyes.
A Friend he had too with him, young and handsome,
Who seeing some Disorder in his Actions, got him away.
—I had almost forgot all Decency,
And started up to call him; but my Quality,
And wanting something to excuse that Fondness,
Made me decline with very much ado.

Gill. Heavens, Madam, I'll warrant they were Heroicks.

L. Lam. Heroicks!

Gill. Cavaliers, Madam, of the Royal Party.

L. Des. They were so, I knew one of 'em.

L. Lam. Ah, *Desbro*, do'st thou? Ah, Heav'ns, that they should prove Heroicks!

L. Des. You might have known that by the Conquest; I never heard any one o't' other Party ever gain'd a Heart; and indeed, Madam, 'tis a just Revenge, our Husbands make Slaves of them, and they kill all their Wives. [*Lovis sees 'em, and starts.*]

Lo. Hah, what have we here?—Women—faith, and handsome too—I never saw a Form more excellent; who e'er they are, they seem of Quality.—By Heav'n, I cannot take my Eyes from her. [*Pointing to* L. Lambert.]

L. Lam. Ha, he's yonder, [237] my Heart begins to fail,
My trembling Limbs refusing to support me—
His Eyes seem fix'd on mine too; ah, I faint—[*Leans on* Desbro.]

Gill. My Lady's Coach, *William*—quickly, she faints.

Lo. Madam, can an unfortunate Stranger's aid add anything to the recovery of so much Beauty? [*Bowing, and holding her.*]

L. Lam. Ah, wou'd he knew how much! [*Aside.*]

Gill. Support her, Sir, till her Ladyship's Coach comes—I beseech ye.

Lo. Not *Atlas* bore up Heaven with greater Pride.

L. Lam.—I beg your Pardon, Sir, for this Disorder,
That has occasion'd you so great a Trouble—

You seem a Gentleman—and consequently
May need some Service done you; name the way,
I shall be glad to let you see my Gratitude.

    Lo. If there be ought in me, that merits this amazing Favor from you, I owe my Thanks to Nature that endow'd me with something in my Face that spoke my Heart.

    L. Lam. Heaven! How he looks and speaks—[*To* Desbro, *aside.*]

    L. Des. Oh, these Heroicks, Madam, have the most charming Tongues.

    L. Lam. Pray come to me—and ask for any of my Officers, and you shall have admittance—

    Lo. Who shall I ask for, Madam? for I'm yet ignorant to whom I owe for this great Bounty.

    L. Lam. Not know me! Thou art indeed a Stranger.
I thought I'd been so elevated above the common Crowd,
it had been visible to all Eyes who I was.

Lo. Pardon my Ignorance.
My Soul conceives ye all that Heaven can make ye,
Of Great, of Fair and Excellent;
But cannot guess a Name to call you by
But such as would displease ye—
My Heart begins to fail, and by her Vanity
I fear she's one of the new Race of Quality:
—But be she Devil, I must love that Form. [*Aside.*]

L. Lam. Hard Fate of Greatness, we so highly elevated
Are more expos'd to Censure than the little ones,
By being forc'd to speak our Passions first.
—Is my Coach ready?

    Page. It waits your Honor.

    L. Lam. I give you leave to visit me—ask for the General's Lady, if my Title be not by that time alter'd.

    Lo. Pistols and Daggers to my Heart—'tis so.

    L. Lam. Adieu, Sir.

[*Exit all but* Lovis *who stands musing.*]

[*Enter* Freeman.]

    Free. How now, what's the matter with thee?

    Lo. Prithee wake me, *Freeman.*

    Free. Wake thee!

    Lo. I dream; by Heaven I dream;
Nay, yet the lovely Phantom's in my View.
Oh! wake me, or I sleep to perfect Madness.

    Free. What ail'st thou? what did'st dream of?

    Lo. A strange fantastic Charmer,
A thing just like a Woman Friend;
It walked and looked with wondrous Majesty,
Had Eyes that kill'd, and Graces deck'd her Face;
But when she talk'd, mad as the Winds she grew,

Chimera in the form of Angel, Woman!

Free. Who the Devil meanest thou?

Lo. By Heav'n I know not, but, as she vanish'd hence, she bad me come to the General's.

Free. Why, this is she I told thee ey'd thee so at the Conventicle; 'tis *Lambert*, the renown'd, the famous Lady *Lambert*—Mad call'st thou her? 'tis her ill acted Greatness, thou mistak'st; thou art not us'd to the Pageantry of these Women yet: they all run thus mad; 'tis Greatness in 'em, *Loveless*.

Lo. And is thine thus, thy Lady *Desbro?*

Free. She's of another Cut, she married, as most do, for Interest—but what—thou't to her?

Lo. If Lightning stop my way:—

Perhaps a sober View may make me hate her. [*Exeunt both.*] [238]

Scene II. *A Chamber in* Lambert's *House.* [239]

[*Enter* Lambert *and* Whitlock.]

Whit. My Lord, now is your time, you may be King; Fortune is yours, you've time itself by th' Fore-lock.

Lam. If I thought so, I'd hold him fast, by Heaven.

Whit. If you let slip this Opportunity, my Lord, you are undone—*Aut Cæsar, aut Nullus.*

Lam. But *Fleetwood—*

Whit. Hang him, soft Head.

Lam. True, he's of an easy Nature; yet if thou didst but know how little Wit governs this mighty Universe, thou wou'dst not wonder Men should set up him.

Whit. That will not recommend him at this *Juncto*, tho he's an excellent Tool for your Lordship to make use of; and therefore use him, Sir, as *Cataline* did *Lentulus*; drill the dull Fool with Hopes of Empire on, and that all tends to his Advancement only: The Blockhead will believe the Crown his own: What other Hopes could make him ruin *Richard*, a Gentleman of Qualities a thousand times beyond him?

Lam. They were both too soft; an ill Commendation for a General, who should be rough as Storms of War itself.

Whit. His time was short, and yours is coming on; Old Oliver had his.

Lam. I hate the Memory of that Tyrant Oliver.

Whit. So do I, now he's dead, and serves my Ends no more. I lov'd the Father of the great Heroic, whilst he had Power to do me good: he failing, Reason directed me to the Party then prevailing, the Fag-end of the Parliament: 'tis true, I took the Oath of Allegiance, as Oliver, your Lordship, Tony, [p. 354] and the rest did, without which we could not have sat in that Parliament; but that Oath was not for our Advantage, and so better broke than kept.

Lam. I am of your Opinion, my Lord.

Whit. Let Honesty and Religion preach against it. But how cou'd I have serv'd the Commons by deserting the King? how have I show'd [240] myself loyal to your Interest, by fooling Fleet-wood, in the deserting of Dick; by dissolving the honest Parliament, and bringing in the odious Rump? how cou'd I have flatter'd Ireton, by telling him Providence brought things about, when 'twas mere Knavery all; and that the Hand of the Lord was in't, when I knew the Devil was in't? or indeed, how cou'd I now advise you to be King, if I had started at Oaths, or preferr'd Honesty or Divinity before Interest and the Good Old Came?

Lam. Nay, 'tis most certain, he that will live in this World, must be endu'd with the three rare Qualities of Dissimulation, Equivocation, and mental Reservation.

Whit. In which Excellency, Heav'n be prais'd, we out-do the Jesuits.

[*Enter* Lady Lambert.]

L. Lam. I'm glad to see you so well employ'd, my Lord, as in Discourse with my Lord Whitlock, he's of our Party, and has Wit.

Whit. Your Honor graces me too much.

Lam. My Lord, my Lady is an absolute States-woman.

L. Lam. Yes, I think things had not arriv'd to this exalted height, nor had you been in prospect of a Crown, had not my Politicks exceeded your meaner Ambition.

Lam. I confess, I owe all my good Fortune to thee.

[*Enter* Page.]

Page. My Lord, my Lord *Wariston*, Lord *Hewson*, Colonel *Cobbet*, and Colonel *Duckenfield* desire the Honor of waiting on you.

L. Lam. This has a Face of Greatness—let 'em wait a while i'th' Antichamber.

Lam. My Love, I would have 'em come in.

L. Lam. You wou'd have 'em! you wou'd have a Fool's Head of your own; pray let me be Judge of what their Duty is, and what your Glory: I say I'll have 'em wait.

Page. My Lord *Fleetwood* too is just alighted, shall lie wait too, Madam?

L. Lam. He may approach: and d'ye hear—put on your fawning Looks, flatter him, and profess much Friendship to him, you may betray him with the more facility.

Whit. Madam, you counsel well. [*Exit* Page.]

[Page *re-enters with* Lord Fleetwood.]

Lam. My good Lord, your most submissive Servant.

Whit. My gracious Lord, I am your Creature—your Slave—

Fleet. I profess ingeniously, I am much engag'd to you, my good Lords; I hope things are now in the Lard's handling, [241] and will go on well for his Glory and my Interest, and that all my good People of *England* will do things that become good Christians.

Whit. Doubt us not, my good Lord; the Government cannot be put into abler Hands than those of your Lordship; it has hitherto been in the hard Clutches of *Jews, Infidels,* and *Pagans.*

Fleet. Yea, verily, Abomination has been in the Hands of Iniquity.

Lam. But, my Lord, those Hands, by my good Conduct, are now cut off, and our Ambition is, your Lordship wou'd take the Government upon you.

Fleet. I profess, my Lord, by yea and nay, I am asham'd of this Goodness, in making me the Instrument of saving Grace to this Nation; 'tis the great Work of the Lard.

L. Lam. The Lard! Sir, I'll assure you the Lard has the least Hand in your good Fortune; I think you ought to ascribe it to the Cunning and Conduct of my Lord here, who so timely abandon'd the Interest of *Richard.*

Fleet. Ingeniously I must own, your good Lord can do much, and has done much; but 'tis our Method to ascribe all to the Powers above.

L. Lam. Then I must tell you, your Method's an ungrateful Method.

Lam. Peace, my Love.

Whit. Madam, this is the Cant we must delude the Rabble with.

L. Lam. Then let him use it there, my Lord, not amongst us, who so well understand one another.

Lam. Good Dear, be pacified—and tell me, shall the Gentlemen without have Admittance?

L. Lam. They may. [Page *goes out.*]

[*Enter* Hewson, Desbro, Duckenfield, Wariston, *and* Cobbet.]

War. Guds Benizon light on yu, [242] my gued Loords, for this Day's Work; Madam, I kiss your white Honds.

Duc. My Lord, I have not been behind-hand in this Day's turn of State.

Lam. 'Tis confess'd, Sir; what would you infer from that?

Duc. Why, I wou'd know how things go; who shall be General, who Protector?

Hews. My Friend has well translated his meaning.

L. Lam. Fy, how that filthy Cobbler Lord betrays his Function.

Duc. We're in a Chaos, a Confusion, as we are.

Hews. Indeed the Commonwealth at present is out at Heels, and wants underlaying.

Cob. And the People expect something suddenly from us.

Whit. My Lords and Gentlemen, we must consider a while.

War. Bread a gued there's mickle Wisdom i'that, Sirs.

Duc. It ought to be consulted betimes, my Lord, 'tis a matter of Moment, and ought to be consulted by the whole Committee.

Lam. We design no other, my Lord, for which Reason at three a Clock we'll meet at *Wallingford* House. [p. 357]

Duc. Nay, my Lord, do but settle the Affair, let's but know who's our Head, and 'tis no matter.

Hews. Ay, my Lord, no matter who; I hope 'twill be *Fleetwood*, for I have the length of his Foot already.

Whit. You are the leading Men, Gentlemen, your Voices will soon settle the Nation.

Duc. Well, my Lord, we'll not fail at three a Clock.

Des. This falls out well for me; for I've Business in *Smithfield*, where my Horses stand; and verily, now I think on't, the Rogue the Ostler has not given 'em Oates today: Well, my Lords, farewell; if I come not time enough to *Wallingford* House, keep me a Place in the Committee, and let my Voice stand for one, no matter who.

War. A gued Mon I's warrant, and takes muckle Pains for the Gued o'th' Nation, and the Liberty o'th Mobily—The Diel confound 'em aud.

Lam. Come, my Lord *Wariston*, you are a wise Man, what Government are you for.

War. Ene tol what ya please, my gued Loord. [Takes him aside.]

Lam. What think you of a single Person here in my Lord *Fleetwood?*

War. Marry, Sir, and he's a brave Mon, [243] but gen I may cooncel, [244] tak't for yar sel my gued Loord, ant be gued for him, 'tis ene gued for ya te.

Lam. But above half the Nation are for him.

War. Bread a gued, and I's for him then.

Fleet. The Will of the Lard be done; and since 'tis his Will, I cannot withstand my Fate—ingeniously.

Whit. My Lord *Wariston*, a Word—What if *Lambert* were the Man? [*Takes him aside.*]

War. Right Sir, Wons and ya have spoken aud; he's a brave Mon, a Mon indeed gen [245] I's have any Judgment.

Whit. So I find this Property's for any use. [*Aside.*]

Lam. My Lord, I perceive Heaven and Earth conspire to make you our Prince.

Fleet. Ingeniously, my Lords, the Weight of three Kingdoms is a heavy Burden for so weak Parts as mine: therefore I will, before I appear at Council, go seek the Lard in this great Affair; and if I receive a Revelation for it, I shall with all Humility espouse the Yoke, for the Good of his People and mine; and so Gad with us, the Commonwealth of *England.* [*Exeunt* Fleetwood, Desbro, Wariston, Duckenfield, Cobbet, Hewson, *and* Whitlock.]

L. Lam. Poor deluded Wretch, 'tis not yet come to that.

Lam. No, my dear, the Voice will go clearly for me; what with Bribes to some, Hypocrisy and Pretence of Religion to others, and promis'd Preferments to the rest, I have engag'd 'em all.

L. Lam. And will you be a King?

Lam. You think that's so fine a thing—but let me tell you, my Love, a King's a Slave to a Protector, a King's ty'd up to a thousand Rules of musty Law, which we can break at pleasure; we can rule without Parliaments, at least chose whom we please, make 'em agree to our Proposals, or set a Guard upon 'em, and starve 'em till they do.

L. Lam. But their Votes are the strangest things—that they must pass for Laws; you were never voted King.

Lam. No, nor care to be: The sharpest Sword's my Vote, my Law, my Title. They voted *Dick* should reign, where is he now? They voted the great Heroicks from the Succession; but had they Arms or Men, as I have, you shou'd soon see what wou'd become of their Votes—No, my Love! 'tis this—must make me King. [*His Sword.*]

Let *Fleetwood* and the Rump go seek the Lard,
My Empire and my Trust is in my Sword.

ACT II.

Scene I. *A Chamber of State in* Lambert's *House.* [246]

[*Enter* L. Lambert, Gilliflower, *and Women-servants.*]

L. Lam. *Gilliflower*, has none been here to ask for any of my People, in order to his approach to me?

Gill. None, Madam.

L. Lam. Madam! How dull thou art? wo't never learn to give me a better Title than such an one as foolish Custom bestows on every common Wench?

Gill. Pardon my Ignorance, Madam.

L. Lam. Again Madam?

Gill. Really, Madam, I shou'd be glad to know by what other Title you wou'd be distinguish'd?

L. Lam. Abominable dull! Do'st thou not know on what score my Dear is gone to *Wallingford* House?

Gill. I cannot divine, Madam.

L. Lam. Heaven help thy Ignorance! he's gone to be made Protector, Fool, or at least a King, thou Creature; and from this Day I date myself her Highness.

Gill. That will be very fine indeed, an't please your Highness.

L. Lam. I think 'twill sute better with my Person and Beauty than with the other Woman—what d'ye call her? Mrs. *Cromwell*—my Shape—and Gate—my Humor, and my Youth have something more of Grandeur, have they not?

Gill. Infinitely, an't please your Highness.

[Enter *Page.*]

Page. Madam, a Man without has the boldness to ask for your Honor.

L. Lam. Honor, Fool!

Gill. Her Highness, Blockhead.

Page. Saucily prest in, and struck the Porter for denying him entrance to your—Highness.

L. Lam. What kind of Fellow was't?

Page. A rude, rough, hectoring Swash, an't please your Highness; nay, and two or three times, Gad forgive me, he swore too.

L. Lam. It must be he. [*Aside.*]

Page. His Habit was something bad and Cavalierish—I believe 'twas some poor petitioning, begging Tory, who having been sequester'd, wou'd press your Highness for some Favor.

L. Lam. Yes, it must be he—ah, foolish Creature! and can he hope Relief, and be a villainous Cavalier? out upon 'em, poor Wretches—you may admit him tho', [247] for I long to hear how one of those things talk.

Gill. Oh, most strangely, Madam—an please your Highness, I shou'd say. [248]

[*Enter* Loveless.]

L. Lam. 'Tis he, I'll swear, *Gilliflower*, these Heroicks are punctual men [249]—how now, your Bus'ness with us, Fellow?

Lo. My Bus'ness, Madam?—

L. Lam. Hast thou ever a Petition to us?

Lo. A Petition, Madam?—Sure this put—on Greatness is to amuse her Servants, or has she forgot that she invited me? or indeed forgot me?—[*Aside.*]

L. Lam. What art thou?

Page. Shall we search his Breeches, an't please your Highness, for Pistol, or other Instruments?

L. Lam. No, Boy, we fear him not, they say the Powers above protect the Persons of Princes. [*Walks away.*] [250]

Lo. Sure she's mad, yet she walks loose about,
And she has Charms even in her raving Fit.

L. Lam. Answer me. What art thou?—
How shall I get my Servants hence with Honor? [*Aside.*]

Lo. A Gentleman—

That could have boasted Birth and Fortune too,
Till these accursed Times, which Heaven confound,
Razing out all Nobility, all Virtue,
Has render'd me the rubbish of the World;
Whilst new rais'd Rascals, Canters, Robbers, Rebels,
Do lord it o'er the Free-born, Brave and Noble.

L. Lam. You're very confident, know you to whom you speak? but I suppose you have lost your Estate, or some such trivial thing, [251] which makes you angry.

Lo. Yes, a trivial Estate of some five and twenty hundred Pound a Year: but I hope to see that Rogue of a Lord reduc'd to his Cobler's-Stall [p. 361] again, or more deserv'dly hang'd, that has it.

L. Lam. I thought 'twas some such Grievance—but you must keep a good Tongue in your Head, lest you be hang'd for *Scandalum Magnatum*—there's Law for ye, Sir.

Lo. No matter, then I shall be free from a damn'd Commonwealth, as you are pleas'd to call it, when indeed 'tis but a mungrel, mangy, Mock-Monarchy.

L. Lam. Is it your business, Sir, to rail?

Lo. You rais'd the Devil, Madam.

Page. Madam, shall I call your Highness's Guards, and secure the Traitor?

L. Lam. No, that you may see how little I regard or fear him; leave us all—[*Exit all but* Gilliflower.] We'll trust our Person in his Hands alone——Now, Sir—Your Bus'ness? [*Smilingly approaches him.*]

Lo. Madam, I waited here by your Commands.

L. Lam. How shall I tell him that I love him, Gilliflower?

Gill. Easily, Madam, tell him so in plain *English*. Madam, 'tis great; Women of your exalted height ever speak first; you have no Equals dare pretend to speak of Love to you.

L. Lam. Thou art i'th' right—Do'st know my Quality, and thy own Poverty? And hast thou nothing to ask that I may grant?

Lo. Sure she loves me! and I, frail Flesh and Blood, Cannot resist her Charms; but she's of the damn'd Party. [*Aside.*]

L. Lam. Are all your Party, Sir, so proud?

Lo. But what have I to do with Religion! Is Beauty the worse, or a kind Wench to be refus'd for Conventickling? [p. 362] She lives high on the Spoils of a glorious Kingdom, and why may not I live upon the Sins of the Spoiler? [*Aside.*]

L. Lam. Sir—you are poor!

Lo. So is my Prince; a Plague on the occasion.

L. Lam. I think you are—no Fool too.

Lo. I wou'd I were, then I had been a Knave, had thriv'd, and possibly by this time had been tugging for rifled Crowns and Kingdoms.

L. Lam. This Satir ill befits my present Bus'ness with you—you—want some Necessaries—as Clothes, and Linen too; and 'tis great pity so proper a Man shou'd want Necessaries. *Gilliflower*—take my Cabinet Key, and fetch the Purse of Broad-pieces that lies in the lower Drawer; 'tis a small Present, Sir, but 'tis an Earnest of my farther Service. [*Gilliflower goes out and returns with a Purse.*]

Lo. I'm angry, that I find one Grain of Generosity in this whole Race of Hypocrites. [*Aside.*]

L. Lam. Here, Sir, 'tis only for your present use; for Clothes—three hundred Pieces; let me see you sweet—

Lo. Stark mad, by this good Day.

L. Lam. Ah, *Gilliflower!* How prettily those Cavalier things charm; I wonder how the Powers above came to give them all the Wit, Softness, and Gallantry—whilst all the great ones of our Age have the most slovenly, ungrateful, dull Behaviour; no Air, no Wit, no Love, nor any thing to please a Lady with.

Gill. Truly, Madam, there's a great Difference in the Men; yet Heaven at first did its part, but the Devil has since so over-done his, that what with the Vizor of Sanctity, which is the gadly Sneer, the drawing of the Face to a prodigious length, the formal Language, with a certain Twang through the Nose, and the pious Gogle, they are fitter to scare Children than beget love in Ladies.

Lo. You hit the Character of your new Saint.

L. Lam. And then their Dress, *Gilliflower*.

Gill. Oh! 'Tis an Abomination to look like a Gentleman; long Hair is wicked and cavalierish, a Periwig is flat Popery, the Disguise of the Whore of *Babylon*; handsome Clothes, or lac'd Linen, the very Tempter himself, that debauches all their Wives and Daughters; therefore the diminutive Band, with the Hair of the Reformation Cut, beneath which a pair of large sanctify'd Souses appear, to declare to the World they had hitherto escap'd the Pillory, tho deserv'd it as well as *Pryn*. [p. 363]

L. Lam. Have a care what you say, *Gilliflower*.

Gill. Why, Madam, we have no Informers here.

[*Enter* Page.]

Page. Madam, here's Old *Noll's* Wife desires Admittance to your Hon—your Highness.

L. Lam. Bid the poor Creature wait without, I'll do her what Good I can for her Husband's sake, who first infus'd Politicks into me, by which I may boast I have climb'd to Empire.

Lo. So, her Madness runs in that Vein I see. [*Aside.*]

Gill. Alack, Madam, I think she's coming.

Crom. [*without*] Does she keep State in the Devil's Name, and must I wait?

L. Lam. Heavens! I shall be scandalized by the Godly. Dear *Gilliflower*, conceal my Cavalier; I would not have a Cavalier seen with me for all the World—Step into my Cabinet. [*Exit* Gilliflower *and* Lovis.]

[*Enter* L. Cromwel, *held back by a Man—to them* Gilliflower.]

Crom. Unhand me, Villain—'twas not long since a Rudeness, Sir, like this had forfeited thy Head.

L. Lam. What wou'd the Woman?

Crom. The Knave, the perjur'd Villain thy Husband, by th' Throat: thou proud, imperious Baggage, to make me wait; whose Train thou hast been proud to bear—how durst thou, after an Affront like this, trust thy false Face within my Fingers reach? that Face, that first bewitch'd the best of Husbands from me, and tempted him to sin.

Gill. I beseech your Highness retire, the Woman's mad.

Crom. Highness in the Devil's Name, sure 'tis not come to that; no, I may live to see thy Cuckold hang'd first, his Politics are yet too shallow, Mistress. Heavens! Did my Husband make him Lord for this? raise him to Honor, Trusts, Commands, and Counsels,

　　　　To ruin all our Royal Family,

Betray young *Richard*, who had reign'd in Peace
But for his Perjuries and Knaveries;
And now he sooths my Son-in-law, soft *Fleetwood*,
With empty hopes of Pow'r, and all the while
To make himself a King:
No, Minion, no; I yet may live to see
Thy Husband's Head o'th' top of *Westminster*,
Before I see it circled in a Crown.

   L. Lam. I pity the poor Creature.

   Crom. Ungrateful Traitor as he is,
Not to look back upon his Benefactors;
But he, in lieu of making just Returns,
Reviles our Family, profanes our Name,
And will in time render it far more odious
Than ever *Needham* [p. 365] made the great Heroicks.

   L. Lam. Alas, it weeps, poor Woman!

   Crom. Thou ly'st, false Strumpet, I scorn to shed a Tear,
For ought that thou canst do or say to me;
I've too much of my Husband's Spirit in me.
Oh, my dear *Richard*, hadst thou had a Grain on't,
Thou and thy Mother ne'er had fall'n to this.

   Gill. His Father sure was seeking of the Lard when he was got.

[Enter L. Fleetwood, *her Train born up.]*

   Crom. Where is this perjur'd Slave, thy Wittal Lord?
Dares he not show his Face, his guilty Face,
Before the Person he has thus betray'd?

   L. Fleet. Madam, I hope you mistake my honor'd Lord *Lambert*, I believe he designs the Throne for my dear Lord.

   Crom. Fond Girl, because he has the Art of fawning,
Dissembling to the height, can sooth and smile,
Profess, and sometimes weep:—
No, he'll betray him, as he did thy Brother;
Richard the Fourth was thus deluded by him.
No, let him swear and promise what he will,
They are but steps to his own ambitious End;
And only makes the Fool, thy credulous Husband,
A silly deluded Property.

[Enter Fleetwood.]

   Fleet. My honor'd Mother, I am glad to find you here; I hope we shall reconcile things between ye. Verily we should live [252] in Brotherly Love together; come, ingeniously, you shall be Friends, my Lady Mother.

   Crom. Curse on th' occasion of thy being a Kin to me.

   Fleet. Why, an please ye, forsooth, Madam?

   Crom. My Daughter had a Husband,

Worthy the Title of my Son-in-Law;
Ireton, my best of Sons: [p. 365] he'd Wit and Courage,
And with his Counsels, rais'd our House to Honors,
Which thy impolitic Easiness pulls down:
And whilst you should be gaining Crowns and Kingdoms,
Art poorly couzening of the World with fruitless Prayers.

    Fleet. Nay, I'll warrant you, Madam, when there is any gadly Mischief to be done, I am as forward as the best; but 'tis good to take the Lard along with us in everything. I profess ingeniously, as I am an honest Man, verily—ne'er stir—I shall act as becomes a good Christian.

    Crom. A good Coxcomb.
Do'st thou not see her reverend Highness there,
That Minion now assumes that glorious Title
I once, and my Son *Richard's* Wife [p. 366] enjoy'd,
Whilst I am call'd the Night-mare of the Commonwealth?
But wou'd I were, I'd so hag-ride the perjur'd Slaves,
Who took so many Oaths of true Allegiance
To my great Husband first, then to *Richard*—
Who, whilst they reign'd, were most illustrious,
Most high and mighty Princes; whilst fawning Poets
Write Panegyricks [253] on 'em; and yet no sooner was
The wondrous Hero dead, but all his glorious
Titles [p. 366] fell to Monster of Mankind, Murderer
Of Piety, Traitor to Heaven and Goodness.

    Fleet. Who calls him so? Pray take their Names down: I profess ingeniously, forsooth, Madam, verily I'll order 'em, as I am here I Willmore

    Crom. Thou, alas! they scorn so poor a thing as thou.

    Fleet. Do they ingeniously? I'll be even with 'em, forsooth, Mother, as I am here I will, and there's an end on't.

    Crom. I wou'd there were an end of our Disgrace and Shame,
Which is but just begun, I fear.
What will become of that fair Monument
Thy careful Father did erect for thee, [*To* L. Fleetwood.]
Yet whilst he liv'd, next to thy Husband *Ireton*,
Lest none shou'd do it for thee after he were dead;
The Malice of proud *Lambert* will destroy all. [254]

    Fleet. I profess, Madam, you mistake my good Lord *Lambert*, he's an honest Man, and fears the Lard; he tells me I am to be the Man; verily he does, after all's done.

    Crom. Yes, after all's done, thou art the Man to be pointed at.

    Fleet. Nay, ingeniously, I scorn the Words, so I do: I know the great Work of Salvation to the Nation is to be wrought by me, verily.

    Crom. Do, cant on, till Heaven drop Kingdoms in thy Mouth: Dull, silly Sot, thou Ruin of our Interest; thou fond, incorrigible, easy Fool.

[Enter *Page.*]

Page. My Lord, the Committee of Safety waits your coming.

Fleet. Why, law you now, forsooth—I profess verily, you are ingeniously the hardest of Belief—tell the Honorable Lords I'm coming: Go, Lady-mother, go home with my Wife; and verily you'll see things go to your wish—I must to Coach.

L. Fleet. Madam, your humble Servant. [*To* L. Lambert.]

Fleet. Honor'd Lady, I kiss your Hands.

[*Exeunt* Cromwel. Fleetwood, *and* L. Fleetwood.]
[Enter *Loveless.*]

Lo. Was this the thing that is to be Protector?
This little sniveling Fellow rule three Kingdoms?
But leave we Politicks, and fall to Love,
Who deals more Joys in one kind happy moment
Than Ages of dull Empire can produce.

L. Lam. Oh Gods! shall I who never yielded yet,
But to him to whom three Kingdoms fell a Sacrifice,
Surrender at first Parley?

Lo. Perhaps that Lover made ye gayer Presents,
But cou'd not render you a Heart all Love,
Or Mind embyass'd [255] in Affairs of Blood.
—I bring no Guilt to fright you from my Embraces,
But all our Hours shall be serene and soft.

L. Lam. Ah, *Gilliflower*, thy Aid, or I am lost;
Shall it be said of me in after Ages,
When my Fame amongst Queens shall be recorded,
That I, ah Heavens! regardless of my Country's Cause,
Espous'd the wicked Party of its Enemies,
The Heathenish Heroicks? ah, defend me!

Lo. Nay—by all that's—

L. Lam. Ah, hold! Do not profane my Ears with Oaths or Execrations, [256] I cannot bear the Sound.

Lo. Nay, nay—by Heav'n I'll not depart your Lodgings, till that soft Love that plays so in your Eyes give me a better Proof—by—

L. Lam. Oh hold, I die, if you proceed in this Abomination.

Lo. Why do you force me to't? d'ye think to put me off with such a Face—such Lips—such Smiles—such Eyes, and every Charm—You've made me mad, and I shall swear my Soul away, if disappointed now.

Gill. Ah, save the Gentleman's Soul, I beseech ye, Madam.

L. Lam. I'm much inclin'd to Acts of Piety—And you have such a Power, that howe'er I incommode my Honor—[*Leaning on him, smiling. He goes to lead her out, Enter* L. Desbro.]—*Desbro* here! How unseasonably she comes?

L. Des. Cry mercy, Madam, [257] I'll withdraw a while.

L. Lam. Ah, *Desbro!* thou art come in the most lucky Minute [258]—I was just on the point of falling—As thou say'st, these Heroicks have the strangest Power—

L. Des. I never knew a Woman cou'd resist 'em.

L. Lam. No marvel then, our Husbands use 'em so, betray 'em, banish 'em, sequester, murder 'em, and every way disarm 'em—

L. Des. But their Eyes, Madam.

264

L. Lam. Ay, their Eyes, *Desbro*; I wonder our Lords shou'd take away their Swords, and let 'em wear their Eyes.

L. Des. I'll move it to the Committee of Safety, Madam, those Weapons should be taken from 'em too.

L. Lam. Still they'll have some to be reveng'd on us.

L. Des. Ay, so they will will; My Lord says, a Cavalier is a kind of *Hydra*, knock him o'th' Head as often as you will, he has still one to peep up withal.

[Enter Page.]

Page. Madam, here's Mr. *Freeman* to speak with your Honor.

Lo. That's a Friend of mine, Madam, and 'twou'd be unnecessary he saw your Highness and I together: let us withdraw—

L. Lam. Withdraw! why, what will *Desbro* say?

L. Des. O Madam, I know your Virtue and your Piety too well to suspect your Honor wrongfully: 'tis impossible a Lady that goes to a Conventicle twice a Day, besides long Prayers and loud Psalm—singing, shou'd do anything with an Heroic against her Honor. Your known Sanctity preserves you from Scandal—But here's *Freeman*—[*Puts 'em in.*]

[Enter Freeman.]

Free. So, Madam—you are very kind—

L. Des. My charming *Freeman*, this tedious Day of Absence has been an Age in love. How hast thou liv'd without me?

Free. Like one condemn'd, sad and disconsolate, And all the while you made your Husband happy.

L. Des. Name not the Beastly Hypocrite, thou know'st I made no other use of him, But a dull Property to advance our Love.

Free. And 'tis but Justice, *Maria*, he sequester'd me of my whole Estate, because, he said, I took up Arms in *Ireland*, on Noble *Ormond's* [p. 369] Side; nay, hir'd Rogues, perjur'd Villains—Witnesses with a Pox, to swear it too; when at that time I was but Eight Years Old; but I escap'd as well as all the Gentry and Nobility of *England*. To add to this, he takes my Mistress too.

L. Des. You mistake, my lovely *Freeman*; I married only thy Estate, the best Composition I cou'd make for thee, and I will pay it back with Interest too.

Free. You wou'd suspect my Love then, and swear that all the Adoration I pay you, were, as we do to Heav'n, for Interest only.

L. Des. How you mistake my Love, but do so still, so you will let me give these—Proofs of it. [*Gives him Gold.*]

Free. Thus, like *Atlante*, you drop Gold in my Pursuit
To Love, I may not over-take you:
What's this to giving me one happy minute?
Take back your Gold, and give me current Love,
The Treasure of your Heart, not of your Purse—
When shall we meet, *Maria*?

L. Des. You know my leisure Hours are when my Honorable Lord is busied [259] in Affairs of State, or at his Prayers; from which long-winded Exercise [p. 370] I have of late withdrawn myself: three Hours by the Clock he prays extempory, [260] which is, for National and Household Blessings: For the first—'tis to confound the Interest of the King, that the Lard wou'd deliver him, his Friends, Adherers and Allies, wheresoever scatter'd about the Face of the whole Earth, into the Clutches of the Righteous: Press 'em, good Lard, even as the Vintager doth the Grape in the Wine-Press, till the Waters and gliding Channels are made red with the Blood of the Wicked. [*In a Tone.*]

Free. And grant the Faithful to be mighty, and to be strong in Persecution; and more especially, ah! I beseech thee confound that malignant Tory *Freeman*—that he may never rise up in judgment against thy Servant, who has taken from him his Estate, his Sustenance and Bread; give him Grace of thy infinite Mercy, to hang himself, if thy People can find no zealous Witnesses to swear him to the Gallows legally. Ah, we have done very much for thee, Lard, thou shoud'st consider us thy Flock, and we shou'd be as good to thee in another thing. [*In a Tone.*]

L. Des. Thou hit'st the zealous Twang right; sure thou hast been acquainted with some of 'em.

Free. Damn 'em, no; what honest Man wou'd keep 'em Company, where harmless Wit and Mirth's a Sin, laughing scandalous, and a merry Glass Abomination?

L. Des. Yes, if you drink Healths, my wicked Brother: otherwise, to be silently drunk, to be as abusive and satirical as you please, upon the Heroicks, is allowable—for laughing, 'tis not indeed so well; but the precise Sneer and Grin is lawful; no swearing indeed, but lying and dissimulation in abundance. I'll assure you, they drink as deep, and entertain themselves as well with this silent way of leud Debauchery, as you with all your Wit and Mirth, your Healths of the Royal Family.

Free. Nay, I confess, 'tis a great Pleasure to cheat the World.

L. Des. 'Tis Power, as divine *Hobbes* calls it.

Free. But what's all this to Love? Where shall we meet anon?

L. Des. I'll tell you, what will please you as well—Your Friend is within with her Highness that shall be, if the Devil and her Husband's Politicks agree about the matter.

Free. Ha, has my cautious Railer manag'd matters so slyly?

L. Des. No, no, the matter was manag'd to his Hand; you see how Heav'n brings things about, for the Good of your Party; this Business will be worth to him at least a thousand Pound a year, or two, well manag'd—But see, my Lady's Woman.

Gill. Oh, Madam, my Lord—[*Running cross the Stage into her Lady's Chamber.*]

Free. Death, how shall I bring my Friend off? he'll certainly be ruin'd.

[*Enter* Gilliflower, Lovis, *and* L. Lambert.]

Gill. Madam, he's coming up.

Lo. Madam, for myself I care not, but am much concern'd for you.

[L. Lambert *takes two Papers out of her Pocket, and gives 'em to* Lovis *and* Freeman.]

L. Lam. Here take these two Petitions, each of you one—Poor Fellows—you may be gone, your Petitions will not be granted.

[*Enter* Lambert.]

Lam. How now, my Dear, what Petitions?—Friends, what's your Bus'ness?

L. Lam. 'Tis enough we know their Business, Love, we are sufficient to dispatch such Suitors, I hope.

Lam. Pardon me, my Dear, I thought no harm; but I saw you frown, and that made me concern'd.

L. Lam. Frown! 'Twou'd make any Body frown, to hear the Impudence of Gentlemen, these Cavaliers—wou'd you think it, my Dear, if this Fellow has not the Impudence to petition for the Thirds of his Estate again, so justly taken from him for bearing Arms for the Man?—

L. Des. Nay, I'm inform'd, that they, but two Nights ago, in a Tavern, drunk a Health to the Man too.

Lam. How durst you, Sirrah, approach my Lady with any such saucy Address? you have receiv'd our Answer.

Lo. Death, I have scarce Patience. [*Aside.*]

Free. We knew, my Lord, the Influence your Ladies have over you, and Women are more tender and compassionate naturally than Men; and, Sir, 'tis hard for Gentlemen to starve.

L. Lam. Have you not able Limbs? can ye not work?

Lo. Persons of our Education work!

Lam. Starve or beg then.

L. Lam. Education! why, I'll warrant there was that young Creature they call the Duke of *Glocester*, [p. 372] was as well educated as any Lad in the Parish; and yet you see he should have been bound Prentice [p. 373] to a Handy-Crafts Trade, but that our Lords could not spare Money to bind him out, and so they sent him to beg beyond Sea.

Lo. Death, I shall do Mischief: not all the Joy she gave me but now, can atone for this Blasphemy against the Royal Youth. [*Aside.*]

Free. Patience—Well, my Lord, we find you are obdurate, and we'll withdraw.

Lam. Do so: And if you dare presume to trouble us any more, I'll have you whip'd, d'ye hear.

L. Des. Madam, I'll take my leave of your Ladyship.

[*Exit* Lovis, Freeman, *and* L. Desbro.]

L. Lam. My Lord, 'twas I that ought to threaten 'em—but you're so forward still— what makes you from the Committee?

Lam. I left some Papers behind.

L. Lam. And they'll make use of your Absence to set up *Fleetwood* King.

Lam. I'll warrant ye, my Dear.

L. Lam. You'll warrant! you are a Fool, and a Coxcomb; I see I must go myself, there will be no Bus'ness done till I thunder 'em together: They want Old *Oliver* amongst 'em, his Arbitrary Nod cou'd make ye all tremble; when he wanted Power or Money, he need but cock in Parliament, and lay his Hand upon his Sword, and cry, I must have Money, and had it, or kick'd ye all out of Doors: And you are all mealy mouth'd, you cannot cock for a Kingdom.

Lam. I'll warrant ye, Dear, I can do as good a thing for a Kingdom.

L. Lam. You can do nothing as you shou'd do't: You want Old *Oliver's* Brains, [261] Old *Oliver's* Courage, and Old *Oliver's* Counsel: Ah, what a politick Fellow was little Sir *Anthony!* What a Head-piece was there! What a plaguy Fellow Old *Thurlo*, [p. 373] and the rest! But get ye back, and return me Protector at least, or never hope for Peace again.

Lam. My Soul, trouble not thy self, go in—
With mine no Power can equal be,
And I will be a King to humor thee. [*Exeunt.*]

ACT III.

Scene I. *A Council-Chamber, great Table, Chairs, and Papers.*

[*Enter two Clerks, who lay Papers in Order, and Doorkeeper.*]

Door. Come, haste, haste, the Lords are coming—keep back there, room for the Lords, room for the honorable Lords: Heav'n bless your Worships Honors.

[*Enter* Lambert, Fleetwood, Whitlock, Wariston, *discoursing earnestly; to them* Duckenfield, Cobbet, Hewson, Desbro, *and others;* Duckenfield *takes* Wariston *by the Hand, and talks to him.*]

War. Bread a gued, Gentlemen, I's serv'd the Commonwealth long and faithfully; I's turn'd and turn'd to aud Interest and aud Religions that turn'd up Trump, and wons a me, but I's get naught but Bagery by my Sol; I's noo put in for a Pansion as well as rest o ya Loones.
Cob. What we can serve you in, my Lord, you may command.
Duc. And I too, my Lord, when the Government is new moulded.
War. Wons, Sirs, and I's sa moold it, 'twas ne'er sa moolded sen the Dam boon'd the Head on't.
Duc. I know there are some ambitious Persons that are for a single Person; but we'll have hot Work e'er we yield to that.
War. The faud Diel take 'em then for *Archibald*; [262] 'tis warse [263] than Monarchy.
Duc. A thousand times: have we with such Industry been pulling down Kings of the Royal Family, to set up Tyrants of our own, of mean and obscure Birth? No, if we're for a single Person, I'm for a lawful one.
War. Wons and ya have spoken aud, my Lord, so am I.
Duc. But *Lambert* has a busy, haughty Spirit, and thinks to carry it; but we'll have no single Person.
War. Nor I, ods Bread; the faud Diel brest the Wem of *Lambert*, or any single Person in *England*. I's for yare Interest, my gued Lords. [*Bowing.*]
Lam. My Lord *Wariston*, will you please to assume the Chair?

[*Enter* Loveless, Freeman, *and others with Petitions.*]

War. Ah, my gued Loord, I's yare most obedient humble Servant. [*Bowing to Lambert all set.*]
All. Hum, hum.
Fleet. My Lords and Gentlemen, we are here met together in the Name of the Lard—
Duc. Yea, and I hope we shall hang together as one Man—A Pox upon your Preaching. [*Aside.*]
Fleet.—And hope this Day's great Work will be for his Praise and Glory.

268

Duc. 'Bating long Graces, my Lord, we are met together for the Bus'ness of the Nation, to settle it, and to establish a Government.

Fleet. Yea, verily: and I hope you will all unanimously agree, it shall be your unworthy Servant.

Lam. What else, my Lord.

Fleet. And as thou, Lard, hast put the Sword into my Hand—

Duc. So put it into your Heart—my Lord, to do Justice.

Fleet. Amen.

Duc. I'd rather see it there than in your Hand—[*Aside.*]

Fleet. For we are, as it were, a Body without a Head; or, to speak more learnedly, an Animal inanimate.

Hews. My Lord, let us use, as little as we can, the Language of the Beast, hard Words; none of your Eloquence, it savoureth of Monarchy.

Lam. My Lord, you must give Men of Quality leave to speak in a Language more gentile and courtly than the ordinary sort of Mankind.

Hews. My Lord, I am sorry [264] to hear there are any of Quality among this honorable Dissembly. [*Stands up.*]

Cob. Assembly, my Lord—

Hews. Well, you know my meaning; or if there be any such, I'm sorry they should own themselves of Quality.

Duc. How! own themselves Gentlemen! Death, Sir, d'ye think we were all born Coblers?

Hews. Or if you were not, the more the pity, for little *England*, I say. [*In a heat.*]

Fleet. Verily, my Lords, Brethren should not fall out, it is a Scandal to the good Cause, and maketh the wicked rejoice.

War. Wons, and theys garr the loosey Proverb on't te, *when loons gang together by th' luggs, gued men get their ene.*

All. He, he, he.

Duc. He calls you Knaves by Craft, my Lords.

War. Bread a gued, take't among ye, Gentlemen, I's ment weel.

Fleet. I profess, my Lord *Wariston*, you make my Hair stand an end to hear how you swear.

War. Wons, my Loord, I's swear as little as your Lordship, only I's swear out, and ye swallow aud.

Duc. There's a Bone for you to pick, my Lord.

All. He, he, he.

Lam. We give my Lord *Wariston* leave to jest.

Des. But what's this to the Government all this while? A dad I shall sit so late, I shall have no time to visit my Horses, therefore proceed to the Point.

Hews. Ay, to the Point, my Lords; the Gentleman that spoke last spoke well.

Cob. Well said, Brother, I see you will in time speak properly.

Duc. But to the Government, my Lords! [*Beats the Table.*]

Lam. Put 'em off of this Discourse, my Lord. [*Aside to* Wariston.]

Des. My Lord *Wariston*, move it, you are Speaker.

War. The Diel a me, Sirs, and noo ya talk of a Speaker, I's tell ye a blithe Tale.

Fleet. Ingeniously, my Lord, you are to blame to swear so.

Lam. Your Story, my Lord.

War. By my Sol, mon, and there war a poor Woman the other Day, begg'd o'th' Carle the Speaker, but he'd give her nought unless she'd let a Feart; wons at last a Feart she lat. Ay marry, quoth the Woman, noo my Rump has a Speaker te.

All. He, he, he.

Duc. But to our Bus'ness—

Des. Bus'ness; ay, there's the thing, I've a World on't. I shou'd go and bespeak a Pair of Mittins and Shears for my Hedger and Shearer, a pair of Cards for my Thrasher, a Scythe for my Mower, and a Screen-Fan for my Lady-Wife, and many other things; my Head's full of Bus'ness. I cannot stay—

Whit. Fy, my Lord, will you neglect the bus'ness of the Day? We meet to oblige the Nation, and gratify our Friends.

Des. Nay, I'll do anything, so I may rise time enough to see my Horses at Night.

Lo. Damn 'em, what stuff's here [265] for a Council-Table?

Free. Where are our *English* Spirits, that can be govern'd by such Dogs as these?—

Lam. Clerk, read the Heads of what past at our last sitting.

War. In the first place, I must mind your Lordships tol consider those that have been gued Members in the Commonwealth.

Fleet. We shall not be backward to gratify any that have serv'd the Commonwealth.

Whit. There's Money enough; we have taxt the Nation high.

Duc. Yes, if we knew where to find it: however, read.

[Clerk reads.] To *Walter Walton,* [266] Draper, six thousand nine hundred twenty nine Pounds six Shillings and five Pence, for Blacks for his Highness's Funeral. [p. 378]

Lam. For the Devil's; put it down for *Oliver Cromwel's* Funeral: We'll have no Record rise up in Judgment for such a Villain.

Lo. How live Asses kick the dead Lion! *[Aside.]*

Duc. Hark ye, my Lords, we sit here to reward Services done to the Commonwealth; let us consider whether this be a Service to the Commonwealth or not?

Lam. However, we will give him Paper for't.

Hews. Ay, let him get his Money when he can.

Lam. Paper's not so dear, and the Clerk's Pains will be rewarded.

War. Right, my gued Lord, 'sbred, that *Cromwel* was th' faudest limmer Loon that ever cam into lour [267] Country, the faud Diel has tane him by th' Luggs for robbing our Houses and Land.

Fleet. No swearing, my Lord.

War. Weel, weel, my Loord, I's larne [268] to profess and lee as weel as best on ya.

Hews. That may bring you profit, my Lord—but, Clerk, proceed.

[Clerk reads.] To *Walter Frost,* [p. 378] Treasurer of the Contingencies, twenty thousand Pounds. To *Thurloe,* Secretary to his Highness—

Duc. To old *Noll.*

[Clerk reads.]—Old Noll, ten thousand Pounds, for unknown Service done the Commonwealth—To Mr. *Hutchinson,* [p. 378] Treasurer of the Navy, two hundred thousand Pounds—

War. Two hundred thousand Pound; Owns, what a Sum's there?—Marry it came from the Mouth of a Cannon sure.

[Clerk reads.] A Present to the Right Honorable and truly Virtuous Lady, the Lady *Lambert,* for Service done to the late Protector—

Hews. Again—say *Cromwel.*

Clerk.—Cromwel—six thousand Pound in *Jacobus's.* [p. 379]

War. 'Sbread, sike a Sum wou'd make me honor the Face of aud *Jemmy.*

Clerk. To Mr. *Ice* [p. 379] six thousand Pound; to Mr. *Loether*, [p. 379] late Secretary to his High—

Whit. To *Oliver Cromwel* say, can you not obey Orders?

Clerk.—Secretary to *Oliver Cromwel*—two thousand nine hundred ninety nine Pounds for Intelligence and Information, and piously betraying the King's Liege People.

War. Haud, haud, Sirs, Mary en ya gift se fast [269] ya'll gif aud away from poor *Archibald Johnson.*

Whit. Speak for yourself, my Lord; or rather, my Lord, do you speak for him. [*To Lambert*]

Lam. Do you move it for him, and I'll do as much for you anon. [*Aside to* Whitlock.]

Whit. My Lord, since we are upon Gratifications,—let us consider the known Merit of the Lord *Wariston*, a Person of industrious Mischiefs to the malignant Party, and great Integrity to us, and the Commonwealth.

War. Gued faith, an I's ha been a trusty Trojon, Sir, what say you, may very gued and gracious Loords?—

Duc. I scorn to let a Dog go unrewarded; and you, Sir, fawn so prettily, 'tis pity you shou'd miss Preferment.

Hews. And so 'tis; come, come, my Lords, consider he was ever our Friend, and 'tis but reasonable we shou'd stitch up one another's broken Fortunes.

Duc. Nay, Sir, I'm not against it.

All. 'Tis Reason, 'tis Reason.

Free. Damn 'em, how they lavish out the Nation!

War. Scribe, pretha read my Paper.

Hews. Have you a Pertition there?

Cob. A Petition, my Lord.

Hews. Pshaw, you Scholards are so troublesome.

Lam. Read the Substance of it. [*To the Clerk.*]

Clerk. That your Honors wou'd be pleas'd, in consideration of his Service, to grant to your Petitioner, a considerable Sum of Money for his present Supply.

Fleet. Verily, order him two thousand Pound—

War. Two thousand poond? Bread a gued, and I's gif my Voice for *Fleetwood.* [*Aside.*]

Lam. Two thousand; nay, my Lords, let it be three.

War. Wons, I lee'd, I lee'd; I's keep my Voice for *Lambert*—Guds Benizon light on yar Sol, my gued Lord *Lambert.*

Hews. Three thousand Pound! why such a Sum wou'd buy half *Scotland.*

War. Wons, my Lord, ya look but blindly on't then: time was, a Mite on't had bought aud shoos in yar [270] Stall, Brother, tho noo ya so abound in *Irish* and Bishops Lands.

Duc. You have nick'd him there, my Lord.

All. He, he, he.

War. Scribe—gang a tiny bit farther.

Clerk.—And that your Honors would be pleas'd to confer an Annual Pension on him—

Lam. Reason, I think; what say you, my Lords, of five hundred Pound a Year?

All. Agreed, agreed.

War. The Diel swallow me, my Lord, ya won my Heart.

Duc. 'Tis very well—but out of what shall this be rais'd?

Lam. We'll look what Malignants' Estates [271] are forfeit, undispos'd of—let me see—who has young *Freeman's* Estate?

Des. My Lord, that fell to me.

Lam. What all the fifteen hundred Pound a Year?

Des. A Dad, and all little enough.

Free. The Devil do him good with it.

Des. Had not the Lard put it into your Hearts to have given me two thousand *per Annum* out of Bishops Lands, and three thousand *per Annum* out of the Marquess's Estate; how shou'd I have liv'd and serv'd the Commonwealth as I have done?

Free. A plague confound his Honor, he makes a hard shift to live on Eight thousand Pound a Year, who was born and bred a Hedger.

Lo. Patience, Friend.

Lam. I have been thinking—but I'll find out a way.

Lo. Or betray some honest Gentleman, on purpose to gratify the Loone.

Lam. And, Gentlemen, I am bound in Honor and Conscience to speak in behalf of my Lord *Whitlock*; I think fit, if you agree with me, he shou'd be made Constable of *Windsor* Castle, Warden of the Forest, with the Rents, Perquisities, and Profits thereto belonging; nor can your Lordships confer a Place of greater Trust and Honor in more safe Hands.

Duc. I find he wou'd oblige all to his side. [*Aside.*]

Has he not part of the Duke of *Buckingham's* Estate [p. 381] already, with *Chelsey* House, and several other Gifts?

Lam. He has dearly deserv'd 'em; he has serv'd our Interest well and faithfully.

Duc. And he has been well paid for't.

Whit. And so were you, Sir, with several Lordships, and Bishops Lands, you were not born to, I conceive.

Duc. I have not got it, Sir, by knavish Quirks in Law; a Sword that deals out Kingdoms to the brave, has cut out some small parcels of Earth for me. And what of this? [*Stands up in a heat.*]

Whit. I think, Sir, he that talks well, and to th' purpose, may be as useful to the Commonwealth as he that fights well. Why do we keep so many else in Pension that ne'er drew Sword, but to talk, and rail at the malignant Party; to libel and defame 'em handsomely, with pious useful Lies,

Which pass for Gospel with the common Rabble,
And edify more than *Hugh Peter's* [p. 381] Sermons;
And make Fools bring more Grist to the public Mill.
Then, Sir, to wrest the Law to our convenience
Is no small, inconsiderate Work.

Free. And which you may be hang'd for very shortly—[*Aside.*]

Lam. 'Tis granted, my Lord, your Merit's infinite—We made him Keeper of the Great Seal, 'tis true, 'tis Honor, but no Salary.

Duc. Ten thousand Pound a Year in Bribes will do as well.

Lam. Bribes are not so frequent now as in Old *Noll's* Days.

Hews. Well, my Lord, let us be brief and tedious, as the saying is, and humor one another: I'm for *Whitlock's* Advance.

Lam. I move for a Salary, Gentlemen, *Scobel* [p. 382] and other petty Clerks have had a thousand a Year; my Lord sure merits more.

Hews. Why—let him have two thousand then.

Fleet. I profess ingeniously, with all my Heart.

Whit. I humbly thank your Lordships—but, if I may be so bold to ask, from whence shall I receive it?

Lam. Out of the Customs.

Cob. Brotherly Love ought to go along with us—but, under favor, when this is gone, where shall we raise new Supplies?

Lam. We'll tax the Nation high, the City higher, They are our Friends, our most obsequious Slaves, Our Dogs to fetch and carry, our very Asses—

Lo. And our Oxes, with the help of their Wives. [*Aside.*]

Lam. Besides, the City's rich, and near her time, I hope, of being deliver'd.

War. Wons a gued, wad I'd the laying o' her, she shou'd be sweetly brought to Bed, by my Sol.

Des. The City cares for no *Scotch* Pipers, my Lord.

War. By my Sol, but she has danc'd after [272] the gued Pipe of Reformation, when the Covenant Jigg gang'd maryly round, Sirs.

Clerk. My Lords, here are some poor malignant Petitioners.

Lam. Oh, turn 'em out, here's nothing for 'em; these Fellows were petitioning my Lady today—I thought she had given you a satisfactory Answer,

Lo. She did indeed, my Lord: but 'tis a hard Case, to take away a Gentleman's Estate, without convicting him of any Crime.

Lam. Oh, Sir, we shall prove that hereafter.

Lo. But to make sure Work, you'll hang a Man first and examine his Offence afterwards; a Plague upon your Consciences: My Friend here had a little fairer Play; your Villains, your Witnesses in Pension swore him a Colonel for our glorious Master, of ever blessed Memory, at eight Years old; a Plague upon their Miracles.

Fleet. Ingeniously, Sirrah, you shall be pillory'd for defaming our reverend Witnesses: Guards, take 'em to your Custody both.

Free. Damn it, I shall miss my Assignation with Lady *Desbro*; a Pox of your unnecessary prating, what shall I do? [*Guards take 'em away.*]

Lam. And now, my Lords, we have finished the Business of the Day. My good Lord *Fleetwood*, I am entirely yours, and at our next sitting shall approve myself your Creature—

Whit. My good Lord, I am your submissive Vassal.

War. Wons, my Lord, I scorn any Man shou'd be mere yare Vassal than Archibald Johnson. [*To* Fleetwood.]

[*Exit All.*]

Scene II. *A Chamber in Lady* Desbro's *House.* [273]

[*Enter* L. Desbro, *and* Corporal *in haste.*]

L. Des. Seiz'd on, secur'd! Was there no time but this? What made him at the Committee, or when there why spoke he honest Truth? What shall I do, good Corporal? Advise; take Gold, and see if you can corrupt his Guards: but they are better paid for doing Mischief; yet try, their Consciences are large. [*Gives him Gold.*]

Cor. I'll venture my Life in so good a Cause, Madam. [*Exit.*]

[*Enter* Tom.] [274]

Tom. Madam, here's Mr. *Ananias Gogle*, the Lay-Elder of *Clement's* Parish.

L. Des. Damn the sham Saint; am I now in Condition to be plagu'd with his impertinent Nonsense?

Tom. Oh! Pray, Madam, hear him preach [275] a little; 'tis the purest Sport—

[*Enter* Ananias.]

Ana. Peace be in this Place.

L. Des. A blessed hearing; he preaches nothing in his Conventicles, but Blood and Slaughter. [*Aside.*] What wou'd you, Sir? I'm something busy now.

Ana. Ah, the Children of the Elect have no Business but the great Work of Reformation: Yea verily, I say, all other Business is profane, and diabolical, and devilish; Yea, I say, these Dressings, Curls, and Shining Habiliments—which take so up your time, your precious time; I say, they are an Abomination, yea, an Abomination in the sight of the Righteous, and serve but as an *Ignis fatuus*, to lead vain Man astray—I say again— [*Looking now and then behind on the Page.*]

L. Des.—You are a very Coxcomb.

Ana. I say again, that even I, upright I, one of the new Saints, find a sort of a—a—I know not what—a kind of a Motion as it were—a stirring up—as a Man may say, to wickedness—Yea, verily it corrupteth the outward Man within me.

L. Des. Is this your Business, Sir, to rail against our Clothes, as if you intended to preach me into my Primitive Nakedness again?

Ana. Ah, the naked Truth is best; but, Madam, I have a little work of Grace to communicate unto you, please you to send your Page away—

L. Des. Withdraw—sure I can make my Party good with one wicked Elder:—Now, Sir, your Bus'ness. [*Exit* Tom.]—Be brief.

Ana. As brief as you please—but—who in the sight of so much Beauty [276]—can think of any Bus'ness but the Bus'ness—Ah! hide those tempting Breasts,—Alack, how smooth and warm they are—[*Feeling 'em, and sneering.*]

L. Des. How now, have you forgot your Function?

Ana. Nay, but I am mortal Man also, and may fall seven times a day—Yea verily, I may fall seven times a day—Your Ladyship's Husband is old,—and where there is a good excuse for falling,—ah, there the fall—ing—is excusable.—And might I but fall with your Ladyship,—might I, I say.—

L. Des. How, this from you, the Head o' th' Church Militant, the very Pope of Presbytery?

Ana. Verily, the Sin lieth in the Scandal; therefore most of the discreet pious Ladies of the Age chose us, upright Men, who make a Conscience of a Secret, the Laity being more regardless of their Fame.—In sober sadness, the Place—inviteth, the Creature tempting, and the Spirit very violent within me. [*Takes and ruffles her.*]

L. Des. Who waits there?—I'm glad you have prov'd yourself what I ever thought of all your pack of Knaves.

Ana. Ah, Madam! Do not ruin my Reputation; there are Ladies of high Degree in the Commonwealth, to whom we find ourselves most comforting; why might not you be one?—for, alas, we are accounted as able Men in Ladies Chambers, as in our Pulpits: we serve both Functions—

[Enter Servants.]

Hah! her Servants—*[Stands at a distance.]*

L. Des. Shou'd I tell this, I shou'd not find belief. *[Aside.]*

Ana. Madam, I have another Errand to your Ladyship.—It is the Duty of my Occupation to catechize the Heads of every Family within my Diocese; and you must answer some few Questions I shall ask.—In the first place, Madam,—Who made ye?

L. Des. So, from Whoring, to a zealous Catechism—who made me? what Insolence is this, to ask me Questions which every Child that lisps out Words can answer!

Ana. 'Tis our Method, Madam.

L. Des. Your Impudence, Sirrah,—let me examine your Faith, who are so saucy to take an account of mine—Who made you? But lest you shou'd not know, I will inform you: First, Heav'n made you a deform'd, ill-favor'd Creature; then the Rascal your Father made you a Taylor; next, your Wife made you a Cuckold; and lastly the Devil has made you a Doctor; and so get you gone for a Fool and a Knave all over.

Ana. A Man of my Coat affronted thus!

L. Des. It shall be worse, Sirrah, my Husband shall know how kind you wou'd have been to him, because your Disciple and Benefactor, to have begot him a Babe of Grace for a Son and Heir.

Ana. Mistake not my pious meaning, most gracious Lady.

L. Des. I'll set you out in your Colours: Your impudent and bloody Principles, your Cheats, your Rogueries on honest Men, thro their kind, deluded Wives, whom you cant and goggle into a Belief, 'tis a great work of Grace to steal, and beggar their whole Families, to contribute to your Gormandizing, Lust and Laziness; Ye Locusts of the Land, preach Nonsense, Blasphemy, and Treason, till you sweat again, that the sanctify'd Sisters may rub you down, to comfort and console the Creature.

Ana. Ah! Am—

L. Des. Sirrah, be gone, and trouble me no more—be gone—yet stay—the Rogue may be of use to me—Amongst the heap of Vice, Hypocrisy, and Devils that possess all your Party, you may have some necessary Sin; I've known some honest, useful Villains amongst you, that will swear, profess, and lye devotedly for the Good Old Cause.

Ana. Yea, verily, I hope there are many such, and I shou'd rejoice, yea, exceedingly rejoice in any Gadly Performance to your Ladyship.

L. Des. This is a pious Work: You are a Knave of Credit, a very Saint with the rascally Rabble, with whom your seditious Cant more prevails, your precious Hum and Ha, and gifted Nonsense, than all the Rhetoric of the Learn'd or Honest.

Ana. Hah!

L. Des.—In fine, I have use of your Talent at present, there's one now in Confinement of the Royal Party—his Name's *Freeman.*

Ana. And your Ladyship wou'd have him dispatch'd; I conceive ye—but wou'd you have him dispatch'd privately, or by Form of Law? we've Tools for all uses, and 'tis a pious Work, and meritorious.

L. Des. Right, I wou'd indeed have him dispatch'd, and privately; but 'tis hither privately, hither to my Chamber, privately, for I have private Bus'ness with him. D'ye start?—this must be done—for you can pimp I'm sure upon occasion, you've Tools for all uses; come, resolve, or I'll discover your bloody Offer. Is your Stomach so queasy it cannot digest Pimping, that can swallow Whoring, false Oaths, Sequestration, Robbery, Rapes, and Murders daily?

Ana. Verily, you mistake my pious Meaning; it is the Malignant I stick at; the Person, not the Office: and in sadness, Madam, it goeth against my tender Conscience to do any good to one of the Wicked.

L. Des. It must stretch at this time; go haste to the Guard, and demand him in my Husband's Name; here's something worth your Pains—having releas'd him, bring him to me, you understand me—go bid him be diligent, and as you behave yourself, find my Favor; for know, Sir, I am as great a Hypocrite as you, and know the Cheats of your Religion too; and since we know one another, 'tis like we shall be true.

Ana. But shou'd the Man be missing, and I call'd to account?—

L. Des. He shall be return'd in an hour: go, get you gone, and bring him, or—no more—[*Exit* Ananias.] [277]

    For all degrees of Vices, you must grant,
    There is no Rogue like your *Geneva* Saint. [*Exeunt.*] [277]

ACT IV.

Scene I. *A Chamber in* L. Desbro's *House. Candles, and Lights.* [278]

[*Enter* L. Desbro *and* Freeman.]

L. Des. By what strange Miracle, my dearest *Freeman*, wert thou set at liberty?

Free. On the zealous Parole of *Rabbie Ananias*; that Rhetoric that can convert whole Congregations of well-meaning Blockheads to errant Knaves, has now mollify'd my Keeper; I'm to be render'd back within this Hour: let's not, my dear *Maria*, lose the precious minutes this Reverend Hypocrite has given us.

L. Des. Oh! you are very gay, have you forgot whose Prisoner you are, and that perhaps, e'er many Days are ended, they may hang you for High-Treason against the Commonwealth? they never want a good thorow-stitch'd Witness to do a Murder lawfully.

Free. No matter, then I shall die with Joy, *Maria*, when I consider, that you lov'd so well to give me the last Proof on't.

L. Des. Are you in earnest, *Freeman?* and wou'd you take what Honor will not suffer me to grant?

Free. With all my Heart, Honor's a poor Excuse. Your Heart and Vows (your better part) are mine; you've only lent your Body out to one whom you call Husband, and whom Heaven has mark'd for Cuckoldom. Nay, 'tis an Act of honest Loyalty, so to revenge our Cause; whilst you were only mine, my honest Love thought it a Sin to press these Favors from you; 'twas injuring myself as well as thee; but now we only give and take our Right.

L. Des. No more, my Husband's old—

Free. Right, my dear *Maria*, and therefore—

L. Des.—May possibly die—

Free. He will be hang'd first.

L. Des.—I hope so—either of which will do our Bus'ness—unreasonable *Freeman*, not to have Patience till my Husband be hang'd a little.

Free. But what if Destiny put the Change upon us, and I be hang'd instead of *Desbro?*

276

L. Des. Why then thou art not the first gallant Fellow that has died in the Good and Royal Cause; and a small taste of Happiness will but turn thee off the Ladder with the sadder Heart.

Free. Hast thou the Conscience, lovely as thou art,
To deal out all thy Beauty to a Traitor?
Is not this Treason of the highest Nature,
To rob the Royal Party of such Treasure,
And give it to our mortal Enemies?
For Shame, be wise, and just,
And do not live a Rebel to our Cause;
'Tis Sin enough to have Society with such a wicked Race.

L. Des. But I am married to him.

Free. So much the worse, to make a League and Covenant with such Villains, and keep the sinful Contract; a little harmless Lying and Dissimulation I'll allow thee, but to be right down honest, 'tis the Devil.

L. Des. This will not do, it never shall be said I've been so much debauch'd by Conventicling to turn a sainted Sinner; No, I'm true to my Allegiance still, true to my King and Honor. Suspect my Loyalty when I lose my Virtue: a little time, I'm sure, will give me honestly into thy Arms; if thou hast Bravery, show it in thy Love.

Free. You will o'ercome, and shame me every way;—but when will this Change come? and till it do, what Pawn will you give me, I shall be happy then?

L. Des. My Honor, and that Happiness you long for, and take but two Months time for their Redemption.

Free. How greedily I'll seize the Forfeiture!

L. Des. But what am I like to get if this Change do come?

Free. A Slave, and whatever you please to make of him.

L. Des. Who knows, in such an universal Change, how you may alter too?

Free. I'll give ye Bond and Vows, unkind *Maria,*—Here take my Hand—Be it known unto all Men, by these Presents, that I, *John Freeman* of *London*, Gent, acknowledge myself in Debt to *Maria Desbro*, the Sum of one Heart, with an incurable Wound; one Soul, destin'd hers from its first Being; and one Body, whole, sound, and in perfect Health; which I here promise to pay to the said *Maria*, upon Demand, if the aforesaid *John Freeman* be not hang'd before such Demand made. Whereto I set my Hand—and seal it with my Lips. [*In a Tone.*]

L. Des. And I, in consideration of such Debt, do freely give unto the above said *John Freeman*, the Heart and Body of the above said *Maria Desbro*, with all Appurtenances thereto belonging, whenever it shall please Heaven to bring my Husband fairly to the Gallows. [*In a Tone.*]

Free. Amen—kiss the Book—[*Kisses her.*]

[Ananias *hums without.*]

L. Des. Hah! that's *Ananias*; sure some Danger's near, the necessary Rascal gives us notice of. [279]

Free. 'Tis so, what wouldst thou have me do?

L. Des. Thou art undone if seen—here, step within this Curtain. [He goes.]

[*Enter Ananias, humming, and spreading his Cloak wide;* Desbro *behind him, puffing in a Chafe.*]

Des. Ads nigs, what a Change is here like to be?—puff, puff—we have manag'd Matters sweetly—to let the *Scotch* General undermine us; puff, puff.

L. Des. What's the Matter?

Des. Nothing, Cockey, nothing, but that we are like to return to our first nothing.

Ana. Yea, verily, when our time's come; but ah, the great Work of Reformation is not yet fully accomplish'd, which must be wrought by the Saints, and we cannot spare one of them until the Work be finish'd.

Des. Yea, yea, it is finish'd I doubt, puff, puff: fie, fie, what a Change is here!

Ana. Patience, ah, 'tis a precious Virtue!—

Des. Patience, Sir! what, when I shall lose so many fine Estates which did appertain to the Wicked; and which, I trusted, had been establish'd ours, and tell'st thou me of Patience? puff, puff. [*Walking fast.*]

Ana. How! lose 'em, Sir? handle the matter with Patience; I hope the Committee of Safety, or the Rump, will not do an illegal thing to one of the Brethren.

Des. No, no, I have been a trusty Knave to them, and so I have found them all to me: but *Monk! Monk!* O that ever we should be such blind Fools to trust an honest General!

Ana. Patience, Sir! what of him?

Des. I just now receiv'd private Intelligence, he's coming out of *Scotland* with his Forces—puff, puff.

Ana. Why, let him come a Gad's Name, [280] we have those will give him a civil Salute, if he mean not honorably to the Commonwealth. Patience, Sir.

Des. But if he proves the stronger, and shou'd chance to be so great a Traitor to us, to bring in the Man—the King.

L. Des. How, the King, Husband! the great Heroic!

Free. Death, this Woman is a Sybil: ah, noble *Monk!*

Ana. Hum—the King!—

Des. Ah, and with the King, the Bishops; and then, where's all our Church and Bishops Lands! oh, undone—puff, puff.

Ana. How, bring in the King and Bishops! my righteous Spirit is raised too—I say, I will excommunicate him for one of the Wicked, yea, for a profane Heroic, a Malignant, a Tory,—a—I say, we will surround him, and confound him with a mighty Host; yea, and fight the Lard's Battle with him: yea, we will—

Des. Truckle to his Pow'r—puff, puff.

Ana. Nay, I say verily, nay; [281] for, in Sadness, I will die in my Calling.

Des. So I doubt shall I—which is Ploughing, Hedging, and Ditching.

Ana. Yea, we have the Sword of the Righteous in our Hand, and we will defend the mighty Revenues of the Church, which the Lard hath given [282] unto his People, and chosen ones—I say, we will defend—

Des. Ah, Patience, Sir, ah, 'tis a pious Virtue—

Ana. Ah, it is Zeal in one of us, the Out-goings of the Spirit.

[Enter *Tom.*] [283]

Tom. Sir, will you go down to Prayers? the Chaplain waits.

Des. No, no, Boy, I am too serious for that Exercise, I cannot now dissemble, Heav'n forgive me.

Ana. How, Sir, not dissemble—ah, then you have lost a great Virtue indeed, a very great Virtue; ah, let us not give away the Good Old Cause—but, as we have hitherto maintain'd [284] it by gadly Cozenage, and pious Frauds, let us persevere—ah, let us persevere to the end; let us not lose our Heritage for a Mess of Pottage, that is, let us not lose the Cause for Dissimulation and Hypocrisy, those two main Engines that have earned on the great Work.

Des. Verily, you have prevail'd, and I will go take counsel of my Pillow: Boy—call my Man to undress me—I'll to Bed, for I am sick at Heart. [*Exit* Tom.]

Free. Death, what shall I do now?

[Desbro *walks, she whispers* Ananias.]

L. Des. You must get my Man off, or we're undone.

Ana. Madam, be comforted, Heaven will bring all things about for our Advantage—[As *Desbro* turns.]

L. Des. But he's behind the Curtains, Man—

[Desbro *turns from 'em.*]

Ana. Ah, let Providence alone—[*Spreads his Cloak wide, and goes by degrees toward the Bed.*]—Your pious Lady, Sir, is doubtful, but I will give her ample Satisfaction.

Des. Ah, do, Mr. *Ananias*, do, for she's a good and virtuous Lady, *certo* she is.

[*Ananias* goes close to the Bed-post, and speaks over his Shoulder.]

Ana. Get ye behind my Cloak—

L. Des. Indeed, Sir, your Counsel and Assistance is very comfortable.

Ana. We should be Help-meets to one another, Madam.

Des. Alack, good Man!

[L. Desbro *goes to coax her Husband.*]

L. Des. Ay, my dear, I am so much oblig'd to him, that I know not, without thy Aid, how to make him amends.

Free. So, this is the first Cloak of Zeal I ever made use of.

[Ananias *going, spreading his Cloak, to the Door*; Freeman *behind goes out.*]

Des. Good Lady, give him his twenty pieces, adad, he worthily deserves 'em. [*Gives her Gold.*]

L. Des. Indeed, and so he does, Dear, if thou knew'st all.—What say you now, do I not improve in Hypocrisy? And shall I not in time make a precious Member of your Church? [*To* Ananias.]

Ana. Verily, your Ladyship is most ingenious and expert.—Sir, I most humbly take my leave. [*Exit* Ananias.]

[*Enter* Tom.]

Tom. My Lord, my Lord *Lambert* has sent in all haste for you, you must attend at his House immediately.

Des. So, he has heard the News—I must away—let my Coach be ready. [Exit *Desbro*]

L. Des. How unlucky was this that *Freeman* should be gone—Sirrah, run and see to o'ertake him, and bring him back. [*Exeunt.*]

Scene II. *A fine Chamber in* L. Lambert's *House.* [285]

[*Enter* Gilliflower *and* Loveless *by dark, richly dressed.*]

Lo. Where am I, *Gilliflower?*

Gill. In my Lady's Apartment, Sir, she'll be with you presently; you need not fear betraying, Sir, for I'll assure you I'm an Heroic in my Heart: my Husband was a Captain for his Majesty of ever-blessed Memory, and kill'd at Naseby, God be thanked, Sir.

Lo. What pity 'tis that thou shouldst serve this Party?

Gill. Bating her Principles, my Lady has good Nature enough to oblige a Servant; and truly, Sir, my Vails [p. 394] were good in old *Oliver's* Days; I got well by that Amour between him and my Lady; the man was lavish enough.

Lo. Yes, of the Nation's Treasure—but prithee tell me, is not thy Lady mad, raving on Crowns and Kingdoms?

Gill. It appears so to you, who are not us'd to the Vanity of the Party, but they are all so mad in their Degree, and in the Fit they talk of nothing else, Sir: we have tomorrow a Hearing as they call it.

Lo. What's that, a Conventicle?

Gill. No, no, Sir, Ladies of the last Edition, that present their Grievances to the Council of Ladies, of which my Lady's chief, which Grievances are laid open to the Committee of Safety, and so redress'd or slighted, as they are.

Lo. That must be worth one's Curiosity, could one but see't.

Gill. We admit no Man, Sir.

Lo. 'Sdeath, for so good a sight I will turn Woman, I'll act it to a hair.

Gill. That would be excellent.

Lo. Nay, I must do't; the Novelty is rare—but I'm impatient—prithee let thy Lady know I wait.

Gill. She's in Affairs of State, but will be here immediately; mean time, retire into her Cabinet, I'll send the Page with Lights, there you may repose till my Lady comes, on the Pallat. [She leads him out.]

Scene III. *A great Chamber of State, and Canopy in* Lambert's *House.* [286]

[*And at a Table, seated* Lambert, Fleetwood, Desbro, Hewson, Duckenfield, Wariston, Cobbet; *all half drunk, with Bottles and Glasses on the Table;* L. Lambert *and* L. Fleetwood.]

Lam. My Lord *Wariston*, you are not merry tonight.

280

War. Wons, Mon, this *Monk* sticks in my Gullet, the muckle Diel pull him out by th' Lugs; the faud Loone will en spoyle and our Sport, mon.

Lam. I thought I had enough satisfied all your Fears; the Army's mine, that is,—'tis yours, my Lords, and I'll imploy it too so well for the Good of the Commonwealth, you shall have Cause to commend both my Courage and Conduct; my Lord *Wariston,* will you accompany me?

War. Ah, my gued Lord, the Honor is too great. 'Tis not but I's dare fight, my Lord, but I love not the limmer Loone, he has a villanous honest Face an's ene; I's ken'd him ence, and lik't him not; but I's drink tol yar gued Fortune; [287] let it gang aboote, ene and ad, Sirs.

[All drink.]

Lam. We'll leave all Discourse of Bus'ness, and give ourselves to Mirth; I fancy good Success from this day's Omen.

[Enters Gilliflower *whispers* L. Lambert *she rises.]*

L. Lam. Waited so long!

Gill. And grew impatient, an't please your Highness; must I go tell him you cannot see him tonight.

L. Lam. Not for the World; my silly Politician will be
Busying himself in the dull Affairs of State;
—Dull in comparison of Love, I mean;
I never lov'd before; old *Oliver* I suffer'd for my Interest,
And 'tis some Greatness, to be Mistress to the best;
But this mighty Pleasure comes *a propos,*
To sweeten all the heavy Toils of Empire.

Gill. So it does, an't please your Highness.

L. Lam. Go, let him know I'm coming—Madam, I must beg your Pardon; you hear, my Lord tomorrow goes on his great Expedition; and, for anything we know, may fall a glorious Sacrifice to the Commonwealth; therefore 'tis meet I offer up some Prayers for his Safety, and all my leisure Hours 'twixt this and that, will be too few—Your humble Servant, Madam. [*Exit* L. Lambert *and* Gilliflower] [288]

L. Fleet. My Dear, I'll leave you too, my time of Devotion is come, and Heav'n will stay for no Body; where are my People? is my Coach ready, or my Chair?

Fleet. Go in your Chair, my Love, lest you catch cold.

L. Fleet. And light your Flambeaus, [289]—I love to have my Chair surrounded with Flambeaus.

[Enter Page.]

Page. Your Chair is ready, Madam.

[She goes out led by Fleetwood.]

Hews. What think ye now, my Lords, of settling the Nation a little? I find my Head swim with Politics, and what ye call ums.

War. Wons, and wad ya settle the Nation when we real [290] ourselves?

Hews. Who, pox, shall we stand making Children's Shoes all the Year? No, no, let's begin to settle the Nation, I say, and go thro-stitch with our Work.

Duc. Right, we have no Head to obey; so that if this *Scotch* General do come whilst we Dogs fight for the Bone, he runs away with it.

Hews. Shaw, we shall patch up matters with the *Scotch* General, I'll warrant you: However, here's to our next Head—One and all. [All drink.]

Fleet. Verily, Sirs, this Health-drinking savoureth of Monarchy, and is a Type of Malignancy.

War. Bread, my Lord, no preaching o'er yar Liquer, [291] wee's now for a Cup o' th' Creature.

Cob. In a gadly way you may; it is lawful.

Lam. Come, come, we're dull, give us some Music—come, my Lord, I'll give you a Song, I love Music as I do a Drum, there's Life and Soul in't, call my Music.

Fleet. Yea, I am for any Music, except an Organ.

War. Sbread, Sirs, and I's for a Horn-pipe, [292] I've a faud Theefe here shall dance ye Dance tol a Horn-pipe, with any States-man a ya aud.

All. He, he, he.

Duc. I know not what your faud Theefe can do; but I'll hold you a Wager, Colonel *Hewson*, and Colonel *Desbro* shall dance ye the Seint's Jigg with any Sinner of your Kirk, or field Conventicler.

War. Wons, and I's catch 'em at that Sport, I's dance tol 'em for a *Scotch* Poond; [293] but farst yar Song, [294] my Lord, I hope 'tis boody, or else 'tis not werth a Feart.

All. He, he, he.

SONG, sung by my Lord *Lambert.*

A Pox of the States-man that's witty,
That watches and plots all the sleepless Night,
For seditious Harangues to the Whigs *of the City,*
And piously turns a Traitor in spite.
Let him wrack, and torment his lean Carrion,
To bring his sham-Plots about,
Till Religion, King, Bishop, and Baron,
For the public Good, be quite routed out.
Whilst we that are no Politicians,
But Rogues that are resolute, bare-fac'd and great,
Boldly head the rude Rabble in open Sedition,
Bearing all down before us in Church and in State.
Your Impudence is the best State-trick,
And he that by Law means to rule,
Let his History with ours be related,
Tho we prove the Knaves, 'tis he is the Fool.

War. The Diel a me, wele sung, my Lord, and gen aud Trades fail, yas make a quaint Minstrel.

All. He, he, he.

War. Noo, Sirs, yar Dance? [*They fling Cushions at one another, and grin. Music plays.*]—Marry, Sirs, an this be yar dancing, tol dance and ne'er stir Stap, the Diel lead the Donce [295] for *Archibald.*

[*When they have flung Cushions thus a while to the Music time, they beat each other from the Table, one by one, and fall into a godly Dance; after a while,* Wariston *rises, and dances ridiculously a while amongst them; then to the Time of the Tune, they take out the rest, as at the Cushion-Dance,* [p. 398] *or in that nature.* Wariston *being the last taken in, leads the rest.*]

—Haud, Minstrels, haud; Bread a gued. I's fatch ad Ladies in—lead away, Minstrels, tol my Lady's Apartment.

[*Music playing before all.*]
[*Exeunt dancing.*]

Scene IV. *Flat.*

[*Enter* Page.]

Page. Cock, Here must I wait, to give my Lady notice when my Lord approaches;— The fine Gentleman that is alone with her, gave me these two fine Pieces of Gold, and bad me buy a Sword to fight for the King withal; and I'm resolv'd to lay it all out in a Sword, not a penny in Nickers, [p. 398] and fight for the Heroicks as long as I have a Limb, if they be all such fine Men as this within. But hark, sure I hear some coming.— [*Exit.*]

[*Flat Scene draws off, discovers* L. Lambert *on a Couch, with* Loveless, *tying a rich Diamond-Bracelet about his Arm: a Table behind with Lights, on which a Velvet Cushion, with a Crown and Scepter cover'd.*]

Lo. This Present's too magnificent: such Bracelets young Monarchs shou'd put on.

L. Lam. Persons like me, when they make Presents, Sir, must do it for their Glory, not considering the Merit of the Wearer: yet this, my charming *Loveless,* comes short of what I ought to pay thy Worth; comes short too of my Love.

Lo. You bless me, Madam—

L. Lam. This the great Monarch of the World once ty'd about my Arm, and bad me wear it, till some greater Man shou'd chance to win my Heart;

Thou art that Man whom Love has rais'd above him;
Whom every Grace and every Charm thou hast
Conspire to make thee mightier to my Soul;
And *Oliver,* illustrious *Oliver,*
Was yet far short of thee.

Lo. He was the Monarch then whose Spoils I triumph in.

L. Lam. They were design'd too for Trophies to the young and gay.
Ah, *Loveless!* that I cou'd reward thy Youth
With something that might make thee more than Man,
As well as to give [296] the best of Women to thee—

[*Rises, takes him by the Hand, leads him to the Table. He starts.*]

—Behold this gay, this wondrous glorious thing.
    Lo. Hah—a Crown—and Scepter!
Have I been all this while
So near the sacred Relicks of my King;
And found no awful Motion in my Blood,
Nothing that mov'd sacred Devotion in me? [*Kneels.*] [297]
—Hail sacred Emblem of great Majesty,
Thou that hast circled more Divinity
Than the great Zodiack that surrounds the World.
I ne'er was blest with sight of thee till now,
But in much reverenc'd Pictures—[*Rises and bows.*]
    L. Lam. Is't not a lovely thing?
    Lo. There's such Divinity i' th' very Form on't,
Had I been conscious I'd been near the Temple,
Where this bright Relic of the glorious Martyr
Had been enshrin'd, 't had spoil'd my soft Devotion.
—'Tis Sacrilege to dally where it is;
A rude, a saucy Treason to approach it
With an unbended Knee: for Heav'ns sake, Madam,
Let us not be profane in our Delights,
Either withdraw, or hide that glorious Object.
    L. Lam. Thou art a Fool, the very sight of this—
Raises my Pleasure higher:
Methinks I give a Queen into thy Arms,
And where I love I cannot give enough; [*Softly.*]
—Wou'd I cou'd set it on thy Head for ever,
'Twou'd not become my simple Lord
The thousandth part so well. [*Goes to put it on his Head, he puts it back.*] [298]
    Lo. Forbear, and do not play with holy things;
Let us retire, and love as Mortals shou'd,
Not imitate the Gods, and spoil our Joys.
    L. Lam. Lovely, and unambitious!
What hopes have I of all your promis'd Constancy,
Whilst this which possibly e'er long may adorn my Brow,
And ought to raise me higher in your Love,
Ought to transform you even to Adoration,
Shall poorly make you vanish from its Lustre?
Methinks the very Fancy of a Queen
Is worth a thousand Mistresses of less illustrious Rank.
    Lo. What, every pageant Queen? you might from thence infer
I'd fall in love with every little Actress, because
She acts the Queen for half an hour,
But then the gaudy Robe is laid aside.
    L. Lam. I'll pardon the Comparison in you.
    Lo. I do not doubt your Power of being a Queen,

But trust, it will not last.
How truly brave would your great Husband be,
If, whilst he may, he paid this mighty Debt
To the right Owner!
If, whilst he has the Army in his Power,
He made a true and lawful use of it,
To settle our great Master in his Throne;
And by an Act so glorious raise his Name
Even above the Title of a King.

L. Lam. You love me not, that would persuade me from My Glory.

[*Enter* Gilliflower.]

Gill. Oh, Madam, the Lords are all got merry, as they call it, and are all dancing hither.

L. Lam. What, at their *Oliverian* Frolics?—Dear *Loveless*, withdraw, I wou'd not give the fond believing Fool a Jealousy of me.

Gill. Withdraw, Madam? 'tis impossible, he must run just into their Mouths.

L. Lam. I'm ill at these Intrigues, being us'd to Lovers that still came with such Authority, that modestly my Husband wou'd withdraw [299]—but Loveless is in danger, therefore take care he be not seen.

Gill. Heav'ns! they are coming, there's no Retreat—

L. Lam. Lie down on the Couch—and cover him you with the Foot-Carpet—So, give me my Prayer-Book.

[*He lies down along on the Couch,* [300] *they cover him with the Carpet:* L. Lambert *takes her Book, sits down on his Feet, and leans on the Back of the Couch reading;* Gilliflower *stands at t'other end, they enter dancing as before.*]

—What Insolence is this? do you not hear me, you—Sots—whom Gaiety and Dancing do so ill become.

War. [*Singing.*] Welcome, *Joan Sanderson,* [p. 402] welcome, welcome. [*Goes to take her out, she strikes him.*] Wons, Madam, that's no part o' th' Dance.

L. Lam. No, but 'tis part of a reward for your Insolence, Which possibly your Head shall answer for—

Lam. Pardon him, my Dear, he meant no Disrespect to thee.

L. Lam. How dare you interrupt my Devotion, Sirrah? Be gone with all your filthy ill-bred Crew.

[Lambert *sits down on* Lovis]

Lam. My only Dear, be patient; hah!—Something moves under me; Treason, Treason! [*He rises.*]

[Lovis *rolls off, and turns* Lambert *over, the rest of the Men run out crying Treason, Treason, overthrowing the Lights, putting 'em out.*]

L. Lam. Treason, Treason! my Lord, my Lord!

Lam. Lights there, a Plot, a Popish Plot, Lights!
L. Lam. The Crown, the Crown, guard the Crown!

[*She groping about, finds* Lovis *by his Clothes, knows him.*]

—Here, take this Key, the next room is my Bed-chamber, Secure yourself a moment.—
[*Exit* Loveless.] Lights there, the Crown—who art thou? [*Takes hold of* Lambert.]

Lam. 'Tis I.
L. Lam. Ah, my Lord, what's the matter?—
Lam. Nay, my Lady, I ask you what's the matter?

[*Enter* Page *with Lights.*]

By Heaven, all is not well; hark ye, my fine she Politician, who was it you had hid
beneath this Carpet?
L. Lam. Heav'ns! dost hear him, *Gilliflower?* Sure the Fellow's mad.
Gill. Alack, my Lord, are you out of your honorable Wits? Heav'n knows, my Lady
was at her Devotion.
Lam. Baud, come, confess thy self to be one. At her Devotion! yes, with a He Saint.
Gill. Ah! Gad forbid the Saints should be so wicked.
L. Lam. Hark ye, thou little sniveling Hypocrite, who hast no Virtue but a little
Conduct in Martial Discipline; who hast by Perjuries, Cheats, and pious Villainies,
wound thy self up into the Rabble's Favor, where thou mayst stand till some more great in
Roguery remove thee from that height, or to the Gallows, if the King return: hast thou the
Impudence to charge my Virtue?
Lam. I know not, Madam, whether that Virtue you boast were lost, or only stak't, and
ready for the Gamester; but I am sure a Man was hid under this Carpet.
L. Lam. Oh Heav'ns, a Man!
Gill. Lord, a Man! Are you sure 'twas a Man, my Lord?—Some villainous
Malignant, I'll warrant.
Lam. It may be so.
Gill. Alack, the Wickedness of these Heroicks to hide under Carpets; why they'll
have the impudence to hide under our Petticoats shortly, if your Highness take 'em not
down. [*To* L. Lambert.]
Lam. I do believe so; Death—a Cuckold? shall that black Cloud shade all my rising
Fame?
L. Lam. Cuckold! Why, is that Name so great a Stranger to ye,
Or has your rising Fame made ye forget
How long that Cloud has hung upon your Brow?
—'Twas once the height of your Ambition, Sir;
When you were a poor-sneaking Slave to *Cromwell,*
Then you cou'd cringe, and sneer, and hold the Door,
And give him every Opportunity,
Had not my Piety defeated your Endeavours.
Lam. That was for Glory,
Who wou'd not be a Cuckold to be great?
—If *Cromwell* leap'd into my Saddle once,

I'll step into his Throne for't: but, to be pointed at
By Rascals that I—rule—'tis insupportable.

    L. Lam. How got this Fellow drunk? call up my Officers!
Who durst deliver him this quantity of Wine?
Send strait in my Name, to summon all the
Drunken Committee of Safety into my Presence.
By Heav'n, I'll show you, Sir—yes they shall
See what a fine King they're like to have
In Honest, Gadly, Sober, Wise *Jack Lambert.*
—Nay, I'll do't; d'ye think to take away my Honor thus?
I, who by my sole Politicks and Management
Have set you up, Villain of Villains, Sirrah.
—Away—summon 'em all. [*To* Gilliflower.]

    Lam. Stay—be not so rash; who was beneath the Carpet?

    L. Lam. I will not answer thee.

    Lam. Nor any living thing?

    L. Lam. No Creature in the Room, thou silly Ideot, but *Gilliflower* and I—at our Devotion, praying to Heav'n for your Success tomorrow—and am I thus rewarded?

[Weeps, Gilliflower weeps too.]

    Lam. My Soul, I cannot bear the Sight of Tears From these dear Charming Eyes.

    L. Lam. No matter, Sir, the Committee shall right me.

    Lam. Upon my Knees I ask thy Pardon, Dear; by all that's good, I wou'd have sworn I'd felt something stir beneath me as I sat, which threw me over.

    L. Lam. Only your Brains turn'd round with too much drinking and dancing, Exercises you are not us'd to—go sleep, and settle 'em, for I'll not deign to Bed with you tonight—retire, as e'er you hope to have my Aid in your Advancement to the Crown.

    Lam. I'm gone—and once more pardon my Mistake. [Bows, and goes out. Exit *Gilliflower*]

    L. Lam.—So, this fighting Fool, so worshipp'd by the Rabble,
How meanly can a Woman make him sneak?—
The happy Night's our own—[*To* Loveless.]

[Enter Gilliflower and Loveless.]

    Lo. Excellent Creature, how I do adore thee!

    L. Lam. But you, perhaps, are satisfied already—

    Lo. Never; shou'dst thou be kind to all Eternity. Thou hast one Virtue more, I pay thee Homage for; I heard from the Alcove how great a Mistress thou art in the dear Mystery of Jilting.

    L. Lam. That's the first Lesson Women learn in Conventicles, Religion teaches those Maxims to our Sex: by this
        Kings are deposed, and Commonwealths are rul'd;
        By Jilting all the Universe is fool'd. [*Exeunt.*]

ACT V.

Scene I. *A Street.* [301]

[*Enter* Corporal, *half dressed; with Soldiers, Joyner, and Felt-maker.*]

Cor. Ha, Rogues, the City-Boys are up in Arms; brave Boys, all for the King now!

Felt. Have a care what you say, Sir; but as to the City's being in Mutiny, that makes well for us: we shall fall to our old Trade of plundering; something will fall to the Righteous, and there is Plunder enough.

Cor. You plunder, Sirrah! knock him down, and carry him into the Guard-room, and secure him.

[*Two Soldiers seize him.*]

1 Sold. They say the Committee of Safety sate all Night at General *Lambert's*, about some great Affair—some rare Change, Rogues.

2 Sold. Yes, and to put off Sorrow, they say, were all right reverendly drunk too.

Cor. I suppose there is some heavenly matter in hand; there was Treason cried out at the General's last night, and the Committee of no Safety all ran away.

1 Sold. Or rather reel'd away.

Cor. The Ladies squeak'd, the Lords fled, and all the House was up in Arms.

Felt. Yea, and with Reason they say; for the Pope in disguise was found under the Lady's Bed, and two huge Jesuits as big as the tall *Irish-man*, [p. 406] with Blunderbusses; having, as 'tis said, a Design to steal the Crown, now in Custody of the General—

2 Sold. Good lack, is't possible?

Joy. Nay, Sir, 'tis true, and is't not time we look'd about us?

Cor. A Pox upon ye all for lying Knaves—secure 'em both on the Guard till farther Order—and let us into th' City, Boys: hay for *Lombard-Street*.

2 Sold. Ay, hay for *Lombard-Street*; there's a Shop I have mark'd out for my own already.

1 Sold. There's a handsome Citizen's Wife, that I have an Eye upon, her Husband's a rich Banker, I'll take t'one with t'other.

Joy. You are mistaken, Sir, that Plunder is reserv'd for us, if they begin to mutiny; that wicked City that is so weary of a Commonwealth.

2 Sold. Yes, they're afraid of the Monster they themselves have made.

[*Enter* Lovis *and* Freeman *in disguise.*]

Cor. Hah, my noble Colonel! what, in disguise!

Free. We have made our Escapes—and hope to see better times shortly, the noble *Scotch* General is come, Boys.

[*Enter* Captain *of the Prentices, and a great Gang with him, arm'd with Swords, Staffs, &c.*]

Capt. Come, my Lads, since you have made me Captain, I'll lead you bravely on; I'll die in the Cause, or bring you off with Victory.

1 Pren. Here's a Club shall do some Execution: I'll beat out *Hewson's* t'other Eye; I scorn to take him on the blind side.

Capt. In the first Place, we must all sign a Petition to my Lord Mayor.—

2 Pren. Petitions! we'll have no Petition, Captain; we are for Club-Law, Captain.

Capt. Obey, or I leave you.

All. Obey, Obey.

Capt. Look ye, we'll petition for an honest Free Parliament I say.

1 Pren. No Parliament, no Parliament, we have had too much of that Mischief already, Captain.

All. No Parliament, no Parliament.

Capt. Farewell, Gentlemen, I thought I might have been heard.

Free. Death, Sirs, you shall hear the Captain out.

All. We obey, we obey.

Capt. I say an honest Free Parliament, not one pick'd and chosen by Faction; but such an one as shall do our Bus'ness, Lads, and bring in the *Great Heroic*.

All. Ay, ay, the Great Heroic, the Great Heroic.

Lo. A fine Youth, and shou'd be encourag'd.

Capt. Good—in the next Place, the noble *Scotch* General is come, and we'll side with him.

Free. Ay, ay, all side with him.

1 Pren. Your Reason, Captain, for we have acted too much without Reason already.

2 Pren. Are we sure of him, Captain?

Capt. Oh, he'll doubtless declare for the King, Boys.

All. Hay, *Viva le Roy, viva le Monk!* [302]

Capt. Next, I hear there's a Proclamation coming out to dissolve the Committee of no Safety.

All. Good, good.

Capt. And I hope you are all brave enough to stand to your Loyal Principles with your Lives and Fortunes.

All. We'll die for the Royal Interest.

Capt. In the next Place, there's another Proclamation come out.

2 Pren. This Captain is a Man of rare Intelligence; but for what, Captain?

Capt. Why—to—hang us all, if we do not immediately depart to our respective Vocations: How like you that, my Lads?

2 Pren. Hum—hang'd! I'll e'en home again.

1 Pren. And I too, I do not like this hanging.

2 Pren. A Man looks but scurvily with his Neck awry.

3 Pren. Ay, ay, we'll home.

Capt. Why, now you show what precious Men you are—the King wou'd be finely hop'd up with such Rascals, that for fear of a little hanging would desert his Cause; a Pox upon you all, I here discharge ye—

—Take back your Coward Hands and give me Hearts. [*Flings 'em a Scroll.*]

I scorn to fight with such mean-spirited Rogues;

I did but try your boasted Courages.

Lo. Brave Boy.

Lo. and Free. We'll die with thee, Captain—

All. Oh, noble Captain, we recant—

1 Pren. We recant, dear Captain, we'll die, one and all.

All. One and all, one and all.

Capt. Why, so there's some trusting [303] to you now.

3 Pren. But is there such a Proclamation, Captain?

Capt. There is; but anon, when the Crop-ear'd Sheriff begins to read it, let every Man enlarge his Voice, and cry, no Proclamation, no Proclamation.

All. Agreed, agreed.

Lo. Brave noble Lads, hold still your Resolution, And when your leisure Hours will give ye leave, Drink the King's Health, here's Gold for you to do so.

Free. Take my Mite too, brave Lads. [*Gives 'em Gold.*]

All. Hay! *Viva* the brave [304] Heroics!

[*Enter* Ananias Gogle.]

Ana. Hum, what have we here, a Street-Conventicle—or a Mutiny? Yea, verily, it is a Mutiny—What meaneth this Appearance in hostile manner, in open Street, by Day-light?

Capt. Hah! one of the sanctify'd Lay Elders, one of the Fiends of the Nation, that go about like roaring Lions seeking whom they may devour.

Lo. Who, Mr. *Ananias* the Padder?

Ana. Bear witness, Gentlemen all, he calls me Highway-man; thou shalt be hang'd for Scandal on the Brethren.

Lo. I'll prove what I say, Sirrah; do you not rob on the High-way i' th' Pulpit? rob the Sisters, and preach it lawful for them to rob their Husbands; rob Men even of their Consciences and Honesty; nay rather than stand out, rob poor Wenches of their Bodkins and Thimbles?

Ana. I commit ye; here, Soldiers, I charge ye in the Name of—of—marry, I know not who, in my Name, and the good People of *England*, take 'em to safe Custody.

Capt. How, lay hold of honest Gentlemen! Noble Cavaliers, knock him down.

All. Knock him down, knock him down.

Free. Hold, worthy Youths; the Rascal has done me Service.

Ana. [*Pulling off his Hat to 'em all.*] Ye look like Citizens, that evil Spirit is entered in unto you, oh Men of London! that ye have changed your Note, like Birds of evil Omen; that you go astray after new Lights, or rather no Lights, and commit Whoredom with your Fathers Idols, even in the midst of the Holy City, which the Saints have prepared for the Elect, the Chosen ones.

Capt. Hark ye, Sirrah, leave preaching, and fall to declaring for us, or thou art mortal.

Ana. Nay, I say nay, I will die in my Calling—yea, I will fall a Sacrifice to the Good Old Cause; abomination ye with a mighty Hand, and will destroy, demolish and confound your Idols, those heathenish Malignants whom you follow, even with Thunder and Lightning, even as a Field of Corn blasted by a strong Blast.

Lo. Knock him down!

All. Down with Dagon, down with him!

[*Enter* Hewson *with Guards.*] [p. 410]

Hews. Ah, Rogues, have I caught ye napping?

[*They all surround him and his Red-Coats.*]

All. Whoop Cobler, Whoop Cobler!

[*The Boys,* Lovis *and* Freeman, Corporal *and* Soldiers *beat off* Hewson *and his Party.* Ananias *gets a Sword, and fights too.*] [305]

Scene II. *Changes to a Chamber in* L. Lambert's *House.* [306]

[*Enter* L. Lambert *and* Gilliflower.]

Gill. I've had no time to ask your Highness how you slept tonight; but that's a needless Question.
L. Lam. How mean you? do you suspect my Virtue? do you believe *Loveless* dares attempt anything against my Honor? No, *Gilliflower*, he acted all things so like a Gentleman, that every moment takes my Heart more absolutely.
Gill. My Lord departed highly satisfied.
L. Lam. She is not worthy of Intrigues of Love, that cannot manage a silly Husband as she pleases—but, *Gilliflower*, you forget that this is Council day.
Gill. No, but I do not, Madam, some important Suitors wait already.

[*Enter* L. Desbro *and* L. Fleetwood.]

L. Lam. Your Servant, Madam *Desbro*, thou'rt welcome—
Gilliflower, are all things ready in the Council-Chamber?
We that are great must sometimes stoop to Acts,
That have at least some show of Charity;
We must redress the Grievance of our People.
L. Fleet. She speaks as she were Queen, but I shall put a spoke in her rising Wheel of Fortune, or my Lord's Politicks fail him.

[*Scene draws off, Table with Papers: Chairs round it.*]

L. Lam. Where are the Ladies of the Council?—how remiss they are in their Attendance on us.
L. Fleet. Us! Heav'ns, I can scarce endure this Insolence!—We will take care to mind 'em of their Duty—
L. Lam. We, poor Creature! how simply Majesty becomes her?

[*They all sitting down, enter* L. Cromwel *angrily, and takes her Place,* L. Lambert *uppermost.*]

—Madam, as I take it, at our last sitting, our Pleasure was, that you shou'd sit no more.
Crom. Your Pleasure! Is that the General Voice? This is my Place in spite of thee, and all thy fawning Faction, and I shall keep it, [307] when thou perhaps, shalt be an humble Suppliant here at my Foot-stool.

L. Lam. I smile at thee.

Crom. Do, and cringe; 'tis thy business to make thee popular.
But 'tis not that—
Nor thy false Beauty that will serve thy Ends.

L. Lam. Rail on; declining Majesty may be excus'd,
Call in the Women that attend for redress of Grievances.

[*Exit* Page.]

[*Enter* Page *with Women, and* Loveless *dress'd as a Woman.*]

Gentlewomen, what's your Bus'ness with us?

Lo. Gentlewomen! some of us are Ladies.

L. Lam. Ladies in good time; by what Authority, and from whom do you derive your Title of Ladies?

L. Fleet. Have a care how you usurp what is not your own!

Lo. How the Devil rebukes Sin! [*Aside.*]

L. Des. From whom had you your Honors, Women?

Lo. From our Husbands.

Gill. Husbands, who are they, and of what standing?

2 Lady. Of no long standing, I confess.

Gill. That's a common Grievance indeed.

L. Des. And ought to be redress'd.

L. Lam. And that shall be taken into consideration; write it down, *Gilliflower*; who made your Husband a Knight, Woman?

Lo. Oliver the first, an't please ye.

L. Lam. Of horrid Memory; write that down—who yours?

2 Lady. Richard the fourth, an't like your Honor.

Gill. Of sottish Memory; shall I write that down too?

L. Des. Most remarkably.

Crom. Heav'ns! Can I hear this Profanation of our Royal Family? [*Aside.*]

L. Lam. I wonder with what impudence *Noll* and *Dick* cou'd Knightify your Husbands; for 'tis a Rule in Heraldry, that none can make a Knight but him that is one; 'tis *Sancha Pancha's* Case in *Don Quixot*.

Crom. How dare you question my Husband's Authority? [*Rises in Anger.*]
Who nobly won his Honor in the Field,
Not like thy sneaking Lord who gain'd his Title
From his Wife's gay Love-tricks—
Bartering her Honor for his Coronet.

L. Lam. Thou ly'st, [308] my Husband earn'd it with his Sword,
Braver and juster than thy bold Usurper,
Who waded to his Glory through a Sea
Of Royal Blood—

L. Des. Sure *Loveless* has done good on her, and converted her.

L. Fleet. Madam, I humbly beg you will be patient, you'll ruin all my Lord's Designs else—Women, proceed to your Grievances, both public and private.

Lo. I petition for a Pension; my Husband, deceas'd, was a constant active man, in all the late Rebellion, against the Man; he plunder'd my *Lord Capel,* [p. 412] he betray'd his dearest Friend *Brown Bushel*, [p. 412] who trusted his Life in his Hands, and several others; plundering their Wives and Children even to their Smocks.

L. Lam. Most considerable Service, and ought to be consider'd.

2 Lady. And most remarkably, at the Trial of the late Man, I spit in's Face, and betray'd the *Earl of Holland* [p. 413] to the Parliament.

Crom. In the King's Face, you mean—it show'd your Zeal for the Good Cause.

2 Lady. And 'twas my Husband that headed the Rabble, to pull down *Gog* and *Magog*, [309] the Bishops, broke the Idols in the Windows, and turn'd the Churches into Stables and Dens of Thieves; rob'd the Altar of the Cathedral of the twelve pieces of Plate call'd the twelve Apostles, turn'd eleven of 'em into Money, and kept *Judas* [p. 413] for his own use at home.

L. Fleet. On my Word, most wisely perform'd, note it down—

3 Lady. And my Husband made Libels on the Man from the first Troubles to this day, defam'd and profan'd the Woman and her Children, printed all the Man's Letters to the Woman with Burlesque Marginal Notes, pull'd down the sumptuous Shrines in Churches, and with the golden and Popish Spoils adorn'd his own Houses and Chimney-Pieces.

L. Lam. We shall consider these great Services.

Lo. To what a height is Impudence arriv'd? [*Aside.*]

L. Lam. Proceed to private Grievances.

Lo. An't please your Honors, my Husband prays too much; which both hinders his private bus'ness at home, and his public Services to the Commonwealth—

L. Lam. A double Grievance—set it down, Gilliflower.

Lo. And then he rails against the Whore of Babylon, and all my neighbors think he calls me Whore.

Crom. A most unpardonable fault.

L. Lam. We'll have that rectify'd, it will concern us.

Lo. Then he never kisses me, but he says a long Grace, which is more mortifying than inviting.

L. Des. That is the fault of all the new Saints, which is the reason their Wives take a pious care, as much as in them lies, to send 'em to Heaven, by making 'em Cuckolds.

L. Fleet. A very charitable Work, and ought to be encourag'd.

[Loveless *gives in a Petition to* Gilliflower.]

Gill. The humble Petition of the Lady *Make-shift.* [*Reads.*]—Heav'ns, Madam, here are many thousand Hands to't of the distressed Sex.

All. Read it.

Gill. [*Reads.*] Whereas there pass'd an Act, *June* 24th, [p. 414] against Fornication and Adultery, to the great detriment of most of the young Ladies, Gentlewomen, and Commonalty of *England*, and to the utter decay of many whole Families, especially when married to old Men; your Petitioners most humbly beg your Honors will take this great Grievance into mature Consideration, and the said Act may be repealed.—A Blessing on 'em, they shall have my Hand too.

L. Lam. We acknowledge, there are many Grievances in that Act; but there are many Conveniences too, for it ties up the villainous Tongues of Men from boasting our Favors.

Crom. But as it lays a Scandal on Society—'tis troublesome, Society being the very Life of a Republic—*Peters* the first, and *Martin* the second. [p. 414]

Lo. But in a Free-State, why shou'd we not be free?

L. Des. Why not? we stand for the Liberty and Property of our Sex, and will present it to the Committee of Safety.

Lo. Secondly, we desire the Heroicks, vulgarly call'd the Malignant, may not be look'd on as Monsters, for assuredly they are Men; and that it may not be charg'd to us as a Crime to keep 'em company, for they are honest Men.

2 Lady. And some of 'em Men that will stand to their Principles.

L. Lam. Is there no other honest Men that will do as well?

3 Lady. Good Men are scarce.

L. Lam. They're all for Heroicks, sure 'tis the mode to love 'em—I cannot blame 'em. [*Aside.*]

Lo. And that when we go to Morning and Evening Lectures, [310] to *Tantlings*, [p. 415] or elsewhere, and either before or after visit a private Friend, it may be actionable for the wicked to scandalize us, by terming of it, abusing the Creature, when 'tis harmless recreating the Creature.

All. Reason, Reason.

Lo. Nor that any Husband shou'd interrupt his Wife, when at her private Devotion.

[*Enter* Page.]

L. Lam. I have been too late sensible of that Grievance.

Gill. And, Madam, I wou'd humbly pray a Patent for Scolding, to ease my Spleen.

Page. An please your Highness, here's a Messenger arriv'd Post with Letters from my Lord the General.

[*Exit* Page.]

L. Lam. Greater Affairs—oblige us to break up the Council. [*Rises, the Women retire.*]

[*Enter* Page *with Messenger*, [311] *or Letters.*]

—What means this haste? [*Opens, and reads 'em.*]

Crom. Hah, bless my Eye-sight, she looks pale,—now red again; some turn to his Confusion, Heav'n, I beseech thee.

L. Lam. My Lord's undone! his Army has deserted him;
Left him defenceless to the Enemies Pow'r.
Ah, Coward Traitors! Where's that brutal Courage, [312]
That made you so successful in your Villainies?
Has Hell, that taught you Valour, now abandon'd ye?
—How in an instant are my Glories fall'n!

Crom. Ha, ha, ha—What, has your Highness any Cause of Grief?

Gill. Call up your Courage, Madam, do not let these things scoff you—you may be yet a Queen: Remember what *Lilly* [p. 416] told you, Madam.

L. Lam. Damn *Lilly*, who with lying Prophecies has rais'd me to the hopes of Majesty: a Legion of his Devils take him for't.

Crom. Oh, have a care of Cursing, Madam.

L. Lam. Screech-Owl, away, thy Voice is ominous.

Oh I cou'd rave! but that it is not great;
—And silent Sorrow—has most Majesty.

[*Enter* Wariston, *huffing.*]

War. Wons, Madam, undone, undone; our honorable Committee is gone to th' Diel, and the damn'd loosey Rump is aud in aud; the muckle Diel set it i'solt, and his Dam drink most for't.

Crom. The Committee dissolv'd! whose wise work was that? [313] it looks like *Fleetwood's* silly Politicks.

War. Marry, and yar Ladiship's i'th' right,'twas en the Work o'th' faud Loone, the Diel brest his Wem for't.

[*Enter* Hewson, Desbro, Whitlock, Duckenfield, *and* Cobbet.]

Hews. So, Brethren in Iniquity, we have spun a fine Thred, the Rump's all in all now, rules the Roast, and has sent for the General with Scissers and Rasor.

Whit. With a Sisseraro, [p. 416] you mean.

Hews. None of your Terms in Law, good Brother.

War. Right; but gen ya have any Querks in Law, Mr. Lyar, that will save our Crags, 'twill be warth a Fee.

Duc. We have plaid our Cards fair.

War. I's deny that; Wans, Sirs, [314] ya plaid 'em faul; a Fule had the shooftling of'em, and the Muckle Diel himself turn up Trump.

Whit. We are lost, Gentlemen, utterly lost; who the Devil wou'd have thought of a Dissolution?

Hews. Is there no Remedy?

Duc. Death, I'll to the *Scotch* General; turn but in time as many greater Rogues than I have done, and 'twill save my Stake yet—Farewel, Gentlemen.

Des. No Remedy?

War. Nene, Sirs, again the King's Evil; Bread, Sirs, ya's ene [315] gan tol yar Stall agen: I's en follow *Duckenfield*—Farewell, Mr. Leyer. [316]

L. Lam. See the Vicissitudes of human Glory.
These Rascals, that but yesterday petition'd me
With humble Adoration, now scarce pay
Common Civilities due to my Sex alone.

[*Enter* Fleetwood.]

Crom. How now, Fool, what is't that makes ye look [317] so pertly? Some mighty Business you have done, I'll warrant.

Fleet. Verily, Lady Mother, you are the strangest Body; a Man cannot please you— Have I not finely circumvented *Lambert?* made the Rump Head, who have committed him to the *Tower*; ne'er stir now that I have, and I'm the greatest Man in *England*, as I live I am, as a Man may say.

Crom. Yes, till a greater come. Ah, Fool of Fools, not to fore-see the danger of that nasty Rump.

L. Fleet. Good Madam, treat my Lord with more Respect.

Crom. Away, fond Fool, born with so little Sense, To dote on such a wretched Idiot; It was thy Fate in *Ireton's* days to love him, Or you were foully scandalized.

Fleet. You are not so well spoken of neither, ne'er stir now, and you go to that. I can be King tomorrow if I Willmore

Crom. Thou liest, thou wo't be hang'd first; mark that I tell thee so. I'll prove *Cassandra* to thee, and prophesy thy Doom; Heav'n pays the Traitor back with equal Measure. Remember how you serv'd my poor Son Richard.

[*Exit* Cromwel *and* Page.]

Fleet. She's mad—Come, my Dear, let's leave the House of this Villain, that meant to have cozen'd me illegally or three Kingdoms—but that I outwitted him at last.

[*Exit* Fleetwood, L. Fleetwood, *and* Page.] [318]
[*Enter* Page.]

L. Lam. Imprison'd too, i'th' Tower! what Fate is mine? [*Leans on* Desbro.]
Page. Madam, the fine Heroick's come to wait on you.
L. Lam. Hah! *Loveless!* let him not see the Ruin of my Greatness, which he foretold, and kindly begg'd I wou'd usurp no more. [*Weep.*] [319]

[*Enter* Loveless.]

Lo. This News has brought me back, I love this Woman,
Vain as she is, in spite of all her Fopperies of State—[*Bows to her, and looks sad.*]
L. Lam. Alas, I do not merit thy Respect,
I'm fall'n to Scorn, to Pity and Contempt. [*Weeping.*]
Ah, Loveless, fly the wretched—Thy
Virtue is too noble to be shin'd on
By anything but rising Suns alone:
I'm a declining Shade—
Lo. By Heaven, you were never great till now;
I never thought thee so much worth my Love,
My Knee, and Adoration, till this Minute. [*Kneels.*]
—I come to offer you my Life, and all
The little Fortune the rude Herd has left me.
L. Lam. Is there such God-like Virtue in your Sex?
Or, rather, in your Party.
Curse on the Lyes and Cheats of Conventicles,
That taught me first to think Heroicks Devils,
Blood-thirsty, leud, tyrannick, salvage Monsters.
—But I believe 'em Angels all, if all like *Loveless*.
What heavenly thing then must the Master be,
Whose Servants are divine?

[*Enter* Page *running.*]

Page. Oh, Madam! all the Heroic Boys are up in Arms, and swear they'll have your Highness, dead or alive,—they have besieg'd the House.

L. Lam. Heav'ns, the Rabble!—those faithless things that us'd to crowd my Coach's Wheels, and stop my Passage, with their officious Noise and Adoration.

[*Enter* Freeman.]

Free. Loveless, thy Aid; the City-Sparks are up;
Their zealous Loyalty admits no Bounds.
A glorious Change is coming, and I'll appear now barefac'd.

Lo. Madam, fear not the Rabble; retire. *Freeman* and I can still 'em. Leads her in, and bows low.

Free. My dear *Maria,* I shall claim ye shortly—

L. Des. Do your worst, I'm ready for the Challenge. [*Go in.*] [320]

[*Exit* Lovis *and* Freeman *another way.*]

Scene III. *The Street.* [321]

[*Enter* Captain *and the rest.*]

Capt. I say we'll have the She-Politician out, she did more mischief than her Husband, pitiful, dittiful *Lambert*; who is, thanks be prais'd, in the Tower, to which place Lord of his Mercy bring all the King's Enemies.

All. Amen, Amen.

[*Enter* Lovis *and* Freeman.]

Lo. Why, how now, Captain, what, besiege the Women! No, let us lead our Force to nobler Enemies.

Capt. Nay, noble Chief, your Word's our Law.

Lo. No, I resign that Title to the brave *Scotch* General, who has just now enter'd the City.

Capt. We know it, Sir; do you not observe how the Crop-ear'd Fanatics trot out of Town?—The Rogues began their old belov'd Mutiny, but 'twould not do.

Lo. A Pox upon 'em, they went out like the Snuff of a Candle, stinkingly and blinkingly.

1 Pren. Ay, ay, let 'em hang themselves, and then they are cold Meat for the Devil.

Capt. But, noble Champion, I hope we may have leave to roast the Rump tonight.

Lo. With all our Hearts, here's Money to make Fires—

Free. And here's for Drink to't, Boys.

All. Hey—*Viva le Roy, viva* [322] *les Heroicks!* [*Go out hollowing.*]

[*Enter* Ananias *peeping,* Felt-maker, *and* Joyner.]

Ana. So, the Rabble's gone: ah, Brethren! what will this wicked World come to?

Felt. Alack, alack, to no Goodness, you may be sure: pray what's the News?

[Fleetwood *peeping out of a Garret-Window.*]

Fleet. Anania, Anania!

Ana. Who calleth *Ananias?* lo, here am I.

Fleet. Behold, it is I, look up. How goeth tidings?

Ana. Full ill, I fear; 'tis a bad [323] Omen to see your Lordship so nigh Heaven; when the Saints are Garretified.

Fleet. I am fortifying my self against the Evil-Day.

Ana. Which is come upon us like a Thief in the night; like a Torrent from the Mountain of Waters, or a Whirlwind from the Wilderness.

Fleet. Why, what has the *Scotch* General done?

Ana. Ah! he playeth the Devil with the Saints in the City, because they put the Covenant-Oath unto him; he pulls up their Gates, their Posts and Chains, and enters.

Felt. And wou'd the wicked City let him have his beastly Will of her?

Ana. Nay, but she was ravish'd—deflower'd.

Joy. How, ravish'd! oh monstrous! was ever such a Rape committed upon an innocent City? lay her Legs open to the wide World, for every Knave to view her Nakedness?

Felt. Ah, ah! what Days, what Times, and what Seasons are here? [*Exeunt.*] [324]

[*Enter* Captain, Corporal *and* Prentice *with Faggots, hollowing.*]

Cor. What say you now, Lads, is not my Prophecy truer than *Lilly's?* I told you the Rump would fall to our handling and drinking for: the King's proclaim'd, Rogues.

Capt. Ay, ay, *Lilly,* a Plague on him, he prophesied *Lambert* should be uppermost.

Cor. Yes, he meant perhaps on *Westminster* Pinacle: where's *Lilly* now, with all his Prophecies against the *Royal Family?*

Capt. In one of his Twelve Houses. [p. 421]

1 Pren. We'll fire him out tonight, Boy; come, all hands to work for the Fire. [*Exit all hollowing.*]

Fleet. Ah, dismal, heavy day, a day of Grief and Woe, Which hast bereft me of my hopes for ay, Ah, Lard, ah what shall I do? [*Exit.*] [325]

Scene IV. *A Chamber in* Lambert's *House.* [326]

[*Enter* Lovis *leading* L. Lambert *in disguise,* Page *and* Gilliflower *disguised,* Lovis *dressing her.*]

Lo. My Charmer, why these Tears,
If for the fall of all thy painted Glories,
Thou art, in the esteem of all good Men,
Above what thou wert then?
The glorious Sun is rising in our Hemisphere,
And I, amongst the crowd of Loyal Sufferers,
Shall share in its kindly [327] Rays.

L. Lam. Best of thy Sex—
What have I left to gratify thy Goodness?

Lo. You have already by your noble Bounty,

Made me a Fortune, had I nothing else;
All which I render back, with all that Wealth
Heaven and my Parents left me:
Which, tho unjustly now detain'd from me,
Will once again be mine, and then be yours.

[*Enter* Freeman.]

Free. Come, haste, the Rabble gather round the House,
And swear they'll have this Sorceress.
Lo. Let me loose among 'em, their rude officious Honesty must be punish'd.
L. Lam. Oh, let me out, do not expose thy Person to their mad Rage, rather resign the Victim. [*Holds him.*]
Lo. Resign thee! by Heaven, I think I shou'd turn Rebel first.

[*Enter* L. Desbro *disguised, and* Tom *with Jewels* [328] *in a Box.*]

L. Des. With much ado, according to thy direction, dear *Freeman*, I have pass'd the Pikes, my House being surrounded; and my Husband demanded, fell down dead with fear.
Free. How, thy Husband dead!
L. Des. Dead as old *Oliver*, and much ado I got off with these Jewels, the Rabble swore I was one of the Party; and had not the honest Corporal convinc'd em, I had been pull'd to pieces.—Come, haste away, Madam, we shall be roasted with the Rump else.
L. Lam. Adieu, dear Mansion! whose rich gilded Roofs so oft put me in mind of Majesty—And thou, my Bed of State, where my soft Slumbers have presented me with Diadems and Scepters—when waking I have stretch'd my greedy Arms to grasp the vanish'd Phantom! ah, adieu! and all my hopes of *Royalty* adieu.—
Free. And dare you put yourself into my Protection? Well, if you do, [329] I doubt you'll never be your own Woman again.
L. Des. No matter, I'm better lost than found on such occasions. [*Exeunt.*]

Scene V. *A Street*; [330] *a great Bonfire, with Spits, and Rumps roasting, and the Mobile about the Fire, with Pots, Bottles, Fiddles.*

1 Pren. Here, *Jack*, a Health to the King.
2 Pren. Let it pass, Lad, and next to the noble General.
1 Pren. Ralph, baste the Rump well, or ne'er hope to see a King agen.
3 Pren. The Rump will baste itself, it has been well cram'd.

[*Enter* Freeman, L. Desbro, Loveless, *and* L. Lambert, Gilliflower, Tom, *Pages,* [331] *&c.*]

Capt. Hah, Noble Champion, faith, Sir, you must honor us so far as to drink the King's Health, and the noble General's, before you go.

[*Enter* Wariston, *dressed like a Peddler, with a Box about his Neck full of Ballads and Things.*]

War. Will ya buy a guedly Ballat or a *Scotch* Spur, Sirs? a guedly Ballat, or a *Scotch* Spur.—'Sbread, I's scapt hitherte weele enough, I's say'd my Crag fro stretching twa Inches longer than 'twas borne: will ya buy a Jack-line to roast the Rump, a new Jack Lambert Line?—or a blithe Ditty of the Noble *Scotch* General?—come buy my Ditties.

Capt. How, a Ditty o'th' General? let's see't, Sirrah.

War. 'Sbread, Sirs, and here's the guedly Ballat of the General's coming out of Scotland.

Capt. Here, who sings it? we'll all bear the bob. [p. 423]

[Wariston *sings the Ballad, all bearing the Bob.*]

[*Enter Ananias crying Almanack.*]

Ana. New Almanacks, new Almanacks.

Capt. Hah, who have we here? *Ananias,* Holder-forth of *Clement's* Parish?

All. Ha, a Traytor, a Traytor.

Lo. If I am not mistaken, this blithe Ballad-singer too was Chair-man to the Committee of Safety.

Capt. Is your Lordship turned Pedlar at last?

War. What mon I do noo? Lerd, ne mere Lerd than yar sel, Sir; wons I show 'em a fair pair of Heels.

[*Goes to run away, they get him on a Colt-staff,* [p. 423] *with* Ananias *on another, Fiddlers playing* Fortune my Foe, [p. 423] *round the Fire.*]

Capt. Play *Fortune my Foe*, Sirrah.

[*Enter* Hewson, *dressed like a Country Fellow.*]

Cor. Who are you, Sirrah? you have the mark o' th' Beast.

Hews. Who aye, Sir? Aye am a Doncer, that come a merry-making [332] among ya—

Capt. Come, Sirrah, your Feats of Activity quickly then.

[*He dances; which ended, they get him on a Colt-staff, and cry a* Cobbler, *a* Cobbler.]

All. A Cobbler, a Cobbler.

Capt. To Prison with the Traitors, and then we have made a good Night's work on't.
  Then let's all home, and to the Powers Divine
  Pray for the King, and all the Sacred Line. [*Exeunt.*]

EPILOGUE

Spoken by Lady *Desbro*.

THE Vizor's off, and now I dare appear.
High for the Royal Cause *in Cavalier;*
Tho once as true a Whig as most of you,
Cou'd cant, and lye, preach, and dissemble too:
So far you drew me in, but faith I'll be
Reveng'd on you for thus debauching me:
Same of your pious Cheats I'll open lay,
That lead your Ignoramus *Flock astray:*
For since I cannot fight, I will not fail
To exercise my Talent, that's to rail.
Ye Race of Hypocrites, whose Cloak of Zeal
Covers the Knave that cants for Commonweal,
All Laws, the Church and State to Ruin brings,
And impudently sets a Rule on Kings;
Ruin, destroy, all's good that you decree
By your Infallible Presbytery,
Prosperous at first, in Ills you grow so vain, [333]
You thought to play the Old Game *o'er again:*
And thus the Cheat was put upon the Nation,
First with Long Parliaments, *next* Reformation,
And now you hop'd to make a new Invasion:
And when you can't prevail by open Force,
To cunning tickling Tricks you have recourse,
And raise Sedition forth without Remorse.
Confound these cursed Tories, *then they cry,* [In a preaching tone.] [334]
Those Fools, those Pimps to Monarchy,
Those that exclude the Saints; yet open th' Door,
To introduce the Babylonian Whore.
By Sacred Oliver *the Nation's mad;*
Beloved, 'twas not so when he was Head:
But then, as I have said it oft before ye,
A Cavalier was but a Type of Tory.
The Curs durst then not bark, but all the Breed
Is much encreas'd since that good Man was dead:
Yet then they rail'd against the Good Old Cause,
Rail'd foolishly for Loyalty, and Laws;
But when the Saints had put them to a stand,
We left them Loyalty, and took their Land:
Yea, and the pious Work of Reformation
Rewarded was with Plunder, Sequestration.
Thus cant the Faithful; nay, they're so uncivil,
To pray us harmless Players to the Devil.
When this is all th' Exception they can make,

They damn us for our Glorious Master's sake.
But why 'gainst us do you unjustly arm?
Our small Religion sure can do no harm;
Or if it do, since that's the only thing,
We will reform when you are true to th' King.

THE END

NOTES ON THE TEXT.

ROVER I.

[1] There is a strange commixture here. The character is familiarly addressed as 'Hal', the scene is Madrid, and he rejoices in the Milanese (not Italian) nomenclature Arrigo = Henry in that dialect.

[2] *Diego, Page to Don Antonio.* Neither 4tos nor 1724 give the page's name, but it is furnished by the stage direction Act ii. I, p. 32. I have added Hellena's page, Belvile's page, and Blunt's man to the list as it appears in 4tos and 1724.

[3] *Angelica.* 4tos give 'Angellica' throughout. I have retained 1724 'Angelica' as more correct.

[4] *my things.* 1724 misprints 'methinks'.

[5] *as those which ...* 4to 1677 prints this as a separate line of blank verse. 4to 1709 italicizes it.

[6] *She often passes ...* 4to 1709 puts this stage direction before Blunt's speech.

[7] *Exit all the Women.* I have added 'except Lucetta' as she is individually directed to make her exit with Blunt later and not at this point.

[8] *Pedro. Ha!* 1724 omits.

[9] *aside.* 1724 omits.

[10] *his shirt bloody.* 1724 gives 'their shirts' but 4tos, more correctly, 'his shirt'. It is only Willmore who has been wounded.

[11] *high i' th' Mouth.* 1724, 1735 misprint 'Month'.

[12] *This last reserve.* 1724 omits 'reserve'.

[13] *by me.* 1724 omits the repetition of 'by me'.

[14] *cure.* 1724 misprints 'curse'.

[15] *Thou art a brave Fellow.* 1724 prints this speech as prose but the 4tos, which I have followed, divide metrically.

[16] *Thou wou't.* 4to 1677. 1724 wrongly reads 'won't'. 1735 'Thou'lt'.

[17] *ago.* 4to 1677. 1724 misprints 'go'.

[18] *starts.* 4tos read 'stares' but I retain 1724 'starts' as more appropriate.

[19] *Expect!* 1724 gives this speech as prose. I follow metrical division of 4tos.

[20] *rally.* 1724 misprints 'railly'.

[21] *Exeunt.* 1724 omits this necessary stage direction.

[22] *Exit.* 1724 misprints 'aside'.

[23] *Enter Sancho.* 4tos, but misprint after Sancho's speech. 1724 omits, but misprints an 'exit Sancho', and gives 'exit' after Blunt's speech instead of 'exeunt'.

[24] *Pimps!* 1724 'Imps'.

[25] *sheer.* 4to 1677. 4to 1709 and 1724 read wrongly 'share'.

[26] *Antonio.* 4to 1677 wrongly gives this speech to Belvile. 4to 1709 and ed. 1724 assign it correctly.

[27] *That Opinion.* 1724 prints this speech as prose. I follow metrical division of 4tos.

[28] *Aside.* 4to 1677. 1724 and 1735 omit this stage direction.

[29] *Masking Habit.* 1724, 1735, 'Masque habit'.

[30] *If you strike.* 1724, 1735 omit this line.

[31] *Belvile Love Florinda!* 4tos give this speech as prose. 1724 metrically.

[32] *Frederick.—'tis he*—1724 and 1735 mistaking 'Fred.' for speech-prefix give this line to Frederick.

[33] *Belvile Vizard ...* 1724, 1735, read 'Vizard falls out on's Hand.'

[34] *Nay, an you ...* 4tos and 1724, print as prose. This speech is obviously metrical.

[35] *I am all Rage!* 4to 1677 divides metrically. 1724 prints as prose.

[36] *unconstant.* 1724, 1735 'inconstant'.

[37] *Aside.* 4tos omit this necessary stage direction.

[38] *Now I perceive.* 1724 prints this as prose. 4tos metrically.

[39] *So, you have made ...* 1724, 1735 prose. 4tos metrically.

[40] *You are mistaken.* 1724, 1735 prose. 4tos metrically.

[41] *continence.* 1724 misprints 'continuance'.

[42] *Willmore.* 1677 misprinting, omits this speech-prefix.

[43] *has Wit.* 1724 misprints 'Whas it'.

[44] *A Woman!* 1724 omits 'A'.

[45] *the Rogue.* 1724 omits 'the'.

[46] *He starts up.* 1677 4to misprints 'she'.

[47] *dexterous.* 1724 misprints 'dexetrous'. 1735 'dextrous'.

[48] *Exeunt.* 1724 wrongly 'exit'.

[49] *Blunt's Chamber.* 4tos 'Chamber'. 1724, 1735, 'Room'.

[50] *as at his Chamber-door.* 1724, 1735, omit 'as'.

[51] *and Belvile's Page.* I have added this entrance which 4tos and 1724 omit, as late in the scene an exit is marked for the page.

[52] *Hah! Angelica!* 4to 1677 mistakenly marks this speech before the stage direction.

[53] *What Devil.* 1724, 1735 'What the Devil', which weakens the whole passage.

[54] *Post-Script.* This is only given in the first 4to (1677).

ROVER II.

[55] I have added to the Dramatis Personæ 'Rag, boy to Willmore', and 'Porter at the English Ambassador's'.

[56] *Scene I.* I have added the locale 'A Street'.

[57] *Campaign.* 4to 1681 'campania'.

[58] *but cold.* 1724 'and cold'.

[59] *embracing.* 1724 omits.

[60] *Philies.* 4to 1681 'Philoes'.

[61] *Brussels.* 4to 1681 'Bruxels'.

[62] *But that.* 1724 prints these two lines as prose.

[63] *Marcy.* 1724 'Mercy'.

[64] *get 'em ready.* 1724 'get it ready'.

[65] *pickl'd Pilchard.* 1724. 'pickle Pilchard'.

[66] *like a Christmas Sweet-heart.* 4to 1681 'boto Christmas Sweet-heart'.

[67] *have I.* 1724 'I have'.

[68] *hot Shot,* 1724 omits 'hot'.

[69] *to receive.* 1724, wrongly, 'to deceive'.

[70] *Scene I.* I have added the locale 'The Street'.

[71] *Harlequin, Scaramouche.* I have added these two names to the stage direction. Harlequin is obviously present from the business. Scaramouche is given in Dramatis Personæ, 4to 1681 and 1724, but in neither is any entry or exit marked throughout

the play. In Killigrew, whom Mrs. Behn is here following very closely, Scaramouche is the quack's servant and appears in this scene. Accordingly I have marked him an entrance.

[72] *Mermaids.* 1724 'Mairmaids'.
[73] *an a Man.* 4to 1681 'and a Man'.
[74] *and falls.* 4to 1681 'who falls'.
[75] *on the Mountebank's Stage.* 4to 1681 'on the stage of the Mountebank'.
[76] *This is flat Conjuration.* 4to 1681 'This flat Conjuration'.
[77] *what's here.* 4to 1681 'what here'.
[78] *Exit Fetherfool and Blunt.* 4to 1681 and 1724 '[Exit.]'
[79] *Scene II. Changes.* 4to 1681 and 1724 'Scene changes'.
[80] *[bis.]* 1724 omits.
[81] *my Cousin Endymion.* 1724 'Endymion's'.
[82] *Sommes.* 4to 1681 and 1724 'somme'.
[83] *Snush.* 1724 'snuff'.
[84] *Gargantua.* 4to 1681 'Garigantua', and omits 'of'.
[85] *and Harlequin attending.* Harlequin's entrance is not marked in 4to 1681 or in 1724, but it is necessary here as he is addressed by the Dwarf.
[86] *Hu, how scornful.* 1724 omits 'Hu'.
[87] *with Harlequin.* Harlequin's exit unmarked in 4to 1681 and 1724.
[88] *Talks to Hunt.* 4to 1681, wrongly, 'Talks to Will'.
[89] *faithless as the Winds.* 1724 'Wind'.
[90] *fixed Resolves.* 1724 'fixt Resolve'.
[91] *he may again rally.* 1724 'railly'.
[92] *them that tries me.* 1724 'them that tire me'.
[93] *set such Price on.* 1724 'set a Price on'.
[94] *I grow weary.* 4to 1681 'I grew weary'.
[95] *sure he knows me not.* 1724 omits 'he'.
[96] *better than an Age of Scorn from a proud faithless Beauty?* 1724 'better from Age of Scorn than a proud faithless Beauty?'
[97] *and all to bekiss me.* 1724 'and kiss me'.
[98] *Laying his hand on his Sword.* 4to 1681 gives stage direction as '[His Sword.]'
[99] *ails he?* 1724 'ye'.
[100] *who wou'st.* 4to 1681 'who'st'. 1724 'wou'st'.
[101] *turn me out despis'd.* 1724 'turn me out so despis'd'.
[102] *Charms shall hold.* 4to 1681 'Charms can hold'.
[103] *she holds him.* 1724 omits 'him'.
[104] *a Purse or hands full of Gold.* 1724 'a Purse of Gold'.
[105] *Ariadne. [feels.] Tis so!* 1724 omits '[feels]'.
[106] *I ever had.* 1724, wrongly, 'I ne'er had'.
[107] *My hope.* 4to 1681 'ever hope'.
[108] *Orange-grove.* 1724 'orange-garden'.
[109] *Was this done.* 1724 'Was not this done'.
[110] *in the Piazza.* 4to 1681 'Piazzo', and always this form.
[111] *and goes out.* 4to 1681 'and ex.'
[112] *whistle to the Birds.* 1724 'whistle to Birds'.
[113] *Aurelia. Well, the Stranger.* 1724 'Ant. Well, the Stranger'.
[114] *that was the Reason then she came.* 1724 omits 'then'.

[115] *The Seigniora perhaps may be angry.* 1724 'Seignior'.

[116] *Damn all dissembling.* 1724 prints this speech as prose.

[117] *Love's diviner Dictates.* 1724 'Love's divine Dictates'.

[118] *false Tenents.* 1724, wrongly, 'False Tenements'.

[119] *Oh, any whither, any whither.* 1724 'anywhere, anywhere'.

[120] *I believed he had.* 1724 'I believe he has'.

[121] *no matter whither 'tis.* 1724 'no matter which 'tis'.

[122] *Abevile sings.* 4to 1681 and 1724 'The Boy sings ...', but his name has already been given.

[123] *To find out this Rest.* 1724 'To find this Rest'.

[124] *La Nuche. 'Tis he whom I expect.* 1724 gives this speech as prose.

[125] *whence I fetched my Gold.* 1724 'whence I fetch my Gold'.

[126] *they are by dark.* 1724 omits.

[127] *What is't to be adorn'd.* 1724 'What 'tis to be adorn'd'.

[128] *Wou'd! by Heaven, thou hast.* 1724 gives this as prose, 1681 metrically. I have followed the 4to, attempting a rather better division of the lines.

[129] *The last indeed.* The first three lines of this speech metrically as 4to 1681. 1724 prints as prose.

[130] *his Youth and Beauty.* 4to 1681 'this Youth and Beauty'.

[131] *not a Landlady. [bis.]* 1724 omits '[bis.]'

[132] *La Nuche. Left by both!* 4to 1681 'Left by both?'

[133] *and Beaumond.* I have added this exit. It is unmarked in 4to 1681 and in 1724.

[134] *in the dark.* 4to 1681 'by dark'.

[135] *un Portavera Poco.* 1724 misprints 'Porsavera'.

[136] *Harlequin. Qui est là?* 4to 1681 'Harlequin. Que et la!'

[137] *I am discover'd.* 1724 'I am discower'd'.

[138] *Fetherfool Hah—my Lady Monster!* 4to 1681 omits to mark at change of scene Fetherfool again as speech-prefix.

[139] *Exit all.* 1724 omits 'all'.

[140] *out of hand. [Aside.* 4to 1681 omits 'Aside'.

[141] *Ariadne!—How vain is all.* 1724 give this speech as prose. I have followed the metrical division of the 4to 1681 with some slight rearrangement of the lines.

[142] *John Potages.* 1724. 'Jean Potages'.

[143] *thou foul filthy Synagogue.* 1724. 'foul-filthy'.

[144] *d'ye see.* 4to 1681 'de see'.

[145] *Myrmidons.* 4to 1681 'Mermidons'.

[146] *wiser than your other Men.* 1724 omits 'your',

[147] *Gets from her.* 1724 omits this stage direction.

[148] *They lay hold on him.* 4to 1681 'of him'.

[149] *nobly throw away.* 1724 'throw a Way'.

[150] *All this won't do.* The concluding twenty lines of the Epilogue are only given in 4to 1681. All subsequent editions omit them.

THE DUTCH LOVER.

[151] I have added to the Dramatis Personæ 'Boy, Page to Marcel, Servant to Carlo, A Friar, Swains, Four Shepherds, Four Nymphs, Dutch men and Dutch women.'

[152] The locale *A Street* is not marked in 4to 1673 or 1724.

[153] *Christian.* 1724 'christian'.
[154] *his nice Honor.* 1724, wrongly, omits 'nice'.
[155] *I must still love on.* 1724 omits 'still'.
[156] *after long Despairs.* 1724 'after long Despair'.
[157] *too much of Joy.* 1724 'Joys'.
[158] *change thy Wonder.* 4to 1673 'Wonders'.
[159] *Marcel is surprised.* 1724 omits this stage direction.
[160] *And thou, Antonio, that has betray'd her.* 4to 1673 'And thou, Antonio, thou hast betray'd her'. 1724 'And thou, Antonio, thou that hast betray'd her'.
[161] *a kind obliging Lady.* 1724 'A kind of obliging Lady'.
[162] *Am I a Dog.* 4to 1673 wrongly marks this line 'aside'.
[163] *I, like the Birds.* 4to 1673 omits 'the'.
[164] *Biscay, a Surgeon.* 4to 1673 omits 'a'.
[165] *Down of Swans.* 1724 'Swan'.
[166] *and lik'd him.* 1724 'and like him'.
[167] *this is the first.* 1724 'this was the first'.
[168] *to his heart.* 1724 omits.
[169] *Prithee instruct.* 4to 1673 as prose.
[170] *Command me.* 4to 1673 as prose.
[171] *My Death.* 1724 'me death'.
[172] *undone its Fame.* 1724 'undone his Fame'.
[173] *the next Morning's Sun.* 4to 1673 'th' Approach of next Morning's Sun'. 1724 'of the next Morning Sun'.
[174] *They go out.* 4to 1673 omits 'they'.
[175] *Come, come.* 1724 prints this speech as prose.
[176] *Look at one another and go.* 1724 omits, reading 'exeunt'.
[177] *very unlucky.* 4to 1673 'very unluckily'.
[178] *Marcel coming towards him jostles him.* 4to 1673 reads 'Marcel coming towards justles him'.
[179] *given him some.* 4to 1673 omits 'him'.
[180] *Of your Victims.* 1724 prints this line and the next as prose.
[181] *Offers her a Dagger.* 1724 omits 'her'.
[182] *a Pox of her terms.* 1724 'A Pox on her terms'.
[183] *Haunce van Ezel.* 1724 'Hance'.
[184] *I cry you Mercy.* 1724 'I cry your Mercy'.
[185] *he does not boast.* 4to 1673, wrongly, 'he does but boast'.
[186] *But do you find her.* 1724 'But do you not find her'.
[187] *'tis certain 'tis so.* 1724 "tis certain so'.
[188] *lest he surprise us.* 1724 'lest he surprises us'.
[189] *Ah, ah, a pox of all Sea-Voyages.* 1724 omits 'all'.
[190] *to our Courages.* 1724 'Courage'.
[191] *over a Leg.* 1724 'over Leg'.
[192] *Rummer.* 4to 1673 'Romer'.
[193] *that's not the Fashion.* 1724 omits 'not'.
[194] *I'll manage her.* 1724 'I manage her'.
[195] *Scene III. Draws off. A Grove.* 1724 omits 'Draws off.' I have added the locale 'A Grove.'
[196] *how darst thou.* 1724 'how durst thou'.

[197] *that could not defend.* 4to 1673 omits 'that'.

[198] *you knew not of my Brother's.* 1724 'you know not my Brother's' and omits '[To Francisca.'

[199] *to see the fair Clarinda [Goes to Clarinda] here, is a Happiness.* 1724 'to see the fair Clarinda [Goes to Clarinda.] Here is a Happiness'.

[200] *Goes out.* 1724 'Exit'.

[201] *Surlily to him.* 1724 'Goes surlily to him'.

[202] *by instinct. [Aside.* 1724 omits 'Aside'.

[203] *Stands looking very simply.* 1724 omits 'very'.

[204] *new-fashion'd Spanish Civility.* 1724 omits 'Spanish'.

[205] *it made my Stomach wamble.* 1724 'it had made'.

[206] *Gaber.* 1724 'Gabor'.

[207] *Fakes, to entertain.* 1724 'Faith'.

[208] *They two dance.* 1724 'They too dance.'

[209] *Runs behind Lovis.* 1724 omits.

[210] *I declare it here upon.* 1724 'Here I declare it upon'.

[211] *who starts as afraid.* 1724 misreads 'as aforesaid.'

[212] *Oh, is it bravely done.* 1724 'Oh, it is bravely done ...' and punctuates ':' instead of '?'

[213] *on this Body.* 1724, wrongly, 'on thy Body'.

[214] *Takes to his Sword.* 1724 'the Sword'.

[215] *Cleonte. Oh my Fears.* 4to 1673 wrongly marks 'aside'.

[216] *Weeps.* This stage direction is not given by 4to 1673.

[217] *How very very wicked.* 1724 'How very wicked'.

[218] *Count d' Olivarez.* 4to 1673 here and elsewhere when the name occurs 'Conte De Olivari's'.

[219] *if you are pleas'd.* 1724 'if your are pleas'd'.

[220] *Carlo's House.* 4to 1673 'House of Carlo'.

[221] *Dormida. As for.* 4to 1673 misreads ' Dormida. As for'.

[222] *Haunce. What a Devil.* 1724 Haunce. What the Devil'.

[223] *Truth. [Goes out.]* 1724 'Exit.'

[224] *God-ha'-Mercy.* 1724 'God-a-Mercy'.

[225] *Go in.* 1724 omits.

THE ROUNDHEADS.

[226] *To The Right Noble Henry Fitz-Roy.* The Dedicatory Epistle only appears in the two 4tos, 1682 and 1698.

[227] *Good Old Couse.* 'Couse' to represent a Cockney pronunciation.

[228] *Ignoramus the 1st and the 2d.* Mrs. Behn deftly compares the verdict of that faction which would have damned her play with the verdict given by the City jury who acquitted Shaftesbury.

[229] *ycleped Hewson.* 4to 'Eclipsed Huson'.

[230] *Dramatis Personæ.* I have added, 'Captain of the Prentices, Page to Lady Fleetwood, A Felt-maker, A Joyner, Doorkeeper, Two Clerks, Three Soldiers, Women Servants to Lady Lambert, Petitioners, Servants, Guards.' The name of Lady Desbro's Page, Tom, is supplied by Act iv, 1. For *Sanctify'd Mobile*, 1724 reads 'Sanctify'd Mobility'.

[231] *Push a Pike.* 1724 'Push of Pike'.

[232] *Go out.* 1724 'Goes out'.

[233] *the rest of the Soldiers.* 1724 'the rest of Soldiers'.

[234] *Love, Wit and Beauty.* 1724 prints these lines as prose.

[235] *A God! altho his outside.* 4tos and 1724 print this speech as prose.

[236] *No, methought he grew.* 1724 prints this speech as prose.

[237] *Ha, he's yonder.* 1724 prints this speech as prose.

[238] *Exeunt both.* 1724 'exeunt', 4tos 'exit both'.

[239] *Scene II. A Chamber in Lambert's House.* 4tos 'Scene a Chamber.' 1724 'Scene. A Chamber.' I have added 'II' and 'in Lambert's House.'

[240] *how have I show'd.* 1724 misprints 'how have show'd'.

[241] *the Lard's handling.* 1724 'the Lord's', 4tos 'Lard's'.

[242] *light on yu.* 1724 'light on you'.

[243] *a brave Mon.* 1724 'a brave Man'.

[244] *I may cooncel.* 1724 'I may counsel'.

[245] *he's a brave Mon, a Mon indeed, gen.* 1724 'he's a brave Mon indeed gen'.

[246] *Scene I. A Chamber of State in Lambert's House.* I have added 'in Lambert's House'.

[247] *admit him tho'.* 1724 omits 'tho''.

[248] *I shou'd say.* 1724 misprints 'I shou'd stay'.

[249] *these Heroics are punctual men.* 1724 omits 'men'.

[250] *Walks away.* 1724 omits this stage direction.

[251] *Some such trivial thing.* 1724 'some such trifling thing'.

[252] *Verily we should live.* 1724 'Verily ye should live'.

[253] *Write Panegyricks.* 1724 prints these concluding four lines as prose. 4tos metrically.

[254] *Lambert will destroy all.* 1724 'Lambert would destroy all'.

[255] *Or Mind embyass'd.* 1724 'Embarass'd'.

[256] *Execrations.* 1724 'Excrations'.

[257] *Cry mercy, Madam.* 1724 omits 'Madam'.

[258] *most lucky Minute.* 1724 'most unlucky Minute'.

[259] *my Honorable Lord is busied.* 1724 'has business'.

[260] *extemporary.* 1724 'extempore'.

[261] *Old Oliver's Brains.* 1724 'Brain'.

[262] *take 'em then for Archibald; 'tis.* 1724 'take 'em then for Archibald? 'tis'.

[263] *warse.* 1724 'worse'.

[264] *Hew. My Lord, I am sorry.* 1724 'Hew. I am sorry'.

[265] *what stuff's here.* 1724 'what's stuff's here'.

[266] *Walter Walton.* 1724 'Walter Walter'.

[267] *ever cam into lour*, read *ever came intol our.* 1724 'ever came into'.

[268] *I's larne.* 1724 'I's learn'.

[269] *se fast.* 1724 'so fast'.

[270] *shoos in yar.* 1724 'shoes'.

[271] *Malignant's Estates.* 1724 'Malignant Estates'.

[272] *she has danc'd after.* 1724 'she has danc'd here after'.

[273] *Scene II. A Chamber in Lady Desbro's House.* 4tos and 1724 'Scene, a Chamber'.

310

[274] *Enter Tom.* 4tos and 1724 'Enter Page' with speech-prefix—'Page.' and 'Exit Page'; but Act iv, 1, 4tos we have 'Enter Page' with speech-prefix 'Tom' and later in the same scene 'Enter Tom Page'.

[275] *hear him preach.* 1724 'here him preach'.

[276] *Beauty.* And later 'falling' to mark the sanctimonious drawl. 1724 prints 'Beauty' and 'falling'.

[277] *Exeunt.* 4tos omit. 1724 omits 'Exit Ana.'

[278] *A Chamber in La. Desbro's House.* 4tos and 1724 'Chamber, Candles and Lights'.

[279] *gives us notice of.* 1724 'gives us notice of it'.

[280] *come a Gad's Name.* 1724 'come in Gad's Name'.

[281] *Nay, I say verily, nay.* 1724 'I say verily, nay'.

[282] *the Lard hath given.* 1724 'the Lard has given'.

[283] *Enter Tom.* 1724 'Enter Page', speech-prefix 'Page', and 'Exit Page'; 4tos 'Enter Page', speech-prefix 'Tom', 'Exit Tom Page'.

[284] *we have hitherto maintain'd.* 1724 omits 'hitherto'.

[285] *A fine Chamber.* I have added to 4tos and 1724 'in La. Lambert's House'.

[286] *A great Chamber.* I have added to 4tos and 1724 'in Lambert's House'.

[287] *I's drink tol yar gued Fortune.* 1724 'to yar gued Fortune'.

[288] *Exit L. Lambert. and Gilliflower.* I have added 'and Gilliflower.

[289] *light your Flambeaus.* 1724 'your Flambeau'.

[290] *when we real.* 1724 'when we reel'.

[291] *o'er yar Liquer.* 1724 'Liquor'.

[292] *I's for a Horn-pipe.* 1724 omits 'for'.

[293] *Scotch Poond.* 1724 'Pound'.

[294] *yar Song.* 1724 'your Song'.

[295] *lead the Donce.* 1724 'lead the Dance'.

[296] *As well as to give.* 1724 'As well as give'.

[297] *Kneels.* 4to 1698 and 1724 omit this stage direction.

[298] *he puts it back.* 4tos 'he put it back'. 1724 'he puts it off'.

[299] *my Husband wou'd withdraw.* 1724 'my Husband cou'd withdraw'.

[300] *He lies down along on the Couch.* 1724 'He lies down on the Couch'.

[301] *Scene I. A Street.* 1724 'Scene I. Street'.

[302] *Viva le Roy, Viva le Monk!* 4tos 'Via la Roy, Via la Monk.'

[303] *Why, so there's some trusting.* 1724 omits 'so'.

[304] *Viva the brave.* 1724 'Vive the brave'.

[305] *Ananias gets a Sword, and fights too.* 1724 'and fights 'em'.

[306] *Scene II. Changes to a Chamber in La. Lambert's House.* 4tos and 1724 'Scene changes to a Chamber'.

[307] *and I shall keep it.* 1724 omits 'I'.

[308] *L. Lambert. Thou ly'st.* 4tos and 1724 print this speech as prose, but it admits of metrical division.

[309] *Gog and Magog.* 4tos 'God and Magog'.

[310] *Morning and Evening Lectures.* 4tos 'Mornings and Evenings Lectures'.

[311] *Enter Page with Messenger.* 1724 'Enter Page with Messengers'.

[312] *Where's that brutal Courage.* 1724 'the Brutal Courage'.

[313] *whose wise work was that?* 1724 'whose wise work's that?'

[314] *Wans, Sirs.* 1724 'Wons, Sirs'.

[315] *ya's ene.* 1724 'ye's ene'.

[316] *Mr. Leyer.* 1724 'Mr. Lyar'.

[317] *makes ye look.* 1724 'makes you look'.

[318] *L. Fleetwood and Page.* 1724 omits 'and Page.'

[319] *no more. [Weep.]* 1724 omits 'Weep'.

[320] *Go in.* 1724 only marks 'Exit' for all characters.

[321] *Scene III. The Street.* 4tos and 1724 'Scene the Street'.

[322] *Viva le Roy, viva.* 1724 'Vive le Roy, vive'.

[323] *ill, I fear; 'tis a bad.* 1724 'ill, I fear 'tis a bad'.

[324] *are here? [Exeunt.* 4tos and 1724 omit 'Exeunt'. I supply this as, obviously, these characters must leave the stage when the Prentices rush on.

[325] *ay, Ah, Lard, ah what.* 4tos 'ay, ah Lard, what'. 1724 'ay. Lard, ah what'.

[326] *Scene IV. A Chamber in Lambert's House.* 4tos and 1724 'Scene, A Chamber'.

[327] *share in its kindly.* 1724 'share its kindly'.

[328] *and Tom with jewels.* 4tos and 1724 'Page with jewels'.

[329] *Well, if you do.* 1724 'Why, if you do'.

[330] *Scene V. A Street.* 4tos and 1724 'Scene, a Street'.

[331] *Gilliflower, Tom, Pages, &c.* I have inserted Tom's name here.

[332] *come a merry-making.* 1724 'come merry-making'.

[333] *you grow so vain.* 1724 'you grew so vain'.

[334] *In a preaching tone.* 1724 'In a preachin tone'. The dropped 'g', is not intentional here, but a misprint.

NOTES: CRITICAL AND EXPLANATORY.

[The page numbers referenced here refer to the page noted in the original edition.]

ROVER I.

p. 7 *Rabel's Drops.* Monsieur Rabell, as he is sometimes termed, was a famous empiric of the day. A description of his medicaments may be found in '*Pharmacopoeia Bateana*; or, Bate's Dispensatory. Edited by William Salmon, London, 1700.' Rabell's name occurs on the title-page of this book, and in Section VI of the Preface Rabell's 'Styptick Drops' are alluded to as having been added to the recipes found in the original volume by G. Bate. An account of the manufacture and use of this particular remedy appears in the same volume, Lib. I, chap. x, under 'Sal Stypticum Rabelli'. Salmon, who edited this pharmacopoeia, was himself an irregular practitioner of some notoriety. He took part in the great controversy with the doctors which raged about 1698 and earlier. He finds a sorry place in Garth's *Dispensary*, canto III, l. 6, wherein his works are alluded to as 'blessed opiates'.

p. 8 *Cits in May-day Coaches.* On May-day it was the custom for all sorts and conditions of persons and pleasure parties to visit Hyde Park in coaches or at least on horse-back, cf. Pepys *Diary*, 1 May, 1663: 'We all took horse, and I ... rode, with some trouble, through the fields, and then Holborn, etc., towards Hyde Park, whither all the world, I think, are going; ... there being people of all sorts in coaches there, to some thousands.... By and by ... I rode home, coaches going in great crowds to the further end of the town almost.'

p. 9 *Sancho, Pimp to Lucetta. Mr. John Lee.* There were at this time two actors and two actresses of the name Lee, Leigh, who, especially in view of the eclectic spelling of seventeenth-century proper names, need to be carefully distinguished. John Lee, who appeared in the small rôle of Sancho and also took the equally unimportant part of Sebastian in *Abdelazer* this same year, had, according to Downes, joined the Duke's Company about 1670. He never rose above an entirely insignificant line, and we find him cast as Alexas in Pordage's *Herod and Mariamne*, 1673; Titiro in Settle's *Pastor Fido*, 1676; Pedro in Porter's *The French Conjurer*, and Noddy in *The Counterfeit Bridegroom*, 1677. He was, it is almost certain, the husband of the famous Mrs. Mary Lee. Downes' entry runs as follows: '*Note*, About the year 1670, Mrs. *Aldridge*, after Mrs. *Lee*, after Lady *Slingsby*, also Mrs. *Leigh* Wife, Mr. *John Lee*, Mr. *Crosby*, Mrs. *Johnson*, were entertain'd in the Dukes House.' There is of course some confusion here. Antony Leigh, it may be noted, is not mentioned in the *Roscius Anglicanus* for another three years to come (1673), and there can be little doubt that the above passage should read 'also Mrs. Leigh's [Lee's] husband, Mr John Lee'. If this were not so, there would be no point in Downes mentioning so minor an actor at this juncture and in such a list. Crosby and Mrs. Johnson were both performers of great merit, in fact Downes, a page later, has a special warm word of praise for the lady whom we find cast as Carolina in Shadwell's *Epsom Wells* (1672). Crosby played such parts as Mr. Cleverwit, Lucia's lover, in Ravenscroft's *Mamamouchi* (1672), Alonzo in *Abdelazer* (1677), Leander Fancy in *Sir Patient Fancy* (1678). John Lee disappears entirely after 1677, and his widow is first billed as Lady Slingsby in 1681. For a full account of this great tragedienne see note on *Abdelazer*, Vol. II.

Mrs. Elizabeth Leigh, Moretta in *The Rover*, Part I, who is so persistently confused with Mrs. Mary Lee, was the wife of Antony Leigh, the celebrated comedian. In Betterton's comedy, *The Revenge* (1680), when she acted Mrs. Dashit, she is billed as Mrs. A. Lee. Her husband died in December, 1692. Their son Michael also gave great promise on the boards. The lad's name occurs in the cast of Shadwell's *The Amorous Bigot* (1690) as 'young Leigh', when he played Diego, a servant, to his father's Tegue o' Divelly, the Irish friar. Unfortunately he died at an early age, probably in the winter of 1701, but his younger brother Francis attained considerable success. Frank Leigh made his debut at Lincoln's Inn's Fields, 31 December, 1702, as Tristram in the original production of Mrs. Centlivre's *The Stolen Heiress*. He died in the autumn of 1719. Mrs. Leigh was herself an actress of no small eminence, her special line being 'affected mothers, aunts, and modest stale maids that had missed their market'. Says Cibber, 'In all these, with many others, she was extremely entertaining'. After 10 June, 1707, when she acted Lady Sly in Carlile's *The Fortune Hunters*, her name is no longer to be found in the bills, and in October, 1707, Mrs. Powell is playing her parts. Mrs. Leigh's repertory was very large, and amongst her roles were Lady Woodvil in Etheredge's *The Man of Mode* (1676); Lady Plyant in *The Double Dealer* (1694); the Nurse in *Love for Love* (1695); the Hostess in Betterton's revival of *Henry IV*, Part I (1699); and Lady Wishfort in *The Way of the World* (1700). In comedies by Mrs. Behn, Mrs. Leigh only appears twice, Moretta, *The Rover*, Part I (1677); and Mrs. Closet, *The City Heiress* (1682).

In and about 1702 another Mrs. Leigh, perhaps Frank Leigh's wife, made a brief appearance. She was at first cast for good parts but soon sank into obscurity. Thus on 21 October, 1702, she sustained Mrs. Plotwell in Mrs. Centlivre's *The Beau's Duel*; on 28 April, 1703, Chloris in the Hon. Charles Boyle's insipid *As You Find It*. She may have been the Mrs. Eli. Leigh who with other performers signed a petition to Queen Anne in 1709. Of Mrs. Rachel Lee, who took the 'walk-on' part of Judy, a waiting-woman, in Southern's *The Maid's Last Prayer* (1693), nothing is known.

p. 9 *Angelica Bianca, a famous Courtesan. Mrs. Gwin.* Anne Quin (or Quyn, Gwin, Gwyn as the name is indifferently spelt) was a famous actress of great personal beauty. She is constantly, but most erroneously, confounded with Nell Gwynne, and the mistake is the more unpardonable as both names twice occur in the same cast. When Nelly was acting Florimel in Dryden's *Secret Love*, produced February, 1667, Mrs. Quin played Candiope. Again, in *An Evening's Love*, June, 1668, Nell Gwynne was Jacinta, and Mrs Quin Aurelia, a role assumed later in the run by Mrs. Marshall. Among Mrs. Quin's more notable parts were Alizia (Alice Perrers) in Orrery's *The Black Prince*, produced 19 October, 1667; 1677, Thalestris in Pordage's *The Siege of Babylon*, and Astrea in *The Constant Nymph*; 1678, Lady Knowell in *Sir Patient Fancy* and Lady Squeamish in Otway's *Friendship in Fashion*; 1682, Queen Elizabeth in Banks' *The Unhappy Favorite*, and Sunamire in Southerne's *The Loyal Brother*. Mrs. Quin appears to have retired from the stage towards the close of the year 1682. There exists of this actress an extremely interesting portrait which was offered for sale at Stevens' Auction Rooms, 26 February, 1901, but not reaching the reserve price, withdrawn. It is mistakenly described in the catalogue as 'Miniature Portrait of Nell Gwynn on copper with original case and 30 cover dresses on talc...' An illustrated article on it, entitled, 'Nell Gwynne's Various Guises', appeared in the *Lady's Pictorial*, 23 March, of the same year, p. 470, in the course of which the writer says: 'Accompanying the miniature are some thirty mica covers in different stages of preservation upon which various headdresses and costumes are painted. The place where, in the ordinary course, the face would come is in all cases left blank, the talc being of course transparent, when it is laid upon the original miniature the countenance of the latter becomes visible, and we are enabled to see Nell Gwynne [Anne Quin] as she would appear in various characters.' The old error has been perpetuated here, but the *Lady's Pictorial* reproduced half-a-dozen of these painted mica covers, and the costumes for the two roles of Queen Elizabeth and Sunamire can be distinctly recognized. Doubtless an examination of the original micas would soon yield an identification of other characters. The miniature, it may be noted, does not in the least resemble Nell Gwynne, so there is bare excuse here for the confusion.

p. 11 *Siege of Pampelona.* Pampluna, the strongly fortified capital of Navarra, has from its geographical position very frequently been a centre of military operations. It will be remembered that it was during a siege of Pampluna in 1521 Ignatius Loyola received the wound which indirectly led to the founding of the Jesuits.

p. 13 *King Sancho the First.* Sancho I, 'the Fat', of Castile and Leon, reigned 955-67: Sancho I of Aragon 1067-94. But the phrase is here only in a vague general sense to denote some musty and immemorial antiquity without any exact reference.

p. 14 *Hostel de Dieu.* The first Spanish hospital was erected at Granada by St. Juan de Dios, founder of the Order of Hospitallers. ob. 1550.

p. 14 *Gambo.* The Gambia in W. Africa has been a British Colony since 1664, when a fort, now Fort James, was founded at the mouth of the river.

p. 17 *Hogoes.* Haut-goût, a relish or savoury.

p. 26 *a Piece of Eight.* A piastre, a coin of varying values in different countries. The Spanish piastre is now synonymous with a dollar and so worth about four shillings. The old Italian piastre was equivalent to 3*s*. 7*d.*

p. 30 *Balcony... each side of the Door.* With regard to the proscenium doors and balconies of a Restoration theatre, our knowledge of these points has been rendered much more exact since the valuable discovery by that well-known authority in stage matters, Mr. W. J. Lawrence, of Sir Christopher Wren's designs for the second Theatre Royal, Drury Lane, 1674. Beyond the proscenium on the apron there are four doors each with its balcony above. The height of these balconies from the stage is considerable, surprisingly so indeed in view of the fact that characters frequently have to climb up into or descend from one of these 'windows', e.g., Shadwell's *The Miser* (1672), Act. iv, when the drunken bullies 'bounce at the Doors', we have 'Squeeze at the Window in his Cap, and undressed,' who cries: 'I must venture to escape at this Window'; 'he leaps down', and yells, as he falls, 'Death! I have broke my Bones; oh! oh!' whilst the scowrers run up, exclaiming: 'Somebody leaped out of a Window', and he is promptly seized. In Ravenscroft's *The London Cuckolds* (1682), Act. v: 'Enter Ramble above in the Balcony'. This gallant, escaping from the house hurriedly, decides 'which way shall I get down? I must venture to hang by my hands and then drop from the Balcony'. Next: 'As Ramble is getting down Doodle enters to look for his glove, Ramble drops upon him and beats him down.' This could hardly have been an easy bit of stage business, although Smith, who acted Ramble, was an athletic, tall young fellow.

Normally no doubt only two of the doors (those nearest the proscenium opening on opposite sides) with their balconies were in constant use by the actors as the exigencies of the play might demand, but if required, all four balconies, and more frequently, all four doors could be and were employed. It is noticeable in Wren's design that the balconies are not stage balconies, but side boxes, a permanent part of the general architectural scheme, and there can be no doubt that, save in exceptional circumstances, the two outermost were occupied by spectators. If the play did not require the use of a balcony at all, spectators would also fill the inner side boxes. In time, indeed, two doors and two balconies only came to be used, but for some decades at least all four were practicable. The present passage of *The Rover* indicates the use of three doors. The bravos hang up two little pictures of Angelica, one at each side of the door of her house, and presently the fair courtezan appears in her balcony above. A little later Don Pedro and Stephano enter by one door at the opposite side, Don Antonio and his page by the second door on the same side as Pedro.

In Etheredge's *She Wou'd if She Cou'd* (6 February, 1668) Act ii, 1, Courtal and Freeman are seen following up Ariana and Gatty in the Mulberry Garden. Presently 'The Women go out, and go about behind the Scenes to the other Door', then 'Enter the Women [at one door] and after 'em Courtal at the lower Door, and Freeman at the upper on the contrary side'.

Three balconies are employed in Ravenscroft's *Mamamouchi* (1672; 4to 1675) Act iv. We have 'Enter Mr. Jorden, musick' obviously in one balcony from the ensuing dialogue. Then 'Cleverwit, in Turk's habit, with Betty Trickmore and Lucia appear in the Balcony' number two. A song is sung and 'Young Jorden and Marina in the Balcony against 'em'. Young Jorden remarks, 'Now, dearest Marina, let us ascend to your Father, he is by this time from his Window convinc'd of the slight is put on you....' 'They retire' and although there has been no exit marked for Mr, Jorden, we find directly, 'Enter Mr. Jorden and Trickmore,' obviously upon the stage itself, to which Mr. Jorden has descended. It must be noted, however, that the use of more than two balconies is very rare.

Mr. W. J. Lawrence in *The Elizabethan Playhouse and other Studies* (First Series) aptly writes: 'No dramatist of the time had a better sense of the theatre than Mrs. Behn, and none made more adroit employment of the balconies.' He then cites the scene of Angelica, her bravos and admirers.

p. 36 *a Patacoone.* A Spanish coin in value about 4*s.* 8*d.*

p. 38 *a Pistole-worth.* The pistole was a gold coin worth about 16*s.*

p. 42 *a shameroon.* A rare word meaning a trickster, a cozening rascal.

p. 54 *bow'd Gold.* Bowed for bent is still used in the North of England: 'A bowed pin.'

p. 57 *disguis'd.* A common phrase for drunk.

p. 75 *cogging.* To cog = to trick, wheedle or cajole.

p. 99 *Tramontana.* Foreign; Italian and Spanish *tramontano* = from beyond the mountains.

p. 101 *upse.* Op zijn = in the fashion or manner of. *Upse Gipsy* = like a gipsy, cf. *The Alchemist,* iv, vi:

> I do not like the dulness of your eye:
> It hath a heavy cast, 'tis upsee Dutch.

p. 101 *Inkle.* Linen thread or yarn which was woven into a tape once very much in use.

p. 106 *Nokes, or Tony Lee.* James Nokes and Antony Leigh, the two famous actors, were the leading low comedians of the day.

p. 107 *Play of the Novella. Novella* is a good, though intricate, comedy by Brome. 8vo, 1653, but acted 1632.

p. 107 *The famous Virgil.* There is a tale, reported by Donatus, that Vergil once anonymously wrote up on the palace gates a distich in praise of Augustus, which, when nobody was found to own it, was claimed by a certain versifier Bathyllus, whom Cæsar duly rewarded, A few days later, however, Virgil again set in the same place a quatrain each line of which commenced 'sic vos non vobis...' but was unfinished, and preceded these by the one hexameter

> Hos ego versiculos feci; tulit alter honores.

All were unable to complete the lines satisfactorily save the great poet himself, and by this means the true author of the eulogy was revealed.

ROVER II.

p. 113 *The Duke.* James, Duke of York, for whom Mrs. Behn, a thorough Tory, entertained sentiments of deepest loyalty. The 'absence', 'voluntary Exile', 'new Exiles', mentioned in the Dedication all refer to James' withdrawal from England in 1679, at the time of the seditious agitation to pass an illegal Exclusion Bill. The Duke left on 4 March for Amsterdam, afterwards residing at the Hague. In August he came back, Charles being very ill. Upon the King's recovery he retired to Scotland 27 October. In March, 1682, he paid a brief visit to the King, finally returning home June of the same year.

p. 114. *young Cesar in the Field.* During the Commonwealth and his first exile James had joined Turenne's army, 24 April, 1652, and was frequently in the field. He distinguished himself by conspicuous bravery. In 1656, at the wish of Charles, he joined the Spanish army.

p. 114 *Some of Oliver's Commanders at Dunkirk.* During the Flanders campaign of 1657, Reynolds, the commander of the English at Dunkirk, sought and obtained an interview with James, whom he treated with the most marked respect and honor. This was reported to Cromwell, much to the Protector's chagrin and alarm.

p. 115. *City Pope.* An allusion to the exploits of Elkanah Settle, who was so notorious at that time for violent Whiggism that in 1680 he had presided over the senseless city ceremony of 'Pope-burning' on 17 November. This annual piece of ridiculous pageantry is smartly described by Dryden in his Prologue to Southerne's *The Loyal Brother* (1682); and in the Epilogue to *Oedipus*, (1679), after enumerating the attractions of the play, he ends—

> We know not what you can desire or hope
> To please you more, but burning of a Pope.

There are many contemporary references to Settle and his 'fireworks'. Otway, in *The Poet's Complaint* (4to, 1680), speaks of Rebellion cockering the silly rabble with 'November squibs and burning pasteboard Popes', canto xi. Duke, in the Epilogue to the same author's *The Atheist* (1683), says that the poet never 'made one rocket on Queen Bess's night'. In Scott's *Dryden*, Vol. VI (1808) is given a cut representing the tom-fool procession of 1679, in which an effigy of the murdered Sir Edmund Bury Godfrey had a chief place. There were 'ingenious fireworks' and a bonfire. A scurrilous broadside of the day, with regard to the shouting, says that "twas believed the echo ... reached Scotland [the Duke was then residing in the North], France, and even Rome itself damping them all with a dreadfull astonishment.' The stage at this juncture of fierce political strife had become a veritable battle-ground of parties, and some stir was caused by Settle's blatant, but not ineffective, melodrama on the subject of that mythical dame *The Female Prelate, being the History of the Life and Death of Pope Joan*, produced at the Theatre Royal, 1680. This play itself is often referred to, and there are other allusions to Pope Joan about this time, e.g., in the Epilogue to Lee's *Cæsar Borgia* (1679), where the author says a certain clique could not have been more resolute to damn his play

> Had he the Pope's Effigies meant to burn,
>
> ....
>
> Nay, conjur'd up Pope Joan to please the age,
> And had her breeches search'd upon the stage.

cf. also Mrs. Behn in her own Epilogue when she speaks of 'fat Cardinals, Pope Joans, and Fryers'; and Lord Falkland's scoff in his Prologue to Otway's *The Soldier's Fortune* (1680):—

> But a more pow'rful Saint enjoys ye now
>
> ....
>
> The fairest Prelate of her time, and best.

Lord Falkland of course points at the play.

p. 116 *lofty Tire.* The Upper Gallery, the price of admission to which was one shilling. It was the cheapest part of the theatre, and is often alluded to in Prologue and Epilogue, but generally with abuse or sarcasm. Dryden, in his Prologue to Tate's *The Loyal General* (1680), caustically advises:—

> Remove your benches, you apostate pit,
> And take, above, twelve pennyworth of wit;

Go back to your dear dancing on the rope,
Or see what's worse, the Devil and the Pope.

p. 117 *Harlequin, Willmore's Man.* Although no actor's name is printed for Harlequin, the part was undoubtedly played by Shadwell's brother-in-law, Tom Jevon, who, at the age of twenty-one, had joined the company in 1673. Originally a dancing-master (Langbaine notes his 'activity'), he became famous in low comedy and particularly for his lithe and nimble Harlequins. In Otway's *Friendship in Fashion* (1677) Malagene, a character written for and created by Jevon, says, 'I'm a very good mimick; I can act Punchinello, Scaramuchio, Harlequin, Prince Prettyman, or any thing.'

Harlequin does not appear in Killigrew's *Thomaso*. Mrs. Behn's mime plays pranks and speaks Italian and Spanish. No doubt she derived the character from the Italian comedians who had been at the Royal Theatre, Whitehall, in 1672-3, as Dryden, in an Epilogue (spoken by Hart) to *The Silent Woman* when acted at Oxford, after a reference to a visit of French comedians, has:—

The Italian Merry-Andrews took their place,
And quite debauched the stage with lewd grimace,
Instead of wit and humors, your delight
Was there to see two hobby-horses fight,
Stout Scaramoucha with rush lance rode in,
And ran a tilt at centaur Arlequin.

They were acting again in July, 1675, and remained some months in England. cf. Evelyn, 29 September this same year, writes: 'I saw the Italian Scaramuccio act before the King at Whitehall, people giving money to come in, which was very scandalous and never so before at Court-diversions. Having seen him act before in Italy many years past, I was not averse from seeing the most excellent of that kind of folly.' Duffett in his Prologue to *Ev'ry Man out of his Humor*, 'spoken by Mr. Hayns', July, 1675, who refers to this second visit—

The Modish Nymphs now ev'ry heart will win
With the surprizing ways of Harlequin
O the fine motion and the jaunty mene
While you Gallants—
Who for dear Missie ne'er can do too much
Make Courtships à la mode de Scarramouch.

and a little later he writes:—

Religion has its Scarramouchys too
Whose hums and has get all the praise and pence.

This Italian troop evidently returned in the following year or in 1677, as we have allusions to Dominique Biancolelli and Fiurelli, 'the Fam'd Harlequin & Scaramouch', in the Prologue to Ravenscroft's *Scaramouch a Philosopher, Harlequin a School-Boy, Bravo, Merchant, and Magician*, a Comedy after the Italian Manner, produced at the Theatre Royal in 1677, with the migratory Joe Haines as Harlequin, and again in *Friendship in Fashion*, Act iii, 1, when Lady Squeamish cries: 'Dear Mr. Malagene, won't you let us see you act a little something of Harlequin? I'll swear you do it so naturally, it makes me think I am at the Louvre or Whitehall all the time.' [Malagene acts.]

p. 117. *Lucia... Mrs. Norris.* In the quarto the name of this actress is spelled Norice. Even if the two characters Lucia and Petronella Elenora were not so entirely different, one being a girl, the second a withered crone, it is obvious that as both appear on the stage at one and the same time Mrs. Norris could not have doubled these rôles. The name Mrs. Norice, however, which is cast for Lucia is undoubtedly a misprint for Mrs. Price. This lady may possibly have been the daughter of Joseph Price, an 'Inimitable sprightly Actor', who was dead in 1673. We find Mrs. Price cast for various rôles of no great consequence, similar to Lucia in this play. She sustained Camilla in Otway's *Friendship in Fashion* (1678), Violante in Leanerd's *The Counterfeits* (1679), Sylvia in *The Soldier's Fortune* (1683), Hippolita in D'Urfey's *A Commonwealth of Women* (1685), and many more, all of which belong to the 'second walking-lady'.

Mrs. Norris, who acted Petronella Elenora, was a far more important figure in the theatre. One of those useful and, indeed, indispensable performers, who, without ever attaining any prominent position, contribute more essentially than is often realized to the success of a play, she became well known for her capital personations of old women and dowagers. Wife of the actor Norris, she had been one of the earliest members of Davenant's company, and her son, known as Jubilee Dicky from his superlative performance in Farquhar's *The Constant Couple* (1699), was a leading comedian in the reigns of Anne and the first George. Amongst Mrs. Norris' many rôles such parts as Lady Dupe, the old lady in Dryden's *Sir Martin Mar-All* (1667), Goody Rash in Crowne's *The Country Wit* (1675), Nuarcha, an amorous old maid, in Maidwell's *The Loving Enemies* (1680), Mother Dunwell, the bawd in Betterton's *The Revenge; or, A Match in Newgate* (1680), all sufficiently typify her special line, within whose limits she won considerable applause.

p. 120 *Crab-Wine.* An inferior tipple brewed from sour apples.

p. 122 *Tantalus better than ever Ovid described him.*

> Quaerit aquas in aquis, et poma fugacia captat
> Tantalus: hoc illi garrula lingua dedit.
> > *Amorum*, ii, 11, 43-4.

> Tibi, Tantale, nullae
> Deprenduntur aquae; quaeque imminet effugit arbos.
> > *Met*, iv, 457-8.

p. 126 *I ... must be this very Mountebank expected.* One may remember Rochester's unpenetrated masquerade as Alexander Bendo, high above 'the bastard race of quacks and cheats,' and Grammont's account of all the courtiers and maids of honor flocking for lotions and potions of perpetual youth to the new empiric's lodgings 'in *Tower-Street*, next door to the sign of the *Black Swan*, at a Goldsmith's house.' In the *Works of the Earls of Rochester, Roscommon and Dorset* (2. vols. 1756), there is a rough cut of Rochester as a charlatan delivering a speech to the assembled crowd. On the platform also stands his attendant, a figure dressed in the diamonded motley of Harlequin.

p. 126 *in querpo.* A Spanish phrase, *en cuerpo* = without a cloak; in an undress or disguise.

p. 133 *old Adam's Ale.* A very ancient colloquialism for water. In Scotland 'Adam's wine' and frequently merely 'Adam'. Prynne in his *Sovereign Power of Parliament* (1648), speaks of prisoners 'allowed only a poor pittance of Adam's ale.' cf. Peter Pindar (John Wolcot), *The Lousiad*, Canto ii, ll. 453-4:—

> Old Adam's beverage flows with pride
> From wide-mouthed pitchers in a plenteous tide.

p. 141 *a Pageant.* Here used to signify a platform or low scaffold.

p. 157 *the Royal Sovereign.* In a Navy List of 1684 the *Royal Sovereign* is classed as one of the 'Nine First Rate' vessels. 1545 tons, 100 guns at home, 90 guns abroad, 815 men at home, 710 men abroad. In 1672 her commander was Sir Joseph Jorden. An authority on nautical matters whom I have consulted informs me that less men and fewer guns were carried to relieve the top hamper of the ship in a sea-way. Most vessels then were inclined to be top heavy, and although able to carry all their guns in the narrow seas, yet when going foreign were glad to leave ten behind, well knowing they would soon lose by scurvy or disease numbers of their crew apart from losses in battle. Although these ships were pierced with ports for, say, 100 guns, it did not follow they always carried so many, as a complete broadside could be fired by running the gun carriages across from one side to another before the fight, so she would not be so heavy above and not so liable to roll and spoil the aim of the guns.

p. 159 *Bezolos mano's, Seignior.* Señor, beso las manos. = Sir, I kiss your hands; the usual Spanish salutation.

p. 165 *brown George.* Coarse black bread; hard biscuit. cf. Urquhart's *Rabelais* (1653), Book IV. Author's prologue: 'The devil of one musty crust of a Brown George the poor boys had to scour their grinders with.' And Dryden, *Persius* (1693), v. 215:—

> Cubb'd in a cabin, on a matrass laid,
> On a Brown George with lousy swabbers fed.

p. 165 *Spanish Pay.* Slang for fair words; compliments, and nothing more.

p. 182 *fin'd.* In a somewhat unusual sense of to fine = to pay a composition or consideration for a special privilege.

p. 198 *Plymouth Cloaks.* Obsolete slang for a cudgel 'carried by one who walked *en cuerpo*, and thus facetiously assumed to take the place of a cloak'. Fuller (1661), *Worthies*, 'Devon' (1662), 248, 'A Plimouth Cloak. That is a Cane or a Staffe whereof this the occasion. Many a man of good Extraction comming home from far Voiages, may chance to land here [at Plymouth] and being out of sorts, is unable for the present time and place to recruit himself with Cloaths. Here (if not friendly provided) they make the next Wood their Draper's shop, where a Staffe cut out, serves them for a covering'. Ray, *Prov.* (1670), 225, adds, 'For we use when we walk *in cuerpo* to carry a staff in our hands but none when in a cloak'. *N.E.D.*, which also quotes this passage of *The Rover*. cf. Davenant:—

> Whose cloak, at Plymouth spun, was crab-tree wood.

p. 199 *Album Græcum.* The excrement of dogs and some other animals which from exposure to air and weather becomes whitened like chalk. It was formerly much used in medicine.

p. 209 *Guzman Medicines.* Trashy, worthless medicines. In *The Emperor of The Moon*, Act iii, 2, 'Guzman' is used as a term of abuse to signify a rascal. The first English translation (by James Mabbe) of Aleman's famous romance, *Vida del Picaro Guzman d'Alfarache*, is, indeed, entitled *The Rogue*, and it had as running title *The Spanish Rogue*. There is a novel by George Fidge entitled *The English Gusman; or, the History of that Unparallel'd Thief James Hind.* (1652, 4to.)

p. 209 *Copper Chains.* In allusion to the trick played by Estifania on the churlish Cacafogo in Fletcher's *Rule a Wife and Have a Wife.* He lends her 1000 ducats upon trumpery which she is passing off as rich gems, and when later he scents the cozenage, he bawls out:—

> Plague of her jewels, and her copper chains,

> How rank they smell!
>> —(Act v, 2.)

The phrase became proverbial for shams.

p. 211 *disembogue*. This word is generally used of the waters of a river or the outlet of a lake pouring into the open sea.

p. 212 *by Play-Bill, summon'd here*. In Restoration times one method of announcing the next day's performance to the public was by putting out bills on posts in the streets adjacent to the theatre. There are allusions to this in Pepys, 24 March, 1662 and 28 July, 1664. The whole subject has been exhaustively treated by Mr. W. J. Lawrence in 'The Origin of the Theatre Programme'—*The Elizabethan Playhouse* (Second Series).

p. 213 *greasing*. Flattery. Settle's post as City Poet, it is well known, did not bring him in any great emoluments. He was, in fact, desperately poor, and even volunteered to join King James' army at Hounslow Heath. In old age he was reduced to writing drolls performed in a Bartholomew Fair booth kept by one Mrs. Minns and her daughter, Mrs. Leigh. He himself acted in these wretched farces, and on one occasion, in *St. George for England*, appeared as a dragon in a green leather case. Eventually he obtained admission to the Charterhouse, where he died 24 February, 1724.

THE DUTCH LOVER.

p. 221 *An Epistle to the Reader*. This amusing and witty Epistle only appears in the 4to, 1673, finding no place in the various collected editions of Mrs. Behn's plays. The writer of comedy—'the most severe of Johnson's sect'—with his 'musty rules of Unity'—at whom she glances pretty freely is Shadwell, who had obtained great success with *The Sullen Lovers* (produced 2 May, 1668; 4to, 1668), and in spite of some mishaps and opposition, made another hit with *The Humorists* (1671; 4to, 1671). An ardent disciple of Ben Jonson, he had in the two printed prefaces to these plays belauded his model beyond all other writers, insisting upon the Unities and the introduction of at least two or three Humors as points essential to any comedy.

p. 221 *Doctor of Malmesbury*. The famous philosopher, Thomas Hobbes (1588-1670), who was born at Westport, a suburb of Malmesbury (of which town his father was vicar).

p. 222 *unjantee*.—'Jantee' obsolete form of 'jaunty': see *N.E.D.*

p. 222 *the mighty Echard*. That facetious divine, John Eachard, D.D. (1636-97), Master of Catherine Hall, Cambridge. His chief work, *The Grounds and Occasions of the Contempt of the Clergy and Religion enquired into. In a Letter to R. L.* (London, 1670), published anonymously, is stuffed full with Attic salt and humor. He has even been censured for a jocosity (at his brethren's expense) beneath the decorum of the cloth.

p. 224 *English Game which hight long Laurence*. To play at Laurence = to do just nothing at all; to laze. Laurence is the personification of idleness. There are many dialect uses of the name, e.g., N.W. Devon 'Lazy's Laurence', and Cornish 'He's as lazy as Lawrence', vide Wright, *English Dialect Dictionary*.

p. 234 *Women must be watched as Witches are*. One of the tests to which beldames suspected of sorcery were put—a mode particularly favored by that arch-scamp Matthew Hopkins, 'Witch-Finder General'—was to tie down the accused in some painful or at least uneasy posture for twenty-four hours, during which time relays of watchers sat round. It was supposed that an imp would come and suck the witch's blood; so any fly, moth, wasp or insect seen in the room was a familiar in that shape, and the poor wretch was accordingly convicted of the charge. Numerous confessions are recorded to have been extracted in this manner from ailing and doting crones by Master Hopkins, cf. *Hudribras*, Part II, canto iii, 146-8:—

> Some for setting above ground
> Whole days and nights, upon their breeches,
> And feeling pain, were hang'd for witches.

cf. again *The City Heiress*, Act i:—

> Watch her close, watch her like a witch, Boy,
> Till she confess the Devil in her,——Love.

p. 235 *Count d'Olivarez.* Gaspar Guzman d'Olivarez was born at Rome, 1587. For many years all-powerful minister of Philip IV; he was dismissed 1643, and died 20 July, 1645, in banishment at Toro.

p. 235 *a Venice Courtesan.* Venice, the home of Aretine and Casanova, was long famous for the beauty and magnificence of her prostitutes. This circumstance is alluded to by numberless writers, and Ruskin, indeed, maintains that her decline was owing to this cause, which can hardly be, since as early as 1340, when her power was only rising, the public women were numbered at 11,654. Coryat has some curious matter on this subject, and more may be found in *La Tariffa delle Puttane di Venegia*, a little book often incorrectly ascribed to Lorenzo Venicro.

p. 245 *They enter at another Door.* Vide note *Rover* I, Act II, I, p. 30.

p. 263 *Beso los manos, signor.* = Beso las manos, señor.

p. 265 *Don John.* The famous hero of Lepanto died, not without suspicion of poison, in his camp at Namur, 1578. Otway introduces him in *Don Carlos* (1676).

p. 271 *Souses.* A slang term for the 'ears'. cf. *The Roundheads*, Act II, I, 'a pair of large sanctify'd Souses.'

p. 271 *Butter-hams.* Apparently from Dutch boterham = a slice of bread and butter. The two narrow strips of trimming on either side of the cloak.

p. 272 *a Rummer of a Pottle.* A jug or goblet holding one pottle = two quarts.

p. 278 *Snick-a-Sne.* A combat with knives amongst the Dutch. Snik: Dutch = a sharp weapon. Dryden in his *Parallel betwixt Painting and Poetry* (4to, June, 1695) speaks of 'the brutal sport of snick-or-sne'. Mrs. Behn has happily put several characteristically Dutch phrases in Haunce's mouth.

p. 278 *Pharamond.* A heroic romance in twelve volumes, the seven first of which are by the celebrated la Calprenède, the remainder being the work of Pierre de Vaumorière. It was translated into English by J. Phillips (London, 1677, folio). Lee has taken the story of Varanes in his tragedy, *Theodosius* (1680), from this romance.

p. 289 *Bethlehem-Gaber.* Bethlen-Gabor (Gabriel Bethlen), 1580-1629, was a Hungarian noble who embraced the Protestant religion, and in 1613, with the help of an Ottoman army, succeeded in establishing himself as King of Transylvania. His reign, although one long period of warfare and truces, proved a most flourishing epoch for his country. Himself a musician and a man of letters, he was constant in his patronage of art and scholars, cf. Abraham Holland's *Continued Inquisition of Paper Persecutors* (1626):—

> But to behold the walls
> Butter'd with weekly Newes composed in Pauls

By some decaied Captaine, or those Rooks
Whose hungry brains compile prodigious books
Of Bethlem Gabor's preparations and
How terms betwixt him and th' Emperor stand.

p. 291 *a Hoy.* A small vessel like a sloop, peculiarly Dutch. Pepys, 16 June, 1661, speaks of hiring 'a Margate hoy'.

p. 323 *a Lapland Witch.* cf. *Paradise Lost*, Book II, l. 666:—

To dance
With Lapland witches, while the laboring moon
Eclipses at their charms.

p. 329 *the German Princess.* Mary Morders, alias Stedman, alias Kentish Moll, a notorious imposter of the day, who pretended to be a Princess from Germany. She had been transported to Jamaica in 1671, but returning too soon and stealing a piece of plate, was hanged at Tyburn, 22 January, 1673. Her adventures formed the plot of a play by Tom Porter, *A Witty Combat; or, The Female Victor* (4to, 1663). Kirkman's *Counterfeit Lady Unveiled* (8vo, 1673), contains very ample details of her career. Pepys went to visit her 'at the Gatehouse at Westminster', 29 May, 1663. In talk he was 'high in the defence of her wit and spirit' (7 June, 1663). 15 April, 1664, the diarist further notes: 'To the Duke's house and there saw *The German Princess* acted by the woman herself ... the whole play ... is very simple, unless, here and there, a witty sprinkle or two.' This piece was doubtless identical with Porter's tragi-comedy.

p. 329 *four Shillings, or half a Crown.* Four shillings was the price of admission to the boxes on the first tier of the theatre; half a crown to the pit. These sums are very frequently alluded to in prologue and epilogue. Dryden in his second epilogue to *The Duke of Guise* (1682), after referring to the brawls and rioting of the pit, says:—

This makes our boxes full; for men of sense
Pay their four shillings in their own defence.

The epilogue (spoken by Mrs. Bontell) to Corye's *The Generous Enemies* (1671), has these lines:—

Though there I see—Propitious Angels sit [points at the Boxes.
Still there's a Nest of Devils in the Pit,
By whom our Plays, like Children, just alive,
Pinch'd by the Fairies, never after thrive:
'Tis but your Half-crown, Sirs: that won't undo.

p. 330 *Rotas.* The Rota was a political club founded in 1659 by James Harrington. It advocated a system of rotation in filling government offices.

THE ROUNDHEADS.

p. 337 *To the Right Noble Henry Fitzroy.* Second son of Charles II by Barbara Villiers, Countess of Castlemaine, afterwards Duchess of Cleveland, was born 20 September, 1663. He married, 1 August, 1672, Isabella, daughter and heiress of Henry Bennet, Earl of Arlington. The bride was then only five years old. In September, 1675, Henry Fitzroy was created Duke of Grafton, and on 30 September, 1680, was installed by proxy as Knight of the Garter. In 1682 he became colonel of the first foot guards. He died 9 October, 1690, from a wound he received under the walls of Cork during Marlborough's expedition to Ireland. Brave and even reckless to a fault, he is said to have been the most popular and the ablest of the sons of Charles II.

p. 341 *noise of Plots.* The ferment occasioned by the pretended Popish Plot of 1678 and the illegal Exclusion Bill was in full blast.

p. 341 *Presbytery.* Presbyterianism.

p. 341 *Forty One.* 1641 was the date of the Grand Remonstrance and Petition to Charles I.

p. 341 *Ignoramus.* When Shaftesbury was indicted for high treason, 24 November, 1681, the grand jury ignored or threw out the bill. Their declaration was 'ignoramus'. cf. Dryden's prologue to *The Duke of Guise* (1682):—
　　　　Let ignoramus juries find no traitors,
and other innumerable references to this verdict.

p. 343 *Fleetwood.* Lieutenant-General Charles Fleetwood was son-in-law to Oliver Cromwell, and for a time Lord-Deputy of Ireland. He was mainly instrumental in the resignation of Richard Cromwell, but so weak and vacillating that he lost favor with all parties. His name was excepted from the general amnesty, and it was only with great difficulty that, owing to the influence of Lord Litchfield, he escaped with his life. He died in obscurity at Stoke Newington, 4 October, 1692.

p. 343 *Lambert.* Major-General Lambert (1619-83) lost his commissions owing to the jealousy of Oliver Cromwell, on whose death he privily opposed Richard Cromwell. In August, 1659, he defeated the Royalist forces under Sir George Booth in Cheshire, but subsequently his army deserted. On his return to London he was arrested (5 March, 1660), by the Parliament, but escaped. Tried for high treason at the Restoration, he was banished to Guernsey, where he died in the winter of 1683.

p. 343 *Wariston.* Archibald Johnston, Lord Wariston, a fierce fanatic, was parliamentary commissioner for the administration of justice in Scotland and a member of Cromwell's House of Peers. On the revival of the Rump he became president of the Council of State, and permanent president of the Committee of Safety. At the Restoration he fled, but was brought back from Rouen to be hanged at the Market Cross, Edinburgh, 23 July, 1663. Carlyle dubs him a 'lynx-eyed lawyer and austere presbyterian zealot', and Burnet says, 'Presbyterianism was more to him than all the world.'

p. 343 *Hewson.* John Hewson, regicide, a shoemaker, was a commander under Cromwell, and afterwards a peer in the Upper House. At the Restoration he escaped to the Continent and died in exile at Amsterdam, 1662, or, by another account, at Rouen.

p. 343 *Desbro.* John Desborough, Desborow, or Disbrowe (1608-80) was Cromwell's brother-in-law. Being left a widower, he married again April, 1658. As he had refused to sit as a judge at the trial of Charles I, he was not exempted from the amnesty; but being considered a source of danger, he was, after the Restoration, 'always watched with peculiar jealousy,' and suffered some short term of imprisonment.

p. 343 *Duckingfield.* Robert Duckenfield (1619-89), a strong Parliamentarian, but one who refused to assist at the King's trial. He had large estates in Cheshire, where he lived retired after a short imprisonment at the Restoration. His son Robert, who succeeded him, was subsequently created a baronet by Charles II, 16 June, 1665.

p. 343 *Corbet.* Although this name is here given as Corbet, Colonel Cobbet occurs Act i, II (p. 355), and we have Cobbet again Act iii, I (p. 374). This character is certainly not Miles Corbet the regicide, but Ralph Cobbet, who was both a colonel and a member of the Committee of Safety. Ralph Cobbet is frequently alluded to in the satires of the time, e.g. *The Gang; or, The Nine Worthies and Champions* (17 January, 1659-60):—

> A man of stomack in the next deal,
>> With a hey down, &c.
> Was hungry Colonel Cobbet;
>> He would eat at a meale
>> A whole commonweale,
>> And make a joint but a gobbet.

p. 343 *Whitlock.* Bulstrode Whitelock (1605-75), keeper of the Great Seal, and in August, 1659, president of the Council of State, was always inclined to royalism, and even advised Cromwell to restore Charles II. At the Restoration he was allowed to retire to Chilton Park, Hungerford, Wilts, and died there 28 July, 1675. According to some accounts his death took place at Fawley, Bucks.

p. 343 *Lady Lambert.* Lady Lambert was Frances, daughter of Sir William Lister, knight, of Thornton in Craven, Yorks. She was married 10 September, 1639. Contemporaries attribute Lambert's ambition to the influence of his wife, whose pride is frequently alluded to. e.g. *Memoirs of Colonel Hutchinson*, edited by C. H. Firth (Nimmo, 1885), Vol. II, p. 189, 'There went a story that as my Lady Ireton was walking in St. James' Park the Lady Lambert, as proud as her husband, came by where she was, and as the present princess always has precedency of the relict of the dead prince, so she put my Lady Ireton below; who, notwithstanding her piety and humility, was a little grieved at the affront.'

p. 343 *Lady Desbro.* Desborough's second wife, whom he married April, 1658, is said, on the dubious authority of Betham, to have been Anne, daughter of Sir Richard Everard, Bart., of Much Waltham. Mrs. Behn's amorous lady, Maria, is, of course, purely fictional.

p. 343 *Lady Fleetwood.* Bridget, eldest daughter of Oliver Cromwell, was married first to Ireton, who died 26 November, 1651, and secondly, in 1652, to Fleetwood. She did not live long after the Restoration, and was buried at S. Anne's, Blackfriars, 1 July, 1662.

p. 343 *Lady Cromwell.* Cromwell married Elizabeth, daughter of Sir James Bourchier, 22 August, 1620. She survived her husband seven years, dying 19 November, 1665. After the Restoration she lived in great seclusion at Norboro', Northamptonshire, the house of her son-in-law, John Claypoole.

p. 343 *Clement's Parish.* Probably St. Clements, Eastcheap. This church, described by Stow as being 'small and void of monuments', was destroyed in the Great Fire and rebuilt 1686. The old church of St. Clement Danes, Strand, being in a ruinous condition, was pulled down in 1680 and built again on the same site. The Puritans always omitted the prefix 'St.' and spoke of churches as 'Paul's', 'Mary's', 'Bartholomew's', 'Helen's' and the like.

The above Note refers to the male character Ananias Goggle, but is printed after the Commentary on the four main female characters.

p. 344 *Gad and the Lord Fleetwood.* Fleetwood, even in an age of Tartuffes, was especially distinguished for the fluency of his canting hypocrisy and godliness. He was a bitter persecutor of Catholics, a warm favorer of Anabaptists and the extreme fanatics of every kidney.

p. 345 *Vane.* Sir Harry Vane (1613-62), the prominent Parliamentarian and a leading member of the Committee of Safety was executed as a regicide, June, 1662.

p. 345 *Fifth Monarchy.* The Fifth Monarchy men were a sect of wild enthusiasts who declared themselves 'subjects only of King Jesus', and held that a fifth universal monarchy (like those of Assyria, Persia, Greece, and Rome) would be established by Christ in person, until which time no single person must presume to rule or be king.

p. 346 *Haslerig.* Sir Arthur Heselrige, one of the Five Members whom Parliament refused to yield to Charles I in January, 1642, was a republican of the most violent type. He died a prisoner in the Tower, 7 January, 1661.

p. 349 *an errant Heroic.* A term for a cavalier or Royalist, cf. Edward Waterhouse's *A Short Narrative of the late Dreadful Fire in London* (1667, 12mo): 'Even so, O Lord, rebuke the evil spirit of these *Sanballats*, and raise up the spirit of the *Nehemiahs* and other such Heroics of Kindness and Ability to consider *London.*' Tatham, in *The Rump* (4to, 1660; 1661), Act ii, 1, has 'The very names of the Cromwells will become far more odious than ever Needham could make the Heroics'.

p. 349 *cuckold the Ghost of Old Oliver.* The intrigue between Cromwell and Lambert's wife is affirmed in '*Newes from the New Exchange; or, the Commonwealth of Ladies* ... London; printed in the year of women without grace, 1650' (4to). Noble, in his *Memoirs of the Cromwell Family* (8vo, London, 1787, 3rd edit., Vol. II, p. 369), says that the lady 'was an elegant and accomplished woman', she was 'suppos'd to have been partial to Oliver the Protector.' A scarce poem, *Iter Australe* (London, 1660, 4to), declares of Cromwell that some

> Would have him a David, 'cause he went
> To Lambert's wife, when he was in his tent.

Some six months before Cromwell's death, when Lambert visited him, Noll 'fell on his neck, kissed him, inquired of dear Johnny for his jewel (so he called Mrs. Lambert) and for all his children by name.' Cromwell's immoralities in youth, when a brewer at Ely, were notorious. Although the parish registers of S. John's, Huntingdon, have been tampered with, the following, under the years 1621 and 1628, remain: 'Oliverus Cromwell reprehensus erat coram tota Ecclesia pro factis.' and 'Hoc anno Oliverus Cromwell fecit penitentiam coram tota ecclesia.' An attempt has been made to erase these.

p. 354 *Tony.* Anthony Ashley Cooper; afterwards first Earl of Shaftesbury.

p. 357 *Wallingford House.* Stood on the site of the present Admiralty. It was so called from Sir William Knollys, Baron Wallingford, Treasurer of the Household to Elizabeth and James I. After Cromwell's death the General Council of the Officers of the Army (Wallingford House Party) met here. Fleetwood actually lived in the house. At the Restoration it reverted to the Duke of Buckingham. The Crown purchased it 1680, and the Admiralty was built about 1720.

p. 361 *Cobler's-Stall.* Hewson, says Wood, had originally been 'an honest shoemaker in Westminster.'

p. 362 *Conventickling.* Conventicle was accentuated upon the third syllable. This, of course, led to innuendo, cf. 1 *Hudibras* (1663) Canto ii, 437:

> He used to lay about and stickle
> Like ram or bull at conventicle

and Dryden, in *The Medal* (1682):—

> A tyrant theirs; the heaven their priesthood paints
> A conventicle of gloomy sullen saints.

p. 363 *Pryn.* William Prynne (1600-69) had been sentenced to severe punishment in February, 1634, for the scandals and libels contained in his dull diatribe, *Histriomastix.* He lost both his ears in the pillory.

p. 365 *Needham.* Marchamont Nedham, 'the Commonwealth's Didaper', was a graduate of All Souls, Oxon, and sometime an usher at Merchant Taylors' school. He also seems to have been connected with the legal profession. 'The skip-jack of all fortunes', neither side has a good word for this notorious pamphleteer, the very scum of our early journalism. When *Mercurius Britannicus* temporarily ceased publication with No. 50, 9 September, 1644, Nedham recommenced it on the 30th of the same month with No. 51 (not No. 52 as is sometimes stated). No. 92, 28 July-4 August, 1645, and the number 11-18 May, 1646, revile the King in such scurrilous terms that Nedham was haled to the bar of the House of Lords and imprisoned. Later he turned Royalist, but in 1650 published *The Case of the Commonwealth Stated,* a defence of the regicides, for which he received a pension of £100 a year. He fled to Holland, April, 1660, but being pardoned, returned to England. He died in Devereux Court, Temple Bar, November, 1678, and is buried in St. Clement Danes. Wood characterizes him as 'a most seditious, mutable and railing author,' whilst Cleveland terms him 'that impudent and incorrigible reviler'.

p. 365 *Ireton, my best of Sons.* Noble, in his *Memoirs of the Cromwell Family,* says that the fact Fleetwood had not the abilities of her first husband gave his wife much concern, as she saw with great regret the ruin his conduct must bring on herself and her children.

p. 366 *Richard's Wife.* Richard Cromwell at the age of 23 married Dorothy, daughter of Richard Major, of Hursley, Hampshire.

p. 366 *glorious Titles.* Cromwell's wife was, as a matter of fact, very averse to all grandeur and state. The satires of the time laugh at her homeliness and parsimony.

p. 369 *Ormond.* James Butler, Duke of Ormond, was lord-lieutenant of Ireland, 1643-47.

p. 370 *Exercise.* A common term amongst the Puritans for worship; a sermon or extemporary prayer. As early as 1574. Archbishop Whitgift speaks of the exercises of 'praying, singing of psalms, interpreting and prophesying', cf. Davenant, *The Wits* (4to 1636):—

> I am a new man, Luce; thou shalt find me
> In a Geneva band....
> And squire thy untooth'd aunt to an exercise,

and also:—

> [she] divides
> The day in exercise.—Mayne's *City Match* (1639), iv, v.

p. 372 *Duke of Glocester.* Henry of Oatlands, Duke of Gloucester, youngest son of Charles I. Born 8 July, 1639, he died of smallpox at Whitehall 13 September, 1660. The Parliament sent him to the continent on 11 February, 1653.

p. 373 *he should have been bound Prentice.* A proposition was actually made in Parliament that the young Duke of Gloucester should be bound to a trade, in order, as it was impudently expressed, 'that he might earn his bread honestly.' Fortunately saner counsels prevailed, in which his fate was happier than that of the Dauphin committed to the cruelties of Citizen Simon, cordwainer.

p. 373 *Old Thurlo.* John Thurloe (1616-68), Secretary of State to Cromwell; M.P. for Ely 1654 and 1656. He died 21 February, 1668.

p. 378 *Highness's Funeral.* A large portion of the debt incurred for Oliver Cromwell's magnificently extravagant funeral ceremonies fell on Richard, who was obliged to retire for a while to the continent to avoid arrest and await some settlement. These obsequies cost in all the huge sum of £60,000, which there was a great difficulty in paying. The chief undertaker's name was Rolt. See note on *The Widow Ranter*— 'Trusting for Old Oliver's funeral,' Act i. (Vol. IV.)

p. 378 *Walter Frost.* Walter Frost, secretary to the Republican Council of State, was quondam manciple of Emmanuel, Cambridge, and acted as spy-master and manager of the 'committee hackneys,' which hunted down and betrayed Royalists. This infamous fellow, who dubbed himself Esquire and Latinized his name to Gualter, was authorized to publish (i.e. write) 'intelligence every week upon Thursday according to an Act of Parliament for that purpose.' He licensed *A Briefe Relation* (No 1, 2 October, 1649) from its second number until 22 October, 1650. This is certainly one of the most evil and lying of the Republican diurnals.

p. 378 *Hutchinson.* Richard Hutchinson, deputy treasurer to Sir Henry Vane. He succeeded as Treasurer to the Navy in 1651 and continued to hold office after the Restoration. He is several times mentioned by Pepys.

p. 379 *Jacobus.* A gold coin value 25s., first current in the reign of James I.

p. 379 *Mr. Ice.* Perhaps Stephen Isles who was appointed a Commissioner for the London Militia, 7 July, 1659. The name 'Mr. Ice' occurs in Tatham's *Rump* in the same context.

p. 379 *Loether.* Sir Gerard Lowther, who, once a loyalist, became a republican, and in 1654 was one of the Three Commissioners of the Great Seal in Ireland. He acquired large estates and died very wealthy on the eve of the Restoration.

p. 381 *Duke of Buckingham's Estate ... with Chelsey House.* Bulstrode Whitelocke actually had obtained the Duke's sequestered estate, and stood for Bucks in Parliament. During the Commonwealth Chelsea House was bestowed upon him as an official residence, and he lived there till the Restoration, when it reverted to the Duke, to whose father it had been granted in 1627 by Charles I. He sold it in 1664 to the trustees of George Digby, Earl of Bristol. In 1682 it became the property of Henry, Marquis of Worcester, afterwards Duke of Beaufort, and was renamed Beaufort House. Sir Hans Sloane purchased it in 1738, and it was demolished two years later.

p. 381 *Hugh Peters.* This divine, who had been chaplain to Sir Thomas Fairfax, was notorious for his fanatical and ranting sermons. Having openly advocated and preached the death of Charles I, he was, at the Restoration, excluded from the general amnesty, tried for high treason, and executed 16 October, 1660.

p. 382 *Scobel.* Henry Scobell, clerk to the Long Parliament. His name appeared as the licenser of various newsbooks, and he superintended the publication of *Severall Proceedings in Parliament*, No. 1, 25 Sept.-9 Oct., 1649. Scobell died in 1660, his will being proved 29 Sept. of that year.

p. 394 *Vails.* Avails; profits. Money given to servants: 'tips'.

p. 398 *Cushion-Dance.* A merry old English round action dance common in the sixteenth and seventeenth centuries.

p. 398 *Nickers.* Or knickers, marbles generally made of baked clay. cf. Duffet's farce, *The Mock Tempest* (1675), Act iv, I:—

Enter *Hypolito playing with Nickers.*

Hypolito. Anan, Anan, forsooth—you, Sir, don't you stir the Nickers. I'll play out my game presently.

p. 402 *Joan Sanderson.* The air to which the Cushion Dance was usually performed. It may be found in Playford's *Dancing Master*, 1686. Sometimes the dance itself was known as Joan Sanderson.

p. 406 *The Tall Irishman.* Oliver Cromwell's porter, yclept Daniel, was a giant. This fellow, through poring over mystical divinity, lost his wits: he preached, prophesied, and raved until finally he was incarcerated in Bedlam, where, after a while, his liberty was allowed him. A famous item amongst his books was a large Bible presented by Neil Gwynne. D'Urfey in his Prologue to *Sir Barnaby Whigg* (1681), has: 'Like Oliver's porter, but not so devout.' There is a rare, if not unique, portrait of Daniel in the Print Room, British Museum. The reputed portrait in Pierce Tempest's *Cryes of the City of London* (No. 71. Un insensé pour la Religion. M. Lauron del. P. Tempest ex.) is not that of a remarkably tall man.

p. 410 *Enter Hewson with Guards.* 5 December, 1659, Hewson did actually suppress a rising of London prentices, two or three of whom were killed and some score wounded. This made him very unpopular.

p. 412 *Lord Capel.* Arthur, Lord Capel, Baron Hadham, a gallant royalist leader, was, after the surrender of Colchester, treacherously imprisoned. He escaped, but was betrayed, and beheaded 9 March, 1649.

p. 412 *Brown Bushel.* A sea captain. Originally inclined to the Parliament, he became a royalist. In 1643 he was taken prisoner, but after being exchanged lived quietly and retired till 1648, when he was seized as a deserter, and after three years captivity, tried, and executed 29 April, 1651.

p. 413 *Earl of Holland.* Henry Rich, Earl of Holland (1590-1649), a staunch royalist, was executed 9 March, 1649, in company with Lord Capel and the Duke of Hamilton.

p. 413 *Judas.* The piece of plate dubb'd Judas would be gilded, cf. Middleton's *Chaste Maid in Cheapside*, (4to, 1630), iii, 2.

3rd Gossip. Two great 'postle-spoons, one of them gilt.

1st Puritan. Sure that was Judas then with the red beard.

Red is the traditional colour of Judas' hair. cf. Dryden's lines on Jacob Tonson the publisher:—

With two left legs and Judas-coloured hair.

p. 414 *an act, 24 June.* Cromwell's parliament passed Draconian Acts punishing adultery, incest, fornication, with death; the two former on the first offence, the last on the second conviction. *Mercurius Politicus*, No. 168. Thursday, 25 August—Thursday, 1 September, 1653 (p. 2700), records the execution of an old man of eighty-nine who was found guilty at Monmouth Assize of adultery with a woman over sixty. It is well known that under the Commonwealth the outskirts of London were crowded with brothels, and the license of Restoration days pales before the moral evils and cankers existing under Cromwell. The officially recognized independent diurnals *Mercurius Democritus, Mercurius Fumigosus*, have been described as 'abominable'. In 1660, when the writers of these attempted to circulate literature which had been common in the preceeding decade, they were promptly 'clapt up in Newgate'.

p. 414 *Peters the first, Martin the Second.* Hugh Peters has been noticed before. Henry Martin was an extreme republican, and at one time even a Leveller. He was a commissioner of the High Court of Justice and a regicide. At the Restoration he was imprisoned for life and died at Chepstow Castle, 1681, aged seventy-eight. He was notorious for profligacy and shamelessness, and kept a very seraglio of mistresses.

p. 415 *Tantlings.* St. Antholin's (St. Anthling's), Budge Row, Watling Street, had long been a stronghold of puritanism. As early as 1599, morning prayer and lecture were instituted, 'after the Geneva fashion'. The bells began at five in the morning. This church was largely attended by fanatics and extremists. There are frequent allusions to St. Antholin's and its matutinal chimes. The church was burned down in the Great Fire. Middleton and Dekker's *Roaring Girl* (1611): 'Sha's a tongue will be heard further in a still morning than Saint Antling's bell.'

> She will outpray
> A preacher at St. Antlin's.—Mayne's *City Match* (1639), iv, v.

Davenant's *News from Plymouth* (fol. 1673, licensed 1635), i, I:—

> Two disciples to St. Tantlin,
> That rise to long exercise before day.

p. 416 *Lilly.* William Lilly (1602-81). The famous astrologer and fortune-teller. In Tatham's *The Rump* (1660), he is introduced on the stage, and there is a scene between him and Lady Lambert, Act iv.

p. 416 *sisseraro.* More usually sasarara. A corruption of *certiorari*, a writ in law to expedite justice. 'If it be lost or stole ... I could bring him to a cunning kinsman of mine that would fetcht again with a sesarara,'—*The Puritan* (1607). 'Their souls fetched up to Heaven with a sasarara.'—*The Revenger's Tragedy*, iv, 2 (1607), *The Vicar of Wakefield* (1766), ch. xxi: '"As for the matter of that," returned the hostess, "gentle or simple, out she shall pack with a sussarara".'

p. 421 *Twelve Houses.* Each of the astrological divisions of the heavens denoting the station of a planet is termed a house.

p. 423 *bear the bob.* To join in the chorus. Bob is the burden or refrain of a song.

p. 423 *Colt-staff.* Or col-staff (Latin *collum*). A staff by which two men carry a load, one end of the pole resting on a shoulder of each porter. cf. *Merry Wives of Windsor*, iii, 3, 'Where's the cowl-staff?'

p. 423 *Fortune my Foe.* This extremely popular old tune is in Queen Elizabeth's *Virginal Book*; in William Ballet's MS. Lute Book; in *Bellerophon* (1622), and in numerous other old musical works. There are allusions to it in Shakespeare and many of the dramatists.

THE END

CPSIA information can be obtained at www.ICGtesting.com
Printed in the USA
LVOW101854310712

292374LV00010B/35/P